Contacts, Collisions and Relationships

Britons and Chileans
in the Independence era, 1806–1831

Liverpool Latin American Studies

Series Editor: Matthew Brown, University of Bristol
Emeritus Series Editor: Professor John Fisher

Liverpool Latin American Studies, New Series 19

Contacts, Collisions and Relationships

*Britons and Chileans
in the Independence era, 1806–1831*

Andrés Baeza Ruz

LIVERPOOL UNIVERSITY PRESS

First published 2019 by
Liverpool University Press
4 Cambridge Street
Liverpool
L69 7ZU

British Library Cataloguing-in-Publication data
A British Library CIP record is available

ISBN 978 1 78694 172 5

Typeset by Carnegie Book Production, Lancaster
Printed and bound in Poland by BooksFactory.co.uk

Contents

Acknowledgements

This book is a revised version of my doctoral dissertation titled 'Britain and Chile in the Independence Era: A Cultural History, 1806–1831', which I completed at the University of Bristol in 2016. Several people and institutions have contributed to both the completion of the dissertation and its development into this book.

In Bristol I found a very supportive, lively and friendly academic environment which allowed me to successfully complete the research upon which this book is based. Prof. Matthew Brown and Dr Jo Crow from the Hispanic, Portuguese and Latin American Studies Department (HiPLA) were more than my supervisors. They were constantly engaged in both my research progress and my well-being. If this book has some merit this is mostly because of their wise advice, careful reading, insightful feedback and infinite patience. My gratitude to their families is extensive as well. Dr Caroline Williams, from the HiPLA Department, allowed me to teach some of the ideas of this book to undergraduate students and along with Prof. Robert Bickers, from the History Department, gave me really helpful advice when this book was just a project. I also owe my gratitude to Prof. Simon Potter (University of Bristol) and Prof. Patience Schell (University of Aberdeen), my examiners whose valuable feedback allowed me to substantially improve the original version of my dissertation and guided it to this final form. Carmen Brauning, Luis Bustamante, Bárbara Castillo, Warren Craig, Jimena Lobo-Guerrero, Marcela Ramos and Juan Andrés Guzmán were all very generous friends and helped me in different ways and moments when I needed it.

Outside Bristol, I am especially grateful to Dr Karen Racine (University of Guelph, Canada), who encouraged me to apply and come to Bristol. She has constantly supported my progress and her own work has also been an inspiration for this book. Prof. Marcelo Caruso (Humboldt University of Berlin, Germany) gave me very useful suggestions regarding the Monitorial system of education and helped me to realise that the scope of my original proposal needed to be broadened. Dr Graciela Iglesias-Rogers (universities of Winchester and Oxford) has also been a generous colleague during and after my doctoral studies and gave useful suggestions in the preparation of this book. She also invited me to join the fabulous research project *The Hispanic Anglosphere: Transnational Networks, Global Communities (Late 18th to Early 20th Century)* in 2017, allowing me to share and discuss the ideas of this book with other historians. Prof. Scarlett O'Phelan (Pontificia Universidad Católica del Perú) kindly invited me to present and discuss some of the material of Chapter 3 in a panel she convened at the Asociación de Historiadores Latinoamericanistas Europeos (AHILA) conference in Berlin (2014). In Chile, Pilar Aylwin, Juan Luis Ossa, Macarena Ponce de León, Andrés Estefane, Marcelo Casals, Luis Thielemann and Joaquín Fernández, although not directly involved in this book, were all supportive friends and colleagues during its preparation.

This book was made possible thanks to the financial support of the Commission for Scientific and Technological Research in Chile (CONICYT) and its scholarship programme, *Becas Chile*, which funded my stay and studies in Bristol (2011–2015). The Banco Santander Travel Grant scheme, the Alumni Foundation and the Faculty of Arts at the University of Bristol, and the Society for Latin American Studies provided me crucial funding for my research trips to Chile and for the presentation of substantial parts of this book in different conferences and seminars in Geneva, Berlin, London, Southampton and Santiago. Such financial support was crucial to research at the National Archives at Kew Gardens, the National Archives of Scotland in Edinburgh; the British and Foreign School Society Archive at Brunel University; the British and Foreign Bible Society Archive held at Cambridge University Library; the Archivo General de Indias at Seville, the British Library; and the Archivo Nacional Histórico and the Biblioteca Nacional in Chile. I appreciate the valuable help and advice of the staff of such institutions and the generous authorisation from the Earl of Dundonald to use the archival sources related to Lord Thomas Cochrane in Chapter 2. I am also grateful to Liverpool University Press and particularly to Chloe Johnson and the anonymous readers of the manuscript. All of them made it possible to improve this book even more.

I express my greatest gratitude for the unconditional support of my family, and particularly to my parents Eduardo and Angélica, for all their help during these years, and to my siblings Tomás and Alejandra. My two sons, Mateo and the Bristol-born Simón, without realising, made easier the preparation, the research and the writing of this book. And finally, none of this would had been possible without my wife, Dr Paula Caffarena, who has always been there and always encouraged me to keep going when more than once I was tempted to give up. This book is dedicated to her.

Abbreviations

ABO	Archivo de don Bernardo O'Higgins
AGI	Archivo General de Indias
ANH-CG	Archivo Nacional Histórico de Chile, Fondo Capitanía General
ANH-FV	Archivo Nacional Histórico de Chile, Fondo Varios
ANH-MH	Archivo Nacional Histórico de Chile, Fondo Ministerio de Hacienda
ANH-MI	Archivo Nacional Histórico de Chile, Fondo Ministerio del Interior
ANH-MM	Archivo Nacional Histórico de Chile, Fondo Ministerio de Marina
BFBS	British and Foreign Bible Society
BFSS	British and Foreign School Society
NAS	National Archives of Scotland
TBL	The British Library
TNA	The National Archives at Kew
TWA	The Wellington Archive
SCL	Sesiones de los Cuerpos Legislativos de la República de Chile

Preface

Karen Racine, University of Guelph, Canada

The streets of London have long been an outpost of Chilean domestic politics. The city has attracted Chilean writers and rebels, artists and atrocity-makers, politicians and tourists for more than two hundred years. In return, British bankers, merchants, miners, farmers and other emigrants have moved to South America in search of new lives there while retaining their own strong cultural and familial links back home. The historic relationship between the two countries, their institutions and their people, is one of the longest-standing international associations in modern times. Chileans of British descent (including Scottish, Welsh and Irish), are estimated to make up approximately 5% of the country's population with surnames like: Aylwin, Blest, Bunster, Cheney, Collingwood, Condell, Cox, Edwards, Hardy, Mackenna, Mackintosh, Miller, Ross, Simpson, Tupper, Walker, Williams and Wood. In the pages that follow, Andrés Baeza Ruz expertly outlines the early years of this connection, characterising the experience as one of contact and collision. It is an apt description and one that extends well beyond the foundational period that he studies here.

The distant Chilean land and its people have had a long presence in the British literary public's mind. At the beginning of the seventeenth century, George Carew attempted the first English translation of *La Araucana* (*The Araucaniad*), Alonso de Ercilla's epic account of the sixteenth-century conquest. Spanish colonial historians Pedro Cieza de León and Alonso de Ovalle wrote chronicles that created the enduring impression of Chile as a fierce, wild and beautiful place. Throughout the eighteenth century, London booksellers stocked these accounts on their shelves, while fashionable magazines regularly excerpted them to be read as erudite after-dinner entertainment.[1] Daniel Defoe literally and figuratively put Chile on the cultural map of British literature when he used one of the Juan Fernández Islands as the fictional setting for his novel *Robinson Crusoe* in 1719; this

---

1 See, for example, *The Universal Museum; or, Gentleman's and Ladies Polite Magazine of History, Politicks and Literature for 1762, Vol. I*, ed. by A. Young and J. Seally (London, 1762), 98–99.

cultural connection remains so powerful that the Chilean government formally renamed it Robinson Crusoe's Island in the 1960s.[2] The naturalist Charles Darwin spent time in Chile during his expedition on the *Beagle*; his diary of the voyage and things he observed there had monumental implications for global science. In London, Kew Gardens has an extensive collection of Chilean plants that were obtained as gifts or through scientific exchanges from the nineteenth century onwards. In 1847, Thomas de Quincey, the famous 'opium eater' of English Romanticism, published a biographical study of Catalina de Erauso, a young girl who fought alongside the Spanish conquistadors in Chile. These close literary connections continued into the twentieth century. Chilean author Blanca Santa Cruz Ossa wrote a children's book called *Cuentos ingleses* (*English Tales*) in 1936. Pablo de Rokha met his third wife while in political exile in London. Isabel Allende got an early start in the literary world by translating the romance novels of Dame Barbara Cartland into Spanish. And Joan Turner Jara, the widow of folk singer Víctor Jara, was a British citizen who returned to her native country after his murder in 1973; she kept his legacy alive by releasing his musical recordings and also forming an international public pressure group to advocate for investigation and prosecutions.

Running alongside these literary and artistic entanglements, London has long been a central pole of Chilean diasporic politics.[3] Beginning with the intrigues and enmities between Antonio José de Irisarri and Mariano Egaña in the 1820s, which Baeza discusses in this book, Chileans from across the political spectrum might have found themselves a world away from home but still actively participating in its domestic causes. The issue of the disastrous loans contracted in the 1820s remained a thorny subject on both sides of the Atlantic for decades. In 1925, a military Chilean attaché named Marmaduke Grove and exiled former president Arturo Alessandri met and conspired with President General Carlos Ibáñez (whose surname is a Hispanicised version of the Welsh name Evans) in London; they signed something called the 'Calais Pact' with some other disaffected democratic types, which eventually led to Grove's brief tenure as president of the Socialist Republic of Chile in July 1932.

The most dramatic recent case of contact and collision between British and Chilean politics, however, was the arrest of General Augusto Pinochet when he was in England in August 1998 to receive treatment at a medical clinic. Pinochet was detained under condition of an international warrant for human rights abuses issued by Spanish judge Baltasar Garzón. He was held in London for over a year and a half, a protracted legal and diplomatic

2 'In an ill hour, I went on board a ship bound for London ...', *The Times* (17 September 2005), 54.

3 Carolina Ramírez, 'The Chilean Diaspora of London: Diasporic Social Scenes and the Spatial Politics of Home' (Unpublished PhD dissertation in the Department of Sociology, Goldsmiths, University of London, 2014).

issue that Fernando Labra has called 'the impasse in London'.[4] It certainly was a collision. In January 1999, more than five hundred anti-Pinochet exiles in London and their local supporters held a March for Justice in Trafalgar Square to declare their ongoing resistance to the regime, to express gratitude for the actions of the Spanish judge and British jailers, and to raise a visible fist against those who supported Pinochet. In July 2003, a heated controversy arose again when the Chilean government sent its naval flagship *Esmeralda* on a goodwill world tour with a planned stop at Dartmouth Naval College which was hastily cancelled because of public protests against the presence of a ship that had been linked to training in and the use of torture. The spillover of Chilean politics onto London streets continues to the present day. In May 2016, students and environmental protesters loudly demonstrated against President Michelle Bachelet during her visit to London, hoping to raise awareness of assaults on indigenous Mapuche land rights, human rights violations and ecological devastation back in Chile.

Obviously the subject of Chile's relationship with Great Britain and its impact during the early years of nation state formation is significant. British personnel, including the infamous Lord Cochrane, and British material support helped to establish the Chilean navy. The British government sold at least three vessels to the patriot government, one in 1817 called the *Windham* (renamed the *Lautaro*) and two more in 1818, called the *Cumberland* (renamed the *San Martín*) and the *Lucy* (renamed the *Galvarino*).[5] The Chilean navy even used the British naval code as the basis for its own foundational structure.[6] Bernardo O'Higgins, Supreme Director of Chile during the immediate post-independence years, had been educated in England and retained fond memories of his friends, the British lifestyle and the people he had known there in his youth. Entrepreneurs like Richard Trevethick arrived from Cornwall to exploit the copper and nitrate mines. Travel accounts became a popular and lucrative genre for middle-class readers.

As Andrés Baeza clearly shows in this book, however, connections between the two countries extend far beyond trade, diplomacy and state interactions to encompass educational models, literature, mining and technology, marriages and family networks, and even changing tastes and habits. For example, when English traveller Maria Graham visited Valparaiso in 1821 and 1822, she found that 'English tailors, shoemakers, and inn-keepers hang out their sign in every street, and the preponderance of the English language over every other spoken in the chief streets would make one fancy Valparaiso [to

---

4 Fernando Labra, *Impasse en Londres* (Santiago: Editorial Forja, 2007).

5 Ricardo Donoso, 'Una intriga diplomática', *Revista Chilena de Historia y Geografía*, 125 (1957), 255.

6 Stephen Clissold, *Bernardo O'Higgins and the Independence of Chile* (New York: Praeger, 1969), p. 182.

be] a coast town in Britain'.[7] British influence was ever-present throughout the independence era. Graham also recorded that in 1821 meals were served family-style on shared bowls and plates, but by the time she had returned for her second visit, manners had changed and each diner now received his or her individually plated meal after the English custom.[8] Chilean historian-statesman Benjamin Vicuna Mackenna claimed that Chileans apparently adopted the British habit of drinking tea in the 1820s, as 'a clean and aromatic substitute for the unhealthy and insipid Paraguayan *mate*'. Unfortunately, not everyone made the switch easily; a local-born cook working in the house of Valparaiso's English teacher Mr Richard took the fancy tea the latter had brought with him from India and fried it in a pan.[9] In the 1820s, British residents introduced Chileans to cricket and foot races. Andrew Blest founded Santiago's first brewery in Santiago.[10] These contacts were not without their collisions, however. In 1827, there as a significant row over the British community's efforts to establish a Protestant cemetery.

Volunteer associations and civic societies exist in both countries and represent the ongoing contact and closeness that Baeza identifies in this book. For example, the Anglo-Chilean Society formed in London in 1944, and expanded in 2008 when it absorbed the British-Chilean Chamber of Commerce. Today it holds cultural events, hosts conferences, facilitates commercial connections and provides a perch for visiting Chilean government officials and dignitaries. On the other side of the world, in Chile, the list of British-affiliated organisations is even longer: the Association of British Schools in Chile, the Cambridge Society, Friends of the London School of Economics, the British Alumni Association, the Salvation Army (Ejército Salvación), the Anglican Church, the British Commonwealth Society, The British Council, the Chilean British Chamber of Commerce, the Royal British Legion, Instituto Chileno Británico de Cultura, Instituto Chileno Británico and the Sociedad Anglo-Chileno (both in Viña del Mar), the British Society of Valparaiso, the Prince of Wales Country Club in La Reina and several volunteer fire-fighting associations, including the British and Commonwealth Fire Company.

Andrés Baeza Ruz adds depth, intelligence and insight to the historical experiences of Chileans in London, and his book also makes clear the importance of the British-Chilean international connection. What is significant about this study, apart from the stories of real people well told, is that

7 Maria Graham (later Lady Callcott), *Journal of a Residence in Chile in 1822 and a Voyage from Chile to Brazil in 1823* (London: Printed for Longman, Hurst, Rees, Orme and Brown, and John Murray, 1824), p. 131.

8 S. Samuel Trifilo, 'Early Nineteenth-Century British Travellers in Chile: Impressions of Santiago and Valparaíso', *Journal of Inter-American Studies*, 11:3 (1969), 405.

9 Benjamín Vicuña Mackenna, *The First Britons in Valparaiso: 1817–1827* (Valparaíso: Gordon Henderson and Company, 1884), pp. 36–37.

10 Vicuña Mackenna, *The First Britons*, p. 38.

Baeza has returned our attention to activities of Chileans in London during the independence period. There are dozens of studies on the activities of the British in Chile and elsewhere in South America during the early era of informal empire, but this book reminds us that Chileans not only travelled internationally themselves, but were engaged and active partners in both connections and the collisions that resulted.

Introduction

In April 2014, during the third year of my doctoral studies, I made a research trip to Edinburgh with my family to review the documents of Thomas Cochrane that are held in the National Archive of Scotland. We had always wanted to visit the city and it seemed like a good opportunity. We also travelled at a particular time, only a few months before the referendum to decide whether Scotland would remain in the United Kingdom. This was really significant. I could witness how a considerable part of Scottish society was calling into question the idea of a British 'nation', whose existence I was convinced of after reading Linda Colley's classic *Britons*[1] and witnessing the Olympic Games that took place in London in 2012. The possibility of reviewing Cochrane's personal documents, the beauty of the city and this historical moment made of our trip an unforgettable experience.

However, our trip to Edinburgh was unforgettable for another reason. Coincidentally, one of my supervisors at the University of Bristol was on holiday nearby and we agreed to spend a day with him and his family. In the middle of a conversation about the purpose of my trip, he remembered that the town where Thomas Cochrane was born, Culross, was relatively close. His father knew the place and gave us the references to get there. It took us forty-five minutes to reach the middle of the town, a royal burgh with no more than 5,000 inhabitants and whose central square occupies a large part of its territory. For me, a Chilean historian concerned with the relations between my country and Great Britain in the independence era, being there was impressive.[2] I was in the middle of Scotland, in a small town in whose

---

1 Linda Colley, *Britons. Forging the Nation, 1707–1837*, 3rd ed. (London: Vintage Books, 1996).

2 I am using the term 'independence era' throughout this book in a practical way. I do not intend to say that Chileans and Spanish Americans were struggling for their independence from 1806. Indeed, one of the arguments of the book is that independence is the result of the dynamic and changing nature of the period and after the 1808 crisis, independence was only one possibility amongst many others. However, many scholars (i.e. Felipe Fernández de Armesto, Rory Miller and Karen Racine)

central square there was a magnificent bust of Thomas Cochrane accompanied by the Scottish and Chilean flags.

I never expected to find a Chilean flag waving in a place like that. It is usual to see the Chilean flag around the world in football stadiums, tennis courts, university campuses, but not in the central square of a British village. I was surprised – and amazed – and some questions quickly came to my mind: How was it possible that the Chilean flag formed part of the everyday life of the inhabitants of this small village? What did they really know about what Cochrane did in Chile? What did they know and think about my country, besides that Cochrane was there? At that moment I realised that my own research could contribute to answering these questions. If in 2014 the Chilean flag was still waving in the middle of Scotland, it was because there are close connections between Chile and Britain that need to be explained historically. Yet I convinced myself that such connections needed to be understood in all their complexity and not simply as a story in which Britons struggled for Chileans' liberty, nor as the story of an evil empire aiming to subjugate people from Latin America. These were the typical narratives about the role played by Great Britain in the independence struggles. However, if we can learn anything about the relations between Chile and Great Britain in the independence era, it is that this story was not written in black and white, it is not a story of good and bad, of victims and victimisers. It is a story written in grey tones and in which these binary categories rather disappear. The purpose of this book is precisely to contribute to such an understanding.

This book delves into the relations between Britain and Chile during the shifting and dynamic years of Spanish American independence (1806–1831).[3]

---

use the term 'independence era' to refer to the period, avoiding other more complex terms that could make the reading of this book more difficult.

3 In most cases the starting point of Chile's independence era is fixed in 1808, when Napoleon invaded Spain and King Ferdinand VII was imprisoned in Bayonne. Likewise, the end point is fixed either in 1818, with the Battle of Maipú, or in 1826, when Chilean troops eventually captured Chiloé and expelled the remaining Spanish troops from the territory. I have started my analysis in 1806 because, as shown throughout this book, I argue that the British invasion of Buenos Aires, in 1806, had significant consequences in Chile related to the independence process. With regard to the end point, I have chosen 1831 because it signals the recognition of Chile's independence from Great Britain, a decision that had been persistently sought by Chilean leaders since the outset of the independence process. See Simon Collier, *Ideas and Politics of Chilean Independence (1808–1833)* (New York: Cambridge University Press, 1967); Juan Luis Ossa, *Armies, Politics and Revolution. Chile, 1808–1826* (Liverpool: Liverpool University Press, 2014); Vasco Castillo, *La creación de la República. La filosofía publica en Chile, 1810–1830* (Santiago: Lom ediciones, 2009); Sergio Villalobos, *Tradición y reforma en 1810*, 2nd ed. (Santiago: Ril editores, 2006); Alfredo Jocelyn-Holt, *La independencia de Chile. Tradición, modernización y mito*, 3rd ed. (Santiago: Debolsillo, 2009); Eduardo Cavieres, *Sobre la independencia en Chile. El fin del antiguo régimen y los orígenes de la representación moderna* (Valparaíso: Ediciones Universitarias de Valparaíso,

I explore how Britons and Chileans perceived each other from the perspective of cultural history, considering the consequences of these 'cultural encounters' for the subsequent nation-state building process in Chile. The overarching argument is that British and Chilean relations during the struggles for independence were characterised above all by a dynamic and changing nature. Imperialism was only one dimension of this relationship and is therefore not the only way to define it. From 1806 to 1831, both British and Chilean 'state' and 'non-state' actors interacted across several different 'contact zones', thereby configuring this relationship in multiple ways. These interactions reveal that although the extensive presence of 'non-state' actors was a manifestation of the 'expansion' of British interests to Chile, it was not necessarily an expression of any British imperial policy. During this period Chileans held multiple attitudes, perceptions, representations and discourses on the role played by Britain in the world, which changed depending on the circumstances. Likewise, for Britons, Chile was represented in multiple ways, the most predominant image being that of Chile as a pathway to other markets and destinations. All these had repercussions in the early nation-building process in Chile.

With regard to the problem of what it was to be Chilean or Briton in this period, my interest is not to discuss in detail the existence of a nation called Chile *vis-à-vis* a nation called Britain. I accept the idea that both were under construction and that any attempt to define what these nations were in this period would be fatuous. Neither of these nations existed as a clear and defined cultural entity during the overarching period of this book. Linda Colley has made clear that our notion of what Great Britain is today is the result of a complex nation-building process that took place between 1807 and 1837. In Colley's words, 'it was an invention forged above all by war. Time and time again, war with France brought Britons, whether they hailed from Wales, or Scotland or England, into confrontation with an obviously hostile Other and encouraged them to define themselves collectively against it'.[4] This means that in this period the British nation did not even exist as such, but was still in a process of configuration. However, in the eyes of a Spanish American or a Chilean, the distinctions between English, Scottish, Welsh or even Irish were not relevant. They simply made contact, and established relationship with 'others' who spoke English and were Protestant. On the Chilean side, things were not so different. There is a general consensus in recent historiography on the idea that nations were not the cause, but the outcome of the independence.[5] Hence, it is hard to identify an 'imagined

---

2012). Neither Jocelyn-Holt nor Cavieres refers explicitly to a year, but it can be inferred from their texts that their analyses do not start in 1806.

4 Colley, p. 5.

5 See Manuel Chust and José Antonio Serrano, 'Un debate actual, una revisión necesaria', in *Debates sobre las independencias iberoamericanas*, ed. by Manuel Chust and José Antonio Serrano (Madrid: Iberoamericana – AHILA, 2007), pp. 9–26 (p. 19).

community' of Chileans in this period as we probably do today. As Colley has said, inspired by Eric Hobsbawm, 'identities are not like hats. Human beings can and do put on several at a time'.[6] In the independence era multiple identities and loyalties overlapped in the same individual: the town, the country or kingdom, the continent and even the *patria* (Spain). In the Chilean case, the most influential interpretation of the nation building-process suggests that the Chilean nation was constructed by the state during the nineteenth century, warfare being one of the key factors that shaped this process.[7] This interpretation, however, dismisses any relevance of 'otherness', whereas for recent researchers, including Colley, this was crucial factor in understanding how nationhood is shaped. Therefore, I argue that contacts, conflicts and relationships between Chileans and Britons influenced the first stage of the nation-building process in Chile.

In a first moment (1806–1808), interactions occurred on an inter-state level and were expressed in both plans to invade Chile and to defend it. The course of the Napoleonic wars in Europe determined the way British policymakers envisioned their approach to Chile. On the other hand, the changing alliances and relationships between the European powers during the Napoleonic wars determined the way Chileans perceived and represented the role of Britain and Britons. British policy regarding Chile was primarily defined by imperialism and British policymakers outlined a plan to invade and incorporate this territory into the Empire due to its privileged location connecting the Atlantic and the Pacific. This was a means to undermine the power of the Spanish Empire as well as to expand British trade routes to the Pacific.

From 1808 to 1818 interactions mainly occurred between 'non-state' actors as a result of Britain's policy of neutrality which restrained state actors from interfering in the struggles for Spanish American independence. When France invaded Spain in 1808, relations between the European powers were reconfigured and Britain and Spain became allies. This led Chileans to change their perceptions of and attitudes towards Britain and to focus on the defence of their territory on behalf of their king, although older suspicions remained for a brief period. When the conflict between Spain and its colonies ignited, Britain declared said policy of neutrality, which restrained any British aggression towards Chile. As a result, during the war for Chile's independence (1812–1818) the relationships between Chile and Britain mainly (but not exclusively) occurred at the 'non-state' level. The newly established Congress of Chile (1811) sent an envoy to London – Francisco Antonio Pinto – in order to obtain support from Britain, but his political status remained unclear and ambiguous since Chile did not declare its independence until February 1818. In other words, Chile, as with the other Spanish colonies, was not yet a state, but a rebel Spanish colony and the British government did not recognise

6 Colley, p. 6.
7 Mario Góngora, *Ensayo histórico sobre la noción de Estado en Chile en los siglos XIX y XX* (Santiago: Editorial Universitaria, 1981).

Pinto as the representative of any state. On the British side, different actors such as missionaries, educators, soldiers, sailors and merchants arrived in Chile for different purposes and established several types of 'cultural encounters' – short-lived, long-standing, troubled, or friendly – with locals.[8] These encounters were spheres in which both Britons and Chileans interacted, exchanged and mutually influenced their respective cultures, expressed in language, ideas, beliefs, costumes and attitudes. This fits well with Eliga H. Gould's analysis of the 'entangled histories' of Britain and Spain, which were 'concerned with mutual influencing, reciprocal or asymmetric perceptions, and the intertwined process of constituting one another'.[9] These exchanges had significant repercussions in the configuration of a Chilean national identity, since they fostered some of the first reflections and debates on Chileans' place in the wider world. Many Chileans had to interact with people that spoke another European language, professed another religion and had different ideas about trade, education and politics.

From 1818 to 1831, state and non-state actors overlapped as a result of both the inauguration of negotiations for British recognition of independence and the opening of trade, which encouraged hundreds of British traders to settle in Chile. Once the independence of Chile was achieved and declared (1818), relations between Britain and Chile again occurred in a 'state' level, whilst non-state encounters continued – and even increased – as Chileans began to lobby for British recognition of their independence. This also led them to promote a new image of a country characterised by order, progress and stability which would become the basis of Chile's future national identity.[10]

8 For a discussion on this see the next section of this Introduction, 'Definitions'.

9 Eliga H. Gould, 'Entangled Histories, Entangled Worlds: The English Speaking Atlantic as a Spanish Periphery', *The American Historical Review*, 112:3 (2007), 764–86 (p. 766). For an analysis on 'mutual influences' in this period see Matthew Brown and Gabriel Paquette, 'The Persistence of Mutual Influence: Europe and Latin America in the 1820s', *European History Quarterly*, 41:3 (2011), special issue: 'Europe and Latin America in the 1820s', ed. by Matthew Brown and Gabriel Paquette, 387–96. See also Brown and Paquette, 'Introduction: Between the Age of Revolutions and the Age of Empire', in *Connections after Colonialism: Europe and Latin America in the 1820s* (Tuscaloosa, AL: The University of Alabama Press, 2013), pp. 1–28 (p. 5).

10 A recent contribution to the literature on self-denomination is Maria José Schneuer, 'Los ingleses del Pacífico. Identidad, guerra y superioridad en el discurso político chileno durante el siglo XIX' (unpublished doctoral dissertation, Pontificia Universidad Católica de Chile, 2014). The allegory of the 'English of the Pacific' has been widely used in Chile. Benjamin Vicuña Mackenna suggests that it was the Britons who settled in Valparaíso in the 1820s at the foot of Mount Pleasant (*Cerro Alegre*) who started to call the city 'The England of the Pacific'. See 'La Inglaterra chica i la Inglaterra grande. Como un sarjento de artillería contribuyo al reconocimiento de la independencia de Chile por la Gran Bretaña', in Benjamín Vicuña Mackenna, *Chile. Relaciones históricas. Colección de artículos I tradiciones sobre asuntos nacionales*, 2nd series (Santiago, Lima and Valparaíso: Rafael Jover editor, 1919), pp. 615–47 (p. 621).

This schematic explanation illustrates one of the main points of this book: that it is necessary to study on their own terms the relations between Great Britain and Chile in the dynamic years of the independence struggles, rather than considering the latter as the foundational period of a later relationship defined by imperialism. This is because there is a common assumption about the 'outcome' of the independence struggles according to which after breaking free from Spanish dominion, the former Spanish American colonies inevitably felt under a new (British) imperial yoke. According to dependency theory scholars like Stanley and Barbara Stein, the new Spanish American elites – including the Chileans – compromised their economic (and political) independence and brought the new states into the orbit of the British Empire as new markets, depots and suppliers of raw materials.[11] The Chilean case seemed to be the best example of this subordination, as pointed out by Hernán Ramírez Necochea, for whom 'since its separation from Spain, [Chile] experienced vigorous and growing British penetration, which ended up making our country a satellite of the English economic system'.[12] More recently, postcolonial theorists have refashioned this conception under the framework of a 'neo-colonial pact' between Latin American and European elites during the nineteenth century.[13] They hold that the colonial condition has been a permanent feature of Latin Americans' identities, and colonialism as a practice has remained 'uninterrupted' to the point that 'it has marked Latin American history from its beginning'.[14] In cultural terms, according to scholars like Walter Mignolo and Aníbal Quijano, independence meant nothing but a 're-articulation of the coloniality of power over new institutional bases'.[15]

However, as Alan Knight points out, 'colonies that have attained independence rarely succumb to renewed colonial rule'.[16] It is therefore not so simple to claim that what characterised the relations between Chile and Great Britain after independence necessarily represented a neocolonial or neo-imperial

11 Stanley J. Stein and Barbara H. Stein, *The Colonial Heritage of Latin America: Essays on Economic Dependence in Historical Perspective* (New York: Oxford University Press, 1970), p. 136.

12 Hernán Ramírez Necochea, *Historia del imperialismo en* Chile, 2nd ed. (Havana: Edición revolucionaria, 1966), p. 23. See also Gabriel Salazar, *Mercaderes, empresarios y capitalistas: Chile, siglo XIX*, 2nd ed. (Santiago: Editorial Sudamericana, 2011).

13 Mabel Moraña, Enrique Dussel and Carlos Jáuregui, 'Colonialism and its Replicants', in *Coloniality at Large: Latin America and the Postcolonial Debate*, ed. by Mabel Moraña, Enrique Dussel and Carlos Jáuregui (Durham, NC and London: Duke University Press, 2008), pp. 1–22 (p. 10).

14 Ibid., pp. 8–9.

15 Anibal Quijano, 'Coloniality of Power, Eurocentrism and Social Classification', in *Coloniality at Large*, ed. by Mabel Moraña, Enrique Dussel and Carlos Jáuregui (Durham, NC and London: Duke University Press, 2008), pp. 181–224 (p. 215).

16 Alan Knight, 'Rethinking Informal Empire in Latin America (Especially Argentina), in *Informal Empire in Latin America: Culture, Commerce and Capital*, ed. by Matthew Brown (Oxford: Blackwell Publishing, 2008), pp. 23–48 (p. 38).

relationship. Of course, this was one clear possibility, but to assume that neocolonialism was the 'obvious', only and inevitable outcome of independence implies starting the analysis from a predetermined end, overshadowing the different and unpredictable possibilities experienced by Chileans during this period.[17] This also might lead us to regard the independence years as mere background to the further imperialistic advances exerted by Great Britain over Chile in the second half of the nineteenth century, particularly during the so-called 'Nitrate era' (c. 1880–1930).[18] A careful analysis of the period demonstrates instead that there were many different ways in which Britain and Chile related to each other that were determined by changes in the geopolitical sphere resulting from the development of the Napoleonic wars in Europe.

Thus, the questions that this study intends to resolve are: What was the role of the British Empire in the making of Chile? To what extent were the relations between Britain and Chile shaped by imperialism? What was the role of the interaction between Britons and Chileans during the struggles for independence in the configuration of a distinctive national identity? To what extent was British imperialism experienced in Chileans' everyday lives? How were those Britons who arrived in Chile in this period perceived by Chileans? What repercussions did Britain's interactions with Chileans have for its self-representation as an imperial power? What were the consequences for British imperial policy of interaction with Chile?

Imperialism or Expansion?

The role of Great Britain in the Spanish American independence struggles cannot be overlooked. In geopolitical terms the overarching period of this book is coincident with the most expansionist period of the British Empire, which C.A. Bayly has referred to as the 'imperial meridian'.[19] Even though Spanish and British imperial rivalry had started early in seventeenth century, the outbreak of the independence process in Spanish America (1808) was seen as a new opportunity to weaken Spanish power.[20] This is what Rafe Blaufarb calls the 'Western Question', which was 'less about the question of independence per se than about how the conflict would affect the geopolitical

---

17 I am using the term 'Chilean' only to refer to the people who inhabited the territory today called Chile. In strict terms, 'Chile' did not exist as a political and distinct entity until the end of the independence process.

18 This view is found in the work of authors like John Mayo, Gabriel Salazar and Hernán Ramírez Necochea, all of whom are quoted in this Introduction.

19 C.A. Bayly, *Imperial Meridian: The British Empire and the World, 1780–1830* (London: Longman, 1989).

20 This is the overarching argument of Peggy K. Liss, *Atlantic Empires: The Network of Trade and Revolution, 1713–1826* (Baltimore, MD: Johns Hopkins University Press, 1983).

order'. In this context, the role of Great Britain seemed critical as all the other powers, such as Spain, France and even the United States, feared that it 'would achieve global hegemony by turning South America into a "second Hindoustan"'.[21] Anick Lempérière has even claimed that this context was so crucial that the new Spanish American states were the 'final product and even the protagonists of a long inter-imperial struggle'.[22]

British imperialism has then been regarded as a crucial factor in understanding the outcome of the independence struggles, although there are divergent interpretations of the role played by Britain in this process. Whereas many scholars see Spanish American independence as nothing other than a means to secure British imperial and commercial supremacy over the new-born states,[23] many other authors maintain that independence was somehow 'given' to Spanish Americans as a result of the spread of British values like liberty and progress. In the late nineteenth century this was exaggerated to the point that one of the first works on Anglo-South American relations emphasised 'how much South America is indebted to Englishmen, in arts, arms and commerce'.[24]

An alternative approach emerged in the 1950s, when John Gallagher and Ronald Robinson published their seminal article 'Imperialism of Free Trade', in which they laid the ground for further debates on British 'informal' imperialism, defined as 'trade with informal control if possible, trade with rule when necessary'.[25] Simon Potter makes clear that this was not a different 'pacific' phase of British imperialism in the mid-nineteenth century, as suggested by some scholars, but a single policy that used different means when necessary, with 'formal rule' the last resort.[26] This approach has been very influential in the understanding of British and Latin American relations in the nineteenth century. Alan Knight, for example, claims that 'informal empire' depends on a 'repertoire of informal pressures and influences (which may include coercion and the threat of coercion)'.[27] Therefore, coercion and threat, two elements that characterise 'formal' imperialism, were not necessary conditions

21 Rafe Blaufarb, 'The Western Question: The Geopolitics of Latin American Independence', *The American Historical Review*, 112:3 (2007), 742–63 (p. 747).

22 Annick Lempérière, 'Presentación: Hacia una nueva historia transnacional de las independencias hispanoamericanas', in *Las revoluciones americanas y la formación de los estados nacionales*, ed. by Jaime Rosenblitt (Santiago: DIBAM, 2013), pp. 13–27 (p. 18).

23 An example is Liss, pp. 209–22. See also Leslie Bethell, 'Britain and Latin America in Historical Perspective', in *Britain and Latin America: A Changing Relationship*, ed. by Victor Bulmer-Thomas (Cambridge and New York: Cambridge University Press, 1989), pp. 1–24.

24 Michael G. Mulhall, *The English in South America* (Buenos Aires: Standard Office; London: Stanford, 1878), p. 14.

25 John Gallagher and Ronald Robinson, 'The Imperialism of Free Trade', *The Economic History Review*, 6:1 (1953), 1–15 (p. 13).

26 Simon Potter, *British Imperial History* (London: Palgrave, 2015), pp. 21–26.

27 Knight, p. 28.

to define the British policy regarding Spanish America as 'imperialist'. More important instead would be the 'perceived mutual interests' of the elites in a relation that was above all shaped by commercial interests. Rory Miller has well explained the difficulties that this interpretation caused for the understanding of the relations between Britain and Latin America. First, it was challenged early by other British scholars like D.C.M. Platt, who claimed that there were significant differences between the interests of government and businessmen. Second, this interpretation had little influence over Latin American scholars, who developed their own interpretations of the role played by Britain. Third, it left open many questions about the relations between businessmen and Latin American elites and left unresolved the marginal place that Latin America occupies in the historiography of British imperialism.[28]

However, this is not the only way to understand the nature of British and Chilean relations during the independence era. Indeed, as an analytical tool, informal imperialism seldom appears in the historiography of independence.[29] The original ideas of Gallagher and Robinson actually apply to the mid-nineteenth century onwards, leaving less explored the extent to which this approach suits the early nineteenth century. In *The Making and Unmaking of Empires*, Peter J. Marshall offers some key insights about British imperial interests in the late eighteenth century. Marshall's focus is primarily on the loss of the 13 North American colonies and the British expansion to India. He claims that concepts like 'expansion' and 'empire' should not be confused or conflated. Marshall's distinction between the roles of 'private' actors and the 'state', which do not necessarily pursue the same interests, is particularly useful for the approach adopted in this book. Marshall argues that 'empire' is a concept that should be used carefully since 'coercion' and 'rule' are key elements defining it and are not always present. Chile is therefore a good case where some of these insights can be applied, even though it does not form part of Marshall's study. Private British actors such as privateers and smugglers were present in Chile from the sixteenth century and others such as merchants, missionaries, military, seamen and educators began to arrive during the struggles for independence. Their presence did not necessarily represent the 'empire', but they were connected to the expansion of British interests in Chile in a period in which imperial ambitions were not always clear or explicit. As Marshall says, 'expansion and empire, private enterprise and state action, were closely linked and mutually dependent. In most cases, however, expansion had preceded the empire'.[30]

28 Rory Miller, *Britain and Latin America in the 19ᵗʰ and 20ᵗʰ Centuries* (Oxford and New York: Routledge, 2013), pp. 17–20.

29 A recent exception is Deborah Besseghini, 'Commercio britannico e imperialismo informale in America latina. Robert P. Staples tra Río de la Plata, Perù e Messico (1808–1824)' (unpublished doctoral dissertation, University of Trieste, 2015).

30 Peter J. Marshall, *The Making and Unmaking of Empires: Britain, India and America, c. 1750–1783* (New York: Oxford University Press, 2005), p. 13.

This book demonstrates that the encounters that took place between 1806 and 1831 are closer to what Marshall calls 'expansion' than to 'empire'. The presence of private or 'non-state' actors contributed to the expansion of British interests, but elements such as coercion and rule were not applied by them. The only moment in which the British authorities aimed to rule Chile with coercion was in 1806–1807, when they outlined a plan to invade and incorporate its territory into the British dominions and to rule the local population.

The Historiography

Chile's independence process has recently been an object of renewed historical research, but it still lacks a more explicit consideration of the wider geopolitical context of the period. The bicentennial celebrations in 2010 contributed to that cause, although with clear limitations in terms of scope. Compared to other countries like Mexico or Argentina, the production of academic works on the independence of Chile was clearly limited and the perspectives were not always original.[31] One critical reason might be that, as Eduardo Cavieres said, liberal nineteenth-century historiography still influences the debates on Chile's independence and there is a clear tendency among Chilean historians to 'close' the topics that have already been researched, avoiding any possibility of a revision, or to engender more serious debate regarding a problem.[32] Likewise, as Paula Caffarena and I have argued elsewhere, the persistence of the 'classic works' on Chilean independence – namely, Villalobos's, Collier's and Jocelyn-Holt's monographs – represents a constraint for any new major debate on the independence process as a whole, and most of their ideas are taken for granted.[33] This is why most of the newest works have focused on the 'understudied' actors of independence, like women, indigenous peoples and the *bajo pueblo* (lower classes), or the role of the provinces in opposition to Santiago, without questioning the overarching paradigms.[34] The recent contribution of Juan Luis Ossa Santa Cruz returns to the role of soldiers, broadening the scope of the subject and

---

31 For a discussion on this see my article co-authored with Paula Caffarena, 'La independencia de Chile en su Bicentenario', *Tiempos de America. Revista de Historia, Cultura y Territorio*, 20 (2013) special issue: 'Las Revoluciones de Independencia: un bicentenario a debate', ed. by Manuel Chust, 91–98.

32 Cavieres, *Sobre la independencia en Chile*, p. 15.

33 Baeza and Caffarena, 91–98.

34 Leonardo León, *Ni patriotas ni realistas. El bajo pueblo durante la independencia de Chile: 1810–1822* (Santiago: Centro Diego Barros Arana, 2012); Patricia Peña, 'Y las mujeres, ¿dónde estuvieron? Mujeres en el proceso independentista chileno', *Anuario de Posgrado Universidad de Chile*, 2 (1997), 235–52; Hugo Contreras, 'Artesanos mulatos y soldados beneméritos. El batallón de infantes de la patria en la guerra de independencia de Chile', *Historia*, 44:1 (2011), 51–89.

examining their role in the armies that fought for independence, as political actors who would play a fundamental part in the construction of the new republican state during the 1820s. Ossa's argument, shared by this book, transcends the limits imposed by Chile's current national boundaries as a point of reference and adopts a transnational approach in order to gain a better grasp of the independence process.[35]

The role of foreign powers like Britain, France or the US in the struggles for Chilean independence remains understudied. What we know about the British-Chilean connections during this period remains fragmented and scattered across different articles and monographs which are, at the same time, written from a wide range of perspectives and underscored by different theoretical frameworks. No particular monograph analyses the nature of these relations in depth. There are many relatively old works on the political and diplomatic influence of Great Britain on Chilean independence, the life and adventures of Lord Thomas Cochrane in the 'liberation' of Chile, the adoption of Lancaster's system of education, the role of merchants and, above all, the role of trade in shaping the connections between Great Britain and Chile.[36] More recently, there has been a renewed interest in British cultural influence on the heritage of Valparaíso (Chile's most important port city).[37]

In fact, Chile is a country in which large communities of Britons settled in different cities, like Valparaíso from the 1820s and where British commercial intervention was a key element of its economic history. Therefore, informal imperialism has seemed to be a suitable analytical tool to study these relations, albeit not for the early nineteenth century. John Mayo, who focuses on British trade and investment in Chile from the mid-nineteenth century, argues that the 'anatomy' of this relation was 'informal dominion',[38]

---

35 Ossa, *Armies, Politics and Revolution*, especially section I.I, '1808–1810: Internal Responses to Imperial Crisis', pp. 16–23. This need was also explicitly indicated by Lempérière in order to situate the independence process in both its inter- and intra-imperial contexts, but also to withdraw from any notion of 'nation' when assessing the role of the actors involved. See Lempérière, p. 17.

36 In this section I will refer to the general works on the subject while the specific works on each of the topics of this book will be discussed in each chapter accordingly. Some of the most relevant works are: Ricardo Montaner Bello, *Historia diplomática de la independencia de Chile* (Santiago: Editorial Andrés Bello, 1961); Brian Vale, *Cochrane in the Pacific: Fortune and Freedom in Spanish America* (London: I.B. Tauris, 2008); Domingo Amunátegui, *El sistema de Lancaster en Chile y otros países sudamericanos* (Santiago: Imprenta Cervantes, 1895); John L. Rector, 'Merchants, Trade, and Commercial Policy in Chile: 1810–1840' (unpublished doctoral dissertation, Indiana University, 1976).

37 Michelle Prain Brice (ed.), *El legado británico en Valparaíso* (Santiago: Ril-Instituto Chileno Británico de Cultura, 2011).

38 John Mayo, 'Britain and Chile, 1851-1886: Anatomy of a Relationship', *Journal of Inter-American Studies and World Affairs*, 23:1 (1981), 95–120 (p. 117).

whereby Chile became part of Britain's informal empire through economic dependence. With regard to the independence era, he only states that it must be regarded as the 'background' to the further asymmetrical relations between these two states.[39] Despite this, in another work about the merchant communities in Coquimbo during the 1820s Mayo did not even mention the word 'empire', nor did he consider informal imperialism as an analytical tool to understand the role of these merchants in Chile's economic and political development in this period.[40] This certainly makes it more difficult to determine whether for Mayo informal imperialism was the way to define British and Chilean relations in early nineteenth century. Claudio Llanos, for his part, has addressed the close connections between scientific knowledge of Chile among British scientific societies and informal imperialism since 1830, but left the independence period unexplored.[41] Although he did not tackle informal imperialism itself, Gabriel Salazar has studied the role of the ruling elite composed of 'entrepreneurs, merchants and capitalists' in the making of the Chilean state and how their interests were shaped by their subordination to the British merchant houses.[42] The role of merchants in the 1820s is a fundamental part of his study, although clearly situated as the starting point of further intervention later in the nineteenth century.

Apart from these works, approaches to British imperialism and Chile are largely absent from historical debates. This absence is also evident in the historiography of the British Empire. Since Latin America, and particularly Chile, did not form part of the 'formal' British Empire, the region still occupies a marginal place in histories of the British Empire in the nineteenth century.[43] On the other hand, contributions on British and Chilean relations are limited to the fields of diplomatic, economic and naval histories without engaging in debates on imperialism.[44] William Edmundson's account of the British 'presence' in Chile from the sixteenth to the nineteenth century is an attempt to systematise the different aspects involved, but it lacks an engagement with these debates.[45] Only in 2013 Marcelo Somarriva has tackled

---

39 Ibid., p. 99.
40 John Mayo, 'The Development of British Interests in Chile's Norte Chico in the Early Nineteenth Century', *The Americas*, 57:3 (2001), 363–94.
41 Claudio Llanos, 'Imperialismo inglés y ciencia. La Sociedad Geográfica Real de Londres, 1830–1870', *Boletín Americanista*, 60 (2010), 209–25.
42 Salazar, *Mercaderes, empresarios y capitalistas*, pp. 79–160.
43 A good example of the absence of Chile in these debates is found in *Settlers and Expatriates: Britons over the Seas*, ed. by Robert Bickers, The Oxford History of the British Empire, Companion Series (Oxford and New York: Oxford University Press, 2010).
44 The major contributions to each of these fields will be discussed throughout the book.
45 William Edmundson, *A History of the British Presence in Chile: From Bloody Mary to Charles Darwin and the Decline of the British Influence* (New York: Palgrave Macmillan, 2009).

these relations between 1808 and 1830 from a cultural theory perspective.[46] Somarriva's major concern lies in the field of 'cultural representations', using mainly written and published sources, such as newspapers, articles, speeches and travel writing, to illustrate the way British and Spanish American elites configured their image of each other. In the Introduction of his thesis it is asserted that:

> it was [...] a relationship profoundly shaped by culture, in which, from the British point of view, travel books and private letters published in newspapers were often the most valuable sources of information available for the public about regions which were becoming increasingly attractive. From the perspective of the Southern Cone, Great Britain became a powerful reference point and in relation to which many of their political, economic and cultural aspirations were modelled.[47]

Somarriva makes a significant contribution to our understanding of British and Chilean relations in the early nineteenth century, demonstrating that many debates that took place in Chile and were published in British newspapers influenced policymaking regarding trade and commerce with Spanish America.

Building on this work, my book explores the interactions that took place in different physical and intellectual 'contact zones', moving beyond the exclusive focus on 'representations' that tend to be more evident when drawing upon published sources and newspapers. Many of the sources used here are unpublished ones like manuscripts and private correspondence, which are not often included in the field of cultural representations, including but moving beyond the study of culture. This study is an attempt to systematise the analysis of British-Chilean relations between 1806 and 1831, taking into account different spheres of interaction rather than trying to demonstrate any particular influence of British culture in the making of Chile as a new nation state. The result is a new interpretation of the subject based upon the perspectives of cultural and transnational histories, drawing scattered fragments together and considering the whole over the *longue durée*.

Contacts, Collisions and Relationships

I agree with Somarriva's suggestion that 'culture' is fundamental in rethinking our understanding of British-Chilean relations. In most cases scholars focus mostly on the political and economic interests of the British Empire, leaving

---

46 See Gabriel Salazar, *Construcción de estado en Chile (1760–1860): Democracia de 'los pueblos', militarismo ciudadano, golpismo oligárquico* (Santiago: Editorial Sudamericana, 2005); Julio Pinto and Verónica Valdivia Ortiz de Zarate, *¿Chilenos todos? La construcción social de la nación (1810–1840)* (Santiago: Ediciones Lom, 2009); León, *Ni patriotas ni realistas*.

47 Somarriva, p. 5.

less explored how Chileans themselves were affected by this.[48] Matthew Brown, drawing upon concepts advanced by 'cultural historians' of imperialism like Mary Louise Pratt, Ricardo Salvatore and Carlos Aguirre, stresses the need to incorporate 'culture' into the analysis, relating the concept to the everyday lives and the mindset of the actors involved. In his view, 'informal empire must be lived, and known, if it is to exist'.[49] Thus, any analysis of these relations needs to take into account both the policies and practices of imperialism embedded in its 'agents'– if such a thing actually defined this relationship – and their reception by those locals who interacted with them.

Nonetheless, the very use of the term 'culture' and some related concepts such as 'cultural encounters and 'cultural history' might be problematic. There is no single way to define and use these concepts, which are also characterised by their elusiveness. Some scholars have linked the term 'culture' to the way Spanish American elites followed Britain as a 'cultural model', from which they took different ideas, values and concepts in the nation-state building process. Karen Racine, for example, has demonstrated how some concepts like 'tradition, property, hierarchy and controlled change' were often associated with British reformism and were seen by the Spanish American leaders as values to be adopted.[50] Yet this was not simply a unidirectional influence. If this occurred it was because many of the leaders of Spanish American independence had actually lived and were educated in London, and if they admired Britain it was due to their own life experience. Bernardo O'Higgins, for example, who was the Supreme Director of Chile between 1817 and 1823, was of Irish descent and had been educated in London.[51]

48 Two classic works on the role of Britain in Spanish American independence, although they only consider British policy as a driving force, are: Charles K. Webster, *Britain and the Independence of Latin America, 1812-1830*, 2 vols (London: Oxford University Press, 1938) and William W. Kaufman, *British Policy and Latin American Independence, 1808-1824* (New Haven, CT: Yale University Press, 1951). In Chile, this is evident even in Ramírez Necochea and Salazar's approaches, but also in others informed by theories of informal imperialism, although they focus on the processes that took place from 1850 onwards. In this regard, see John Mayo, *British Merchants and Chilean Development, 1851-1886* (Boulder, CO: Westview Press, 1987).

49 Matthew Brown, 'Introduction', in *Informal Empire in Latin America: Culture, Commerce and Capital*, ed. by Matthew Brown (Oxford: Blackwell Publishing, 2008), p. 21.

50 Karen Racine, 'This England and This Now: British Cultural and Intellectual Influence in the Spanish American Independence Era', *Hispanic American Historical Review*, 90:3 (2010), 423–54 (p. 442); Karen Racine, 'Proxy Pasts: The Use of British Historical References in Spanish American Independence Rhetoric, 1808–1828', *The English Historical Review*, 132:557 (2017), 863–84. See also Stein and Stein, p. 167.

51 Racine, 'This England and this Now', pp. 435–41. An analysis of how having lived and being educated in London influenced O'Higgins see Karen Racine, 'The Childhood Shows the Man: Latin American Children in Great Britain, 1790–1830', *The Americas*, 72:2 (2015), 279–308 (pp. 282–85).

During his government the new navy of Chile and the new educational system were organised under British models that he knew well from living in London.

Matthew Brown and Louise H. Gunther have paid more attention to the dimension of everyday life, for the Colombian and Brazilian cases respectively. Brown has studied the cultural encounters between the locals and the more than 7,000 British adventurers who joined Bolívar's army, challenging the old assumptions about the unidirectional influence of Great Britain on the country's independence.[52] For his part, Guenther has investigated the role of British merchant communities that settled in Brazil in the early nineteenth century with a clear focus on cultural and social life.[53] In both cases the focus is on cultural encounters and interpersonal relations between Britons and locals, which illustrate the ground that this approach has gained in the historiography of Latin America.[54] Although not from the perspective of cultural history, the work of Alina Silveira has shed light on the integration of the British communities in Buenos Aires during the wars of independence by focusing on social life and the formation of the first associations.[55] For the Chilean case it is more difficult to find contributions like these. Marcelo Somarriva, for example, explicitly states that he is focusing on 'cultural representations', which led him to pay less attention to interpersonal relations.[56] Even though it focuses on the period from the 1830s onwards, Patience Schells's *The Sociable Sciences: Darwin and his Contemporaries in Chile* is one of the few works that fits into this perspective.[57] Her emphasis on interpersonal relations between British scientists like Charles Darwin and Chilean locals, and the mutual influences that resulted, fits well into a recent historical trend which considers these types of relations as critical to understanding wider nation-building processes.

52 Matthew Brown, *Adventuring through Spanish Colonies: Simón Bolívar, Foreign Mercenaries and the Birth of New Nations* (Liverpool: Liverpool University Press, 2006).

53 Louise H. Guenther, *British Merchants in Nineteenth-Century Brazil: Business, Culture, and Identity in Bahia, 1808–50* (Oxford: Centre for Brazilian Studies, University of Oxford, 2004).

54 Ibid.; Brown, *Adventuring through Spanish Colonies*.

55 Alina Silveira, 'Ingleses y escoceses en Buenos Aires. Movimientos poblacionales, integración y practicas asociativas (1800–1880)' (unpublished doctoral dissertation, Universidad de San Andrés, Buenos Aires, 2014).

56 Marcelo Somarriva, '"An Open Field and Fair Play": The Relationship between Britain and the Southern Cone of America between 1808 and 1830' (unpublished doctoral dissertation, University College London, 2012), pp. 5–14.

57 Patience A. Schell, *The Sociable Sciences: Darwin and his Contemporaries in Chile* (New York: Palgrave Macmillan, 2013). Another recent contribution that has (re)positioned Chile in global history is Paula Caffarena, 'Viruela y vacuna. Difusión y circulación de una práctica médica. Chile en el contexto hispanoamericano, 1780–1830' (unpublished doctoral dissertation. Pontificia Universidad Católica de Chile, 2015).

The incorporation of everyday life is crucial to the understanding of culture adopted in this book. Particularly, I follow Raymond Williams's social dimension of culture, defined as 'a description of a particular way of life, which expresses certain meaning and values not only in art and learning but also in institutions and ordinary behaviour'.[58] The other two dimensions of culture, the 'ideal' and the 'documentary', are not absent from my analysis.[59] If anything characterised the expansion of the British Empire, it was its 'civilising' discourse (ideal dimension), expressed in travel diaries and memoirs written by its agents, that reinforced the supposed supremacy of the British Empire (a documentary dimension of culture).

My concern is, however, how these entangled dimensions of culture were also embedded in the lives of those Britons who reached Chile during the struggles for independence and those Chileans who interacted with them.[60] I am using the term 'everyday life' in a relatively limited way and not considering all aspects of the private life of the protagonists of this book. My focus is their perceptions, discourses and representations of the other when they came into contact, as well as their self-image when entering into a relationship with the other, rather than the way they ate, lived or dressed. These were also aspects that emerged in their ordinary life that are not often included in the narratives of British-Chilean relations. Fears of being invaded by Britain, the obligation of adopting a foreign language as members of a navy, the presence of Protestant missionaries or British merchants and diplomats with different beliefs, values and perceptions of Chile and the debates that they triggered, are some examples of these dimensions studied here.

This clarification also permits us to be more precise when explaining why this books is a sort of 'cultural history' of British-Chilean relations. As Peter Burke admits, it seems that nowadays most cultural historians study culture in its wide range of manifestations of 'everyday life'. From this perspective, one of the strengths of cultural history is that 'it privileges encounters, dialogues, viewpoints, conflicts, misunderstandings and translations (including mistranslations)'.[61] The focus on 'encounters' is precisely the one privileged in this book as it offers good opportunities to analyse representations, discourses and interactions between peoples of different backgrounds and origins. Following Burke, 'from a methodological point of view, encounters reveal more clearly than usual major differences of viewpoint, mentality

58 Raymond Williams, 'The Analysis of Culture', in *Cultural Theory and Popular Culture: A Reader* ed. by John Storey, 2nd ed. (Athens, GA: The University of Georgia Press, 1998), pp. 48–56 (p. 48).

59 The 'ideal' concept refers to a certain stage of human perfection and universal values, whereas the 'documentary' relates to 'body of intellectual and imaginative work'. See Williams, 'The Analysis of Culture', p. 48.

60 Raymond Williams, 'Culture Is Ordinary', in *The Everyday Life Reader*, ed. by Ben Highmore (London and New York: Routledge, 2002), p. 93.

61 Burke, 'Strengths and Weaknesses of Cultural History', p. 9.

or assumptions between people from different cultures, making open or explicit what is normally hidden or implicit'.[62]

Considering that this book deals with different ambits such as military, naval, religious, educational, economic and diplomatic histories, the approach of 'cultural encounters' permits a transcendence of the boundaries imposed by the particular methodology of each approach. The case of John James Barnard, who arrived in Chile in 1812, is a good demonstrative example. He is often regarded as a British merchant, but he was also an arms trafficker who sold weapons to the patriots, a Bible seller, a Monitorial school benefactor and one of the funders of the Liberation Expedition of Peru. In other words, he appears in almost every chapter of this book, one reason why it was necessary to adopt a thematic approach that transcends disciplinary divisions.

One model of 'cultural encounters' was advanced by the Swiss historian Urs Bitterli, whose typology of contact, collision and relationship from 1492 to 1800 is useful for understanding the nature of the relations that took place in the overarching period of this book.[63] Bitterli defines 'contact' as an 'initial, short-lived or intermittent encounter' often characterised by peacefulness and mutual goodwill. Most of the initial contacts between Europeans and non-Europeans, he claims, ended up in a 'collision', in which 'the weaker partner, in military and political terms, was threatened with the loss of cultural identity, while even its physical existence was jeopardised and sometimes annihilated altogether'. If a contact did not end up in a collision (although a collision could also produce the same effect), the outcome was a 'relationship', defined as 'a prolonged series of reciprocal contacts on the basis of political equilibrium or stalemate'. On the European side, Bitterli adds, these relationships 'were sustained [...] by traders and missionaries'.[64]

However, as this book shows, British missionaries did not necessarily establish 'relationships' with their counterparts, but short-lived encounters or 'contacts'. At the same time, the encounters that took place within the Chilean navy were characterised by complexity, and both collision and relationships are suitable analytical tools there. This was even more evident in the case of traders, many of whom did establish long-term relationships with Chileans and were also integrated into society. Still, it cannot be denied that many of them acted as imperial agents representing British expansionist interests. Bitterli's approach is useful for conceptualising the analysis of a cultural encounter, despite his not recommending the term's use for post-1800 encounters, perhaps because he did not regard them

---

62 Ibid., p. 9.
63 Urs Bitterli, *Cultures in Conflict: Encounters between European and Non-European Cultures, 1492–1800*, trans. by Ritchie Robertson (Stanford, CA: Stanford University Press, 1989).
64 Ibid., pp. 20–51.

as proper encounters. This is why the conceptualisation of the 'contact zone' advanced by Marie Louise Pratt, defined as space where 'peoples geographically and historically separated come into contact with each other and establish ongoing relations, usually involving conditions of coercion, radical inequality, and intractable conflict', is also useful.[65] As with Bitterli, Pratt's approach emphasises conflict as the core element of these encounters, although she accepts that the relationships established by different peoples are much more complex. This book focuses precisely on the latter. Despite conflict seeming to be a core element of any cultural encounter, there were many instances of non-conflictive interactions. Therefore, contact, collision and relationship formed part of the same complex process of encounters and interactions.

Widening the Scope

The focus on cultural encounters implies going beyond the limitations imposed by the 'nation state' approach and rather adopting a 'transnational' perspective. A transnational approach allows us to study the sites and instances of encounters as spaces of dynamic interaction, in which flows and movements of peoples and ideas were the norm. As pointed out by Gabriel Paquette, this approach has 'breathe[d] new life' into the studies of Spanish American independence and its relation with the world.[66] Eugenia Roldán Vera, for example, has made a major contribution to our understanding of British and Spanish American 'networks' in the post-independence period, through her study of the circulation of textbooks from a transnational perspective.[67] However, there is much more work to do, as is recognised by other scholars like Lauren Benton, who openly calls for a 'reorientation of world history' and for 'repositioning Latin America within it'.[68] This book seeks to contribute to positioning rather than 'repositioning' the history of Chile in the early nineteenth century in a wider scenario of transnational interactions. Transnational (and also global) histories of different aspects of the history of Chile have just recently begun to appear with a clear preference for processes that took place in the twentieth century, particularly during the 'Cold War'.[69] An exception is Ricardo Salvatore, who focuses

---

65 Ibid., pp. 6–7.
66 Gabriel Paquette, 'The Dissolution of the Spanish Atlantic Monarchy', *The Historical Journal*, 52:1 (2009), 175–212 (p. 204).
67 Eugenia Roldán Vera, *The British Book Trade and Spanish American Independence: Education and Knowledge Transmission in Transcontinental Perspective* (Aldershot: Ashgate, 2003).
68 Lauren Benton, 'No Longer Odd Region Out: Repositioning Latin America in World History', *Hispanic American Historical Review* 84:3 (2004), 423–30 (p. 426).
69 See Tanya Harmer and Alfredo Riquelme (eds), *Chile y la Guerra fría global* (Santiago: Ril Editores-Instituto de Historia Universidad Católica, 2015).

on both 'experiences' and 'representations' to understand the nature of imperialism in Latin America.[70]

Yet the use of a transnational perspective is not free of trouble. C.A. Bayly, for instance, calls into question whether the use of the term 'transnational' for the study of the processes that took place before 1850 because 'large parts of the globe were not dominated by nations so much as empires'.[71] Despite this, although the term transnational may seem confusing, it is reasonable to use it as an analytical tool for processes in which national identities were under construction, as was the case of Spanish America in the early nineteenth century. In addition, the transnational approach has methodological advantages since, as claimed by Isabel Hofmeyr, it 'opens up broader analytical possibilities for understanding the complex linkages, networks and actors in the Global South'.[72]

Notwithstanding, this might also be an advantage of other approaches of wide scope such as 'global history'. For John Darwin, a 'new global history' focuses on 'regions or oceans, long-distance trades, networks of merchants, the tracks of wandering scholars, the traffic of cults and beliefs between cultures and continents', all features that are found in this book.[73] The empire seems, therefore, a suitable entry route for global processes of exchange and flows of goods and peoples.[74] In this sense, the characterisation of global history advanced by John De Vries as a 'house of many mansions' helps to clarify which concept better suits this book. The penthouse represents the history of globalisation and the mega-processes of integration, whilst the ground floor is more like the history of transnational interactions on a more 'modest scale'. Since this book seeks to connect two different regions of the globe and not to link the history of Chile to the whole globe, 'transnational history' suits this study better.[75] Even so, there

---

70 Ricardo Salvatore, 'The Enterprise of Knowledge: Representational Machines of Informal Empire', in *Close Encounters of Empire: Writing the Cultural History of U.S.-Latin American Relations*, ed. by Gilbert Michael Joseph, Catherine LeGrand and Ricardo Salvatore (Durham, NC: Duke University Press, 1998), pp. 71–104.

71 C.A. Bayly, Sven Beckert, Matthew Connelly, Isabel Hofmeyr, Wendy Kozol and Patricia Seed, 'AHR Conversation: On Transnational History', *The American Historical Review*, 111:5 (2006), 1441–64 (p. 1442). This is not surprising considering the marginal place occupied by Latin America in Bayly's *The Birth of the Modern World, 1780-1914: Global Connections and Comparisons* (Malden, MA, Oxford and Carlton, Blackwell Publishing, 2004).

72 Hofmeyr, 'AHR Conversation', p. 1444.

73 John Darwin, *After Tamerlane: The Global History of Empire since 1405* (New York: Bloomsbury Press, 2008), p. 12.

74 See Benton, p. 428. Benton considers 'global empires' to be one of the trends that have reshaped world history.

75 John De Vries, 'Reflections on Doing Global History', in *Writing the History of the Global: Challenges for the 21ˢᵗ Century*, ed. by Maxine Berg (Oxford: Oxford University Press, 2013), pp. 32–47 (p. 32).

are some parts for which references to wider continental and transoceanic contexts are also necessary.

The 'transnational turn' has resulted in major advances in recent historical debates on Spanish American independence, but there remains a clear lack of research adopting this perspective for the Chilean case. In addition, this transnational approach is still limited to the processes that took place within the boundaries of the Spanish Empire, without expanding the scope to interactions with other foreign powers like the British Empire. This is still a major challenge for Chilean historiography if we take into account the progress that has been made elsewhere in this respect.[76] Klaus Gallo's *Great Britain and Argentina: From Invasion to Recognition (1806–1826)* is an example of a comprehensive monograph devoted to examining the relations between Argentina and Great Britain between 1806 and 1826 (although primarily concerned with the political, economic and diplomatic spheres).[77] Daniel Gutierrez, for his part, has offered new insights into the diplomatic relations between Colombia and both European and American states and the pursuit for political recognition. Gutierrez not only tackles the diplomatic perspective, but also public opinion and other discourses on the subject.[78]

All these examples suggest that the cultural history methodology adopted here, combined with a transnational approach, will best allow us to explore the meanings and consequences of Spanish American independence within its global context. This combination has significant methodological consequences for the structure of this book. I have defined different sites and instances of interaction between Chileans and Britons rather than trying to embrace all the aspects involved in these relations. Some were physical encounters, like that experienced by the Chilean navy, whilst others occurred in domains in which the presence of Great Britain was perceived, imagined and contested by Chileans, as was the case of the plans to invade Chile and their repercussions. From here onwards, the subsequent diplomatic, naval, religious, educational and commercial ambits are used to analyse the imbricated interactions and interrelations between Chileans and Britons during and after the wars for the independence of Chile.

All these spheres are analysed by applying a 'cultural approach' to determine the ways in which Chileans perceived, received, adopted, adapted and represented different ideas, models, and practices brought by those Britons who arrived in Chile between 1806 and 1831. This implies going beyond British 'influence' and focusing on the entangled and troubled nature

76 See Paquette, pp. 204–05.

77 Klaus Gallo, *Great Britain and Argentina: From Invasion to Recognition (1806–1826)* (Basingstoke and New York: Palgrave-St Antony's College, Oxford, 2001).

78 Daniel Gutiérrez Ardila, *El reconocimiento de Colombia: diplomacia y propaganda en la coyuntura de las restauraciones (1819–1831)* (Bogotá: Universidad Externado de Colombia, 2012).

of such relations. This sheds light on the debates about the construction of Chile's national identity as a prosperous and stable country, a topic that has not been sufficiently addressed from the point of view of the interaction with foreign actors. If this experience offered anything, it was the possibility of interacting with an 'other', and as many scholars have suggested, 'otherness' is a key element in the configuration of any national identity.[79] This is not to say that by the end of the 1820s Chile's national identity was completely configured, but there was at least a first moment of self-differentiation from 'others' who were not Spanish Americans. Thus, an analysis based on the 'contact zones' allows an exploration of the troubled interactions between Chileans and Britons during this period. This implies treating the testimonies of both groups at the same level and to see whether their mutual perceptions, discourses and representations of each other led to a configuration of a mixed or hybrid entity, rather than determining the influence of one group upon the other.

This book draws upon a wide range of primary sources. It brings to light unknown sources from archives in Chile, Great Britain and Spain, and reassesses others that are more well-known. Archival sources, such as official correspondence, personal letters, reports, judiciary files, court martial records, etc. are the most abundant across this study, although some published sources such as compilations of primary sources,[80] annual reports,[81] travel literature[82] and newspapers are also used. The source

---

79 See Anna Trainafyllidou, 'National Identity and the Other', *Ethnic and Racial Studies*, 21:4 (1998), pp. 593–612 (p. 596). This article discusses the main ideas of some of the most relevant scholars who have dealt with issues of the nation, national identities and nationalism like Ernst Gellner and Anthony Smith, and concludes that the existence of the 'other' is an implicit assumption in their theories. However, nationalism is not applicable to the context of Spanish American independence, thus I am not saying that the 'Chilean nation' was constructed in reference to 'another' nation. My point is that the interaction between locals and foreigners (seen as 'others') during Chile's struggles for independence might be seen as a process of differentiation – as were many other factors – that eventually lead to the configuration of a national identity. On the role of foreigners in the process of national identity formation in Gran Colombia, and insights that can also be applied to the Chilean context, see Matthew Brown, 'Not Forging nations but Foraging for them: Uncertain Collective Identities in Gran Colombia', *Nations and Nationalism*, 12:2 (2006), 223–40. A good review of the historiography of national identity in Latin America is Nicola Miller 'The Historiography of Nationalism and National Identity in Latin America', *Nations and Nationalism*, 12:2 (2006), 201–21.

80 Francisco Javier González (ed.), *Archivo de don Bernardo O'Higgins* (Hereafter, *ABO*), vol. 35 (Santiago: Academia Chilena de la Historia, 2001).

81 Mainly the *Annual Reports* of both the British and Foreign School and Bible societies.

82 John Miers, *Travels in Chile and La Plata. Including Accounts Respecting the Geology, Statistics, Government, Finances, Agriculture, Manners and Costumes and the Mining Operations in Chile. Collected During a Residence of Several Years in These Countries,*

material is therefore vast and diverse, and it has been difficult to incorporate all of it, simply because of the amount of information that could possibly be drawn from these sources. In other words, both despite and because of the number of available archival sources, this book does not attempt to offer a comprehensive survey of all the aspects of British-Chilean relations in the independence era, but rather, a theoretically informed analysis of the themes and problems derived from those relations on a case study basis.

This also represents a methodological opportunity to explore different ways, spaces and realms in which Chileans and Britons interacted during the struggles for independence. For example, consular reports about the social and political life of Chile, letters and reports of the difficulties experienced by sailors who joined the Chilean navy, correspondence between Protestant missionaries and their headquarters, plans to invade Chile and reports from Chile about the British menace, all allow us to understand the complex and divergent interactions between Chileans and Britons, which went beyond simple commercial interests and diplomatic negotiations. Most of these sources contain valuable information about some 'unknown' actors of the period, rather than the most renowned characters involved in these interactions (i.e. Thomas Cochrane and Bernardo O'Higgins). These testimonies are seldom found in the scholarship on the subject, yet they are privileged here.

A Note on the Structure, Some Absences and Terminology

Considering that this book has been conceived on a case study basis, its structure is predominantly thematic. Chapters 1 and 5, however, follow a chronological pattern as well, since they are conceived as the starting and end points respectively.

The book is organised in five chapters, each one dealing with a different aspect of the main problem of this investigation. The first chapter analyses British imperial policy towards Chile and its repercussions, as well as the involvement of 'state actors' in these relations. It concludes that this was a realm of 'virtual' interaction in which Britain was seen first as an enemy and gradually as an ally. Debates and interactions undertaken between 1806 and 1814 led to a gradual reconfiguration of both the image of Britain as an ally and Chile as a differentiated community. Chapters 2, 3, 4 and 5 delve into different 'physical' ambits of interaction between Britons and Chileans, most of whom were 'non-state' actors, ranging from the Chilean navy (Chapter

---

2 vols (London: Baldwin Cradock and Joy, 1826); Maria Graham, *Journal of a Residence in Chile in the year 1822 and a Voyage from Chile to Brazil in 1823* (London: Longman, 1824); Peter Schmidtmeyer, *Travel into Chile Over The Andes in the Years 1820 and 1821, With Some Sketches of the Production of Agriculture; mines and Metallurgy; Inhabitants, History, and Other Features of America, Particularly of Chile, and Arauco* (London: Longman, Hurst, Rees, Orme, Brown and Green, 1824).

2) to, education and religion (Chapter 3), trade (Chapter 4) and diplomacy (Chapter 5). In all these chapters the focus is on how ideas about British imperialism were based on a civilisational discourse, and were contested, debated and sometimes appropriated or even rejected in the Chilean context. In Chapter 2 the focus is on the reception of the British model for the organisation of the navy, the troubled relations between British and Chilean seamen, and the way Cochrane represented Chilean interests as a catalyst for a proto-national identity. In Chapter 3 I analyse the complex process of reception of British Protestant societies' civilisational projects in the realms of education and religion. The effects of missionaries' expectations and views on Chile, as well as the way they interacted with the locals, had significant consequences for the construction of a national education system and the consolidation of Catholicism as the official religion. In Chapter 4 I delve into the settlement of the British community of traders in the 1820s, with a particular focus on the way their particular interests were or were not perceived as representative of British imperialism. The way they interacted with the locals and defended their own interests, as well as the way in which they were perceived by these locals, calls into question the idea that they were 'bridgeheads' of the Empire. Chapter 5 relates Chile's independence process to the complex geopolitical context in which Britain exerted a hegemonic role. Chileans sought recognition from the beginning of the process, which led them to publicise their country in many divergent and even contradictory ways, using images of Chile as a stable and unified country, but also as a poor and distant territory.

There are some absences in this book that require further explanation. One of them is the absence of a chapter on travel writing, considering the extensive presence of British travellers in Chile throughout the period.[83] One reason is that Marcelo Somarriva has done a significant work on this and I had few considerations to add. Another reason lies in the troubled meaning of the term 'travelling'. In this book there are many travellers who are not regarded as such in the accounts of travel literature. If we accept Carl E. Thompson's definition of travelling as 'the negotiation between self and other that is brought about by movement in space', most of the characters involved in each chapter were in fact travellers, which renders redundant an exclusive chapter on the subject.[84]

In addition, there is another dimension that has been left aside in this book, which requires further research, but which also has been recently tackled by some scholars, like Patience Schell and Sarah Chambers.[85] Kinship and

---

83 For a comparative analysis of the account of these travellers see S. Samuel Tirifilo, 'Early Nineteenth-Century British Travelers in Chile: Impressions of Santiago and Valparaíso', *Journal of Inter-American Studies*, 11:3 (1969), 391–424.

84 Carl Edward Thompson, *Travel Writing* (London: Routledge, 2011), p. 9.

85 See Schell; Sarah Chambers, *Families in War and Peace: Chile from Colony to Nation* (Durham, NC: Duke University Press, 2015). See also Mary Lowenthal Felstiner,

marriages were significant factors in the way Britons were incorporated into Chilean society and a more thorough analysis of this area would shed further light on the nature of British and Chilean relations. Although some examples are quoted here, this book focuses on other ambits of interaction which have been more typically associated with empire. Schell's and Chambers's contributions represent significant advances, although they did not focus on the independence period (Schell) or exclusively on British and Chilean relations (Chambers). That is why further research is still needed. This book aspires to provide the foundations for such a study.

Something similar might be said about gender analysis. It is clear that, aside from Maria Graham, women are almost absent from this book. A study of the construction of masculinities through independence might also have added to the analysis, especially with regard to the 'citizen' or the 'sailor', both of whom were conceived in masculine terms. I have chosen other approaches to the construction of national identities. The work of Claire Brewster, Catherine Davies and Hilary Owen shows that research in this line can yield impressive insights.[86]

Finally, with regard to terminology, two terms are used on almost every page of this book: Britons and Chileans. Although in this book I mainly refer to 'Britain' or 'Britons', without specifying any particular nationality, Irish nationality is highlighted in some cases. This is because there were certain episodes in which conflicts arose between 'English' and 'Irish', even while they were interacting with Chileans. Britons were not a homogenous entity and at particular moments Irishmen reinforced their identity by entering into conflict with their English fellows. Even overseas, Britons and Irishmen were constructing their national identities. These distinctions, however, were not important for Chileans, who mainly used the term 'English' – perhaps because of their use of this language – to refer to both Britons and Irishmen, although in some cases the term 'Briton' was also used.[87] When I speak of 'Chileans', I am not saying that this term was actually used during the independence struggles. This is a quite complex issue, since the literature on national identity and the nation-building process widely accepts the assumption that the Chilean 'nation' was actually configured after and not before

'Kinship Politics in Chilean Independence Movement', *Hispanic American Historical Review*, 56:1 (1976), 58–80.

86 Some contributions are Matthew Brown, 'Adventurers, Foreign Woman and Masculinity in the Colombian Wars of Independence', *Feminist Review*, 79 (2005), 36–51 and Catherine Davies, Claire Brewster and Hilary Owen (eds), *South American Independence: Gender, Politics, Text* (Liverpool: Liverpool University Press, 2006).

87 On the complex relations between Ireland and the British Empire see Stephen Howe, 'Minding the Gaps: New Directions in the Study of Ireland and Empire', *The Journal of Imperial and Commonwealth History*, 37:1 (2009), 135–49. On the role of Irishmen in the construction of the Spanish Empire see Oscar Recio Morales, *Ireland and the Spanish Empire, 1600–1815* (Dublin: Four Court Press, 2009).

independence. Therefore, when I use the term 'Chilean', I do so in a very pragmatic way, simply to designate those who were born in or were somehow (perhaps emotionally) linked to the land that in independence's aftermath would be called Chile.

CHAPTER 1

Invasions, Negotiations and Conspiracies

British-Chilean Relations in an Era of Change, 1806–1817

1.1 Introduction

Relations between Britain and Chile began in the sixteenth century when, according to several testimonies, smugglers, privateers and scientific travellers from Britain and Ireland frequently met and interacted with Chileans.[1] The period in which Chile and the rest of the Spanish colonies in America fought to establish themselves as new political entities represented a new stage in this relationship. This chapter analyses the relations between Great Britain and Chile between 1806 and 1817. In this period, Chile was not yet an independent state, but still a Spanish colony. The inhabitants of Chile, for their part, were still subjects of King Ferdinand VII and behaved as such. Between 1806 and 1817, ideas about Chile's place in the world were discussed and debated, resulting in a revolutionary movement that ultimately achieved independence from colonial rule. As subjects of the king of Spain, Chileans shaped their first attitudes and reactions towards Britain during these years. Their views of Britain and Britons were determined by the British invasions of Buenos Aires – the capital of the Viceroyalty located on the other side of the Andes, next to the General Captaincy of Chile – that took place in June 1806.

These invasions had almost immediate consequences for both Britain and Chile. Firstly, the initial success of the invasions led the British authorities to outline a plan to invade Chile in order to consolidate a trade route to connect the Atlantic and the Pacific. There had been British proposals to invade Chile before, but in 1806 the British state was directly involved in the very design and delivering of such a plan. This is clear evidence – overlooked by the existing historiography both in Britain and Chile – that British policy regarding Chile went through an explicit, if brief, 'imperialist' phase. This was not simply an 'economic influence', as suggested by Antony McFarlane, but an outright plan to transform Chile into a British

1 Edmundson, pp. 7–26.

colony.[2] The plan itself – discussed in detail in this chapter – clearly states that the British forces must occupy Chile, and that the British monarch must rule the local population.

Secondly, their knowledge of the very presence of the British forces on the other side of the Andes and the threat of an invasion to Chile, led the Chilean authorities to organise the defence of the territory. The aim was not independence at this stage, but to keep the colony free and safe from the expected invasion of an unfriendly, foreign imperial power. The defence plan was designed in the context of the imperial rivalry between Spain and Britain, which meant that in defending their territory, Chileans were actually defending the Spanish Empire.[3] At this stage, the relationship between Chile and Britain was defined and experienced primarily at the interstate level. On both sides, the authorities were involved in the design of plans that aimed either to invade or to defend the territory.

This period was characterised by quick political and geopolitical developments. The Napoleonic wars in Europe brought about significant changes in the relationship between Chile and Great Britain. Firstly, the overthrow of King Ferdinand VII by Napoleon in May 1808 reconfigured relations between Spain and Britain, making the two powers staunch allies against the French threat. This meant that, in theory at least, Britain should no longer be an enemy to Spanish Americans but rather a new ally in the defence of their territories. The behaviour of the Governor Francisco García Carrasco between 1808 and 1810 reveals that the new role assumed by Britain was not totally accepted. On the one hand, he suspected Britain's motivations and delivered some anti-foreigner and anti-British policies. On the other, he defended the free trade agreement with Britain on the grounds that this would help to overcome the economic crisis brought about by Napoleon's invasion of Spain. This demonstrates that representations of Britons were not monolithic but divergent and often contradictory.

In the Chilean case, the period between 1808 and 1810 was rather confusing as news filtered across the Atlantic and groups jockeyed for position. The official colonial authorities remained in their posts until July 1810. Governor Francisco García Carrasco had managed to rule the territory, but failed to obtain the support of Santiago's *hacendados* (landowners) and merchants. His involvement in acts of repression and corruption led the Royal Audience of Chile to demand his resignation. After this, the *vecinos* or 'neighbours' of

---

2 Antony McFarlane, *The British in the Americas, 1480–1815*, Studies in Modern History (London and New York: Longman, 1994), pp. 303–04. See also Leslie Bethell, 'Britain and Latin America in Historical Perspective', in *Britain and Latin America: A Changing Relationship*, ed. by Victor Bulmer-Thomas (Cambridge and New York: Cambridge University Press, 1989), pp. 1–24.

3 For a general account of British-Spanish relations and the way they mutually influenced each other see John Elliott, *Empires of the Atlantic World: Britain and Spain in America, 1492–1830* (New Haven, CT: Yale University Press, 2006).

Santiago (those who owned a plot within the city), led by the oldest military officer, Mateo de Toro y Zambrano, decided to call for an open meeting of the *Cabildo* (Council) to decide the next steps. At that time, Caracas and Buenos Aires had formed their own *junta* governments (on 11 April and 15 May 1810, respectively) and it was necessary to decide whether Santiago would do the same.[4] Eventually, on 18 September of 1810, the Cabildo of Santiago decided to form a *junta* which would rule the territory on behalf of the captive king.

When the Junta of Santiago was formed in September 1810, some Creoles approached Britain, accepting its proposal to serve as intermediary between Spain and its unsettled colonies. As the Junta gradually became a 'revolutionary' movement and ideas of independence began to spread, the leaders of the process quickly initiated the first diplomatic negotiations with Britain in order to obtain its support. This led the provisional institutions established in the period, such as the National Congress of Chile (1811), to send diplomatic envoys to London to negotiate British support for their cause. However, Britain's new policy of neutrality in the conflict between Spain and its colonies meant that their overtures were in vain.

The adoption in 1808 of neutrality regarding Spain's conflict with its colonies, as D.A.G. Waddell argued, is the principal explanation for the shift in relations between Britain and Chile at both state and individual levels.[5] If, in 1806–1807 the British state was keen on invading Chile as a means to undermine Spanish power and to expand its commercial markets, from 1808, it remained neutral and was unwilling to give any support to Spanish Americans. Officially, therefore, Chile was no longer of any particular interest and the initial aggressive approach to Chile was abandoned. Henceforth, British and Chilean relations were shaped primarily by 'non-state' actors. Relationships and representations were formed at the everyday level, by the few Chileans who travelled to Britain, and the much greater number of Britons who travelled to Chile with a wide range of interests. They interacted with Chileans in many different places and spheres and at all of the levels defined by Bitterli – contacts, conflicts and relationships. These merchants, soldiers, skilled workers, seamen, educators and missionaries are the subject of chapters two, three and four of this book.

---

4 The term *junta* is almost untranslatable into English, but in this context it refers to a group of people who were nominated by the Cabildo to rule the territory on behalf of the absent monarch. The rationale of this measure was that the monarch's sovereignty 'returned' to the people in case he was absent or even if he became a tyrant. *Juntas* were formed across the Spanish Empire in many cities, towns and villages. Spanish Americans defended their right to form their own *juntas* since they were all subjects of the king. Even though they accepted the initial leadership of the Central *Junta* of Madrid, they gradually demanded more autonomy to make their own decisions.

5 D.A.G. Waddell, 'British Neutrality and Spanish-American Independence: The Problem of Foreign Enlistment', *Journal of Latin American Studies*, 19:1 (1987), 1–18.

In the initial period 1806–1817, to be analysed in this chapter, we can see that the 'state' and 'non-state' levels of the relationship overlapped. We can also see that in this period several different types of encounter coexisted in parallel. For instance, it was in this period that the first British officers, soldiers and sailors arrived in Chile to join the wars of independence, and the first merchants travelled to take advantage of new trade regulations passed by the Junta. None of them arrived as part of an official British expedition or due to any explicit policy of the British state. They came because of changes in the attitude of the Chilean authorities, who now 'invited' them to enter their territory.

All this also had consequences in the cultural sphere, not least in affecting the wide range of ideas that were exchanged between Chile and Britain and mutual representations. Between 1806 and 1808, when the threat of an invasion was present and feared, Chileans reflected on different topics related to their identity. Firstly, when establishing the plan to defend the territory, the authorities hoped to deter potential aggressors by emphasising the image of Chile as a poor, marginal and isolated country, inhabited by 'savages' who had nothing to offer to invaders. Secondly, whilst British forces were based in Buenos Aires (1806–1807), the Chilean authorities received requests for assistance from their neighbours, which catalysed a broad debate about whether Chileans should or could respond. In response to the British threat, Chileans discussed the extent to which the inhabitants of Buenos Aires formed part of the same community or *patria*, or whether Chileans were a separate community with their own identity. By 1808, the answers were still not clear. But the threat of British invasion had triggered a debate about Chile's incipient configuration of a (proto-)national identity as something different from their *porteño* neighbours, which had long-term significance. This debate ran parallel to and informed the development of various representations of Britain and Britons in Chile, ranging from 'enemies', 'evil', and 'empire', to 'allies' and 'neutral power'. This chapter performs the first analysis of these significant developments in relations between Chile and Britain during a period of massive political and military upheaval.

1.2 A Threat on the Other Side of the Andes: The British Invasions of the River Plate, 1806–1807

As Marcelo Somarriva says, the independence of Chile is eminently a transnational history, since we cannot tell its story without reference to processes that took place elsewhere.[6] The British invasions of Buenos Aires are a good example since these determined many reactions, decisions and attitudes of the population of Chile based on the fear of being invaded in

---

6 Somarriva, p. 12.

turn. The British invasions of Buenos Aires and Montevideo took place between June 1806 and July 1807. This episode has been widely analysed by historians interested in its consequences in Argentina, but little has been said about its repercussions elsewhere.[7] In Buenos Aires, the invasions mobilised the entire population to defend the city and most historians agree that the *porteños* realised that they were acting completely alone in the defence of the Spanish king's territory and sovereignty, which was crucial for the war of independence that took place later on. The most radical interpretation suggests that it was at this moment when a 'new nation' was born.[8] Beyond this, the very presence of British forces in one of the key ports and cities in South America was seen as a threat to the surrounding territories of Buenos Aires, among them the General Captaincy of Chile (see Map 1).

Both the civil authorities and military officers of the General Captaincy of Chile interpreted these invasions as the first step of a wider British plan of expansion in South America, which included Chile as a possible destination. During the first month of the occupation of Buenos Aires, the British forces seemed to have the entire situation under control. The British authorities were then confident of the plausibility of further expansion of their operations in South America and Chile began to be seen as a new target. The Chilean authorities reacted immediately to set up a plan to repel a possible attack from the other side of the Andes. In doing so, they elaborated a particular representation of their own country, in which they emphasised the negative aspects of the population and territory. The image of Chile as a marginal and poor place, inhabited by savage people, was used as a means to discourage the invasion. The reactions generated by the presence of an occupying army on the other side of the Andes focused on the practical defence of the Chilean territory itself, without an appeal to defend the wider American *patria* (as happened later, in 1808, when the threat of a new invasion of Buenos Aires was latent, as discussed below in Section 1.4).

Certainly, this was not the first time that Chileans had feared an invasion by the British, and the events of 1806–1807 chimed with existing memories of British activities. Since the sixteenth century the presence of pirates and privateers like Francis Drake along the coasts of Chile had been significant. In some cases, they even attacked the coastal towns, which led Chileans to fear their presence.[9] Furthermore, records survive of at least four official plans authorised by the British government to invade Chile before the events of 1806. According to Mario Barros, a group of merchants from Glasgow acquainted with the strategic position of Chile had requested permission to organise an invasion of Chile in 1780. The invasion never happened, for

---

7 Gallo, pp. 150–60.

8 Ben Hughes, *The British Invasions of the River Plate, 1806–1807: How the Redcoats Were Humbled and a Nation Was Born* (Barnsley: Pen and Sword, 2013).

9 Edmundson, pp. 7–24.

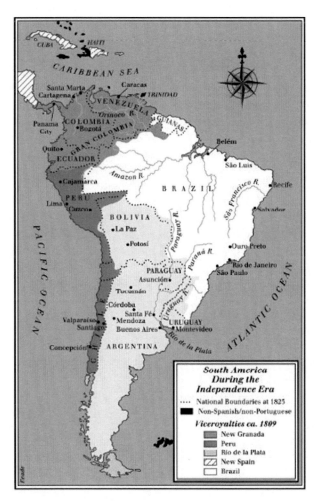

Map 1 South America in the Independence era

reasons that remain unexplained. In 1788, there were fears of an invasion in La Serena, in northern Chile, in response to which the governor Ambrosio O'Higgins activated a defensive plan designed by the Irishman Tomás Shee.[10] In 1797, the British Secretary of State and War Henry Dundas (Lord Melville) devised a plan to occupy the entire zone south of Valdivia with the idea of dominating trade in the Southern Pacific, especially that with India and New South Wales. According to Barros, this expedition was about to set out to Chile with three warships and 5,500 men when the war between Spain and Britain restarted in 1804.[11] It had to be postponed 'until 1806' to avoid igniting an insurrection.[12]

The most well-known plan to invade Chile, the 'Maitland Plan', was brought to light by the Argentinian scholar and politician Rodolfo Terragno. In his view, this plan was devised in 1801 by General Thomas Maitland and involved invading Chile by crossing the Andes after occupying Buenos Aires and Mendoza. Once Chile was taken, the next step was to set out northwards to Peru by sea, and to continue with Ecuador.[13] In his view, the attempt to invade Chile in 1804 was not based on the plan of 1797, but was developed by Henry Popham, inspired by Maitland. The new plan included an invasion of Venezuela led by Francisco de Miranda but, as noted, it was postponed until 1806. The Maitland plan was very similar to the strategy followed later by José de San Martín, who led the Liberation Army across the Andes from Mendoza in Argentina between January and February 1817 to liberate Chile and then Peru. This was the first plan to consider an invasion from the Andes and not from the Pacific. Its similarities to that of San Martín have been claimed as evidence that he learnt about the latter while living in London. The most exaggerated interpretation suggests that this would demonstrate that the independence of Spanish America was a plan conceived and designed by Great Britain, and particularly by the Freemasons. Terragno himself does not provide enough evidence to support this. He only speculates about the possibility of San Martín being a Freemason with access to all the secrets of British masonry. Although Terragno admits that there is no evidence that San Martín actually read

---

10 Both were Irishmen in the service of the Spanish Crown. Their original names were Ambrose O'Higgins and Thomas O'Shee respectively. The plan is reproduced by Juan Luis Ossa, 'La criollización de un ejército periférico, Chile, 1768–1810', *Historia (Santiago)*, 43 (2010), 413–48 (p. 425).

11 See the anonymous *An Authentic Narrative of the Proceedings of the Expedition Under the Command of Brigadier–Gen. Craufurd, Untils its Arrival to Montevideo, With an Account of the Operations Against Buenos Aires Under the Command of Liut. Gen. Whitelocke. by an Officer of the Expedition* (London: G.E. Miles, 1808), pp. 1–3.

12 Mario Barros, *Historia diplomática de Chile, 1541–1938* (Santiago: Andrés Bello, 1970), pp. 41–42.

13 Rodolfo H. Terragno, *Maitland y San Martín*, 3rd ed. (Bernal: Universidad Nacional de Quilmes Ediciones, 2001).

or heard about the plan, these coincidences have encouraged the idea that Spanish American independence was a British-masonic conspiracy.[14]

Little is said about Maitland's plan in the literature on Chile's independence. Instead, there is a sort of consensus that Sir William Windham's plan represents the moment at which a British invasion to Chile came closer than ever before. Based on a sketchy comparison, Terragno claims that this plan was influenced by Maitland's but, again, he does not provide any evidence to go beyond speculation.[15] Instead, this plan to invade 'the Provinces of Chili' seems to have been a revival of Melville's idea and was proposed as a result of the success of the British invasions of Buenos Aires. As with Melville's plan, it was directly managed by the British government and it was Lord Windham himself who passed it on to Brig. Gen. Robert Craufurd in October 1806. The military and naval necessities of the Napoleonic wars had catalysed the British state and its 'official mind' to take a more active role in the relationship with Chile, rather than leaving it to individual agents of empire such as privateers, travellers or adventurers. Thus, this was a relatively brief but significant moment in which British policymakers thought actively about Chile and considered incorporating it into the British dominions. Only when negotiations for British recognition of Chile's independence began in 1817 would British policymakers again focus on Chile.

The possibility of an invasion of Chile was at its most real in 1806–1807, when British troops were physically stationed in Buenos Aires. Historians agree that the presence of the British army in Buenos Aires obliged the Governor of Chile, Luis Muñoz de Guzmán, to call his military advisors to design a plan to defend the territory from a British invasion.[16] The operations of the British state in the South Atlantic triggered a reaction from the authorities of the General Captaincy of Chile, as well as changing individual perceptions of Britain's role as a global power. As the authorities drew up the plans to defend the territory, they elaborated a particular image of the territory they were trying to defend. In September 1806, Muñoz de Guzmán called 'the colonels of the militias, both the disciplined and the urban ones, to the presence of both the judge advocate general and the Secretary of the General Captaincy of Chile'.[17] His main concern was

---

14 This is the case of some 'historical' novels on the period recently published in Chile, which are mainly nurtured by conspiracy theories rather than history. See Francisco Ortega, *Logia* (Buenos Aires: Planeta, 2014) and Waldo Parra, *Masones y libertadores* (Buenos Aires: Planeta, 2016).

15 Terragno, pp. 21–28.

16 For a first account of the consequences of the British invasions of Buenos Aires in Chile, see Diego Barros Arana, *Historia general de Chile*, 16 vols, 2nd ed. (Santiago: Rafael Jovet Editores, 1886), VII, 294–306.

17 'Informe de Luis Muñoz de Guzmán para defender el reino de los ingleses, en vista del peligro que reviste una invasión luego de la ocupación de Bs. As.', Santiago,

the precarious condition of the military forces of the kingdom of Chile,[18] which Muñoz de Guzmán had become aware of during his first years in the post. Shortly after he had taken office he analysed 'the state of the forces of the kingdom', which he found 'not only weak, but without contingent to strengthen them'.[19]

Two other factors made Chile vulnerable to an invasion at this moment. Firstly, a royal decree from November 1804 had declared that the defence of the Spanish American territories must be organised by local governments using their own militias, without any aid from the Iberian Peninsula.[20] The second factor was the destruction of at least ten Spanish ships during the battle of Trafalgar (out of 15 that joined the battle). There were also 1,050 casualties and 2,436 wounded at Trafalgar, which made it difficult to mobilise an expedition from the Peninsula to South America.[21] Therefore, any invasion from an external enemy had to be resisted with the scarce resources available in Chile.[22] That is why, as the principal authority of the General Captaincy of Chile, Muñoz de Guzmán had to devise his own defensive plan in case the British invaded from Buenos Aires.

Different plans were proposed by the military officers, but it was that of Judas Tadeo Reyes, the commander of the militias of Chile, that Muñoz de Guzmán followed. Tadeo Reyes's plan, dated 14 September 1806, was explicitly designed to defend the kingdom from an 'English invasion'.[23] Both the condition of the population and the precarious economic situation of the territory were relevant factors to consider in its defence. In the first case, Tadeo Reyes characterised the men who composed the militias as undisciplined and proposed that they be trained by veteran officers. He nevertheless regarded such a feature as an advantage since these men could appear to enemies as fierce and fearsome warriors. They had to be armed with 'knives, lances and machetes' in order to organise a cavalry and a battalion of *cuchilleros* (knifemen). This recalled the image of the fierce and brave *mapuche* or *araucano* warriors who allegedly never gave in to the Spaniards during

27 October 1806, Archivo Nacional Histórico de Chile, Fondo Varios (hereafter, AHN-FV), vol. 237, fol. 183.

18 During the colonial era different denominations for Chile were in use: General Captaincy, Kingdom and Governance.

19 'Informe de Luis Muñoz de Guzmán para defender el reino de los ingleses, en vista del peligro que reviste una invasión luego de la ocupación de Bs. As.', Santiago, 27 October 1806, AHN-FV, vol. 237, fol. 183.

20 Ossa, 'La criollización de un ejército periférico', pp. 442–46.

21 Luis E. Iñigo Fernández, *Breve historia de la Batalla de Trafalgar. La batalla naval que cambió el destino del mundo* (Madrid: Ediciones Nowtilus, 2014), pp. 231–32.

22 Ibid., pp. 442–46.

23 'Informe sobre el defensa nacional expedido por don Judas Tadeo Reyes en 1806 para resguardos contra ataques de los ingleses', Santiago, 14 September 1806, Archivo Nacional Histórico de Chile, Fondo Sergio Fernández Larraín (ANH-SFL), vol. 144, piece 6.

the conquest of Chile.[24] The poverty of the territory also formed part of this defensive plan. One of the threads of this plan was the destruction of the harvests located near to the coasts and moving cultivation towards the mountains in order to make privateers and pirates believe that there were not even agricultural goods to take from the territory. This was an old tactic to discourage them, 'relying on the very poverty of the colony to make it unattractive to potential enemies'.[25]

On 27 October 1806, Luis Muñóz de Guzmán circulated a report in which he made official the plan to defend Chile based on Judas Tadeo Reyes's ideas, in the event of a British invasion.[26] Even though the invasion never took place, the very presence of British troops in Buenos Aires had significant consequences in Chile. In the first place, Chileans realised that they had to defend themselves on their own in case of invasion. At best, they could find some support from the population of neighbouring territories like the United Provinces of La Plata. Indeed, both Buenos Aires and Montevideo had sought military support from their Chilean counterparts. At the same time, the Chilean authorities realised how difficult the defence of the territory would be, considering the militias' lack of training, the precarious economic condition of the territory and the extent of Chile's coasts. In the second place, the rapid (although short-lived) success of the British troops in Buenos Aires led the British authorities to believe that the expansion of their operations in South America was plausible. Chile had a long Pacific coast, but its location also allowed for a connection of the trade routes between the Atlantic and the Pacific. Therefore, the next step in their expansionist project in South America would be the invasion and occupation of Chile. The outline of William Windham's plan to invade Chile is held in the National Archives at Kew Gardens and is relatively well known to historians of Chile's independence. A careful analysis of its contents reveals what British policymakers believed to be the role of Chile in their imperial project.

On 30 October 1806, that is, three days after Luis Muñoz de Guzmán circulated his defensive plan, Brigadier General Robert Craufurd of the British army received from the Secretary of State for War and the Colonies, William Windham, the 'Instructions' to invade Chile. The object of the expedition was clear and explicit: 'the capture of the sea ports and fortresses and the reduction of the province of Chili'.[27] Diego Barros Arana held that

---

24 The term *Araucano* was used by the Spaniards during the conquest to refer to the native population of southern Chile, who called themselves *Mapuche* (People of the land).

25 David Cubitt, 'Lord Cochrane and the Chilean Navy, 1818–1823, with an Inventory of the Dundonald Papers Relating to his Service with the Chilean Navy' (PhD dissertation: University of Edinburgh, 1974), p. 15.

26 'Informe de Luis Muñoz de Guzmán', 27 October 1806, ANH-FV, vol. 237, piece 4472.

27 'Instructions to Craufurd', 30 October, 1806, The National Archives at Kew (TNA), War Office (WO) 1/161, fols 136–54.

Map 2
Chile in the Independence era

knowledge of this plan in Chile led the local population to fear an invasion at the end of 1807: 'the militias were armed everywhere, and the most serious military preparations were made: all talk was of an English invasion that should arrive soon with identical purposes to the one that had attacked Buenos Aires shortly before'.[28] However, Craufurd had reached the La Plata estuary by 11 June 1807 and even returned to England on 7 July, when the occupation of Buenos Aires had already come to a definitive end. It is unlikely that at the end of the same year the Chilean authorities were unaware of this and were still expecting an invasion that would never occur. Another possibility is that it was known that a new expedition was set to depart from Cork in December 1807. However, debates about the activation of plans to defend the territory from this invasion only started in May 1808. Hence, these fears spread at the end of 1807 because the 'spectre' of an invasion was still latent, not because Windham's plan was known.[29] Indeed, there is no evidence to maintain that Muñoz de Guzmán was informed about the plan, so Chileans were not awaiting Craufurd's specific expedition, but rather a potential British invasion. The memory of the many occasions the British had planned to invade Chile combined with the physical presence of British troops on the other side of the Andes to create this vigilance. At the same time, the long-standing presence of British smugglers, travellers and privateers along Chile's coasts had led Chileans to expect a massive presence of Britons at any moment. The geopolitical context between 1806 and 1807 had made the possibility of an invasion a real threat as well.

In April 1807 news of the fall of Montevideo to the British reached Chile. General Samuel Auchmuty had invaded the city on 16 January 1807 and accepted its surrender after two weeks of resistance on 3 February. The Cabildo of Santiago received a letter from the Cabildo of Montevideo asking for help and immediately organised a brigade to join the defence of the city.[30] The occupation of Montevideo was crucial as it was from there that the second invasion to Buenos Aires would take place. Eventually, the British forces in Buenos Aires were defeated on 7 July 1807 by local militias. News of the British defeat arrived in Santiago at the end of that month and the triumph was celebrated and commemorated as if it had been the Chileans' own victory. The Cabildo of Santiago declared on 30 July 1807 that:

> On the occasion of seeing a letter from the Illustrious Cabildo of Buenos Aires, in which it informs of the glorious victory won on the fifth of this month by the arms of His Majesty against the English troops [...], they said that it was fair to thank God for this singular triumph and agreed to

---

28 Diego Barros Arana, *Historia Jeneral de la Independencia de Chile*, 2 vols (Santiago: Imprenta Chilena, 1854), I, p. 1.

29 See Ibid., I, pp. 1–3; Ossa, 'La criollización de un ejército periférico', p. 443.

30 ANH-FV, vol. 239. Unfortunately, this volume is missing, so this information is drawn from references from the catalogue.

celebrate a solemn mass in this Holy Cathedral Church. One of the best preachers of the capital will say a panegiric prayer and His Excellency Mr President and all other bodies will be invited.[31]

This service paid tribute to all the men who had died during the defence of Buenos Aires, and cost 1,000 pesos in total. In addition, the Cabildo decided to make a contribution of 2,000 pesos to begin a subscription to help the 'very many unfortunate women who lost their husbands and sons in that action'.[32] The significance of this ceremony lies in the fact that the defeat of the British forces in Buenos Aires was celebrated as it had been the Chileans' own victory. The threat of the invasion had subsided, at least for a while.

All of these reactions from Chileans were generated by information and rumours. There was little 'real' contact between Chileans and Britons during these events apart from the presence of British smugglers and travellers in Chile, and a few Chileans who travelled to Britain. In terms of representations, it is clear that at least for the authorities of Chile, Britain was seen as an enemy, a threat to internal peace and their king's sovereignty. Also, they developed a defensive plan publicising an image of Chile that was the exact opposite of that which would be promoted by Chilean diplomats in the 1820s negotiating for the recognition of their independence (this is discussed in Chapter 5). At that time, Chilean envoys tried to demonstrate that Chile was an example of order, stability and progress. Muñoz de Guzmán and Tadeo Reyes preferred to use the image of Chile as a poor territory with nothing to offer to its enemies and a local population lacking discipline and order.

1.3 The Spectre of an Invasion: Robert Craufurd and the Instructions to Capture and Reduce the 'Province of Chili'

Muñoz de Guzmán's plan to defend Chile was established as a result of the presence of British forces in Buenos Aires and the assumption that Chile could be invaded from there either by sea or land. Chile's governor did not know with certainty whether British authorities were planning an invasion, but he behaved as if one was imminent. William Windham's plan to invade Chile was also a result of the British invasions of Buenos Aires. In James Davey's words, 'this stark and surprising imperial success saw people turn for the first time in the conflict to the possibilities of a war of colonial expansion, and created what can only be described as a "mania" for imperial investment'.[33] The invasion of the isolated, impoverished and remote

---

31 'Actas del Cabildo de Santiago', 30 July 1807, available at: http://www.historia.uchile. cl/CDA/fh_indice/0,1387,JNID%253D27,00.html.

32 Ibid.

33 James Davey, *In Nelson's Wake: The Navy and the Napoleonic Wars* (London: Yale University Press, 2015), p. 127.

territory of Chile was seen as an opportunity to extend British dominion in South America and as a means to weaken the power of the Spanish Empire. William Kaufmann has suggested that this reflected a mixture of factors: 'the precariousness of the situation in Europe, the pressure from the mercantile community, and the fact that Popham was a British officer, acting with British troops for purely British ends'.[34] As the 'Instructions' delivered by Windham to Craufurd reveal, Chile was seen as a territory that offered many benefits to both British authorities and merchants. It was an entry route to the Pacific and a 'pathway' to other major markets like Peru, which would allow for the establishment of internal trade routes with Buenos Aires.

This document, which contains the plan to invade Chile, is also a representation of the place that Chile occupied in the British imperial project. In contrast to the image promoted by Muñoz de Guzmán, it is clear that Chile was not seen as a marginal place but as an advantageous territory for the expansion of trade routes to the Pacific and for their connection to the Atlantic. In addition, it reveals that in the context of imperial rivalry, at this moment Britain intended to incorporate Chile into its 'formal' empire. Hence this plan was not a 'last resort' of imperial policy, but the first. However, it was the last official plan proposing an invasion of Chile. Both France's invasion of Spain and Britain's adoption of neutrality in 1808 were the catalysts for a change of policy. After this, the means used by Britain to achieve the aim of connecting the Atlantic with the Pacific ranged from encouraging merchants to settle in Chile to appointing consuls during the 1820s. As discussed in Chapter 5, not even the idea of Cristopher Nugent – designated British Consul in Valparaíso in 1824 – of invading the island of Chiloé persuaded the British Authorities to use military means to expand their trade routes into the South Pacific.

Windham's plan to invade Chile reveals that for British authorities Chile had many advantages for trade routes. However, the soldiers who were to invade Chile were ignorant of their destination. As the anonymous author of the only account of this expedition described it, they spent several months in Falmouth, Cornwall, awaiting orders to depart to an 'unknown destination'.[35] According to his narrative, Craufurd left the base for London on 24 October 1806, returning on 2 November to join the expedition under the general command of Admiral George Murray. It was during this short trip to London that Craufurd received the 'Instructions' to invade Chile from Windham. However, nobody else knew the objective of the expedition. Firstly, the author of the account stated that before their departure, considering the enthusiasm that the triumph in Buenos Aires had caused in Britain,

> the conjectures at this head were various; but that respecting the commencement of our operations at Vera Cruz, in the Gulph of Mexico,

34 Kaufmann, *British Policy and the Independence of Latin America*, p. 25.
35 *An Authentic Narrative*, pp. 5–6.

appeared to be founded on the best reasoning: at all events there appeared little doubt but that some part of the Spanish possessions in America was to become the theatre of our military operations.[36]

The destination in question was always unclear. For some reason, which is not indicated in the document, Craufurd decided not to tell his men that they were going to Chile. The author explicitly claimed that 'General Craufurd's instructions were never communicated to the world'[37] and later reiterated that 'on leaving *St. Jago* we were in the same state of uncertainty respecting the object of the expedition as we had been at our arrival'.[38] Later on, while near the Cape of Good Hope in South Africa, Craufurd received new dispatches from a Fly-class brig that approached on 2 February 1807. Shortly after, he gave the order to depart towards Saint Helena in the middle of the Atlantic Ocean. It was at this point that many soldiers began to think that Brazil was their destination, since the only thing that seemed clear after this visit was that Craufurd had received an order to change the plan. For many, Brazil appeared an attractive alternative; for others it seemed an unrealistic option considering the strong defensive forts along its coast, which made the repulsion of any attack likely.[39]

When they realised that the destination was the River Plate, 'to repair the disasters encountered by General Beresford, and to make up the losses Sir Samuel Auchmuty had met with in the assault of *Montevideo*',[40] many were disappointed because this meant that they had to continue with a project that someone else had already started. In the words of the anonymous author, 'this was certainly a subject of regret to all parties, as we were anxious to have a new field to ourselves, instead of which we were about to enter one, where neither military glory [n]or personal advantage, could be obtained'.[41] The reasons for this turn were clear: Craufurd had now been committed to back up the troops that had occupied Buenos Aires as the population of the city, led by the Viceroy Santiago Liniers, had defeated the forces of General Beresford on 12 August 1806. According to his new instructions, General Craufurd had to join Auchmuty's forces, which he did on 15 June 1807. Soon after, General John Whitelocke would join too as the new commander.

An initial question that arises from this 'silence' about Chile in the narrative of Craufurd's expedition is why Craufurd decided not to tell his men where they were going. A possible explanation is that the fact they were looking forward to invading Mexico reflects that they hoped to go to the 'mainland'

36 Ibid., p. 4.
37 Ibid., p. 23.
38 Ibid., p. 35.
39 Ibid., pp. 74–75, 82–83.
40 Ibid., p. 46.
41 Ibid., p. 74.

and not to the 'outskirts' of the Spanish Empire. Chile was less well known than Mexico, made famous by stories of its gold and silver, and it is plausible that Craufurd did not want to disappoint his men, even that he kept them in the dark in order to avoid a mutiny. In addition, the 'Instructions' reveal that the only significance assigned to Chile was its strategic location, which would allow for further military and economic operations on the continent. Regarding the military, the first letter stated that 'establishing and retaining a strong military position on the west coast of South America from which future operations may be carried on is the main object of your enterprise'.[42] With regard to trade, the second letter highlighted the position of Chile with respect to Peru and the expectation that its ports should 'become depots of trade to a considerable extent'.[43]

The letters are revealing expressions of the representation of Chile and the place it occupied in Britain's imperial project. The military occupation of the territory was nothing other than a means to consolidate existing trade routes and to open up new ones in South America and the Pacific. From a continental perspective, Peru, and not Chile, was the market which the British government sought to open for its merchant houses. Chile was only seen as a stepping stone to reach this market rather than as a market in itself. The 'Instructions' clearly stated that the goal was 'to encourage the introduction of British goods into Peru from the ports of Chili', adding that 'such an intercourse may furnish many opportunities of impressing the advantages of British connection on the minds of the Peruvians, and disposing them to concur in any measures which may be taken for subverting the Spanish Government'.[44] This confirms Somarriva's assertion about the Southern Cone being a 'new market' in the eyes of the British authorities (although he does not include the plan to invade Chile in his analysis).[45]

The main object of the occupation of Chile being the opening up of trade, Britons were aware of the importance of persuasion rather than imposition as a mechanism to control the inhabitants. This confirms what Marshall says about the absence of coercion in the relations of Britain during the eighteenth century, which also applied to early nineteenth-century South America.[46] Britons attempted not to show themselves as the new 'rulers' of the territory so as not to trigger resistance from the population or 'any act of revolt or insurrection'.[47] According to Mario Barros, this fear had also prevented Lord Melville from carrying out the invasion in 1804 and was one of the reasons for postponing it.[48] The instructions stated that Craufurd must try

42 'Instructions to Craufurd', fols 139–40.
43 Ibid., fol. 149.
44 Ibid., fols 138–39.
45 Somarriva, pp. 15–44.
46 Marshall, p. 4.
47 'Instructions to Craufurd', fol. 157.
48 Barros, *Historia diplomática de Chile*, pp. 40–41.

to persuade Chileans of the convenience of accepting the role of Britain as a protector of free trade, by using every means 'to conciliate the good will of the inhabitants, and to convince them of the superior advantages to be derived from British connection and Government'. However, despite being the order for an invasion, the document also stated that 'it is peculiarly important to abstain from any exercise of the rights of war'.[49] In the second letter, the object was even clearer since Windham stated that Craufurd must 'promote the objects of the British Government that this trade should be protected and kept open, unless interrupted by the enemy'. At the end, it is stated that Craufurd's efforts should be directed 'to the maintenance of internal order and tranquillity' and that he should not take 'any other measures leading to any other change than that of placing the country under his Majesty's protection and government'.[50]

The instructions confirm that a first approach to Chile was to incorporate it into Britain's 'formal' rather than 'informal' empire. This nuances Somarriva's assertion about the importance of informal imperialism to understanding relations between Britain and the Southern Cone even in 1806.[51] As demonstrated here, formal imperialism was also a possibility considered seriously by British policymakers when planning how to approach Chile. Using an army to occupy the territory and replacing the Spanish king's authority with that of the British monarch were the two means of carrying out this plan. It is also evident that the British authorities were conscious of the danger of not considering the context in which this occupation was meant to take place. They did not wish to appear as invaders but as 'protectors', nor to produce 'any impression that booty and not protection was the interest of the British Government'. They were aware of 'the impatience of [the Spanish government] felt by the inhabitants' and that any abusive behaviour could trigger an unmanageable 'spirit of revolt and insurrection'.[52] Therefore, they would respect the 'rights and functions' the locals already held, with a particular emphasis on privileging the 'natives' for any employment under the new government. Craufurd was committed to acting as the representative of a new government who seemingly did not want anything apart from fostering and protecting free trade and 'improving the conditions and conciliating the will of the inhabitants'.[53]

---

49 'Instructions to Craufurd', fol. 140. The document does not specify which rights of war it is referring to. The concept is surely taken from Hugo Grotius's *The Rights of War and Peace*. For Grotius, the right of war 'is properly that which may be done without Injustice with Regard to an Enemy'. See Hugo Grotius, *The Rights of War and Peace* (New York and London: M. Walter Dunne Publisher, 1901 [1625]), Book I, Chapter 1, 3.

50 Ibid., fol. 159.

51 Somarriva, pp. 10–11.

52 Ibid., fol. 138.

53 Ibid., fol. 141.

As stated above, the invasion never took place and there is no evidence either to maintain that this plan became known to the Chilean authorities of the time. The official correspondence of Governor Luis Muñoz de Guzmán, which is held in both Santiago and Seville, never mentions this episode.[54] For his part, John Whitelocke, the commander of the second expedition, in which Craufurd had taken part, was judged in a court martial carried out in February 1808. Craufurd and all the other major officers involved in the expedition gave their testimony at the trial. The records were published the same year in London under the title *The Proceedings of a General Court Martial Held at Chelsea Hospital* and contain both the testimonies of the officers and the 'Instructions' to invade Chile as an appendix.[55] This means that the details of the plan have been publicly available ever since. Coincidence or not, the fact is that Craufurd's expedition only began to be mentioned in the Chilean sources in July 1808. This reinforces the idea that by 1807 Chileans were fearing an expedition by British forces, but not necessarily Craufurd's.

1.4 A New Call from Buenos Aires

In May 1808 the Viceroy of Buenos Aires, Santiago Liniers, wrote to the Cabildo of Santiago to ask for economic aid to defend the city from a new possible invasion. A new expedition commanded by General Arthur Wellesley had been in preparation in Cork since December 1807. This expedition did not sail to Buenos Aires in the end, because it was ordered to join the defence of the Peninsula in the war against France that started in 1808. In addition, the failure to take Buenos Aires, whose population successfully resisted and repelled the invasion, convinced the British authorities that a military strategy was not the most appropriate way to expand their sphere of influence in Spanish America. As James Davey argues, 'only a scheme of "liberating South America", in the process gaining popular support, was workable, but any thought of pursuing such a policy was abandoned following Napoleon's invasion of Spain in 1808, and the subsequent revolt against French rule'.[56] The new strategy, according to McFarlane, consisted of 'supporting creole revolutionaries in efforts to subvert Spanish authority from within'.[57] A key figure in this change of policy was Wellesley himself, who in February 1808 wrote a memorandum stating his views on the 'means

---

54 The correspondence is contained in ANH-FV, vol. 237 and Archivo Nacional Histórico de Chile, Fondo Capitanía General (ANH-CG), vol. 819.

55 *The Proceedings of a General Court Martial Held at Chelsea Hospital ... for the Trial of Lieut. Gen. Whitelocke* (London: J.C. Mottley, 1808).

56 James Davey, 'Atlantic Empire, European War and the Naval Expeditions to South America, 1806–1807', in *The Royal Navy and the British Atlantic World, c. 1750–1820*, ed. by John Mcaleer and Christer Petley (London: Palgrave Macmillan, 2016, pp. 147–73 (p. 165).

57 McFarlane, *The British in the Americas*, p. 304.

of effecting a revolution against the Spanish Crown'.[58] The document, which until now was unknown to historians of Chilean independence, contains several ideas about the state of the Spanish American colonies and how Britain should proceed. One of Wellesley's main conclusions was that

> from what has lately passed at Buenos Ayres and from all that I have read of these countries, I am convinced that any attempt to conquer them with a view to their future subjection to the British Crown would certainly fail; and therefore I consider the only mode in which they can be wrested from the Crown of Spain is by a revolution and by the establishment of an independent government within them.[59]

This reveals that it was clear to the British that in a context of imperial rivalry, the aim of undermining the Spanish Empire could be achieved only through support of revolutionary movements on the grounds that independent governments would then negotiate with Britain to open up their trade. Wellesley's words also reveal that the ultimate aim of such a policy was to subjugate the Spanish colonies to British interests. The problem was the means to achieve it; it seemed more plausible to support them from within rather than through an explicit policy.

Wellesley also thought about the best strategy to start operations in Spanish America. Thus, he suggested that any operation be started in Buenos Aires because of its proximity to Europe and its importance. Chile and Peru were less convenient, firstly because of the 'long voyage nearly round the world' to reach their coasts, and secondly because 'the benefits which would be derived [...] would not be so great as those which would be derived from an attempt on a nearer object'.[60] This clearly represented a major shift in the representation of Chile from Windham's plan, its less attractive character and isolation being emphasised here.

Liniers's concerns were the weakness of Buenos Aires's forces and the scarcity of resources that would allow for another defence of the city. He asked the Cabildo of Santiago 'to help us with some amount [of money] for some objectives that are in both your and our interest'.[61] He clearly tried to persuade the Chileans that their own safety relied on the capacity of Buenos Aires to defend itself, which many Chileans believed as well. This petition was received by the new Governor of Chile, Francisco Antonio

---

58 Arthur Wellesley, 'Memorandum by Major General Sir Arthur Wellesley on the means of effecting a revolution against the Spanish Crown in its colonies in Central America and South America with British support and the proposed constitution of the countries', 8 February 1808, The Wellington Archive (TWA), University of Southampton Library, Special Collections, WP1/192/37.

59 Ibid., fols 4–5.

60 Ibid., fols 7–8.

61 'Santiago Liniers to the Cabildo de Santiago', Buenos Aires, 28 May 1808, ANH-CG, vol. 819, fol. 9.

García Carrasco, who had taken over after the death of Luis Muñoz de Guzmán in February 1808. Unlike the reactions generated by the invasions of 1806–1807, in this instance there were many contested ideas about patriotism and an incipient national identity under debate. The dilemma for the Chilean authorities and representatives of the main governmental bodies was whether they had to defend their own land only, as they had in 1806–1807, or to contribute to the defence of Buenos Aires both economically and militarily. On both sides of the argument there were different notions about the *patria* under discussion. Some appealed to the American *patria* given that, in the context of Spanish dominion, Buenos Aires and Chile formed part of a single community under the authority of the same king, but others started to think of Chile as a distinctive community and expressed the more nuanced idea that people from both sides of the Andes belonged to the same family.

On 20 June 1808, García Carrasco commissioned Judas Tadeo Reyes to hold a consultation with all the governmental bodies of General Captaincy of Chile about whether they considered it appropriate to contribute to the defence of Buenos Aires. These corporations were the Cabildo of Santiago, the Cabildo Eclesiástico, the University of San Felipe, the Tribunal del Consulado, the Real Audiencia and the Tribunal de Minería. All of these bodies received letters from Judas Tadeo Reyes, on behalf of the Governor, encouraging them to join the cause. As a result, the consultation fostered debates about how to defend the territory in case of a new invasion, what the Chileans had learnt from the experience of Buenos Aires the year before, how the concept of *patria* should be understood and why Britain was still the enemy of Spanish Americans. The responses reveal that there was no consensus regarding how to reply to Liniers. There were different interests and views of the situation, especially regarding the understanding of *patria*.

Judas Tadeo Reyes appealed to a continental American *patria* to convince the corporations to contribute to the defence of Buenos Aires. When writing to the University of San Felipe he claimed that 'we are sons of the same mother and individuals of the same family' in reference to their condition as subjects of the same king.[62] He also highlighted certain cultural elements of this *patria*, like 'language and religion', which were not shared with the British, who were usually depicted as the 'enemies of religion'.[63] The latter was also one of the main arguments used to persuade the Cabildo Eclesiástico to help Buenos Aires. Tadeo Reyes began by saying that 'the inhabitants [of Buenos Aires] are our brothers and sisters and in this fraternity they always were the model of the most Catholic country. If we grade

---

62 'Judas Tadeo Reyes to the University of San Felipe', Santiago, 4 July 1808, ANH-CG, vol. 819, fol. 15. In a letter to the Cabildo de Santiago, he wrote: 'we are subjects of the same king' (Santiago, 4 July 1808, ANH-CG, vol. 819, fol. 10).

63 'Judas Tadeo Reyes to the Cabildo Eclesiático', Santiago, 4 July 1808, ANH-CG, vol. 819, fol. 10.

our necessities, nothing is more serious than a Catholic population under threat of destruction'.[64]

Some of the responses also stressed Spanish American patriotism as an argument for supporting Buenos Aires. Antonio Alvarez Jonte, Rector of the university, mentioned the Viceroyalty of New Spain (Mexico) as an example: 'we know that when a city or port in New Spain was exposed to an enemy invasion, all the Spanish continent endeavoured to help'.[65] The members of the Tribunal del Consulado, although reluctant to accept Tadeo Reyes's proposal, commenced their letter by stressing the 'pure patriotism, love and fidelity of the inhabitants of the Kingdom', who were 'united by the heroic sentiments of its fellow countrymen and neighbours, forming one single body in spite of the cold mountains that separate them'.[66] This shows that an incipient patriotism was emerging among some representatives of the main bodies of the General Captaincy of Chile, although it was still conceived on a continental scale. Tadeo Reyes provided an ambiguous version of this narrative. When he wrote to the university, he claimed that his aim was to 'assist in the defence of this distraught capital with pecuniary resources so that the good reputation of the inhabitants of Chile is preserved in that nation [Argentina], and to offer new evidence of patriotism'.[67] On the one hand, he insisted on this broader idea of the *patria*, but on the other, he believed that the Chileans would merit a reward for their help. This reward was a good opinion of the inhabitants of this particular community called Chile.

This nascent patriotism was even more explicit in other replies, which revealed major concerns about both Chile's weak military strategy and lack of economic resources. The very existence of Chile in this threatening context was under discussion, which led Tadeo Reyes to persist with the idea that Chile's future rested on the fate of Buenos Aires. To justify his petition, he wrote in one letter that 'this kingdom more than any other is linked by its situation to the fate of that capital [Buenos Aires]'. For Tadeo Reyes,

64 Ibid., fol. 11.
65 'Antonio Alvarez Jonte to the Rector of the University', Santiago, 6 July 1808, ANH-CG, vol. 819. fols 19–22. Alvarez Jonte was born in Madrid in 1784, but spent most of his life in Buenos Aires. According to the historian of the university, he gained his doctorate in law at the University of San Felipe in Santiago in 19 February 1808. Then he returned to Buenos Aires and a year later he was designated by the *junta* of Buenos Aires as its representative in Santiago, as is shown in Section 1.6 of this chapter. For the record of his degree, see José Toribio Medina, *Historia de la Real Universidad de San Felipe de Santiago de Chile, Vol. 1* (Santiago: Sociedad Imprenta y Litografia Universo, 1928), p. 551. For a short biography, see Juan Lucio Torres, *El español como soldado argentino. Participación en las campañas militares por la libertad e independencia* (Madrid: Ediciones de la Torre, 2014), p. 52.
66 'Juan Rodrigo Ballesteros, Santiago Aldunate, Manuel de Irigoyen, José Concha to the Cabildo de Santiago', Santiago 25 July 1808, ANH-CG, vol. 819, fols 38–39.
67 'Judas Tadeo Reyes to the University of San Felipe', Santiago, 4 July 1808. ANH-CG, vol. 819, fol. 11.

the conquest of Buenos Aires would cause serious difficulties for Chilean communications with the metropolis. In most cases, correspondence from Spain reached Chile via Buenos Aires across the Andes, and not through the Pacific. Thus, he wrote, 'should the English invade and dominate the capital Buenos Aires our communication with Spain would be dislocated or even destroyed'.[68] This testimony reinforces the marginality of Chile in the context of the Spanish dominion. Despite facing the Pacific, this was not seen as a means of connecting Chile to the rest of the world. The connection with the United Provinces of La Plata through the Cordillera de los Andes was the privileged route of communication with Spain. This means that Chile depended to a certain degree on Buenos Aires to effectively form part of the Spanish Empire.

Muñoz de Guzmán was so concerned about communications with Buenos Aires that he commissioned Luis de la Cruz, the mayor of Concepción, to organise an expedition from Concepción to Buenos Aires in 1806, 'to clarify all the points of utility and convenience that may result for the two kingdoms, concerning communication and direct trade through this new path'.[69] This implied finding new routes between Concepción and Buenos Aires, and gaining the support of the indigenous population of the zone (*Pehuenches*) to open up the route. It was during this journey that De la Cruz learned that Buenos Aires had been occupied by British troops.

Despite Tadeo Reyes's persistence in linking the fate of Chile to that of Buenos Aires, the biggest fear of the other Chilean authorities was an invasion by sea, regardless of the fate of the other capital. Craufurd's expedition was mentioned in the discussion to demonstrate the plausibility of such an eventuality. The members of the Tribunal de Minería argued that:

> we must agree to defend our kingdom and that capital [Buenos Aires] equally, without losing sight of the danger of imminent invasion via our coasts. We know that Colonel [*sic*] Craufurd came with a section destined for Chile when he unexpectedly joined that of General Whitelocke against Buenos Aires.[70]

Tadeo Reyes argued that an invasion by land departing from Buenos Aires was more plausible than by sea, because the Argentine capital was 'the gate by which we would be invaded by land on an adequate scale so that their squadrons reach intact the ports of the south [of Chile]'.[71]

68 'Judas Tadeo Reyes to the Consulado de Comercio', ANH-CG, Santiago, 4 July 1808, vol. 819, fol. 12.

69 Luis de la Cruz, *Viage a su costa, del Alcalde Provincial del muy Ilustre Cabildo de la Concepción de Chile, D. Luis de la Cruz* (Buenos Aires, Imprenta del Estado, 1835), p. 5.

70 'Gerónimo, Pedro Pérez Infante, Joaquín Fernández de Leiva to Francisco García Carraco', Santiago, 23 July 1808, ANH-CG, vol. 819, fol. 36.

71 'Judas Tadeo Reyes to Pedro Flores and Francisco García Carrasco', Santiago, 11 July 1808, ANH-CG, vol. 819, fol. 13.

Two visions were confronted in this discussion. Tadeo Reyes stressed the importance of the connections between Chile and Buenos Aires as the main means of communicating with the Iberian Peninsula. In this view, Chile seemed more connected to the Atlantic than to the Pacific. The members of the Tribunal de Minería instead stressed the importance of the Pacific Ocean as the means by which Chile was connected to other events. For them, it was obvious that any invasion had to be by sea rather than by land as Tadeo Reyes believed. For the British designers of the plan to invade Chile, both interpretations converged into one single vision. Chile and Buenos Aires formed part of the same trade space, and the territory in between was seen as a corridor to connect the Atlantic and the Pacific. They were not concerned about the individual identities of each territory. In their view, this was one territory.

Besides the mention of Craufurd's example, the same tribunal argued that 'regardless of what is happening in Europe and on these shores, Chile must be wary in all things. It must keep at a distance the trouble of war by energetically assisting the threatened point [Buenos Aires] because in doing so it will distract the attention of the enemy'.[72] For them, the idea was to concentrate the war in the city of Buenos Aires in order to keep the enemy away from Chile. This was the only reason to join the defence of that city, as the Chilean governor himself, García Carrasco, also suggested:

> It is therefore necessary to keep the enemy away from us while giving us time to prepare ourselves to fight. We keep the enemy in Buenos Aires. There is the vanguard of our army: those brave men form the first columns of the great army that has to defend this part of America and should be considered dispersed in their vast provinces, united by common interest.[73]

García Carrasco was speaking as a Spanish authority, emphasising that there was only a single army formed by different sections across the Continent, one of these being in Buenos Aires. Ultimately, regardless of the territory they were living in, they were all defending the Spanish king's sovereignty. However, García Carrasco's words reveal that he was more concerned about the community he was in charge of and support for Buenos Aires was only suggested as a means to keep the enemy away from Chile. Hence, in spite of being a Spanish authority he was acting as a member of a particular and different community.

The latter was only one way to understand the role of each territory in the conflict and reveals the contested ideas about patriotism and proto-national identities that began to emerge amidst the conflict. The staff members of the University of San Felipe warned that 'the cost of this relief must be assumed

72 'José María Linares to Francisco García Carrasco', Santiago, 18 July 1808, ANH-CG, vol. 819, fol. 18.

73 'Francisco García Carrasco to all the Corporations of Santiago', Santiago, 11 July 1808, ANH-CG, vol. 819, fol. 28.

by the assisted and not by the taxpayers',[74] stressing that the university did not count on extraordinary funds to contribute to this cause. Others, in turn, highlighted that Chile was a poor province to justify its incapacity to provide relief to Buenos Aires. Bernardo de Vera y Pintado, a professor at the university who was born in Santa Fe in one of the United Provinces of La Plata, claimed that Chile 'is a poor kingdom, subject to a purely passive trade and considerably subsidised'.[75] Chile had to 'reserve the taxes that might help it if invaded. Thus, [Buenos Aires] could not criticise Chile for its loyal situation (which is the best apology of Chilean patriotism)'.[76] The main fear was that any help to Buenos Aires might lead to an increase in Chilean taxation. Antonio Alvarez Jonte, for example, considered this 'impracticable and arbitrary',[77] while the Tribunal del Consulado went further, warning that 'since money is scarce in this agricultural kingdom, its inhabitants will agitate in case of any taxation'.[78] There were also those who expressed the opposite feeling, that is, that Chileans should not defend Buenos Aires, but concentrate on the defence of Chile. In this respect, the Tribunal de Minería pointed out that 'Chile has all it needs to be respected. There are arms that might be easily distributed, strong and belligerent men who do not obey any military corps and an excellent youth'.[79]

All of these ideas about the place of Chile in the context of continental warfare were debated between May and September 1808. During these months the Peninsula had been occupied by the French army and the Spanish royal family, including King Ferdinand VII, had been sent to Bayonne by Napoleon. As a result, the war of Spanish independence started in the Peninsula on 2 May 1808. This news only reached Chile,

---

74 'The University of San Felipe to Francisco García Carrasco', Santiago, 18 July 1808, ANH-CG, vol. 819, fol. 13.

75 'Bernardo Vera y Pintado to the Rector of the University of San Felipe', Santiago, 11 July 1808, ANH-CG, vol. 819, fol. 29. Vera y Pintado was born and grew up in Santa Fe in the Viceroyalty of La Plata. Like Alvarez Jonte, he moved to Santiago to get his doctorate in law and became a professor. He did not go back to the Viceroyalty, but remained in Chile. When the *Junta* of Buenos Aires designated him its representative in Santiago he was already living there. He spent the rest of his life in Chile, becoming a key political figure, and was elected deputy of the Congress in 1824. He wrote Chile's first national anthem in 1819. An account of his life can be found in Miguel Luis Amunátegui, 'D. Bernardo Vera i Pintado', in *La Semana. Revista noticiosa, literaria i científica*, 10 (23 July 1859), 147–50.

76 'Bernardo Vera y Pintado to the Rector of the University of San Felipe', Santiago, 11 July 1808, ANH-CG, vol. 819, fol. 29.

77 'Antonio Alvarez Jonte to the Rector of the University of San Felipe', Santiago, 6 July 1808, ANH-CG, vol. 819, fol. 19.

78 'Juan Rodrigo Ballesteros, Santiago Aldunate, Manuel de Irigoyen, José de Santiago Concha ANH-CG, Santiago, 21 July 1808, vol. 819, fol. 38.

79 'Tribunal de Minería to Francisco García Carrasco', Santiago, 8 July 1808, ANH-CG, vol. 819, fol. 18.

via Buenos Aires, in September, which meant that both the inhabitants of Buenos Aires and Chile had been seriously considering the possibility of a new British invasion for at least four months, unaware that Britain was now an ally of Spain. When news of the new geopolitical situation in Europe arrived in Chile, the attitudes of both the authorities and the members of the main bodies of the General Captaincy of Chile began to change and now fears were of a possible invasion by France. Judas Tadeo Reyes expressed this fear in a letter dated 10 September 1808, in which he stated that it was necessary to resume the plan he had designed when the enemy was Britain to defend Chile from external invasion. He wrote that, 'taking into account the latest news provided by the Viceroy [of Buenos Aires] in his proclamation', he thought it better to 'help this capital [Santiago] and take it to the highest level of defence in case of invasion by our enemies'.[80]

All this shows that in the early nineteenth century the relations between Britain and Chile were shaped by different attitudes. The British had a clear interest in expanding their commercial networks and markets, and the location of Chile represented a good opportunity to take control of the trade routes in the South Pacific. This also led to the undermining of the Spanish Empire's power in a period of imperial rivalry. Chileans, for their part, who were used to interacting with British smugglers, were again facing the possibility of an invasion. In a word, fear was the most widespread attitude, especially once the authorities learnt that there was an actual plan to invade the territory. In addition, all these plans to defend the territory and debates about the idea of *patria* demonstrate that in these early years the relationship between Britain and Chile was mainly defined at the state level. That is because it was Britain itself, as an imperial power, which was being represented as a threat for both Chile and Chileans.

1.5 The Anti-foreigner Policy

The perception of Britain as an enemy remained even after 1808, when it became an ally of Spain in the war against France, but not all Chileans were persuaded about this new role. Images and representations of Britain were changing and for some Chileans, Britain's place in the world remained ambiguous. Indeed, the image of Britain as an enemy, which was determined by its role as a rival empire, coexisted with the image of Britain as an ally. Representations about Britain began to be contradictory because of the changing nature of the geopolitical context of this period. For García Carrasco, for example, Britain remained an enemy, not because it was an imperial power, but because it was synonymous with degeneracy and barbarism. At the same time, he defended free trade agreements with Britain

---

80 'Judas Tadeo Reyes to the Cabildo de Santiago', Santiago, 10 September 1808, ANH-CG, vol. 819, fol. 54.

in spite of the Decree of 1778, which only authorised trade between specific ports in Spanish America and Spain.

Francisco García Carrasco replaced Luis Muñoz de Guzmán in the government when he died on 11 February 1808. He was a military man from Concepción who assumed his post after internal struggles between Santiago's and Concepción's elites.[81] García Carrasco was the Governor of Chile when Napoleon invaded Spain in May 1808 and behaved as a loyal authority committed to preserving the rights of King Ferdinand VII under any circumstance. However, he was a disastrous governor, unable to maintain the stability of the General Captaincy of Chile during the uncertain months after the invasion of the Peninsula. Manuel Manso, a customs officer at that time, declared that from the first moment, García Carrasco 'showed that he was entirely unworthy of such an important position'.[82] García Carrasco punished and prosecuted anyone who questioned his authority or that of the metropolis, which eventually would lead to several conflicts with the elite of Santiago. The most famous episode was the imprisonment of three remarkable figures of the period in May 1810, Juan Antonio Ovalle, Bernardo Vera y Pintado and José Antonio Rojas, for rebelling against the authorities. This episode angered many among the elite of Santiago, who protested against the governor, eventually provoking his fall.[83]

In the context of the political crisis of the Spanish monarchy and the French invasions of the Peninsula, García Carrasco pursued a repressive policy towards foreigners. All foreigners began to be seen as potential enemies of the kingdom, despite the changed situation in Europe and the fact that Britain and Spain had become allies since May 1808. On 13 July 1808, García Carrasco decided to undertake a census of 'all the foreigners present in the Kingdom for any reason',[84] on the grounds that many old laws, which were not being enforced, explicitly prohibited the entry of foreigners into Spanish America without authorisation. García Carrasco wrote in the preamble of his decree of 'the persistence of the war in Europe, its spread to America and the efforts made by the English against this southern region'.[85] He was reluctant to recognise that the situation had changed, to accept the

---

81 Barros Arana, *Historia general de Chile*, VIII, pp. 41–57.

82 'Manuel Manso to the Central Junta of Seville', Santiago, 4 February 1809, Archivo General de Indias (AGI), Seville, Fondo Chile, vol. 206.

83 'Proceso seguido por el Gobierno de Chile en 25 de Mayo de 1810, contra don Juan Antonio Ovalle, don José Antonio Rojas y el doctor don Bernardo Vera y Pintado por el delito de conspiración', in *Colección de Historiadores y Documentos relativos a la Independencia de Chile, Vol. 30*, ed. by Guillermo Feliú Cruz (Santiago: Imprenta Universitaria, 1939).

84 These documents are included in Miguel Luis Amunátegui, *La crónica de 1810* (Santiago: Imprenta de la República de Jacinto Núñez, 1876), Appendix 'Espulsion de extranjeros', II, pp. 330–35.

85 Ibid., p. 331.

new role played by Britain in the war, and started a persecution of Britons and other foreigners.

García Carrasco feared that the excessive presence of foreigners of 'all nations and professions' as well as 'prisoners and deserters of privateer and smuggler ships' or from 'the hostile invader expeditions of the River Plate' could destabilise the internal situation.[86] This was not conceived as an abstract threat though, but a very concrete one: '[foreigners], with their doctrines and bad habits are the cause of perversion of the natives, they who serve as emissaries, translators and even as agents of smugglers'.[87] Thus, foreigners, and particularly the British, who were clearly linked to the activities listed by García Carrasco, were represented as degenerate elements in Chilean society. They were not simply members of a rival military or naval force, but people involved in illegal activities like contraband and with 'bad habits' derived from their religious beliefs. Chileans must therefore be kept away from the danger they represented.

The form that all foreigners had to fill out in the census aimed to determine what kind of habits they had and whether they were 'useful' for the kingdom. Some questions requested specific data, such as origins ('nation', 'city or town' or 'kingdom'), religion ('old Catholic, Reconciled Catholic or another religion'), the length of their stay in the kingdom, place of stay, and reasons for being in Chile (i.e. 'deserter'). Others aimed to delve more deeply into their character, appearance and habits: 'What has been your religious and civic behaviour? Do you have any prevailing vice or any particular skill in foreign languages, sciences or mechanical arts? [Please list] your height, physiognomy and features that makes you recognisable'.[88] The census revealed a wide range of origins amongst the 79 foreigners registered: Americans (or *bostonenses*), Russians, Germans, Austrians, Danish, French, Italians, Portuguese, Maltese, Swedish, Hungarians, Dutch, Irish, Scottish and English. Only six were Britons (one Englishman living in Copiapó, two in Santiago, two in Rancagua, one in Valparaíso and one Scot in Valdivia) and four Irish (one in Talca, one in Talcahuano and two in Valdivia). Eventually, García Carrasco decided that all foreigners were to be expelled 'without lenience or dissimulation, regardless of their nation'.[89] However, some foreigners were entitled to remain in Chile: those who were naturalised, those who were authorised by special laws or by the special privileges of the king, those who were married with children, single Catholics with 20 years of residence in Chile who could certify their good behaviour, the elderly and the ill, and 'those who practise mechanical crafts that are useful to the republic'.[90] These exceptions made clear that one of the threats that García

86 Ibid., pp. 331–32.
87 Ibid., p. 331.
88 Ibid., p. 332.
89 Ibid., p. 333.
90 Ibid., pp. 334–35.

Carrasco was trying to face was religious infidelity. With few exceptions, only Catholics could remain in the territory, which can be inferred from the fact that in Chile in 1808 it was only possible to be married under the Catholic rite, and because to be a subject of the Spanish king meant to profess the Catholic religion. García Carrasco also made an exception for people with practical and useful knowledge that might be used in times of war. A good example is that of smiths, many of whom were involved in the making of arms, some of whom were Britons. The persecution carried out by García Carrasco was short-lived and there is no indication of the extent to which foreigners were actually expelled from the territory. Considering the new geopolitical context after Napoleon's invasion of Spain, it is unlikely that a persecution against Britons would have succeeded.

García Carrasco's anti-foreigner policy reveals that attitudes and perceptions towards Britons were still influenced by the earlier threats of invasion and the massive presence of smugglers on the coasts. Even in a new geopolitical context, Britons were still regarded as enemies and García Carrasco used a new language to define their role as such. Unlike subsequent representations of Britons as members of the 'civilised' world, García Carrasco depicted them as degenerate elements of Chilean society. Britain was not regarded as a cultural model to follow, but as an infidel land. Britons were likewise regarded as delinquents who did not deserve to be accepted in Chile. All of this had a clear purpose: to benefit from the construction of the image of the smuggler as a criminal. Shortly after the announcement of his plan to prosecute foreigners, in July 1808, García Carrasco joined a plot against a British privateer, Tristan Bunker, the commander of the *Scorpion*. This was an infamous scandal and the fact that García Carrasco was involved only discredited him further.[91]

However, García Carrasco's attitude towards Britain demonstrates that the geopolitical context was a crucial factor in understanding how Chileans perceived its role. His perceptions and decisions about Britain changed according to the circumstances and his actions before the news of Napoleon's invasion to the Peninsula would be completely different to what he did once news of the new geopolitical scenario arrived in Chile. Recent research has made clear that in mid-1809, when news of the situation at the Peninsula had already spread, García Carrasco's policy towards Britain had changed considerably. At that time, due to the economic crisis after Napoleon's invasion of Spain, García Carrasco seriously considered the possibility of opening free trade to British merchants, something that had not been part of his plans before news about the invasion arrived in Chile. His views were so radical in this matter that some prominent merchants like Agustín de Eyzaguirre criticised this idea and defended the trade monopoly established by the Spanish crown. For him, the complex scenario which unfolded

91 The details and repercussions of this scandal are analysed in Chapter 5.

after the 1808 crisis made it necessary to take protectionist measures to boost local production. Eyzaguirre was so concerned about this matter that he described García Carrasco as 'an enemy to be defeated', became one his most renowned rivals and was an instigator of his overthrow in 1810 once he took over as the mayor of the Cabildo of Santiago.[92] Despite the efforts of Eyzaguirre and other merchants, the Junta of Santiago decided to adopt a free trade policy with neutral states in 1811. As discussed in Chapter 5, this policy encouraged British merchant houses to send consignees to Chile, which would be the beginning of a new stage of British and Chilean relationships.

1.6 Early Diplomatic Negotiations after the 1808 Crisis

In mid-1808, Napoleon had already invaded Spain, King Ferdinand VII was imprisoned and the geopolitical dimension of the conflict in both Europe and Spanish America had changed rapidly. Since June 1808 Britain and Spain had been allies in the war against France. The possibility that Napoleon would invade South America was always latent, and mobilised Spanish Americans to reorganise their defensive plans. For Chile this meant that Britain was no longer the enemy, and new attitudes towards its intermediary role during the war began to emerge. In this new context, Britain was seen as a natural ally in the war against Napoleon, but not when the conflict between the Spanish American colonies and the metropolis broke out. Britain held a 'neutral' policy in this latter conflict, although its interests in Spanish America, mainly related to expanding its trade routes, remained intact. This neutrality also reveals the extent to which the 'British state' was committed to expanding its empire to South America, and to incorporating Chile into its dominion. If this was evident in 1806–1807, from 1808 onwards the situation changed. As a neutral state, Britain did not interfere in the internal affairs of Chile and other colonies, but assumed an intermediary role during the wars of independence.[93] Despite neutrality, however, the pervasive perception among Spanish Americans that Britain was the supreme empire persisted. The intervention of British agents in political affairs in South America was clear proof that its role as the leading empire of the world also affected Spanish Americans. Chileans accepted Britain's neutral stance, but also tried to take advantage of the British interest in the continent by offering something in exchange for their support in the struggles for independence. This led Chileans to promote a new image of Chile as a stable country, with enough room to receive British migrants if necessary. Even though a first diplomatic approach was attempted

---

92 Details of the dispute between Agustín Eyzaguirre and Francisco García Carrasco can be found in Juan Luis Ossa, 'Miguel Eyzaguirre: las redes de un chileno reformista en la Lima del virrey Abascal, 1803–1816, *Revista de Indias*, 57:269 (2017), 137–67 (pp. 145–48).

93 See Waddell, p. 6; Blaufarb, p. 755.

in the period covered by this chapter, diplomacy was not a success until the late 1820s. By that time, Chile was an independent state and its authorities sought and demanded recognition.

News of the French invasion of the Iberian Peninsula reached Santiago via Buenos Aires on 6 September 1808.[94] Santiago Liniers, the Viceroy of Buenos Aires, informed García Carrasco in a letter dated 17 August 1808. The Chilean governor replied a month later, stressing 'the willingness of the inhabitants to unite their efforts to defend the just cause of our beloved King Ferdinand the seventh'.[95] In his reply, dated 16 October 1808, Liniers included new information about the crisis. He enclosed 'four copies of the letter I received from the serene Princess Carlota Joaquina of Bourbon and my own reply'.[96] In these letters, Carlota expressed her gratitude to Liniers for preserving 'the rights of my royal house and of my family', signing the letter with her original surname, Bourbon.[97] Carlota was the sister of Ferdinand VII, the imprisoned king of Spain, and was married to the regent Prince of Portugal Joao VI, who became king of Portugal in 1822. With the aid of the British navy, who were aware of Napoleon's intentions to invade the Peninsula, the entire Portuguese court set off to Río de Janeiro on 29 November 1807, arriving on 7 March 1808. While in Río, Carlota learnt of the imprisonment of her brother, in May 1808, and the political crisis it triggered in his dominions. Since she was the only member of the Bourbon family in America, she sent emissaries to all the colonies to demand their loyalty.

The issue was controversial since Carlota was settled in Río de Janeiro as a member of the royal family of Portugal, the Braganzas, and her act was seen as an attempt to undermine the power of the Spanish monarchy. Carlota devised a plan to set up a new monarchy in the Viceroyalty of Buenos Aires with the advice and support of the British Admiral Sidney Smith and the *porteño* Saturnino Rodrígues Peña. Her secret agent in Buenos Aires was the British physicist James Paroissien, who had arrived in Río de Janeiro from Montevideo after the failure of the British invasions of the River Plate.[98]

94 Barros Arana, *Historia Jeneral de la Independencia de Chile*, 1, p. 125.

95 'Francisco García Carrasco to Santiago Liniers', Santiago, 17 September 1808, British Library (BL), Additional Manuscripts (Add MS) 32608, fol. 36.

96 'Liniers to García Carrasco', Buenos Aires, 16 October 1808, BL, Add MS 32608, fol. 41.

97 'Carlota Joaquina to Santiago Liniers', Río de Janeiro, 16 September 1808 (Buenos Aires: Real imprenta de los niños expósitos, 1808), p. 3.

98 R.A. Humphreys, *Liberation in South America, 1806–1827: The Career of James Paroissien* (London: The Athlone Press, 1952), pp. 15–32. Paroissien is one of the more interesting characters of the period. He travelled to Spanish America from Britain to join the British invasion of Buenos Aires, went on to become a secret agent of Carlota Joaquina and would join San Martin's Army of the Andes to liberate Chile and Peru, even becoming one of Carlota Joaquina's closest advisors. During 1822–1823 he would also be the Peruvian envoy to London to negotiate recognition.

Paroissien would later join San Martín's liberation army during the wars of independence and became a central figure in Peruvian mining operations. According to Marcela Ternavasio, the Viceroyalty of Buenos Aires was where Carlota Joaquina had most support. Revolutionary leaders in 1810 seriously considered the possibility of accepting the regency of Carlota because it would secure their 'independence' – an ambiguous term at that time – from the Spanish monarchy. For Ternavasio, the *carlotista* project was much more significant than it was thought and was far from being a mere anecdote in this complex scenario. Colonial authorities and revolutionary leaders were somewhat forced to debate its plausibility, which also made them reflect on their links with the Spanish monarchy.[99]

Carlota's attempts to gain support in Chile were unveiled by García Carrasco, who sent a letter to Liniers dated 23 November 1808: 'the English frigate *Higgins* has arrived in the port of Valparaíso with cargo trade and dispatches from the serene lady Princess of Brazil, Carlota. The supercargo Federico Dowling has been instituted as her cabinet postman'.[100] Dowling not only delivered Carlota's correspondence, but also tried to gain more support from some of the notables of Chile after the negative response from the Real Audiencia. To this end he wrote down the most important names in a list so that Carlota Joaquina could send them personal letters. This list included García Carrasco himself; Luis Muñoz de Guzmán's daughter, Luisa; and Ignacio de la Carrera, the father of José Miguel Carrera, who became the first leader of Chile's independence movements. All replied in respectful terms that they were loyal to their king, Ferdinand VII, as the Real Audiencia had.[101] However, they could not ignore the fact that the letters had been brought by a British navy officer, which was clear proof of Britain's intermediary role in the continent.

By July 1810 the early British mediation in Chilean affairs would be even more explicit, when the British warship *Standard* brought the commander Elphinstone Fleming to Valparaíso.[102] He acted as an intermediary between the acting government in the Iberian Peninsula (the Consejo de Regencia) and the government of Chile, still in the hands of García Carrasco. Elphinstone Fleming had been commissioned to ask for financial aid to defend the Peninsula from the French and to transport the elected deputies who were to represent the General Captaincy of Chile to the Cortes of Cádiz,

99 Marcela Ternavasio, *Candidata a la Corona. La infanta Carlota Joaquina en el laberinto de las revoluciones hispanoamericanas* (Buenos Aires: Siglo veintiuno editores, 2015).

100 'García Carrasco to Liniers', Santiago, 23 November 1808, BL, Add MS 32608, fol. 140.

101 The letters were sent on May 1809. See Roberto Hernández Ponce, 'Carlota Joaquina de Borbón. Apuntes en torno al epistolario carlotino y a un epistolario chileno inédito, 1808–1816', *Historia*, 20 (1985), 137–65.

102 All this is narrated by Barros Arana, *Historia General de Chile*, VIII, pp. 264–66.

a sort of parliament composed of deputies from all the Spanish kingdoms. The Chileans were reluctant to accept these demands. Firstly, resources were scarce, and it was more urgent to use them in the defence of their own territory. A few years ago, these same British had invaded Buenos Aires and had settled on a plan to invade Chile, so there were strong reasons to maintain such a reluctance. Secondly, the Chileans did not consider it necessary to elect deputies to the Cortes as two of them were already in the Peninsula: Joaquín Fernández de Leiva and Miguel Riesco. They had travelled to the Peninsula for different reasons, but once there they had been designated 'acting deputies'.[103] Indeed, no other deputies represented Chile in the Cortes, so Fleming's mission was in vain. In his *Diplomatic History of the Independence of Chile* the historian Ricardo Montaner Bello maintained that Fleming 'had a bad impression of what he saw, and he surely passed this on to the viceroy [Fernando] Abascal, because that was when the military plan to forcibly suppress the Chilean authorities was put into action'.[104]

Abascal was the Viceroy of Peru and began to see the formation of the Junta of Santiago as a threat to the king's sovereignty, referring to it as a 'revolutionary' and 'insurgent' move. In December 1812 Abascal decided to invade Chile to overthrow the revolutionary Junta. This marked the actual beginning of the war of independence in Chile since Chileans had to organise themselves in order to defend their territory and their revolution. After four months of warfare in southern Chile, a peace treaty was signed by both forces on 3 May 1814. The details of this treaty are well known to historians: it basically stated that both forces had to stop the attacks and could not continue to approach each other. It also stated that Chile must send deputies to the Cortes of Cádiz and the Chileans had to reinforce their loyalty to the king Ferdinand VII. For their part, royalists had to recognise the provisional government of the Junta.[105]

The treaty was drafted by Commodore James Hillyar, a Royal Navy officer stationed in the South Pacific to safeguard the interests of British merchants. At that moment, Britain and the US were embroiled in the Anglo-American war (1812–1815), some of whose battles were fought in the South Pacific. One confronted the British ship *Phoebe*, commanded by Hillyar, and the *Essex*, commanded by the US navy officer Captain David Porter. After defeating the *Essex* in March 2014, which secured British interests in the South Pacific, Hillyar sailed to Callao to meet Viceroy Abascal to manifest his concern about the situation between the Viceroyalty of Peru and the General Captaincy of Chile. Since the conflict was affecting British interests and mercantile

103 See Paula Caffarena, 'Las Cortes de Cádiz y Chile. Encuentros y desencuentros a partir de sus diputados Joaquín Fernández de Leiva y Miguel Riesco, *Historia 396*, 2 (2012), 223–44.
104 Montaner Bello, p. 15.
105 The treaty is available in *Colección de historiadores y documentos de la independencia de Chile* (Santiago: Imprenta de Cervantes, 1909), XV, pp. 328–33.

activities in the Pacific, he tried to persuade Abascal about the convenience of ending it. This was also justified on the grounds that both armies needed at least a truce. Abascal eventually accepted the deal and Hillyar drafted the treaty to be negotiated and signed by both forces. On the Chilean side, Bernardo O'Higgins and his Irish officer Juan Mackenna led the negotiations on behalf of the Junta, now presided by Francisco de la Lastra. On the royalist side, negotiations were undertaken by Commander Gabino Gaínza. The treaty itself stated that both armies must acknowledge the role played by Hylliar in 'suppressing the hostilities, restoring peace, good harmony and close friendship between the governments of Lima and Santiago'.[106] Historians agree that ultimately the treaty was a complete failure. It did not stop the war and both sides disavowed what they had signed. However, its signing is clear proof that Britain's role as an intermediator in the conflict was accepted by both armies. In other words, the Chileans' perception of the role played by Britain had changed completely since 1806.

These examples show that from the outset, the political dimension of the conflict was far from being exclusively a matter for the Spanish monarchy and its colonies. We can see *peninsulares*, Spanish Americans, Portuguese, British and French involved in a single episode, such as in Carlota Joaquina's requests for loyalty. In these years it became evident that the 'intermediary' role of the British Empire was difficult to avoid. The formation of the first local *junta* on 18 September 1810 after the fall of García Carrasco reinvigorated this idea. From then on, Chileans resolved to make their own decisions without consulting the metropolis. However, this degree of autonomy also led them to realise that their situation was fragile and any defence of their territory, against a possible invasion by either France or Spain, would need external support. This meant that, subsequently, they would have to seek that support and not await an intervention to send representatives to negotiate the involvement of an external foreign power. In other words, to 'beg' for help, which reinforced Britain's self-perception as the new ruling power of the world.

The establishment of Chile's first Congress in 1811 was the first step towards this development. Francisco Antonio Pinto, who later on became Vice President of Chile (1827–1830), was appointed as the first diplomatic representative of Chile to Buenos Aires in the session held on 9 July 1811. According to the Congress's records, this appointment was made not only to seek to establish diplomatic relations with Buenos Aires, but to collect information about the situation in the Peninsula, in Europe and Brazil. Buenos Aires was better connected than Santiago and news arrived more quickly, which was stated as the main reason for the Congress to appoint Pinto as envoy to Buenos Aires:

> Being of the utmost importance to have in the capital Buenos Aires one person assigned to examine with interest the genuine state of things, to

106 Ibid., pp. 332–33.

inquire on the news from Spain as well as from other European powers, [and] the Court of Brazil, to announce the truth to all in due time, and based on all this, to form an idea of what is most advantageous for this country and its relations [...] We proceed to the election and Mr Francisco Antonio Pinto, captain of the infantry militias, was elected.[107]

Likewise, Buenos Aires designated Antonio Alvarez Jonte – the same rector of the University of San Felipe who had replied in Tadeo Reyes's consultancy – as its representative in Santiago; he arrived in October 1810. However, his behaviour and involvement in the internal affairs of the Junta led its members to ask the Junta of Buenos Aires for his removal.[108] In June 1811 he was recalled by Buenos Aires and replaced with Bernardo Vera y Pintado, a professor at the University of San Felipe who was already living in Santiago.[109]

Events in Europe urged the Chilean authorities to modify Pinto's mission and send him as their representative to the 'courts of Rome, France and England' in order to gain recognition of their cause.[110] Pinto left Buenos Aires by the end of July 1813 on a British merchant ship, and arrived in London in October. His instructions contained three sections: politics, economy and religion.[111] The 'political section' reflected Chile's doubts about the role of Britain in the ongoing conflict. They feared that 'England thought of some colonial system and of monopoly with respect to the Americas, which would bring about the evils suffered by the Asian people'. Chileans sought to open up trade with Asia, accepting Britain's role as the wardens of free trade, but not a monopoly nor a colonial system. They aimed to 'procure for themselves cotton manufactures, which they probably lacked'.[112]

The instructions also included one of first Chile's disseminations of 'propaganda', portraying the country as an example of peace, stability and prosperity. This offered a stark contrast with the negative image of Chile publicised by Luis Muñoz de Guzmán and Judas Tadeo Reyes as part of their defensive plans. In this instruction, the situation of Chile was compared to that of Switzerland: 'the political harmony of Chile must be like that

---

107 'Acuerdo del Congreso Nacional de Chile', Santiago, 11 October 1811, in Melchor Martínez, *Memoria histórica sobre la revolución de Chile: desde el cautiverio de Fernando VII hasta 1814* (Valparaíso: Imprenta europea, 1848), pp. 356–57.

108 Barros Arana, *Historia General de Chile*, VIII, p. 250.

109 Amunátegui, 'D. Bernardo Vera i Pintado', p. 150.

110 The life of Francisco Antonio Pinto during the independence years has been studied by Juan Luis Ossa, 'Francisco Antonio Pinto en los albores de la República, 1785–1828' (unpublished dissertation, Santiago: Pontifica Universidad Católica de Chile, 2006).

111 'Instrucción remitida al encargado de negocios en la Corte de Londres y enviado extraordinario don Francisco Antonio Pinto', in Montaner Bello, *Historia diplomática de la independencia de Chile*, pp. 441–46.

112 Ibid., p. 442.

established in Switzerland in Europe, notwithstanding that given the ongoing convulsion and dangers in America it will defend the American System with all its power until it is consolidated'. For the members of the Junta, the most efficient way to successfully defend the Spanish American territories was the establishment of 'a confederation of at least all South America'.[113] The fact that in London there were delegates from the rest of the Spanish American territories would facilitate this formation, but always via British mediation and without caring whether it was monarchical or not.[114]

The 'economic section', apart from the statements made in favour of free trade, stressed the need to attract skilled Britons to Chile, reinstating the idea of 'usefulness' advanced by García Carrasco in 1808, when he sought to expel foreigners from the territory. Although the document did not exclusively refer to Britons, it stated that it was easier to attract Britons than continental Europeans due to the 'oppression and losses brought about by the war in France'. Pinto's instructions refer to skilled artisans and men educated in the fields of 'chemistry, botany, mineralogy and other useful sciences'. The government considered granting certain privileges to make Chile a more attractive destination, such as empty lands and taxation benefits.[115] The flax industry ('the principal and only one of the kingdom') needed skilled workers, but also 'a powerful trade house, able to sustain the project'. Mining was also a major concern for the Chilean government, which expressed the need to 'have artists for the mineral products that can be applied to arts and other industries, for which it would be really important to have a chemistry teacher to spread this science in the kingdom'.[116] Such improvements also required access to information, for which reason Pinto was requested to bring periodicals, manuals, machines and tools, as well as 'political papers about American businesses'.[117]

Pinto's instructions reveal that by 1813 Chilean leaders hoped to win the support of Great Britain by expanding the scope of the conflict to a transcontinental scale, and trying to persuade the British to intervene directly in their favour. However, they did not foresee that Lord Castlereagh would take a cautious approach to the revolutions in the Spanish American colonies, which has been labelled 'neutral'.[118] This neutrality has been called into question in recent years. Martin Robson has stressed the point that Britain had an urgent need to expand its sphere of influence to Spanish America, because of the French blockade of British-European trade. The need to establish new trade

113 Ibid.
114 Ibid.
115 Ibid., pp. 442–43.
116 Ibid., p. 443.
117 Ibid., p. 444.
118 R.A. Humphreys, 'Presidential Address: Anglo-American Rivalries and Spanish American Emancipation', *Transactions of the Royal Historical Society*, fifth series, 16 (1966), 131–56.

routes and markets was a matter of survival, so this obliged the British to approach the insurgent colonies in a 'not-so-neutral' manner.[119]

Pinto's instructions also reflect a definite turn in the perceived image of Britain among the Chilean authorities. For García Carrasco, foreigners, including Britons, had represented a threat to the country's internal situation and were perverting Chileans, with the exception of those who had useful knowledge for the kingdom. By 1813, the exception became the rule and the Junta manifested its interest in attracting skilled foreigners, even offering privileges. If in 1809 the privilege was simply the right to remain in the territory, by 1813 this was no longer sufficient. Moreover, the instructions issued to Pinto reveal that Chile needed to offer something in exchange for the help it was asking for. The only thing available was Chile's landscape, constructed as an attractive destination for those skilled Britons who sought new opportunities. All this also reveals that in the period 1806–1814, 'non-state' agents began to serve as intermediaries in the relations between Britain and Chile. Chileans began to 'invite' Britons to travel to Chile in order to collaborate in different economic activities. As revealed in subsequent chapters, this was also the result of the preconceptions that many Chileans held regarding Britain and Europe in general: that they formed part of the 'civilised world' and could help to improve the Chilean economy.

1.6 The Conspiracy of the English

The 'offer' made by Pinto to the British authorities consisted of bringing skilled workers to live in Chile. It is not clear to what extent they took up the offer, but some sources reveal that in 1814 there were skilled British workers living in Chile and that some had even joined the army. This was the first time the army worked as a 'contact zone' between people from different places and backgrounds. By 1814, many foreigners had been enrolled in the patriotic forces, although it is difficult to determine exactly how many of them were British. One testimony suggests that there were '40 officers from all nations, another 40 French artisans and 150 seamen'.[120] The episode that is analysed in this section shows that the experiences of some of those Britons who joined the army in the first stage of the war were not determined simply by their origins, but by their social status. The 'conspiracy' mounted against the government by some Britons in the Chilean army was a response to their living conditions, showing that there were no firm loyalties towards any side in the war.

As noted above, the war for Chilean independence began in December 1812, when the Viceroy of Peru, Fernando de Abascal, decided to invade

119 Martin Robson, *Britain, Portugal and South America in the Napoleonic War* (London: I.B. Tauris, 2012), pp. 1–21.

120 Quoted in Douglas Barry and Patricio Vergara, 'De Revolucionarios a Libertadores. Los Oficiales Europeos y Norteamericanos en el Ejército de Chile. 1817–1830', *Anuario de historia militar*, 27 (2013), 87–131 (p. 94).

the territory and sent a military expedition to restore the authority of the absent king Ferdinand VII. Two other expeditions were sent in January and July 1814.[121] Thus, between 1812 and 1814 the war had progressed rapidly, especially in southern and central Chile. This was because the troops departed from Callao and were transported by sea to Talcahuano in the south, so that they could march northward to take Santiago. It has become clear that this war was not between the Spanish and Chileans. It was above all a civil war, which engaged people born in the same land, but with different loyalties. Antonio Pareja, commander of the first expedition, had been commissioned to organise an army with locals from Chiloé and Valdivia who did not adhere to the cause of independence.[122]

On 26 May 1814, six Britons enrolled in the patriotic forces were condemned for conspiring against the Chilean government. Three of them, Pedro Guillermo (William Smith), John Brown and Thomas Bales, were sentenced to death and another three, Jorge Cosme, Tomas Herrera (Thomas Smith) and Guillermo (William) Homes, to ten years in the *galeras* (galleys).[123] There were other Britons involved, like Antonio José, Adam Roche and Bartolome Tuckerman, who were not condemned because they were informers. Another, who was accused of being the instigator, José Diaz (Joseph Smith), was a fugitive. According to the testimonies given at the trial, the conspiracy consisted of taking control of the Plaza de armas, the main square of Santiago, using one of the cannons that was in their charge. After the first shot, all the Britons of the forces – which, according to their testimonies, numbered more than thirty – were to gather in the square in order to take the gunpowder room located at one of its corners. Then they would have to take another cannon, which was stored in the same room, and point both at the palace of the government until the '*Chilotes* troops', the royalist forces, reached the city. The conspirators would then join the Chilotes, who would designate a new governor, likely the officer of the Casa de moneda (Currency House).[124]

The testimonies given by the different actors involved were of course contradictory, since none of them wanted to be punished, and they all defended their innocence and accused another of being the main instigator. The only element they agreed on was the absence of political reasons for carrying out the conspiracy. None of the actors involved provided an explanation for why the Chilean government needed to be overthrown and

121 Collier, pp. 101–17.
122 Ibid.
123 The records of the trial were compiled under the title 'Proceso seguido para el esclarecimiento de una conspiración que tuvo lugar en Santiago i que se denominó de "los ingleses", 1814', in *Colección de historiadores i de documentos relativos a la independencia de Chile*, IX, pp. 323–82.
124 Summary from the testimonies of Adam Roche and Antonio José, 26 April 1814, and John Brown, 29 April 1814, 'Proceso seguido para el esclarecimiento de una conspiración', pp. 324–25, 342.

replaced by a new one. The only reason that emerged from the testimonies was the need to improve their living conditions. Some, like Roche and José, spoke clearly of 'money' as a motivation for conspirators like Guillermo. The soldiers had been invited by Guillermo to join a 'very big business, with a lot of money'.[125] Those who joined the conspiracy did so in the expectation of obtaining easy money, because the supposed new governor would be a very rich man and because one of the targets was the Casa de moneda, 'from where we will take a lot of money'.[126] Others, like Tuckerman, were more ambiguous, indicating the hope of having a better life if they joined the other army. According to his testimony, Guillermo had said that 'should they join the enemy [...] in this way they would be equally happy'. This was justified on the grounds that an unknown *hacendado pudiente* (a very rich estate owner) was coming to Santiago with the royalist troops 'to protect them' and to rescue his brothers who were captives of the patriots.[127] This desire to improve their living conditions by conspiring against a government that apparently did not meet their economic expectations can also be explained by the origins of the conspirers. The six condemned all occupied the lowest military ranks. They had perhaps travelled to Chile in response to the need of skilled foreigners that could be useful to the 'republic' expressed by García Carrasco a few years before. However, this did not mean that they would occupy a privileged rank in the military hierarchy, in stark contrast to the situation of the British seamen who later arrived with Thomas Cochrane in 1818 to join the newly created Chilean navy, many of whom were officers of the highest rank.[128]

Amongst the Britons involved in the plot were others in precarious situations. At least two servants of other Britons were involved in the conspiracy. Jorge Cosme was the servant of Thomas Bale and Ricardo of John James Barnard, who had only arrived in Chile in December 1812.[129] Cosme delivered an important testimony about Bale, which eventually incriminated him. He had been told by Bale that he considered himself more of a leader than Diaz in case of a revolt.[130] Bale was eventually sentenced to death. Barnard informed on Ricardo, revealing that he had been invited by Guillermo to join the plot.[131]

---

125 Testimony of Adam Roche, 26 April 1814, 'Proceso seguido para el esclarecimiento de una conspiración', p. 325.
126 Testimony of Adam Roche, 26 April 1814, 'Proceso seguido para el esclarecimiento de una conspiración', p. 325.
127 Testimony of John Brown, 29 April 1814, 'Proceso seguido para el esclarecimiento de una conspiración', pp. 325, 342.
128 See Chapter 2 of this book.
129 See Chapter 4, Section 4.4, of this book.
130 Testimony of Jorge Cosme, 29 April 1814, 'Proceso seguido para el esclarecimiento de una conspiración', pp. 345–46.
131 Testimony of John James Barnard, 26 April 1814, 'Proceso seguido para el esclarecimiento de una conspiración', p. 336.

This was actually the only testimony against Ricardo, who was not among the condemned. Thus, no sense of loyalty united the participants of the conspiracy. Their relations were fragile and shaped by self-interest rather than by a big cause, as could have been expected given their intent to overthrow a government responsible for their situation. Only in the testimony of Guillermo Homes, the sole American of the group, is it possible to identify a sense of loyalty, for he recognised that he had decided he would join the conspiracy 'if my mates and the Sergeant who had brought me here join it'.[132] Roche, in turn, declared that he could not have joined the conspiracy because, 'being from a free country he could not defend against the liberty of these people and, by contrast, he would always fight with the patriots'.[133] Yet it is difficult to determine whether this was a genuine expression of loyalty to the patriotic cause or he was simply trying to convince the authorities of his innocence, as the testimony shows different uses of the word 'liberty' in this period.

The prosecutor claimed that the conspiracy aimed to 'earn a fortune for the accomplices by surrendering the capital to the enemy'. The crime was considered even more serious in this case because, 'being foreigners who had been admitted to this kingdom by hospitality, getting advantages that they would never have found in their own country, their gratitude should put them in favour of the government, which in representing the people dispenses such benefits to them'.[134] Pedro Guillermo was accused of being the leader and instigator of the conspiracy and his punishment was more humiliating than that of the others: he was sentenced to hanging, before which he was to be paraded through the streets of the city carried on a *bestia de albarda* (likely to be a mule). Dr José Silvestre Lazo, the *procurador de pobres* (attorney for poor people) of the Cabildo of Santiago, wrote a letter seeking clemency on behalf of Guillermo's 'poor family' and his 'four innocent children' who would lose their livelihoods. However, in another part of the letter he appealed to the value of Guillermo's skills as a smith and his utility for the war: 'the *patria* needs workers to make it respectable. She embraces everything, and is even able to forgive a guilty man if he serves a purpose'. In consequence, Guillermo deserved to be forgiven simply because he was a 'useful man for the making of arms'.[135]

132 Testimony of Guillermo Homes, 29 April 1814, 'Proceso seguido para el esclarecimiento de una conspiración', pp. 337–38.

133 Testimony of Adam Roche, 26 April 1814, 'Proceso seguido para el esclarecimiento de una conspiración', pp. 324–25.

134 Testimony of the prosecutor 26 May 1814, 'Proceso seguido para el esclarecimiento de una conspiración', p. 377. Antonio José Irisarri, the judge of the trial, determined that he was going to make a decision based on the declaration of the prosecutor, thus he sentenced the accused with the penalties demanded by him.

135 Letter from José Silvestre Lazo, 27 May 1814, 'Proceso seguido para el esclarecimiento de una conspiración', pp. 379–80.

This is an example of the overlapping of both the 'state' and 'non-state' levels to explain how British and Chilean relations developed during these years. All these soldiers arrived in Chile as a result of an official policy which consisted of attracting skilled workers to the country who could serve and be 'useful' in the army. At the same time, these soldiers arrived as individuals seeking a new life or to improve the one they had. They interacted with locals in the contact zone of the army. These interactions reveal again that seven years after the invasions of Buenos Aires and Montevideo, the relations, interactions and the way Britons and Chileans perceived each other had changed. The presence of British soldiers in the patriotic army is clear proof that they were no longer necessarily seen as enemies. Since the course of the war had changed in Europe, they were now accepted for their 'usefulness' in the construction of the new political entity called Chile. Those involved in the conspiracy were not only soldiers, but skilled smiths who knew how to make arms. However, their situation seemed to be precarious, which led them to conspire against the government in order to improve their living conditions. No reference to a political project was made, only expressions of self-interest. The sentence also reveals the place that foreigners occupied in the Chilean community: they were welcome insofar as they were useful and grateful to the *patria*. If they betrayed the *patria*, their crime was even worse than if the traitor was a Chilean. The conspiracy also reveals that the first 'collision' between Britons and Chileans in a 'contact zone' like the army was determined not only by cultural background, but also by class and the position they occupied in the army. On a much larger scale, this would be even more evident in another contact zone that was configured during the war: the Chilean navy.

1.7 Conclusion

The spectre of an invasion was the catalyst for a wide range of ideas and perceptions regarding the place of Chile in the complex context of the imperial rivalries of the period. The Chileans were preparing for war against the British enemy, were discussing a possible invasion and were studying how to defend the territory from Britain, when Napoleon invaded the Peninsula and the political context changed dramatically. They were still debating the idea of Britain as an enemy when news of the imprisonment of the king reached Chile. Britain changed from being the enemy to a possible ally and from then on there was a new enemy. This, however, did not change the British perception of Chile; they were still interested in opening new trade routes in the South Pacific using Chilean ports.

After the 1808 crisis ignited in the Iberian Peninsula, Chileans – and other Spanish Americans – were also forced to accept Britain's role as the arbiter of international relations, and as a mediator with other foreign powers. The Chileans sent emissaries to negotiate for early political recognition and support for their cause. This attitude reinforced Britain's self-perception as the ruling power of the period, which would become even more evident when the military struggles came to an end in the 1820s. In the Chilean case, once the Junta was formed in 1810, the new authorities realised that it was crucial to find support from foreign powers like Britain. The Chileans had to go to Britain and beg for help, and they had to offer something in exchange. They offered Chile itself, as a land of opportunity for skilled workers. Some of those who went fought for the patriots, although the conspiracy of 1814 revealed that they were simply trying to improve their living conditions. It is evident that these relationships were shaped by self-interest rather than transcendental causes like liberty or patriotism.

Amidst all these tribulations, different representations of the place of Chile in the world that resulted from these encounters. For Britons, Chile was not a country of interest *per se*, but only because it was a well-connected territory which offered good opportunities to expand trade routes to the Pacific. For Chileans, depending on the context, the country was either the poorest, most savage and most marginal in the Spanish Empire, or its most stable and organised society. In the rest of the period studied here, these images of Chile would be alternately contested and promoted, depending on the objective.

This chapter has demonstrated that the moment in which British imperial policy actively contemplated invasion and annexation was significant but brief. Its strongest expression was in the plan for British armed forces to invade Chile. After this, due to its declaration of neutrality during the wars of independence, Britain was no longer considering an invasion, but privileged its role as an intermediary to negotiate with the Spanish colonies. Non-state interactions, of merchants, soldiers, sailors and missionaries, continued unabated. In the Chilean case, the first diplomatic negotiations did not reveal great interest from Britain in maintaining more fluid relations. These efforts resumed only in the 1820s, after the establishment of a series of relationships by non-state actors in the intervening period, to be analysed in the following chapters.

CHAPTER 2

Cultural Encounters Offshore

Britons and Chileans in the Chilean Navy, 1817–1823

2.1 Introduction

As shown in the previous chapter, Britain maintained a policy of neutrality during the wars for independence between Spain and its colonies. As a result, relations between Chile and Britain were largely enacted by 'non-state' actors, like merchants, educators, missionaries, military and seamen, although the Chilean governments of the period still sent envoys to London to negotiate support for the cause. This chapter delves into the role played by one of these 'non-state' actors: British seamen who participated in the newly created Chilean navy from 1817 and their interactions with their Chilean counterparts.

The end of the Napoleonic wars in 1815 was a crucial factor in why there were so many Britons willing to travel to South America to take part in a war that was not directly relevant to them. The reduction of both the Royal Navy and Army left thousands of soldiers and seamen unemployed.[1] The intensification of the war in Spanish America was a new opportunity and many travelled to South America in search of a new 'adventure' and were attracted by the financial benefits offered by the newly independent governments.[2] In the case of Chile, most Britons and Irish who took part in the war for independence joined the newly created Chilean navy (1817). Although some had settled in Chile even before that, the appointment of Thomas

---

1 Peter Kemp, *The British Sailor: A Social History of the Lower Deck* (London: J.M. Dent & Sons Ltd, 1970).

2 Brown, *Adventuring through Spanish Colonies*, pp. 4–8. Brown argues that 'adventurer' is a less politically and ideologically charged term than others often used, such as 'mercenaries', 'errant heroes' or 'volunteers'. I agree, although for this book I simply use the term 'seaman'. For a general overview of the wars of independence and their consequences for Spanish American societies see Clément Thibaud, *Repúblicas en armas. Los ejércitos bolivarianos en la Guerra de independencia en Colombia y Venezuela* (Bogotá: Instituto Francés de Estudios Andinos, 2003) and Anthony McFarlane, *War and Independence in Spanish America* (New York: Routledge, 2014).

Cochrane as Vice Admiral of the Chilean navy (November 1818) led about nine hundred British and Irish seamen to travel to Chile.[3] The involvement of these seamen in the wars of independence was not part of British policy. Indeed, in 1819, the Parliament passed the Foreign Enlistment Act, which sought to prevent British subjects taking part in this war, a law that was obviously linked to the policy of neutrality.[4] Thus, these seamen joined the navy of Chile as individuals rather than as British state agents.

By this point, Chileans' perceptions of and attitudes to Britons had changed quite radically. They shifted according to the development of the war in Europe and the role played by Britain in this conflict. By 1818 the war in Europe had finished and Chile had declared its independence from Spain on 12 February. This was a new reality from the period analysed in the previous chapter. In the new context, Spanish Americans began to see Britain as a possible ally in their own war against Spain. However, since diplomatic contacts had started early in 1813, they were aware that it was almost impossible to persuade the British authorities to take part in the conflict. Chileans soon realised that they would stick to Britain's policy of neutrality and sought instead to persuade those Britons who were no longer fighting in Europe to join their war in South America. British sailors were then 'invited' by the Chilean authorities to organise the navy on the British model. This was not surprising considering that some leaders, like O'Higgins, had lived and been educated in London, and exhibited a clear admiration of Britain.[5] For them, Britain was a cultural model from which to take ideas, practices and expertise to be implemented in Chile in different ambits, like seamanship, industries and education (see Chapter 3).[6]

In this case, relations between Chile and Britain were not interstate since one of the states, Britain, was not yet willing to establish such relations with the newborn state called Chile. However, both 'state' and 'non-state' actors were involved in the relationship. The Chilean 'state' was involved, with its diplomatic representatives in Europe and London, who aimed to recruit mercenaries to join the navy. There was an agreement between the agents representing the Chilean state and the seamen who travelled to Chile as individuals. Thus, in this case, relations between Chileans and Britons must be approached on a 'non-state' or, more specifically, an 'interpersonal' level.

Once on board ship, British seamen entered into 'cultural encounters' with the Chileans who also formed part of the navy. If we apply Bitterli's typology of such encounters, we may say that many different 'contacts', 'collisions' and 'relationships' took place simultaneously. Collisions were clearly marked by cultural differences between the two groups of sailors. They spoke different

3 Based on David Cubitt's estimate for the years 1817–1820, although he recognises that it is difficult to make an accurate estimate. See Cubitt, p. 183.
4 Waddell, p. 17.
5 Racine, 'The Childhood Shows the Man', pp. 282–85.
6 Racine, 'This England and this Now', pp. 438–40.

languages, professed different religions and most of the Chilean sailors did not have a maritime culture.[7] There were also 'class' issues, which led lower-deck seamen, regardless of their origins, to challenge the authority of the British officers. However, 'relationships' were also established, since cultural distinctions such as language and religion were not insurmountable. In the case of language, the role of interpreters as 'cultural mediators' was crucial in overriding the difficulties in communication derived from the use of different languages. As shown in this chapter, the Chilean government also mediated in these conflicts by passing regulations that enabled both groups to preserve their own cultural parameters, like language and religion, within the navy. Overall, the story of the first years of the Chilean navy was one of success. We see important triumphs like the capture of Valdivia and the blockade of Callao, which historians agree would not have been possible if the misunderstandings between Chileans and Britons had been impossible to resolve.[8]

There was, therefore, no binary opposition between British and Chilean sailors within the navy, but a space of mutual exchange of ideas and practices. The analysis of the interpersonal interactions that took place on board allows me to reinforce the argument that the era of Chile's independence cannot be considered a prelude to the neo-imperial relations established in the late nineteenth century. British seamen were rarely seen – and did not see themselves – as imperial agents. The navy worked as a 'contact zone', following Pratt's argument, in which relationships were troubled. In addition, this had significant consequences for the nation-building process in Chile. The idea of a 'Chilean nation' was not fixed during this period, but was still very much under construction.[9] What emerged from such interactions was not a new nation, but it might be argued that the experience of being confronted with an 'other', in this case represented by Britons, brought about a sense of difference. This supplements Juan Luis Ossa's assertions about the configuration of the Chilean 'national' army partially as a result of the fragmentation of the Liberation Army of Peru.[10] Likewise, Cochrane's role as the commander of the navy was crucial in shaping and promoting the image

---

7 Some of the studies that have focused on conflicts are Brian Vale *Cochrane in the Pacific*, pp. 85–97; Carlos López Urrutia, *Historia de la marina de Chile* (Santiago: El Ciprés Editores, 2007), pp. 21–34.

8 An emphasis on Chile's maritime power, but without dealing with any internal conflict in the navy, is found in Renato Valenzuela Ugarte, *Bernardo O'Higgins. El Estado de Chile y el poder naval* (Santiago: Editorial Andrés Bello, 1999), pp. 197–215. See also Alamiro de Ávila Martel, *Cochrane y la independencia del Pacífico* (Santiago: Editorial Universitaria, 1976), pp. 151–54; Donald Worcester, *El poder naval y la independencia de Chile* (Santiago: Editorial Francisco de Aguirre, 1971, pp. 75–98.

9 For a discussion on this see Pinto and Valdivia, p. 117.

10 Ossa, *Armies, Politics and Revolutions*, Chapter V 'Becoming a Chilean Army', pp. 148–81.

of Chile as a distinctive political entity, entitled to be recognised as an equal by other nations and destined to rule in the Pacific.

2.2 Building up the Chilean Navy

The Chilean navy became one of the most important 'contact zones' between Chileans and Britons during an era in which the British circulation of goods, ideas, models and peoples was significant. Even prior to the arrival of Cochrane in Chile, interactions between Britons and Chileans were a fundamental feature of the newly created navy. Ships were purchased from Europe, often Britain, and in most cases their officers remained with them and joined the Chilean navy. There were disagreements between some British and Chilean officers due to their different origins. In addition, British merchants were directly involved in the first steps taken by the navy, when it was simply a small squadron.

The Chilean navy was officially established on 20 November 1817, when Bernardo O'Higgins enacted the 'Provisional Regulation for the Navy' to provide a definite organisation to the existing squadron that had been gradually formed after the military triumph of Chacabuco (12 February 1817). Previously, another naval force had been established in 1814 in the United Provinces of La Plata, whose commander was Admiral William (Guillermo) Brown, an Irishman who had arrived in Buenos Aires as a trader.[11] The presence of British and Irish sailors was a significant element in the formation of the Chilean navy. Already in March 1817, a few weeks after the battle of Chacabuco, which secured the liberation of the central valley of Chile and the establishment of Bernardo O'Higgins's government, the need to arm some ships to patrol the coasts began to be evident. The first priority was to liberate those patriots who, after the restoration of the Spanish authorities and the king's sovereignty in October 1814, had been exiled to the Juan Fernández Archipelago in the Pacific. The government decided to use and arm a brig that had been captured during the war called the *El Aguila*, whose commander was the English seaman Raymond Morris, one of the Britons who had been part of the Army of the Andes. The mission lasted from 16 to 31 March 1817, and was a complete success.[12] This was one of the first manifestations of one of the most remarkable features of the first years of the Chilean navy: its heterogeneity. Not only because of the appointment of a Briton as commander of the *El Aguila*, but because, according to the first historian of the Chilean navy, Antonio García Reyes, 'any sailor of any

---

11 For a short biography see the chapter 'William Brown and the Argentinian Navy', in Moises Enrique Rodriguez, *Freedom's Mercenaries: British Volunteers in the Wars of Independence of Latin America* (Lanham, MD: Hamilton Books, 2006), II, pp. 531–70.

12 Antonio García Reyes, *Memoria sobre la primera Escuadra nacional* (Santiago: Imprenta del Progreso, 1846), p. 10.

nationality found on the beach was thrown [into the *El Aguila*]'.[13] Thus, even before the significant arrival of British and Irish sailors along with Cochrane, relations between Britain and Chile during the war of independence were on an 'interpersonal' level.

Despite most of the Spanish navy having been destroyed in the Battle of Trafalgar (1805), the Chilean authorities still believed that a naval expedition from Spain was possible, considering the support given by other powers to the King of Spain after the Congress of Vienna in 1815. In addition, they feared a blockade of Valparaíso and San Antonio, the principal ports of Chile, by the Spanish ships stationed in Callao, like the *Venganza*, the *Esmeralda*, the *Sebastiana*, the *Resolución*, the *Veloz*, the *Pezuela* and the *Portillo*. These fears became real when the blockade eventually started in March 1817. The government had already sent agents to Europe and North America to purchase guns and ships, and to recruit officers to reinforce the sea defence. One of the agents, José Antonio Alvarez Condarco, managed to purchase a ship that belonged to the East Indian Company, the *Windham*, and sent it to Valparaíso. According to García Reyes, the ship entered the bay during the blockade as it was not a warship and used a British flag. The British and North American traders already settled in Valparaíso were outraged because of the harm caused by the blockade and 'they decided to arm the *Windham*, which they had bought in conjunction with the government, and gave it the name *Lautaro*'.[14] The commander of this ship was an Irishman, George O'Brien, a former officer of the Royal Navy. The ship was also provided with 'one hundred foreign seamen and two hundred and fifty Chileans'.[15] O'Brien attempted to capture the *Esmeralda* on 27 April 1818 but failed, and was fatally wounded trying to board it. The blockade came to an end but the government was further convinced that the organisation of a proper and professional navy was an urgent matter. One of the fears was that after the triumph of Maipú (5 April 1818), the Viceroy of Peru would attempt to rescue the remaining royalist forces that had fled southwards after rendering Santiago to the patriots. These men could gather in Talcachuano and wait for a new expedition from Callao.[16]

During 1818, then, the government devoted itself to building up a new navy, in spite of the lack of both economic resources and experienced and trained men. The *Lautaro* became the base for a small squad. Its new commander was the Briton John Higginson, who was also the chief of all the ships. The other ships were the *El Aguila* (renamed the *Pueyrredon* after the Director of the United Provinces of La Plata), the sloop *Coquimbo* (renamed the *Chacabuco*), the brig *Columbus* (brought by the North American Charles Wooster, as a result of José Miguel Carrera's negotiations in the United States

13 Ibid., p. 12.
14 Ibid., p. 13.
15 Ibid.
16 Ibid., pp. 10–11.

to receive aid, and renamed the *Araucano*) and finally the *Cumberland* (a ship of the East India Company purchased in London and renamed the *San Martín*).[17] Its commander, William Wilkinson, also travelled to join the new navy. In August 1818 the navy was comprised of five ships, the most powerful being the *San Martín*. Wilkinson commanded the *San Martín*, Higginson the *Lautaro*, Morris the *Araucano* and the Chileans Francisco Diaz and Fernando Vasquez commanded the *Chacabuco* and the *Pueyrredon* respectively. In addition, the government had to decide who would be the commander of this small navy, a matter that was not easy to solve. There were many experienced and trained British, Irish and North Americans officers, like Charles Wooster, to take over the post. However, as William Miller, the commander of the marines at that time, asserted, 'foreigners who were candidates for the command, were so exorbitant in their conditions, and so much divided amongst themselves, that the government was unable to select a proper person from amongst those in Chile'.[18]

Wooster considered himself one of the most serious candidates, but the government decided to appoint Manuel Blanco Encalada to the post. The latter was born in Buenos Aires and had been a soldier and a midshipman of the Spanish navy during the Napoleonic wars. He later on joined the Army of the Andes commanded by San Martín, and had a significant role as an artillery officer during the war in Chile.[19] Many testimonies, like Wooster's, suggest that Blanco's appointment frustrated the ambitions of the foreign officers.[20] Wooster had complained about Blanco Encalada's lack of maritime skills since he was only a soldier. Blanco defended himself several years later in a letter saying that his knowledge of seamanship, gained in the academy 'which produced the Juanes, the Ulloas, the Mazarredos, the Mendozas!!' gave him right to be appointed commander of the squadron.[21] In other words, Blanco Encalada claimed that he belonged in a different and respectable maritime culture, the Spanish, which was going to collide with the image British seamen had about the superiority of their own maritime culture.

It was under Blanco Encalada's command between 23 June 1818 and Cochrane's arrival in November 1818, that the Chilean navy had its first victory: the capture of the *Maria Isabel*, the most powerful Spanish ship in the South Pacific, in October 1818. This triumph led O'Higgins to make Blanco

---

17 Vale, *Cochrane in the Pacific*, pp. 43–44; López Urrutia, *Historia de la marina en Chile*, pp. 21–34.

18 John Miller, *Memoirs of General William Miller in the Service of the Republic of Peru* (London: Longman, 1828), p. 192.

19 Benjamín Vicuña Mackenna, *El Almirante don Manuel Blanco Encalada* (Santiago: Ediciones de la Revista Chilena, 1917), pp. 15–20.

20 Quoted by Barros Arana, *Historia General de Chile*, XII, p. 142.

21 Manuel Blanco Encalada, *Contestación del Vice-Almirante Blanco Encalada a la vindicación apolojética del Capitán Wooster inserta en el número 37 de* El Barómetro de Chile (Santiago: Imprenta de la opinión, 1836), p. 3.

a rear admiral of the new navy. The *Maria Isabel* was incorporated into the fleet, renamed the *O'Higgins*. In the same month a new ship, the *Galvarino*, joined the squad. It was a British ship under the command of Martin Guise, who had purchased it from the East Indian Company as the *Lucy* and used it in the Napoleonic wars under the name *Hecate*. He had tried to sell this ship along with its crew to the Buenos Aires government, but after failing in his attempt, the Chilean officer appointed in that city, Miguel Zañartu, purchased the ship and appointed Guise as a new officer for the navy. Guise travelled by land to Chile, while his lieutenant, John Spry, reached Talcahuano in command of the ship. A month later, the *Intrepido*, a ship that belonged to the Provincias Unidas, was offered to the Chilean government as a contribution to the cause, as part of a loan.[22] Therefore, Blanco Encalada's command was successful, not only because of his triumph, but because the squadron grew in size considerably.[23]

Nevertheless, at the time Blanco assumed his post as commander of the navy, Alvarez Condarco had already agreed with Thomas Cochrane his appointment as Vice Admiral of the Chilean navy. On 12 January 1818 he wrote to José Ignacio Zenteno, the Chilean Minister of Maritime Affairs, that 'Lord Cochrane, one of the most famous and perhaps the most valiant seaman [*sic*] in Great Britain has determined to travel to Chile in order to direct our navy'.[24] The fact that the Chilean navy was commanded by a Briton with a clear preference for his compatriots when it came to nominating officers had many consequences for life on board the ships. Even though both Britons and Chileans had coexisted within the Chilean navy since its foundation, Cochrane reinforced the differentiation between the groups. He not only exhibited a clear preference for British officers, but also demanded of the Chilean government that these Britons must be permitted to preserve their culture and identity by professing their own religion, speaking the English language and being ruled according to the British regulations.

2.3 Lord Thomas Cochrane and the 'Liberation' of Chile

Cochrane arrived in Chile because he was appointed by Bernardo O'Higgins's government to accomplish a specific assignment: to lead the newly created navy. Although some biographers have stressed his 'radicalism' to explain his sympathy for the cause of independence, Cochrane was experiencing difficult times when he was contacted by Alvarez Condarco.[25] In 1814 he was involved in the 'stock exchange scandal', which eventually caused his dismissal from

22 Carlos López Urrutia, 'El Bergantín Intrépido', *Revista de Marina*, 1 (2007), 66–75 (p. 67).

23 López Urrutia, *Historia de la marina de Chile*, p. 65.

24 Quoted by Vale, *Cochrane in the Pacific*, p. 32.

25 Christopher Lloyd, *Lord Cochrane: Seaman, Radical and Liberator. A Life of Thomas, Lord Cochrane, 10th Earl of Dundonald* (London, New York & Toronto: Longmans,

both the Royal Navy and Parliament.[26] Thereafter, he had no place in Britain to undertake his activities either as a seaman or a politician. This shows that the involvement of Britons like Cochrane in the war for independence did not necessarily respond to the policy of the British state, but could be, as in this case, the personal decision of someone who needed a change in his life. Under the circumstances, the offer from Chile to take over the highest position in the navy offered him the chance to clear his name and restart his career as a seaman. As Vice Admiral of the Chilean navy he was commissioned to organise this branch according to the British model. As Christopher Lloyd has pointed out, in Chile 'at last there was a chance to return to his own profession, to win honour in battle, and at the same time to pursue his crusade for freedom in the active sort of life he loved and for which his talents eminently fitted him'.[27]

This background opens some questions regarding the extent to which the presence of a Briton like Cochrane in Chile was seen as a manifestation of British imperialism, or whether he was or not an agent of the British Empire. This linkage is rarely found in the sources, but it is possible to envision that the extended presence of British mercenaries in Spanish America was another more subtle means of influencing and infiltrating for British imperialism. In Cochrane's case it is evident that his presence in Chile was a result of a disgrace, rather than of a planned policy. In this respect, he might be seen as a sort of 'cast-off' of the Empire rather than an agent, or part of a deliberate strategy to establish a 'bridgehead', of the Empire.[28] His self-perception as a 'liberator' of an 'oppressed' people and the use of ideas about 'civilisation' to justify his mission made him look like an imperialist. As Catherine Hall has argued, the very appeal to the idea of civilisation is a construction made in the context of imperialism.[29] Agents of the British Empire used this idea to justify their global activities and Cochrane shared this explanatory discourse. In this case, his discourse was shared by members of the local elite who also used a political discourse based on ideas of civilisation and liberty to justify their new political project. This explains also why Chile's

---

1947), pp. 138–39; Brian Vale, *The Audacious Admiral Cochrane: The True Life of a Naval Legend* (London: Conway Maritime Press, 2004), pp. 62–73.

26 This scandal arose in 1814, when Cochrane found himself involved in a fraud when rumours about Napoleon's death began to spread in Britain. The expectations of peace made share prices rise very quickly and a committee to investigate the case discovered that some people had sold their shares in the meantime, among them Cochrane. A good account can be found in Richard Dale, *Napoleon Is Dead: Lord Cochrane and the Great Stock Exchange Scandal* (Stroud: The History Press, 2006).

27 Lloyd, p. 139.

28 John Darwin, 'Imperialism and the Victorians: The Dynamics of Territorial Expansion', *English Historical Review*, 112:447 (1997), 614–42 (p. 629).

29 Catherine Hall, *Civilising Subjects: Metropole and Colony in the English Imagination, 1830–1867* (Cambridge: Polity, 2002), p. 10.

ruling elite was eager to 'invite' Britons like Cochrane to Chile. Cochrane was seen not only as a seaman with the expertise to organise the navy, but as someone who defended the same principles and ideas about liberty that the local elite used to legitimise their republican project.

Cochrane's behaviour during his stay in Chile shows that he perceived his mission as a transcendental one, a 'crusade for freedom' in Lloyd's words. He repeatedly claimed that it was the cause of independence what 'called' him to Chile, managing to appear as a man engaged by elevated principles, rather than mundane matters. In a letter written in England several years after his stay in Chile he claimed that without his aid, 'the establishment of the independence of those states could not, beyond all comparison, have been so speedily and cheaply accomplished'.[30] He truly perceived himself as a 'liberator' of Chile and so did some of his compatriots. John Miers, for example, stressed this idea when referring to Cochrane in his diary: 'fortunately for Chile, Lord Cochrane, whose attachment to the cause of liberty, and, whose wishes for the emancipation of South America were well known, accepted the proposal of the deputies to become the Admiral of Chile, and sailed from England, in August, 1818, to take command of the naval force of that country'.[31] Maria Graham exaggerated the nature of this mission, going beyond the naval ambit. For her, 'he did his utmost to enlighten the countries he protected, and to teach them the principles of rational freedom'.[32] This idea has been repeated by almost all of his biographers, most of whom have approached Cochrane from the point of view of his heroism.[33]

The question remains, however, whether this perception of Cochrane's mission in Chile was shared by the people who, according to Graham, were learning ideas of liberty and rational freedom from him. Many testimonies from Chileans show that his figure was indeed linked to a 'liberating mission'. Shortly after his arrival, for example, Cochrane was the protagonist in a heroic deed, the capture of Valdivia on 3–4 February 1820, which was heavily reported by the press.[34] On 19 February the *Gazeta ministerial de*

30 Thomas Cochrane, *Observations on Naval Affairs and on Some Collateral Subjects; including Instances of Injustice Experienced by the Author: With a Summary of his Naval Service: and a Copious Appendix* (London: James Ridgway, 1857), p. 83.

31 Miers, p. 20.

32 Graham, p. 104.

33 See Ávila Martel, *Cochrane y la independencia del Pacífico*, p. 141; David Cordingly, *Cochrane the Dauntless: The Life and Adventures of Thomas Cochrane, 1775–1860*, 2nd ed. (London, Berlin & New York: Bloomsbury, 2008), pp. 269–95; Ian Grimble, *The Seawolf: The Life of Admiral Cochrane* (London: Blond & Briggs, 1978), pp. 188–214; Lloyd, *Lord Cochrane: Seaman*, pp. 143–60; Vale, *The Audacious Admiral Cochrane*, pp. 92–112; Vale, *Cochrane in the Pacific*, pp. 138–41.

34 For an account of the importance of the battle see Ximena Rojas, *Lord Cochrane y la liberación de Valdivia* (Santiago: Instituto de Historia de la Pontificia Universidad Católica de Chile-Instituto Chileno-Británico de Cultura, 1970).

Chile reproduced all the documents and reports from the ships during the battle, as well as a speech in which O'Higgins congratulated the 'sons of Valdivia' on behalf of 'the Chilean nation'.[35] Likewise, the *Instituto Nacional* – the leading educational institution at that time – organised a public ceremony to praise the hero of Valdivia. There the speaker, Professor Juan Egaña, said, '[We are] amazed to receive and congratulate the philosopher hero who abandoned his amenities and distinctions to uphold the rights of the oppressed portion of humanity'.[36] O'Higgins himself sent a letter to Cochrane in which he wrote that 'the eyes of the liberal world are over the Argonauts of the Pacific, and from their efforts they hope to shake themselves from oppression in its extensive coasts'.[37] Even the Minister José Ignacio Zenteno, whom Cochrane considered an enemy, claimed that the Chilean state had put in his hands 'the best support of its political existence, which is the Squadron, on which it has based its independence as well as its further aggrandisement'.[38] These words also reveal that the recruitment of Britons like Cochrane was seen as a fundamental step in consolidating the very existence of the new Chilean state. Local authorities saw in the appointment of non-state agents like Cochrane a means of securing the state's safety and integrity.

The binary conception of liberty and oppression was employed in the rhetoric of the new leaders of the newborn Republic of Chile, in order to justify their project. Simon Collier argued that rather than political theorists, independent leaders were 'patriotic propagandists' and used these ideas as part of a 'revolutionary ideology', which included an 'anti-Spanish' outcry, to justify independence.[39] Vasco Castillo suggests that the idea of liberty was conceived as part of a more sophisticated republican ideology, in which the 'plan for liberty' had been elaborated from the outset.[40] This was far from Cochrane's conception of liberty though. On February 1819, during the navy's first campaign in Callao, Cochrane demanded from the Viceroy of Peru, Joaquin de la Pezuela, a more humane and fair treatment of the prisoners captured during the war. Pezuela replied, expressing his 'surprise that a British nobleman should come to fight for a rebel community unacknowledged by all the powers of the globe'.[41] Cochrane's reply was eloquent: 'a

35 *Gazeta Ministerial de Chile*, 19 February 1820.
36 Juan Egaña, 'Elogio de Lord Alejandro Cochrane, Vicealmirante de Chile y General en jefe de de la Marina pronunciado en el Instituto Nacional', Santiago, 1819, available in Memoria Chilena, Biblioteca Nacional de Chile, http://www.memoriach-ilena.cl/602/w3-article-71971.html (accessed 2 June 2015).
37 'O'Higgins to Cochrane', Santiago 3 March 1819, *ABO*, Vol. 35, doc. 44.
38 'Zenteno to Cochrane', Valparaíso, 21 June 1819, *ABO*, Vol. 35, doc. 61.
39 Collier, pp. 130, 192.
40 Castillo, pp. 17–21.
41 Thomas Cochrane and H.R. Fox Bourne, *The Life of Thomas Cochrane, Tenth Earl of Dundonald G.C.B.* (London: Richard Bentley, 1869), I, p. 159.

British nobleman was a free man and therefore had the right to assist any country which was endeavouring to re-establish the rights of the aggrieved humanity'.[42] For Cochrane there was a close connection between being a 'British nobleman' and a 'free man', but in this case he only expressed that he was willing to help a community to restore its right of self-determination, regardless of whether the political regime was republican or monarchical.

When quitting Chile in November 1822, Cochrane said to Chileans: 'It is now four years since the sacred cause of your independence called me to Chile. I assisted you to gain it; I have seen it accomplished, it only now remains for you to preserve it'.[43] He only justified his role as that of helping Chileans to gain their independence, without any reference to the political regime to be adopted. Moreover, after serving in Chile, Cochrane participated in the independence struggles of Brazil, which in October 1822 had proclaimed its first 'Emperor', Pedro I. His goal there was to help Brazilians to gain their independence, irrespective of the regime they had adopted. Cochrane's self-perception as a liberator and Graham's claims about him teaching the principles of 'rational freedom' were part of their own legitimising discourse, which was coincident with the ideas of liberty already defended by the Chilean elite in order to justify their political project. This is why he was not perceived as an 'imperialist' by locals, but as a coadjutor in their cause. However, as I show in this chapter, these ideas of liberty were seldom held by the crews of the navy, who were in a permanent condition of privation and were often punished for not knowing the 'British way' of being a seaman.

2.4 The Composition of the Navy

The appointment of Cochrane as Vice Admiral of the Chilean navy was not without trouble. This was because the navy was composed of many individuals with different interests, beliefs and expectations, irrespective of their origins. Some historians, like Antonio García Reyes, have explained conflicts on the grounds of Cochrane's origins and Chileans' resentment of his appointment:

> Cochrane was a foreigner and it did not seem prudent to entrust the command of the forces to an individual who did not give a guarantee of his loyalty. His interest in the republic was not to be presumed, since he had a different religion, language and different customs as a citizen.[44]

However, this explanation appears weaker when considering who complained most about his appointment. According to Brian Vale, Martin Guise, an Englishman and former officer of the Royal Navy, and Charles Wooster, a

42 Quoted Ibid., I, p. 159.
43 'Lord Cochrane's Proclamation of quitting Chile', reproduced by Miller, *Memoirs*, p. 387.
44 García Reyes, p. 28.

North American, were those who most explicitly criticised his appointment, saying that Blanco Encalada was the most appropriate individual for this position.[45] Other testimonies suggest that Guise was not happy with Blanco's previous appointment either, as he wrote in a letter to Cochrane on 21 December 1819 that '[Blanco] was not an experienced navy officer'.[46] Brian Vale added that even Cochrane's personality could be part of the problem, as he

> may have exerted great personal magnetism on those immediately around him, but he seemed unable to inspire those who were not. With close friends or inferiors he was affable and interesting, but others remember him as being tall and round shouldered with an awkward manner and a monosyllabic mode of speech that was uninspiring.[47]

This shows that even within the group of 'foreigners', composed mainly of English, Scottish, Irish and North Americans, relations were complex. In the particular case of British and Irish, it is clear that they were not a homogeneous group and many conflicts emerged during their service in the Chilean navy. This was similar to what happened in the Colombian army, where the same conflicts between English and Irish arose.[48] In addition, this shows that at an interpersonal level, conflicts were explained by a wide range of reasons. Hence, the conflicts experienced within the navy cannot simply be reduced to the coexistence of two different groups, namely 'locals' and 'foreigners'. There were conflictive relations within each group as well. The extremely poor conditions that the Chilean navy had to face, as well as the differences in treatment and privileges between officers and sailors, were also elements that explain these troubled relations. Nevertheless, the very heterogeneity of the navy's composition reinforces the idea that it can be seen as a contact zone between people of different cultural backgrounds, allowing experiences of dialogue, conflicts, misunderstanding, translations, negotiations, borrowing and exchanges to take place. All this had significant consequences for the configuration of a Chilean national identity, which at this stage was still incipient.

Thomas Cochrane took over in November 1818, at which point the operations of the navy had already started under the leadership of Manuel Blanco Encalada. Cochrane's impressions of this experience were summarised in a letter he sent to the President of Chile several years later:

> I am compelled to inform you or to remind you of the peculiarly arduous position in which I was placed as Commander of your squadron the crew of which was composed of an heterogeneous assemblage of natives and

45 See Vale, *Cochrane in the Pacific*, pp. 40–42.
46 Quoted by Barros Arana, *Historia general de Chile*, VIII, p. 141.
47 Vale, *Cochrane in the Pacific*, p. 87.
48 See Brown, *Adventuring through Spanish Colonies*, pp. 115–16.

foreigners and were subjected to privations of which there is no parallel in the naval service of European states, nor even in the merchant service of any country.[49]

For Cochrane, one of his main challenges was to deal with the 'assemblage' of native and foreign seamen. Most of them were Chileans and Britons, which means that they spoke different languages, professed different religions – although some Britons and Irishmen were Catholics – and had different backgrounds and experiences as seamen, peasants or fishermen. In other words, they had different cultural parameters, but had to enter into 'contact' in a shared common space represented by each of the ships that constituted the navy. Collisions were common, mainly manifested in linguistic troubles and abuse of power by the officers, but exacerbated by the privations that characterised the first years of the Chilean navy.

The appointment and arrival of Cochrane was a significant turn for the composition of the navy. Due to the commitment of the government to Cochrane's appointment, Blanco Encalada was obliged to step aside, but agreed to remain as the rear admiral of the navy. In his memoirs, Cochrane expressed gratitude to Blanco Encalada, recognising that 'nothing but the Chilian [sic] admiral's disinterested patriotism prevented a serious rupture'.[50] In addition, when Blanco was later judged in a court martial after abandoning the blockade of Callao, Cochrane did not push the issue and as the president of the court he managed to absolve him (see Section 2.5 below).

However, Cochrane did not rely on the locals to assume the leadership of the fleet. Indeed, he agreed with the government the grant of his liberty to appoint his own officers. Alvarez Condarco wrote to him that 'your Lordship may be able to appoint all the navy officers [...] all the appointments of officers made by your Lordship shall be confirmed by the Chilean government'.[51] The preferences of Cochrane were clear as he mainly recruited British officers, especially to command the ships. The two Chilean officers who had taken command of the *Chacabuco* and the *Pueyrredón*, Francisco Díaz and Francisco Vásquez, were immediately removed by Cochrane, as it is possible to deduce from Table 1 below.[52] With Cochrane, all of the ships' commanders were British (or Irish, like Thomas Carter), with the exception of the Frenchmen Tortel and Prunier, from the Channel Islands, who commanded the *Chacabuco* (1820) and the *Pueyrredon* (1819–1820), respectively.

49 'Thomas Cochrane to the President and Government of the Republic of Chile', [n.d.], National Archive of Scotland, Edinburgh (hereafter NAS), Dundonald Papers, GD233/31/237. There is also a Spanish version of the letter: 'Al Presidente y Gobierno de la República de Chile', 3 February 1845, available at: http://www.memoriachilena. cl/archivos2/pdfs/mc0034410.pdf (accessed 14 December 2013).
50 Cochrane, *The Life of Thomas Cochrane*, p. 151.
51 Cubitt, p. 66.
52 Based on information provided by García Reyes, Cubitt and Vale.

Table 1: Commanders of Chilean navy ships 1818–1820

Ship	November 1818 Commander: Blanco	January 1819 Commander: Cochrane	September 1819 Commander: Cochrane	August 1820 Commander: Cochrane
San Martin	William Wilkinson	William Wilkinson	William Wilkinson	William Wilkinson
Lautaro	Charles Wooster	Martin Guise	Martin Guise	Martin Guise
Chacabuco	Francisco Díaz	Thomas Carter	Thomas Carter	Jean Joseph Tortel
Araucano	Raymond Morris	James Ramsay	Thomas Crosbie	Thomas Carter
O'Higgins		Robert Forster	Thomas Cochrane	Thomas Crosbie
Galvarino	John Spry	John Spry	John Spry	John Spry
Pueyrredon	Fernando Vásquez	William Prunier	William Prunier	William Prunier
Independencia			Robert Forster	Robert Forster
Montezuma			Robert Casey	George Young
Maipú	Thomas Carter			

Other officers like John Pascoe Grenfell, Henry Cobbett and Robert Simpson had been all Royal Navy officers.[53] A later volunteer was Richard Longeville Vowell, who had participated in the wars of independence in New Granada and joined Cochrane in 1822.[54] The rest of the crews were recruited by different means, such as impressment and voluntarily enrolment.[55] Foreigners were recruited in different places, although many of them, roughly five hundred, were recruited by Zañartu in Buenos Aires.[56] As said previously, the participation of agents of the Chilean state in the recruiment of seamen shows that 'state-level' relations between Britain and Chile were still one-sided.

David Cubitt has made the most reliable estimate – based on ample analysis of primary sources – of the make-up of the navy. He concluded that, on average, the Chilean navy 'was manned by one third British or North Americans, one third Chilean seamen, and one third Chilean marines'.[57] In the first campaign to Callao, in January 1819, there were 1,106 men aboard four ships, the *O'Higgins*, the *San Martín*, the *Lautaro* and the *Chacabuco*. Of these, 828 were Chileans and 278 were foreigners, although Cubitt did not distinguish between specific nationalities in this latter group and did not provide a breakdown for each ship.[58] The relevant fact, though, is that amongst the officers there were only seven Chileans as opposed to 24 foreigners. In the case of the seamen, 331 were Chileans and 254 were foreigners.[59] For the year 1820, Cubitt provided a more detailed picture, including a breakdown of the crews of the most important ships up to February and of two of the ships before the departure of the Liberation Army of Peru (see Table 2).

Table 2 shows that there were more Chileans than foreigners, although not excessively so, the number being more than double on only four occasions: the *Araucano* in June 1819, the *San Martín* in February 1820, and the *Lautaro* and the *Independencia* in August 1820. In the first case, the proportion of Chileans was more than twelve times larger, the *Araucano* being perhaps the most 'Chilean' ship of the fleet. The only case in which the proportion of foreigners was larger was the *Maipú* in February 1820. This ship had just joined the fleet, in November 1819, and its crew was

53 Ávila Martel, *Cochrane y la independencia del Pacífico*, p. 109.
54 Páez Víctor, pp. 113–28.
55 Cubitt, pp. 193–95.
56 Ibid., p. 183.
57 Ibid.
58 Ibid., p. 189.
59 In the Chilean group there were also 137 grummets, 128 gunners and 225 soldiers. García Reyes provides some data, estimating that in total the first campaign was composed of 1,130 men, of whom 264 were foreign seamen in contrast to 461 Chileans. He does not distinguish the origins of the officers, but states that in total there were 31 officers on the four ships. The rest were grummets, gunners and soldiers. See García Reyes, p. 104.

Table 2: David Cubitt's estimates of the proportion of Chilean and foreign seamen in the Chilean navy under Lord Cochrane's command

Ship	June 1819			February 1820			August 1820		
	Chile	Other	Total	Chile	Other	Total	Chile	Other	Total
O'Higgins	228	151	379	164	96	260			
Araucano	64	5	69	60	35	95			
Maipú				35	40	75			
Montezuma				–	–	87			
Lautaro				182	111	293	179	63	242
Independencia				137	73	210	169	56	225
San Martin				170	42	212			
Intrepido				35	40				

composed of all those foreigners who had not been able to travel on the *Galvarino* a few days before. In addition, the proportion of foreigners after 1820 was clearly declining. This can be explained by the desertions that occurred after the first two expeditions to Peru, discussed in Section 2.7. The Chilean government could not pay the wages and prizes it owed, so many decided to desert the navy. As for July 1821 – although not shown in the table – the internal situation was even more dramatic, as nearly all the British officers deserted to join the navy that San Martín decided to establish as the 'Protector of Peru'.

The information above reveals that, despite the navy being composed of a wide range of people of different backgrounds and origins, most of the conflicts occurred between two majority groups: Britons and Chileans. Although it would be simplistic to say that these groups were rivals, the fact that most naval officers and commanders were Britons triggered a series of conflicts in which Chileans suffered most because they were more numerous within the crews. This also reveals that, apart from origins, class issues were also a factor in explaining most of the 'collisions' within the navy. It would therefore be simplistic to reduce the conflicts experienced within the navy to the coexistence of two rival groups as Alamiro de Ávila and David Cubitt do.[60] Although this factor is important, conflicts were experienced primarily as between individuals, and followed different patterns according to their protagonists. In addition, none of these conflicts seemed to be impossible to overcome. Mediation was a fundamental factor in resolving conflicts, which enabled the minimising of any resentment between groups.

2.5 Spanish vs English: The Cultural Mediation of the Interpreter

Many conflicts within the navy can be explained on the grounds of the difficulty of communication between people who spoke different languages and did not understand the language of the other. Broadly speaking, it is possible to say that regardless of their specific birthplace, there were mainly two groups in the Chilean navy: those who spoke Spanish and those who spoke English. This was much more problematic for the 'Spanish speakers', since despite being the majority group, most of them were obliged by their officers to use the English language on shipboard. As shown in the Section 2.2, the official language within each ship was that of its commander and virtually all of the commanders were English speakers. William Miller claimed that 'naval officers were nearly all English or North American, who spoke the Spanish language imperfectly, or not at all'.[61]

In addition, as shown below, 'English speakers' did not show any interest in dealing with the Spanish language and most of the controversies between both groups had to be eventually sorted out by the cultural mediation of an

60 Ávila Martel, pp. 165–67; Cubitt, pp. 210–12.
61 Miller, *Memoirs*, p. 193.

interpreter. This was crucial because in this case the mediation of the government, which declared that the spoken language on each ship must be that of its commander, seemed to be even more problematic. The conflict remained latent, especially after Cochrane decided that almost all the commanders would be native English speakers. The mediation of interpreters was required in order to partially solve the problems and to facilitate more fluent communication between the two groups. A clear example was Miller himself, who spoke both languages – although not perfectly – as well as Cochrane. Blanco Encalada said in a letter that 'Miller was my interpreter in the conferences with the officers'.[62] In his own personal account, Cochrane described the meeting he had with San Martín in Peru on 4 August 1821:

> San Martín knit his brows, and turning to his ministers, García and Monteagudo, ordered them to retire, to which his Lordship [Cochrane] objected, stating, that as he was not master of the Spanish language, he wished them to remain as interpreters, fearful that some expression not rightly understood might be considered offensive.[63]

Cochrane's words reveal that he spoke Spanish, but not perfectly, which explains his desire for García and Monteagudo to remain as interpreters to avoid any misunderstanding in the conversation with San Martín. Something similar occurred in some of the courts martial, where some officers acted as interpreters. William Prunier, commander of the *Pueyrredón* in 1820, and Albert Morris agreed to 'accept and promise to faithfully accomplish the role of interpreter'.[64] Thomas Clark was requested by Ramón Freire, the Intendant of Concepción, to translate one of Guise's reports from English into Spanish.[65] Sometimes the presence of an interpreter did not solve the problem because many of the crews were unfamiliar with seamanship and could not understand orders, even in their own language. Blanco Encalada suffered this problem when he was the commander of the navy and most of the crews were foreigners. On one occasion he recognised that he gave the command of the *San Martín* to Charles Wooster, a North American captain, because 'nobody understands me here'.[66] Miller, who was on board, explained that

---

62 Blanco Encalada, p. 7.

63 Cochrane, *The Life of Thomas Cochrane*, p. 194.

64 'Causa criminal en contra del autor y cómplices de una conspiración de la Lautaro en contra la Patria', Concepción, July 1819, Archivo Nacional Histórico de Chile, Fondo Ministerio de la Marina (ANH-MM), vol. 30, n.fol. It has been difficult to find further information about them. According to Vale, Prunier was born in the Channel Islands and Cubitt said he was a 'Jerseyman', so he could speak both French and English. He would later join the Peruvian navy. Unfortunately, it remains unclear how he learnt Spanish. See Vale, *Cochrane in the Pacific*, p. 43; Cubitt, p. 59. I have not found more details on Albert Morris.

65 'Causa criminal', ANH-MM, vol. 30, n.fol.

66 Blanco Encalada, p. 7.

the only naval officer on board, excepting the commodore, was the first lieutenant, Ramsay, who on the day before, had become deaf from the effects of the fringe, and now became dumb, or at least so hoarse as to be unable to make himself heard; and the commodore, being ignorant of the English language, could not himself give orders to the foreign seamen. Miller, the surgeon, Mr. Green and the purser, were therefore the only three officers capable of communicating an order: but as none of them understood anything of seamanship, the scene became truly distressing.[67]

The inconvenience generated by the use of different languages became gradually more serious. The reason can be deduced from the information in Table 1 in the previous section, which shows that some of the commanders of the first squadron were British and Irish, and some Chilean. In addition, the data collected by Cubitt show that most of the sailors were Chileans. Higginson, appointed chief of the ships in 1817, always tried to impose English as the official language of the navy, which caused a clash with Blanco Encalada, who privileged the use of Spanish. Eventually, it was agreed that each ship would be managed in the language of its commander, which meant that on the *Chacabuco* and the *Pueyrredón* all the orders would be given in Spanish, and in English on the *San Martín*, the *Lautaro* and the *Araucano*. García Reyes claimed that as a result, 'Higginson openly divided such a newly founded squad into two factions'.[68] The truth is, however, that there were more 'factions', since not all of the conflicts were triggered by linguistic problems, but also class differences which, as shown in the next section, led some English-speaking sailors to rebel against British officers because they suffered the same ill treatment as Chileans.

As already noted, upon his arrival in November 1818, Cochrane removed the Chilean commanders and replaced them with Britons. This meant that, following the aforementioned agreement that each ship had to be managed in the language of its commander, since all of these were English speakers, this language became the official tongue of the navy. Illiterate fishermen and peasants who had joined the Chilean navy found themselves having to follow orders in a foreign language. In May 1821, a British officer of the South American Station reported that 'the whole of the duty in the squadron is carried out in the English language, and the uniform is as much like ours as possible'.[69] After English became the 'official' language of the navy, several conflicts derived from the impossibility of understanding this non-native language, and this affected both groups and all ranks.

67 Miller, *Memoirs*, pp. 201–02.
68 García Reyes, p. 18.
69 'Thomas Hardy to John Wilson Croker', 17 May 1821. Gerald Graham and R.A. Humphreys (eds), *The Navy in South America, 1807–1823: Correspondence of the Commanders-in-Chief on the South American Station* (London and Colchester: Navy Records Society, 1952), p. 332.

Blanco Encalada, the rear admiral of the navy, remained in an ambiguous situation, since he was the highest ranking officer after Cochrane, but did not command his own ship. This also generated some serious inconvenience. Indeed, Blanco Encalada was judged in a court martial in July 1819 because he allegedly abandoned the blockade of Callao, disobeying Cochrane's orders to remain there whilst he was involved in other operations.[70] Blanco Encalada was the highest ranking officer of the fleet that stayed at Callao, but even so, he had to deal with Guise, Spry, Wilkinson and their language. The files of the trial held at the National Archive of Chile show that historians who have discussed this episode, like Alamiro de Ávila Martel, consider only the allegations, but not all the other aspects of the conflict.[71] The allegations were that Blanco Encalada left Callao for Valparaíso in disobedience of Cochrane's orders, a decision he made after realising that the ships were running out of provisions. Blanco Encalada claimed that this decision was made on the grounds that Wilkinson had informed him that all the food remaining on the *San Martín* was rotten. Also, he added that he and Guise had concluded that Pisco, a village close to the port, was a 'miserable town' that had nothing to offer to them. All of these claims and counterclaims were mediated by interpreters. Blanco Encalada claimed that he had the conference with Wilkinson and Guise in the presence of Prunier, who acted as both witness and interpreter of the meeting. Another interpreter mentioned in the file is Nataniel Belez, First Lieutenant of the *San Martín*. Guise claimed that he had said that it was possible to find some provisions in Pisco before the return of Cochrane, an opinion he transmitted 'by means of an interpreter', and therefore, 'there could not be any mistake'.[72] Nevertheless, in his statement, Belez confirmed the version of Blanco Encalada, saying that all were convinced about how miserable Pisco was. Eventually, the sentence handed down by Jean Joseph Tortel, the judge of the trial, a former French privateer who had joined the navy, absolved Blanco Encalada, taking into account the opinions of both interpreters.[73] This decision was confirmed in the court martial that took place later on, which was headed by Cochrane. He declared that 'it is my vote to absolve the Vice Admiral from each and every charge'.[74] It is possible that Cochrane's decision was influenced by Blanco's behaviour when he gave up his post as commander to Cochrane.

---

70 The expedient of the trial is in ANH-MM, vol. 30, fols 42–60.

71 Ávila Martel, pp. 179–81.

72 'Guise to Blanco', Valparaíso, 18 June, 1819, ANH-MM, vol. 30, fol. 54.

73 Juan José Tortel (1763–1842) was French-born, but spoke Spanish because he had arrived in Chile on a privateering ship in 1802. He joined the navy at its very origins, remained in Chile after the wars and was elected deputy of the Congress representing Valparaíso in 1826. See J. Horacio Balmelli, 'Juan José Tortel: Nuestro primer capitán de puerto' in *Revista de Marina*, 2 (1999), available at: http://revistamarina. cl/revistas/1999/2/balmelli.pdf (accessed 14 July 2015).

74 Cochrane, Valparaíso, 22 July 1819, ANH-MM, vol. 30, fol. 68.

However, the linguistic problems within the navy were not resolved, thry remained in place within the crews.

The trial of Francisco de Paula Valdivieso in August 1820 also reveals these linguistic problems. De Paula was the *contador mayor* (purser) of the *Araucano* and responsible for the provisions and rations of the ship. In a rather confusing incident for all involved, de Paula was accused of abandoning his duties on the *Araucano* as he did not return to his position. Indeed, he had gone to the *Chacabuco* since he was not willing to stay under the orders of the new commander. He claimed that Thomas Carter, who had been moved from the *Chacabuco* to the *Araucano* along with his entire crew, expelled him from the ship, along with his *maestre de víveres*. Carter, as the new commander of the *Araucano*, wanted all the stock of provisions for him and his men, which de Paula complained about as he was not 'responsible for their business'. His main complaint was that Carter appointed a new English *maestre de víveres*, and that 'because of his language I could not communicate with him'.[75]

It is hard to believe that there were sufficient interpreters on each ship to transmit orders from the officers to the crew. Quite often, this role was assumed in an improvised way, by people who barely knew the other language. Even with an interpreter, or without one, the language barrier was surmounted only with difficulty. Blanco Encalada left Callao in part because the message that each party wanted to transmit was unclear. In the case of de Paula, communication was simply impossible without any interpreter, a difficulty which led him to leave his ship. Henceforth, language would be one of the mechanisms that reinforced the differentiation of two worlds within the same navy, though the mediation of an interpreter did resolve problems in some cases.

Beyond the practical problems derived from this, the coexistence of two languages was a way to shape an embryonic sense of imagined community, in which the Spanish speakers shared a common view and understanding of their place in the world. It was one of the first times in Chile that a group of individuals with common origins, who were fighting for their independence, had to deal with a European language other than Spanish. In this case, an institution of the Chilean state was obliging them to learn and use a language other than their own. This element of obligation may explain many of the 'collisions' between groups and the development of a sort of forced 'differentiation' between English and Spanish speakers. However, between these two groups, the role of interpreters was crucial as intermediaries in everyday life on ship. In courts martial, their role was even more significant as they had to certify the veracity of the versions provided by those who spoke a language unknown to their counterparts.

75 'Sumario seguido contra el Contador mayor del bergantín de Guerra Araucano, don Francisco de Paula Valdivieso', Valparaíso, August 1820, ANH-MM, Vol. 30, n.fol.

2.6 One Navy, Two Regulations: Granting Privileges or Restraining a Cultural Imposition?

Despite the heterogeneity of the seamen who composed the navy, some of the measures adopted tended to divide it into two major groups. During its first years the navy was organised according to the stipulations of two different regulations, the British and the Spanish. This measure was taken on the grounds that Britons were ignorant of the content of the Spanish regulations – the one privileged by Blanco Encalada at the beginning – and refused to work under them. Cochrane and the rest of the British officers wanted to rule the navy according to British regulations. This clashed with the views of both Blanco Encalada and O'Higgins, who were aware of the importance of considering the context where the regulations were being implemented. O'Higgins, although he admired the British way of organising the navy, did not accept such an imposition, but adopted an odd formula in order to preserve the identity of the Chileans, who were more familiar with the Spanish regulations. Unlike the language problem, this issue could only be mediated by the government. Eventually, both regulations came to coexist and the seamen were regulated according to their nationality. This led to many conflicts and collisions and reinforced the perception that Britons were behaving arbitrarily.

When Blanco Encalada was appointed commander of the newly created navy, he had to deal with a basic problem: how to organise it. Most Chilean sailors were peasants or fishermen without experience in naval affairs and who knew little of discipline, ranks and hierarchies. Others were experienced soldiers from the war that had started in 1812. Blanco Encalada was one of the few Chileans with experience in naval warfare, as he had served as midshipman in the Spanish navy during the Napoleonic wars. This explains his preference for the Spanish navy's regulations in organising the new Chilean navy. The document detailing the regulations was the *Real ordenanza naval para el servicio de los baxeles de S.M.*, published in Madrid in 1802.[76] The regulations were not experienced as strange but lent a sense of 'continuity', since many aspects of the social and political life of the newly independent Republic of Chile (as with the rest of Spanish America) were regulated by the old Spanish laws and institutions.[77]

When Cochrane took office, this was one of the first issues he had to face. Given that the majority of the officers he appointed were British, Irish and North American, they were unfamiliar with the Spanish *Ordenanzas*. All of them had been ruled by the *Regulations and Instructions relating to*

76 *Real ordenanza naval para el servicio de los baxeles de S.M.* (Madrid: Imprenta Real, 1802) This was a revised version of the *Ordenanzas Generales de la Armada Naval*, published in 1793 during the reign of Charles IV (1788–1808).

77 For a discussion of these 'continuities' in Spanish America see Jeremy Adelman, 'Colonial Legacies', pp. 1–12.

his Majesty's Service at Sea, published in 1808.[78] This resulted in one of the first clashes between the Britons and the Chileans who formed the navy. Upon Cochrane's arrival, O'Higgins had tried to adapt the structure of the navy to the requirements of the British seaman. The hierarchies of the Spanish *Ordenanzas* only considered two top ranks, General Captain of the Navy, and Lieutenant Colonel, whereas the *Regulations* stipulated three 'flag officer' ranks: admiral, vice admiral and rear admiral. In a communication to the Senate on 12 December 1818, O'Higgins said that 'the best way to succeed in these matters is to imitate the practices of Great Britain, whose paramount knowledge in maritime affairs is recognised by all the nations'.[79] His decision was therefore to incorporate the three ranks of the British system into the navy, replacing the two top ranks of the Spanish hierarchy.

Cochrane demanded that both his wage and prize money rights were ruled according to British law. This was also passed on to the Senate by O'Higgins, who stressed the need of 'paying him the same wage that a chief of an army in the same situation as him gets in England' along with a part of the prize in accordance with 'the standards of the same position'.[80] The Senate finally agreed with Cochrane, arguing that 'his personal merit, his choice for the freedom of America, his family residing in this country, all these made him worthy of exemption and privileges'.[81] In the same session, O'Higgins explained the problems that Cochrane was facing in the extended use of the Spanish *Ordenanzas* in the navy, especially regarding penalties for offenders. O'Higgins claimed that Cochrane 'does not know entirely the rituality of the court martial according to the Spanish regulations, and this is why he has requested to follow the English one'.[82] In other words, Cochrane was not demanding the coexistence of both rules, but the implementation of the British *Regulations* for everyone. Minister Zenteno had warned Cochrane that, despite their 'superiority', 'as some parts of the mentioned regulations must be unsuitable for our situation, customs and character, there will certainly be some modifications'.[83] O'Higgins was cautious on this:

considering the strength of the customs and the trouble that a sudden innovation may cause in this matter, I think that the form of criminal trial

---

78 *Regulations and Instructions relating to his Majesty's Service at Sea* (London, 1808). This was a revised version of the *King's Regulations and Admiralty Instructions*, first published in Great Britain in 1731.

79 'O'Higgins to the Senate', 12 December 1818, ANH-MM, vol. 8, fol. 4.

80 'O'Higgins to the Senate', 16 August 1819, *Sesiones de los cuerpos lejislativos de la República de Chile, Vol. 3 (1819–1820)*, ed. by Valentín Letelier (Santiago: Imprenta Cervantes, 1867), p. 161 (hereafter, *SCL*).

81 Ibid.

82 Ibid.

83 'Zenteno to Cochrane', Valparaíso, 20 July 1819, *ABO*, vol. 35, doc. 104.

prescribed in the English regulation must be adopted with respect to the individuals of such nation, keeping the Spanish one with respect to the sons of this country [Chile].[84]

Eventually, the Senate stipulated that 'English and American delinquents must be judged according to the English Regulations and the sons of the country according to the Spanish one'.[85]

The problem of which rule must be applied to the different groups that formed the navy reveals that Cochrane's interest in preserving the *Regulations* did not simply conform to practical matters, that is, the knowledge of the rules to be applied in case of an offence. He was also interested in preserving the same economic status he had enjoyed serving in the Royal Navy. O'Higgins and Zenteno, who seemed to admire the British model, were conscious that it could not be applied without considering the Chilean context. That is why they demanded an adaptation rather than an imposition of the *Regulations*. Therefore, the coexistence of both sets of rules can be seen as a way to avoid the imposition of a cultural model rather than as a mere concession to Britons. Preserving both rules also implied assuming the existence of two different 'cultures' in one single space. Those cultures were defined by different parameters, such as language, origins and religious beliefs, but also by the very significance of the fact of being a seaman. Chilean seamen were mainly Catholics and Spanish speakers, whereas British seamen were English speakers and professed different confessions that in the Catholic world were labelled as 'Protestant'.

In this regard, religion was a fundamental element of the representations of Britain that persisted in Spanish America. As many testimonies across this book show, for Spanish Americans, being a Briton meant being a Protestant.[86] In some ways, this also meant being an enemy of the Catholic Church, which in most of the newborn Spanish American states remained the official and only permitted religion. In Chile, the Catholic Church prohibited the burial of people of other confessions, either in parishes or in cemeteries. This meant that, given that most of the Britons who joined the Chilean navy were Protestants, they were not allowed to be buried in Chilean territory and many seamen's corpses were simply thrown into the sea or laid unburied at the coast. On 12 July 1819 O'Higgins decided that 'considering that those dead laid unburied or floating at the mercy of the waves due to a lack of a specific site, [Lord Cochrane] proceeded to identify a ground outside this town [...] where those individuals of both the navy or the army who are in that situation can be buried'.[87]

---

84 'O'Higgins to the Senate', 16 August 1819, *SCL*, vol. 3, 162.
85 'Zenteno to Cochrane', Valparaíso, 14 August 1819, *ABO*, vol. 35, doc. 41.
86 See Chapter 3 of this book.
87 'Oficio del Director Supremo Bernardo O'Higgins', Santiago 12 July 1819, *ABO*, vol. 35, doc. 82.

This concession has been regarded as a manifestation of the liberal thought of O'Higgins and as a first step to religious tolerance, which would be one of the enduring ideological struggles during the nineteenth and twentieth centuries. However, this concession did not apply to Chileans because it was assumed that all were Catholics, which would trigger new and further conflicts about religious freedom during the nineteenth century.[88] The British seamen were the first 'group' of Britons to receive such a benefit in Chile, even before the settlement of traders in the 1820s. It can be regarded as a compromise which preserved their identity as British seamen. Burials were part of the *Regulations*, but were accompanied by many symbols, traditions and rituals that were seen as vital for Britons to preserve. These ranged from the number of minute guns to be fired depending on the rank, to the specific ritual according to their religion.[89] Therefore, the mediation of O'Higgins allowed both groups, that is, Chileans and Britons, to preserve their own identities. It allowed Chileans to be ruled according to their own regulations in a moment in which Cochrane was eager to impose the British regulations on everyone.

The coexistence of both regulations probably did prevent many problems, but served to foster others. Unlike the measure adopted to resolve the problem of language, the government decided that each individual must be subject to a particular regulation and *not* that each ship must be subject to the regulations of its commander (as had been the case for language). This generated serious trouble because most commanders were British and were not familiar with the Spanish *Ordenanzas*.

In October 1819, Cochrane had to face a serious controversy between Manuel Blanco Encalada and William Wilkinson. Blanco Encalada, on board the *San Martín* during the second campaign to Callao, understood that as the highest ranking officer he had more authority than Wilkinson, who was the commander of the ship. He also understood that he was entitled to apply the regulation that he found most suitable, and not necessarily follow the *Regulations* in place on the ship in question. That is why he decided to give his instructions according to the Spanish *Ordenanzas*, which led to a conflict with Wilkinson. Blanco Encalada arrested him because, as he

---

88 Throughout the nineteenth century, one of the most relevant doctrinal disputes concerned the dominance of the Catholic Church over the Chilean state. In this dispute, religious tolerance was one of the most contested topics, a matter that began gradually to be resolved during the second half of the nineteenth century. In the case of burials, Protestants were only allowed to be buried at the *cementerio de disidentes* in Valparaíso, and the Santa Lucia Hill at the centre of Santiago also served as a cemetery for non-Catholics. Only in 1883 did the Congress passed the 'Secular Cemeteries Law' which allowed anyone to be buried in a public cemetery. See Sol Serrano, *¿Qué hacer con Dios en la república? Política y secularización en Chile (1845–1885)* (Santiago: Fondo de Cultura Económica, Chapter V, pp. 221–44.

89 *Regulations*, Chapter 2, arts 25–28, pp. 52–53.

explained in a letter to Cochrane, Wilkinson had said that 'the orders given by me, which do not meet the regulations that you stipulated, will not be followed unless you give them in writing'.[90] Wilkinson did not deny these allegations and instead defended himself arguing that as a Briton he was not obliged to follow the Spanish *Ordenanzas* because he was 'totally ignorant of them'.[91] This misunderstanding was caused by the confusing coexistence of two different regulations in the navy and the divergent interpretations which ensued. Wilkinson, the commander of the ship, remained committed to the agreement that each ship must be ruled by the preferred regulation of its commander. Blanco Encalada, instead, understood that as the highest ranking officer on the ship commanded by Wilkinson, he had the right to choose the regulation to be used.

This conflict reveals the difficulties of adopting two different regulations according to the origins of the sailors, since both groups coexisted on all the ships. In practice, each commander adopted the regulation he found most suitable but, as shown above, none of the commanders was Chilean after Cochrane took over. As a rear admiral, Blanco Encalada was the only officer who could challenge this practice, as he did with Wilkinson, but eventually the British *Regulations* were imposed as the official norm for organising the navy. As one of the first historians of the Chilean navy pointed out, 'an organised section of the British officers was transplanted, as it were, to the Chilean ships'.[92] The uniforms, the ranks and the codes of the British model were all adopted by the Chilean navy.

The willingness to allow both groups to follow different regulations should not be understood simply as an imposition by Cochrane. The hundreds of Britons who joined the navy, many of them former officers of the British navy, belonged to a specific community and wanted to preserve their own identity, even in the service of a foreign flag. As Margarette Lincoln has pointed out, seamen were a particular group in the British community, which after several years of wars and victories, had created their own identity:

> British seamen of the period had a strong sense of their own identity and, by the end of the [eighteenth] century, a clear understanding of what constituted a true-bred 'man-of-war's man'. They were tempted to regard landsmen as an inferior species, and used markers of dress, bearing and language to set their own world apart.[93]

Wilkinson probably did not see Blanco Encalada as a seaman. He only saw a 'landsman' trying to be a sailor. For Wilkinson, the problem was not that

---

90 'Informe de Manuel Blanco Encalada a Cochrane', *San Martín* sloop, 28 October 1819, *ABO*, vol. 35, doc. 224.

91 'Wilkinson to Cochrane', *San Martín* sloop, 29 October 1819, doc. 225.

92 García Reyes, p. xiii.

93 Margarette Lincoln, *Representing the Royal Navy: British Sea Power, 1750–1815* (Aldershot and Burlington, VT: Naval Maritime Museum-Ashgate, 2002), p. 7.

he was unacquainted with the *Ordenanzas*, or that he did not understand the Spanish language. The problem was that Blanco Encalada was unacquainted with the *Regulations* and he did not speak English. If Chileans wanted to create a navy, in his view, it was their obligation to adapt themselves to the genuine sailor's way, the British way.

This was even more evident in Cochrane's own behaviour. Apart from demanding the application of the *Regulations* for everyone, he reminded the authorities on many occasions that British officers could not be judged by the Spanish norms. On July 1820 he wrote to Zenteno to remind him that 'according to the English laws', Chilean officers could not carry out a court martial against a British officer.[94] This was a complex issue, especially because allegations from Chileans of the British officers' abusive behaviour were not rare, as shown in the next section below. In most of these cases, such officers alleged that they could not be judged under the Chilean laws and were therefore not punished. On one occasion, Sergeant José Ramon Gormas, an officer of the marines, reported to William Miller, his commander, that soldiers were frequently lashed and tied to a gun for the smallest offence on board. One of the problems he reported was that Chilean marines did not know the British regulations, a reason for which they were physically punished.[95] When Cochrane learned about this, he stated that the allegations 'originate[d] in wilful misrepresentation and falsehood' and demanded that Gormas give clear proof of his allegations.[96] Eventually, O'Higgins intervened and agreed to Gormas personally explaining the situation to Cochrane and demonstrating the facts.[97] Gormas denounced the punishment of Chileans for their ignorance, but Cochrane did not believe the allegations because to accept them would have implied wrongdoing by a British officer. This shows that in spite of the coexistence of both regulations, Chileans suffered serious consequences when they were not familiar with the British *Regulations*; Britons, in turn, might well have been unfamiliar with the *Ordenanzas* without suffering any punishment.

One problem derived from such coexistence was that the *Regulations* and *Ordenanzas* were, above all, written texts that regulated the organisation, discipline, routines and ranks of sailors. Offences and punishment were not clearly specified, which caused trouble for most seamen on board ship. This became an even more serious problem when the commander of a ship was a Briton and the offender a Chilean. The immediate reaction was to apply the punishment they were most familiar with, which was the basis of Gormas's allegations. This also gave place to abuses, since, on several occasions, the punishment applied seemed to be excessive, as will be shown in the next

---

94 'Cochrane to Zenteno', Valparaíso, 14 July 1820, ANH-MM, vol. 30, n.fol.
95 'Gormas to Miller', Valparaíso, 11 February 1820, ANH-MM, vol. 35, fols 17–19.
96 'Cochrane to Zenteno', Valparaíso, 9 March 1820, ANH-MM, vol. 35, fols 20–22.
97 'O'Higgins and Zenteno to Cochrane', Valparaíso, 14 March 1820, ANH-MM, vol. 35, fol. 23.

section. According to Ávila Martel, the judgement of each individual according to his origin resembles the principle applied during the colonial period, in which each 'body' of society had its own *fuero* (charter) or specific rights and privileges granted by the monarch after a negotiation.[98] In the newly created Chilean navy, nobody could claim the principle of 'equality' either, because the punishment to be applied depended on the type of *fuero* granted to his/ her body, that is, the specific regulation that corresponded to each individual. This also led to other instances of inequity, such as differences in payments and prize money according to the regulation in question. That is why Blanco Encalada, the new vice admiral after Cochrane's departure, suggested in 1824 that the government should 'apply the Spanish *ordenanzas* only' so as to give equal treatment to everyone. However, although *fueros* could be seen as a grant of privilege to British seamen, O'Higgins was forced to acquiesce to preserve the old laws and customs that were familiar to Chilean seamen. By means of this measure at least Chileans could be judged according to their own laws and were not obliged to be judged under a regulation they did not know (although in reality sometimes Britons did not follow this). This casts doubt on Ávila Martel's assumption about the *fueros* since ultimately, rather than a simple privilege, it was seen as the only way to preserve Chilean seamen's identities within the navy.

Despite the conflicts brought about by the coexistence of two sets of regulations, both groups were ruled by an unfamiliar regulation, which means that it was a problem for both. This also reinforced the 'differentiation' experienced by both groups on the grounds of language. Individuals from Santiago, Valparaíso or Coquimbo shared not only a common language but also the fact of being subject to the same regulations. In some cases, this was their only defence against the abusive behaviour of British officers who were unwilling to follow the Spanish rules when applying a punishment. The fact that most officers were Britons was a major obstacle for the real implementation of two regulations equally, and in many cases Chileans were punished because they did not know the British regulation. This led them to perceive Britons as abusive, although not necessarily as 'imperialist'. Punishment and abuse also affected other Britons who were lower-deck seamen and not officers, which meant that conflicts were often triggered by class issues, and not simply by cultural differences.

2.7 Penury, Abuses and Desertions

In his *Memoirs*, William Miller dedicated some words to the behaviour of the British officers on board ship: 'With only a very few exceptions, they affected a prejudice against every thing that differed from the rules of the service in

---

98 Ávila Martel, p. 135. The Senate itself used the word *fuero* to refer to the granting of this privilege. See *SCL*, vol. 3, pp. 160–63.

which they had been brought up'.[99] Miller, a Briton himself, was a soldier, not a seaman, and in spite of his origins he manifested his discontent at his compatriots' extensive abuse of power. This problem, although well known, has not been sufficiently addressed by historians, who have mainly focused on the achievements and organisation of the Chilean navy, and not on conflicts amongst seamen. David Cubitt is one of the few to have tackled this problem from the perspective of a lack of 'discipline', stressing that this was fostered by the 'strong resentments' towards the British officers and seamen felt by the Chileans. The 'harsh discipline' introduced by the British officers, he argues, was one of the motives explaining the Chileans' 'indiscipline', especially before the departure to Callao in 1820.[100] This explanation, however, only considers one dimension of the problem, which is 'discipline'; it does not address the complexity and material destitution of conditions of everyday life on board ship. These conditions triggered many of the conflicts within the navy, which often resulted from physical punishment by the British officers of both Chilean and British crew members.

British officers' abuse of power, particularly expressed in corporal punishment, was an extensive practice during the first years of the Chilean navy, as many of the primary sources used for this chapter reveal. A number of cases are reported in the official records. Violence was exerted because of cultural and material conditions and not simply because a specific group had a particular nationality. Peter Kemp has made it clear that during the Napoleonic wars, the coexistence of different nationalities within the Royal Navy was rather common, so British officers were used to sharing the same space with foreigners. At the same time, he explains the recurrent use of physical punishment by captains after the end of the war, as a means to maintain a strict discipline on the ships in order to win promotion to a higher rank, which in peacetime seemed more difficult. Therefore, the use of physical punishment also formed part of the 'maritime culture' in which many of the British sailors who entered the Chilean navy had become seamen.[101]

The extremely poor material conditions under which the Chilean navy was formed also explains the use of violence. Delays of payments and prizes are often mentioned as motives for discontent among both officers and crews.[102] However, it was mainly the lack of essential provisions for survival, like food and clothing, which catalysed the discontent in both groups; especially during the campaigns at Callao, when ships reportedly ran out of such goods. Under this context of penury, the Chileans' outrage was triggered by the privileges of the British officers, who were seen to receive more than them. Some mutinies started as protests about the delays of payment, but others were responses to the unequal treatment between officers and the crews,

99 Miller, *Memoirs*, p. 193.
100 Cubitt, p. 226.
101 Kemp, pp. 160–62; 188–91.
102 Cubitt, pp. 316–18.

irrespective of their origins. The reasons triggering violence must not obscure the importance of its consequences, which cannot be reduced to a lack of discipline or poor morale. Violence catalysed different attitudes in terms of how each group perceived the other, and what this represented in the context of a period in which identities where changing. This meant that any conflict experienced in the navy on the grounds of culture, such as language, religion or regulations, might have been distorted by the destitute conditions in which the interactions between Chileans and Britons took place. In such conditions, any privilege granted to a British officer might well have triggered a mutiny which in most cases ended up in courts martial and executions.

One of the most reported mutinies took place in January 1819 on the *Chacabuco* sloop.[103] The commander Thomas Carter sent a very detailed report to Cochrane about what happened on board:

> Once I could get silence, I asked the crew what reasons they had for this disturbance at such an hour and they said only that the government is unwilling to pay either their salary or prizes, and that they would be paid and would excuse themselves, because they did not want to serve under my orders, and in a squad commanded by foreigners. Then they raised again their voices, crying out, 'long live the Patria and death to the English'.[104]

The instigators, all Chileans, were executed and others sent to land. These were summary executions ordered by the government. In a letter sent to Cochrane, Zenteno said that the wish of the government was that the leaders of the mutiny should die by firing squad and that the rest be *quintados*, which meant that one in five mutineers should be executed randomly. Finally, they wanted 'their corpses to be exhibited to the public by hanging them in the yardarm of the sloop'.[105] In this case, the mutiny started because of delay in payment, but reveals the Chileans resentment of the British officers.

The case of Francisco de Paula in August 1820, who, as mentioned in Section 2.5, had been expelled by Thomas Carter from the *Chacabuco* for abandoning his duties, also reveals the conflictive coexistence of different groups. During the court martial, he claimed that Thomas Carter had behaved 'in a very violent and informal manner, demanding everything without giving me the inventory receipt [for food]', adding that 'foreigners procure to maintain a balance which is prejudicial to the interests of the nation'.[106] De Paula referred to 'foreigners' as a different group that pursued their own interests. In addition, he expressed the feeling that their behaviour

---

103 See Worcester, p. 79; Cubitt, p. 73.

104 'Carter to Cochrane', *Chacabuco* vessel, 29 January 1819, *ABO*, vol. 35, doc. 37. I consulted a source that was translated into Spanish by the editor of the *ABO*. This is my own translation of the Spanish text.

105 'Zenteno to Cochrane', Valparaíso, 25 February 1819, *ABO*, vol. 35, doc. 38.

106 'Sumario seguido contra el Contador mayor', ANH-MM, vol. 30, n.fol.

was against the interests of the 'nation'. De Paula's words echoed some of the ideas that had been previously stated by the governor Francisco García Carrasco in 1808 when he targeted all foreigners, and particularly Britons, as a bad influence on Chileans.[107] De Paula's attitude might be attributed to a reaction against behaviour he considered abusive, but the way he referred to foreigners also makes clear that in 1820, despite the image of Britain as an 'enemy' having changed, some old ideas remained.

At first sight, it might look like both episodes, which occurred on the same ship and under the same commander, were cultural 'collisions' between two different groups reflecting Chileans' 'resentment' of the British officers for the simple fact that they were Britons, as stated by Cubitt.[108] However, as argued, perceptions and representations during the independence period changed rapidly and there were also differences based on origins that were more nuanced. This challenges Cubitt's assertion of resentment being the main factor explaining the conflicts on board ship.

In July 1819 a conspiracy was carried out on board the *Lautaro*. A group of sailors conspired to rebel against the British officers, aiming to replace Martin Guise with a new commander. The leaders of the mutiny were the Chilean sergeant José Vega and the Irish surgeon's mate John Anderson, who would become the new commander. They were followed by a part of the Chilean crew and by one English midshipman, Edward Bradley. The most important complaint was the cruelty of the English officers, who apparently treated Chileans badly and punished them very harshly. Some testimonies speak of Chileans 'working as slaves' and being used by officers for personal work that had nothing to do with their duties. The language problem was also latent, as shown by the first statement on the case, which says that the mutiny was carried out by 'various individual nationals of this state, and not having on board any official who properly understands the language'.[109] Other testimonies from the court martial stressed the privileged position of the English compared to the Chileans. In his declaration, Anderson maintained that the Sergeant Díaz asked him 'whether I could not see the bad treatment suffered by Chileans, who worked all day long and who only received one ration of *aguardiente*, whilst Englishmen got four'.[110] Bradley testified that he had told Anderson that the commander had punished him with two hundred lashes and that he 'he would rather shoot himself than be lashed'.[111] Eventually, both Vega and Anderson were sentenced to death in a court martial.

This trial also shows the undefined nature of the national identities of the sailors involved, which was closer to a vague sense of patriotism. When

---

107 See above, Chapter 1.
108 Cubitt, p. 225.
109 'Causa criminal en contra del autor y cómplices de una conspiración de la Lautaro en contra la Patria', ANH.MM, vol. 30, n.fol.
110 Ibid.
111 Ibid.

the prosecutor asked them about their *patria*, they spoke of the city they were born, as did the midshipman Juan Aguirre, born in Coquimbo. This was not the case for Anderson, for whom the *patria* was Ireland, or for Bradley, whose *patria* was England. This also reveals that in the group of English speakers there were many latent conflicts. One had to do with their own national rivalries and the fact that Irishmen and Englishmen were also constructing their own national identities at the time, often in opposition to each other.[112] The Chilean defendants referred to themselves as 'Chilenos' involved in a conflictive relation with the English officers. At the same time, Anderson and Bradley's insurrection against the British officers also reveals class-related disputes within the navy. Regardless of their common origins with the officers, they rebelled because they had more in common with the lower-ranking Chileans than with the privileged British officers. Physical punishment was in this case a shared experience between low-ranking sailors with different origins. Therefore, this case reveals that the representations and perceptions of Britons were not fixed and in some cases followed other factors apart from origins, such as class. Thus, assertions made by historians like Cubitt and Ávila Martel, both of whom have stressed seamen's different origins to explain conflicts within the navy, must be called into question. Material conditions and class issues also triggered conflicts within a group of the same nationality.

In another case, the role of British officers was twofold: some of them punished Chilean seamen while others defended them. In November 1822, a group of seamen from the *Lautaro* ended up in the hospital of Valparaíso seriously injured. One of them, Felix Palacio, declared that he had been 'unjustly punished with a rope's end by Lieutenant Williamson of the *Lautaro*, that he received very severe stripes on the face and neck, which ha[d] produced considerable inflammation and swelling of those parts, difficulty in deglutition and external ulceration'.[113] Officers Brown and Vowell – who were at the hospital at the time – also wrote to Cochrane to bring to his attention the testimonies of the wounded who were in the hospital:

> Transito Hernández of the carpenter crew, states that he received four dozen lashes with the end of the main sheet by which he considers his life in danger.
> Francisco Duarte, seaman, states that he also was so severely punished on board, that he is now in hospital in consequence.
> Feliz Palacios, seaman, states that he was most severely cut in the face, neck and throat by a rope's end, which places are in a state of ulceration. He states also that he was at the time of punishment knocked down the main gateway.

---

112 See Brown, *Adventuring through Spanish Colonies*, pp. 115–16.
113 Wilkinson to Cochrane, Valparaíso, 6 November 1822, NAS, Dundonald Papers, GD233/36/253.

Ramon Seguero, seaman, also states that in consequence of similar irregular punishment, the consequences of which we were eye witnesses to, he is now in hospital.[114]

Another five seamen reportedly died on board, including a 'boy' called José Valencia. Another sailor, José María Muñoz, had been left 'in a dying state on board' after being 'twice knocked down the main gateway'.[115] This was clearly a serious case. Closer analysis of the surviving material demonstrates the complicated nature of the events, in which British officers played contradictory roles. The officers of the *Lautaro* behaved with such cruelty that their compatriots Vowell and Brown reported the case to Cochrane and demanded a fair investigation,[116] while Chilean sailors observed that some of the British officers were aggressive and others were compassionate. Events like this made it clear for the Chilean sailors that Britishness was by no means a guarantee of respect and justice.

These episodes reveal that abuse of power affected Chilean seamen not only as Chileans, but because punishment formed part of the maritime culture and mostly affected lower-ranking seamen. In some cases, it also affected seamen of other nationalities like Irish. Sometimes violence was even exerted among British officers. Thomas Woolridge wrote to Cochrane from Valdivia on 16 May 1822 to denounce Captain Cobbett, stating that he 'has frequently treated his officers in the most unbecoming manner by calling them "beasts" and "ubbers" and on all occasions condemning them to "hell" as well as indulging his temper by placing them under an arrest for trifles, and ordering them to their duty whenever it became a matter of convenience to himself'.[117] This, again, challenges what historians like Ávila Martel and Cubitt have said about the nature of the conflicts within the navy. In this case, a British officer insulted some of his compatriots because they were 'ubbers' (derived from 'landlubber'), that is, people with no experience at sea. In other words, in Cobbett's eyes, some British officers did not share the maritime culture that he believed any British sailor must have.

It is plausible that many of the desertions reported before 1822, the year in which San Martín founded the Protectorate of Peru, were the result of both extreme living conditions and abuse of power. On 7 April 1820, Captain Guise reported to Cochrane that 'so many acts of insubordination, robbery and desertion have been committed by the marines embarked onboard the *Lautaro* under my command that unless a stop be speedily put to such proceedings the most serious consequences may

---

114 'Brown and Vowell to Cochrane', Valparaíso 1 November 1822, NAS, Dundonald Papers, GD233/36/253.
115 Ibid.
116 Ibid.
117 'Woolridge to Cochrane', Valdivia, 16 May 1822, NAS, Dundonald Papers, GD233/36/254.

happen to the squadron'.[118] This might be explained on the grounds of the different positions that each group occupied in the hierarchy of the navy. According to Lincoln, in the culture of the British Navy, 'only officers had a permanent connection with the Navy as a service. Ordinary seamen viewed themselves primarily as members of a ship's company and often moved from the navy to the merchant service as circumstances and individual preference dictated'.[119] Going beyond these considerations, this was not a problem of being a mercenary or not. In the eyes of Chilean seamen, it was a matter of being an officer, someone who had privileges and abused their power. In addition, some of the deserters, as reported by Captain Robertson to Guise, only went to land and were sheltered by soldiers of a regiment. The following account reveals the 'solidarity' of Chilean soldiers, even officers, with the deserters:

> At this moment, two officers, Lieut. José Ma Madariaga, and Sub Lieut. Ollasu [Oyarzun] presented themselves, who also refused me admittance and treated me in derision and with contempt. I encouraged the soldiers around them to treat me, in like manner [...] I requested the deserter to be given up; but they refused unless by an order from the commandante. I remained in the house of the commandante and received an order for his release and on my presenting this to the said two officers (who had assured me they would be responsible for the prisoner) they informed me they had suffered him to escape.[120]

In some critical moments, penury was also shared by both groups alike, regardless of rank and origins. On 8 September 1821 Paul Delano, commander of the *Lautaro*, wrote to Cochrane that 'the officers as well as the men, are dissatisfied having been a long time on the cruise and at present without any kind of meat or spents [*sic*] onboard and a long time without pay that they are not able to provide for themselves any longer and having no petty officers their duty has been truly hard and until starved without a murmur'. In such conditions, warned Delano, it was difficult to keep them on board or even to guarantee the safety of the ship, for which reason 'I do not hold myself responsible for any accident that may happen on the ship until the difficulties are removed'.[121] Delano not only complained about the lack of food and unpaid wages, he also revealed that there was a lack of petty officers in the navy, which meant that the division between officers and lower-ranking sailors was even starker than usual. Petty officers were crucial in intermediating between officers and sailors. Their absence from the ships also explains

---

118 'Guise to Cochrane', Valparaíso, 7 April 1820, NAS, Dundonald Papers, GD233/36/253.
119 Lincoln, p. 12.
120 'Robertson to Guise', 1 May 1820, NAS, Dundonald Papers, GD233/36/253.
121 'Delano to Cochrane', On board, Callao 8 September 1821, NAS, Dundonald Papers, GD233/32/240.

why most of the mutinies and insurrections analysed in these sections started amongst the low-ranking sailors and not the officers. Eventually, on 24 September 1821 Cochrane reported the outcome of this episode and warned Zenteno about the extremely weak conditions of the squadron:

> It is impossible to exist on the ships in their present state. In addition of having the Lautaro been abandoned as I informed you, I tell you now that all the foreign seamen of the Valdivia after making a mutiny, disobeying my and their officers' orders, and behaving in the most dangerous way for the safety of their ship, they were left on ground by Captain Cobbett, aided by his officers and the marines.[122]

According to this testimony, the mutiny was carried out by 'seamen' of different nationalities, who rebelled against the captain and the officers of the *Lautaro*. The extremely poor conditions, and the delay of payments, made it difficult to guarantee the loyalty of the officers, who had to deal with the discontent of the crews. On one occasion during which Cochrane 'resigned', his officers gave clear proof regarding their self-perception in the construction of the Chilean navy.[123] In a meeting held on board the *Independencia* on 19 July 1820, captains Cobbett, Wilkinson, Hunter, Grenfell, Still, Coulthan and Lawson, and another 23 officers, resolved:

> 1st that the pronounced safety and interest of the Navy of Chile entirely rest on the abilities and experience of the present commander in chief.
> 2nd That the feelings of unbounded confidence and respect which we entertain for the present commander in chief and which cannot be transferred to another have induced us to come to the resolution of resigning our commissions and of transmitting the same to government through the hands of his Lordships.[124]

For them, the navy could only be built up by British officers, reinforcing Lincoln's assertion about British officer's identity as the true-bred 'man-of-war'. The reinforcement of this identity, the delay of payment and the scarcity of the resources they counted on to control the crews were all problems that explained the massive desertions that took place at the end of the cruise to Callao. García Reyes stressed the 'mercenary' character of the British officers, stating that they only went to Chile for money, to explain the massive desertions during the campaigns in Peru.[125] The establishment of the

---

122 'Cochrane to Zenteno', Callao, 24 September 1821, NAS, Dundonald Papers, GD233/31/239.

123 Cochrane threatened to resign on 13 July 1820 because of the delay in payment. See Barros Arana, *Historia general de Chile*, VIII, p. 451. He made the same threat on two other occasions.

124 'Cobbett, Wilkinson, Hunter, Grenfell, Still, Coulthan, Lawson, etc. to Cochrane', Valparaíso, 20 July 1820, NAS, Dundonald Papers, GD233/31/237.

125 García Reyes, p. xii.

Protectorate of Peru by San Martín was a crucial moment, because for the first time during the war a new entity might have disputed the loyalty of the British officers and seamen with attractive offers. Cochrane wrote in 1822:

> numerous desertions of officers and men had occurred and continued to occur occasioned by their disgust at the apparent neglect of the Chilian [*sic*] government, and by the seductive promises of San Martín, who sought to get the squadron into his own power and place it under the flag of Peru; of which state he at that time undoubtedly contemplated constituting himself the Imperial chief.[126]

Cochrane was convinced that San Martín was conspiring against the Chilean squadron and was sending agents to persuade British officers to join the Peruvian navy. One of them was William Kennedy, a former member of the crew of the *Scorpion* who had survived the conspiracy and killing of its commander Tristan Bunker and his crew in 1809, in which governor García Carrasco was involved (see chapter 1).[127] In a letter to Joaquín Echeverría, Cochrane complained that 'San Martín's intention is to ruin the naval service of Chile, taking advantage of the privations of the officers, and of the nudity and destitute state of the crews'.[128] Eventually, on 16 July 1822, Zenteno reported to Cochrane the desertion of 15 officers, most of them Britons.[129] Cochrane blamed both the government, who seemed ignorant of what was going on, and the persistence of penury on ship as the main causes of desertions. In a letter to the officers on 1 January 1823, he claimed:

> Your patience and perseverance under privations of all kinds are such as Chile had no right to expect, and such as no other country experiences even from its native subjects. In all maritime states the strictest attention to the necessities of officers and then, regularity of pay and adequate reward for services are deemed necessary as excitements to perseverance and the achievement of effective and heroic exploits; but your exertions and performances have been independent of all these inducements.[130]

Cochrane ceased serving the Chilean navy on 20 November 1822 and set out for Brazil in January 1823 to take part in its independence struggles. From there, he wrote to the Chilean authorities expressing his anger about how everything had turned out, especially in relation to the treatment of foreigners: 'for with regard to foreign seamen, such is the disgust they

---

126 'Cochrane to the President of Chile', NAS, Dundonald Papers, GD233/31/237.
127 See above, Chapter 1.
128 'Cochrane to Echeverría', Valparaíso, 4 October 1822, NAS, Dundonald Papers, GD233/31/239.
129 'Zenteno to Cochrane', Valparaíso, 16 July 1822, NAS, Dundonald Papers, GD233/32/240.
130 'Cochrane to the Captains and Officers of the Navy of Chile', 10 January 1823, NAS, Dundonald Papers, GD233/32/240.

entertain for a service in which they have been so neglected and deceived, that I am confident the ships of Chile will never again be effectually supplied with men of that description'.[131] Through this letter, Cochrane also showed that his main concern was the situation of the officers and the unpaid wages, rather than the extreme living conditions of the entire navy. He did not complain about the abusive behaviour of some officers or the violence they exerted upon lower-deck seamen. All this reveals that on an interpersonal level, reactions, attitudes, ideas and behaviours varied according to the circumstances. There were many factors that catalysed violence, such as the different cultural backgrounds in each group. The decisive factor, however, was the destitute conditions experienced by the seamen.

2.8 Cochrane and the National Significance of the Navy

The geopolitical context of the independence era was quite complex. Chilean independence was not recognised by Great Britain until 1831, and when Cochrane arrived in Chile in 1818, British foreign policy regarding Chile was still unclear and ambiguous. Cochrane's role in this context was also ambiguous. He was a Briton in the service of Chile who had also been granted Chilean citizenship, but sometimes, as shown in the previous section, he was more concerned about the loyalty of the British officers in the Chilean navy than about the crews. As the commander of the navy, he had to defend Chile's interests even if this implied confronting other Britons, like the commanders of the ships of the Royal Navy who were stationed in the Pacific to protect the interests of British merchants. By means of the Chilean navy and whenever he had to confront a ship from another country, Cochrane configured and promoted the idea that Chile was a political entity that must be respected and recognised on equal terms by other states. This undermines the conception of Cochrane as an imperial agent, since he demonstrated that, even against his own compatriots, he defended the rights of Chile to exist and to be respected as an independent state. Furthermore, along with O'Higgins he was one of the first to suggest the idea that Chile should rule the Pacific, based on its maritime power. This would automatically lead to competition with Britain and the US, who were also interested in controlling trade in the Pacific. Here there is another overlap between the different levels on which British and Chilean relations took place. Cochrane indeed acted as an agent of the Chilean state, and defended its interests even against his British compatriots. As an individual he acted at the state level to foster the image of Chile as an independent and sovereign state. On an individual level, this was also a way for him to assert his own status. He had not taken a step down, but rather a step across.

---

131 'Cochrane to the Minister of Marine of Chile', Bahia, June 1823, NAS, Dundonald Papers, GD233/32/240.

The incident of the 'flag's salute' is clear proof of how, through the navy, Cochrane aided in the construction of the image of Chile as a new political entity. Soon after his arrival in December 1818, the North American vessel *Ontario* reached Valparaíso, commanded by Captain James Biddle. When the *Ontario* was trying to leave the port, Cochrane delayed the authorisation for a rather trivial reason, which nevertheless presented a strong symbolism. Cochrane reminded Biddle that 'whenever a warship of a foreign nation reached a friendly port, the custom has always been to publicly salute its flag'.[132] Biddle replied by saying that while he was aware of this custom, he would only do it as requested 'if this is responded to with an equal number of gunshots'.[133] In Cochrane's view, the 'host port' had always replied with two fewer gunshots than the visiting ship, which Biddle was not willing to accept. Cochrane's final response was that 'in any port of a civilised nation the power that is being saluted responds with the same number of gunshots'.[134] Cochrane was demanding that Chile be recognised as an equal by the United States. Chile deserved the same treatment as any other 'civilised nation' and Cochrane did not hesitate to request this of the commander of a North American ship. Considering that Chile had only declared its independence on 12 February 1818, a few months before this incident, this was one of the first occasions on which another state was confronted with the idea of Chile as an existing community.

Considering Cochrane's British origins, it might be argued that, in part, this incident conveyed an animosity towards North America, a territory that had been part of the British Empire and was now a new and rising international power. However, Cochrane displayed similar behaviour when facing his own compatriots. In December 1818 he carried out the blockade of Callao. In this period there was no clear international law, but most states followed the principles of *The Law of the Nations* published in 1783 by Emerich de Vattel. One of the subjects was the rights of a state that started a blockade in the context of warfare, and the control over the sea surrounding the blocked port. The most complex issue was how to treat neutral ships and what to do if they were carrying a load belonging to the enemy. During the blockade of Callao several British ships transited throughout the Pacific and were considered neutral. However, Captain Donat O'Brien, a Royal Navy officer stationed on the Pacific coast of South America, complained to Cochrane that some British merchant ships under his protection had been captured by the Chilean squadron under Cochrane's command. O'Brien reminded Cochrane of his condition as a British subject, but Cochrane had already warned him that his duty was 'to investigate under which circumstances neutral ships have entered into the coasts of the Viceroyalty

132 'Cochrane to John Biddle', *Ontario*, 27 December 1818, reproduced in *Gazeta Ministerial de Chile* (Santiago, 23 January 1819), *ABO*, vol. 12. pp. 28–33.
133 'Biddle to Cochrane', 28 December, 1818, *ABO*, vol. 12, pp. 28–33.
134 'Cochrane to Biddle', 28 December 1818, *ABO*, vol. 12, pp. 28–33.

of Peru'.[135] In his reply, Cochrane asserted that he only acted 'against those neutrals that violate the blockade or carry contraband of the enemy'.[136] The same thing happened on several occasions afterwards. On 17 June 1821 Cochrane responded to a letter regarding a similar conflict, demanding from Great Britain the same treatment as any other state for Chile:

> I am so warmly interested in the honour and welfare of my native country that I am most willing to hope that the government has not adopted one law for war, and another for convenience in peace; that they have not established one rule for the strong and another for the weak; but that the attributes of England are, as they heretofore have been, those of strict honour and impartial justice.[137]

Again, Cochrane was constructing an image of Chile as a distinctive political entity. Even before independence had been recognised by Great Britain, he responded to his own compatriots as a Chilean, and demanded the same respect deserved by other states according to the principles of the *Law of Nations*.

In Peru, there was another instance in which Cochrane promoted the image of Chile as a new political entity: the crisis with José de San Martín, which most historians argue was triggered by his aversion to paying wages and prizes to the Chilean navy.[138] San Martín was Commander of the Liberation Expedition, and was delegated as its supreme authority by the Chilean Congress. Cochrane was told to obey him under all circumstances. However, when San Martín proclaimed himself the Protector of Peru on 28 July 1821, Cochrane considered that he was acting as the supreme authority of a new political entity and was no longer representing the Liberation Expedition. As a result, he refused to serve as San Martín's subaltern because he was representing another state. Cochrane had been commissioned by the Chilean congress, and could not accept being subordinated to the authority of another state. He later wrote:

> as the existence of this self-constituted authority was no less at variance with the institutions of the Chilian [*sic*] Republic than with its solemn promises to the Peruvians again, I hoisted my flag on board the O'Higgins, determined to adhere solely to the interests of Chili [*sic*] till they interfere with me in my capacity of the Commander-in-Chief of the Chilian navy.[139]

135 'Cochrane to O'Brien', 29 September 1819, *ABO*, vol. 35, doc. 212.

136 'Cochrane to O'Brien', 2 October 1819, *ABO*, vol. 35, doc. 218.

137 'Cochrane to Hardy', 17 June 1821, in *The Navy in South America, 1807–1823: Correspondence of the Commanders-in-Chief on the South American Station*, ed. by Gerald Graham and R.A. Humphrey (London and Colchester: Navy Records Society, 1952), p. 337.

138 See Cubitt, pp. 316–17; Ossa, *Armies, Politics and Revolution*, pp. 166–72.

139 Cochrane, *The Life of Thomas Cochrane*, p. 193.

One of San Martín's proposals was to organise a new expedition to invade and conquer the Philippines, which he was convinced had been left abandoned by the Spanish authorities. However, Cochrane refused and left Peru.[140] Cochrane (and, indirectly, San Martín) was defining what Chile was in international terms, an idea that was represented through the navy itself. The clearest proof was San Martín's plan to organise a Peruvian squadron and the offers he made to Cochrane and his men, as shown in the previous section. Cochrane refused, but many of his fellows deserted. The former Chilean navy was now divided into two different navies, these being determined by different nationalities. In Cochrane's eyes, this constituted a threat to Chile's interests and he realised that the idea of the Liberation Expedition as a continental enterprise had come to an end. For him, it was Chile that 'gave' independence to Peru and the Chilean navy under his command that expelled the Spanish forces from the Pacific. This brought benefits for the rest of the states with Pacific coastlines, including Peru, for which reason Chile was thought to deserve some special rights over the Pacific. That is why he rejected the plan to invade the Philippines as part of the Peruvian squadron proposed by San Martín, and sailed without any orders to the coast of Mexico to hunt the remaining Spanish ships. According to Luis Valencia Avaria, after this cruise Cochrane wrote to O'Higgins: 'make yourself an Emperor, a King, a Protector, a President or a Chief, under any title that suits you better. Here is your squadron, which would put at your feet anything that exists in this coast from the Cape Horn'.[141]

Despite refusing to set out to the Philippines under the command of San Martín, Cochrane took the idea and devised a new plan to invade them from Chile. The Peruvian historian Francisco Javier Mariátegui stated that during a visit to Chile during the 1820s, he heard about a plan from General Francisco Pinto to extend the maritime power of Chile across the Pacific. Cochrane proposed that O'Higgins 'launch a new campaign, heading to the Philippines [...], which in the seizure of the islands would capture some ships and with them, the nation would soon recover from what is owed'. Mariátegui also claimed that the plan was discussed between O'Higgins, his ministers and some other politicians, including Pinto, but that it had been rejected.[142] According to O'Higgins's testimony, the plan considered the consolidation of the control of Valdivia and Chiloé, the establishment of some bases in Guayaquil and, most importantly, the invasion of the Philippines. In a letter O'Higgins sent to Cochrane on 12 November 1821, there are some allusions to the plan:

140 Barros Arana, *Historia general de Chile*, VIII, p. 469.

141 Quoted by Luis Valencia Avaria, 'Las Filipinas habrían podido ser para Chile', *En Viaje*, 99 (January 1942), pp. 2–3.

142 Francisco Javier Mariátegui, *Anotaciones a la Historia del Perú independiente de don Mariano Paz-Soldan* (Lima: Imprenta de El Nacional, 1869), p. 78.

If Guayaquil strengthens its relations with Chile in a way that no other government can dissolve, a matter that I leave to your discretion and your military and political talents, then this Republic could dominate and rapidly reach its greatness. Then, not only what is owed to this country will be paid by putting customs wherever we want, but we can also go against the Philippines.[143]

The plan was not carried out. Cochrane left Chile in January 1823 after facing several problems with the Chilean authorities upon his return from Peru. Although there is no evidence to maintain that the above plan was a direct influence, similar arguments were made several years later when the Minister of the Interior and War, Diego Portales, claimed that Chile 'should dominate in the Pacific forever'.[144] His main concern was that Andrés de Santa Cruz, the *caudillo* of the Peruvian-Bolivian Confederation, could threaten the economic ambitions of Chile and the dominance of Valparaíso as the main port of the South Pacific. In a letter written on 10 September 1836 to Manuel Blanco Encalada, who at that time was Admiral of the Chilean navy, he claimed that 'the Confederation must disappear forever'. One of the reasons was that 'this new organisation would try to dominate the Pacific'. Portales claimed at the end of the letter that 'we [Chileans] must dominate the Pacific forever; this must be our motto now and forever'.[145] As a result, Chile's first international war after independence was triggered in 1837.[146]

The performance of Cochrane as Vice Admiral of the Chilean navy was also a complex issue in which matters were neither clear nor well defined. His image as a national hero in Chile coexisted with his aim of organising the Chilean navy under the British model. His decisions to appoint British officers almost exclusively and to rule the navy under the British *Regulations* caused serious difficulties for Chilean seamen and he did not seem concerned about this in his correspondence. As the commander of the navy, he did not deal with everyday issues, except when complaining to the authorities about the penury experienced on board ship. He seemed more concerned with the power and prestige that he imagined the Chilean navy should gain under his admiralcy, envisioning it as a cohesive entity that must represent the interests of the Chilean state. In so doing he also contributed to some of the first definitions of Chile as a distinctive state, in a context of war and international conflict in which he aimed to make it look like independent and respectable.

143 Quoted by Ávila Martel, p. 257.

144 Quoted by Jay Kinsbruner, *Diego Portales: Interpretative Essays on the Man and Times* (The Hague: Springer Science, 1967), p. 84.

145 Portales to Blanco Encalada, Santiago, 19 September 1836, in *Epistolario de Don Diego Portales, Vol. 3: 1834–1837*, ed. by Guillermo Feliú Cruz (Santiago: Dirección General de Prisiones, 1936–1938), pp. 452–53.

146 A good contribution on Andrés de Santa Cruz is Natalia Sobrevilla, *The Caudillo of the Andes: Andrés de Santa Cruz* (Cambridge: Cambridge University Press, 2011).

2.9 Conclusion

This chapter has analysed several interactions that took place within the Chilean navy during the wars of independence. In general, the historiography has tended to focus on the achievements of the army and the navy in battle rather than analysing in depth their internal issues and the way they influenced the nation-building process. In this chapter the focus was on the navy itself, its composition and problems derived from life on board ship rather than achievements or battles. The aim was not to describe the internal features of the navy, but rather to explain the way interactions between Britons and Chileans influenced subsequent interstate relationships and the configuration of national identities.

During the independence struggles the Chilean navy was a 'contact zone' in which people from different cultures interacted. I have focused on two specific 'non-state' actors, Britons and Chileans, whose interactions can easily be regarded as conflictive, because their different origins, languages, and life experiences predetermined the privileged situation of Britons in relation to Chileans. However, this chapter shows that conflicts, although these existed, cannot overshadow the complex ways in which such interactions took place. There were many instances of mediations between the two groups that in some ways nuanced their supposedly difficult coexistence. Linguistic problems were one of the main challenges on ship, but interpreters often worked as cultural mediators. If communication had been impossible, no successes would have been possible either and the fact is that the navy experienced many triumphs in Valdivia and Peru. In addition, linguistic problems also confirmed a lack of knowledge of seamanship in both Chilean seamen − former peasants and fishermen − and some British soldiers on board. The coexistence of different regulations, regarded by some historians as the granting of *fueros* that perpetuated the privileges of Britons over Chileans, also needs to be carefully analysed. Such a measure can also be regarded as a means to prevent the imposition of the British regulations on all, which eventually led to an adaptation of the rules rather than an imposition. Of course, this remained a conflictive issue and led to several reported cases of abuse of power because the captains were all Britons and Chileans were not familiar with the British regulations. Notwithstanding, it has also been demonstrated that officers did not abuse their power over Chileans just because they were Chileans, but because most of them were lower-deck seamen, and in some cases they rebelled alongside Britons who suffered the same conditions of poverty. The destitute condition which affected both groups alike, although to a lesser degree the officers, exacerbated their outrage but also catalysed different attitudes towards conceptions of loyalty and patriotism, which in these years remained undefined and unclear. Therefore, Britons were not simply seen by Chileans as enemies or as 'imperialists' but as seamen with different conditions depending on whether they were officers or not.

Cochrane himself also deserves more careful attention. He was not simply a hero liberating South Americans from the Spanish yoke. Although he presented this image and was convinced that he was infusing ideas of liberty into the 'oppressed' population, these ideas were part of his legitimising discourse and were seldom seen by the crews of the navy. It was hard for Chileans to see their British officers as liberators on board ship, although sometimes they were their only chance of justice after suffering unfair punishment. Despite this, Cochrane's behaviour as commander of the navy also reinforced the idea of Chile as an independent political entity. As such, he had to confront officers from British and North American ships and remind them that Chile had just entered into the world of 'civilised nations', demanding equal treatment. His idea of converting Chile into a maritime power in the Pacific on the grounds of its privileged position on the map echoed some of the ideas in the instructions granted to Craufurd to invade Chile. In this document Chile was seen as a key territory to open new trade routes in the Pacific connected to the Atlantic. However, for both Cochrane and O'Higgins, this was a starting point for building up a new empire, and not a conception that envisioned subjugation to another power.

CHAPTER 3

Bibles, Schools and Citizens

British Protestant Missionaries and Educators in Chile, 1817–1831[1]

3.1 Introduction

The seamen who travelled with Cochrane and arrived in Chile did so as individuals with their own diverse personal projects. All of them joined the navy for different reasons and had different destinies during the war for independence. Some died, others deserted; some went back home and others remained in Chile. None of them were representing others' interests. They travelled to Chile pursuing their own personal goals. This was not the case, however, of all the Britons who travelled to Chile in the period. Some individuals travelled because they were representing the interests of another group of individuals and not only their own personal projects. This was the case of the British Protestant societies that emerged in Britain from the late eighteenth century and sent agents and missionaries to different parts of the world. These societies embarked on what they saw as a global mission aimed at civilising the rest of the world. Some of them, like the British and Foreign Bible Society (BFBS) and the British and Foreign School Society (BFSS), reached South America and Chile when the struggles for independence were coming to an end. This chapter analyses the process of interaction and the exchange of ideas and practices between the agents of

---

1   I have expanded upon some of the ideas in this chapter in the following: Andrés Baeza, 'One Local Dimension of a Global Project: The Introduction of the Monitorial System of Education in Post-Independent Chile, 1821–1833', *Bulletin of Latin American Research*, 36:3 (2017) special issue: 'New Perspectives on Political Ideas and Practices in Post-Independence Chile (1818–1830)', ed. by Joanna Crow, 340–53; 'Educational Reform, Political Change, and Penury: Primary Schooling and the Monitorial System of Education in Chile, approx. 1810–1833', in *Classroom Struggle: Organizing Elementary School Teaching in the 19th Century*, ed. by Marcelo Caruso, Studia Educationis Historica, Vol. 2 (Frankfurt am Main: Peter Lang, 2015), pp. 67–90; 'Circulación de biblias protestantes y tolerancia religiosa en la América post-independiente: La mirada de Luke Matthews, un misionero protestante británico, 1826–1829', *Economía y Política*, 3:2 (2016), 5–35.

these societies who travelled to Chile in the 1820s and the Chileans who were involved in the construction of the new state.

The independence of Spanish America was seen as a new opportunity to expand the sphere of influence of these societies beyond the boundaries of the British Empire. A territory that had previously been ruled by the Spanish king and subject to the power of the Catholic Church was now regarded as a potential land for an evangelising mission. The more 'liberal' environment brought about by the new ruling elites and the supposed declining power of the Catholic Church in the new political context were seen as the main factors that would facilitate their mission. However, the reality that British Protestant missionaries found in Spanish America was much more complex. On the one hand, the Catholic Church still exerted a great degree of power and influence and many clergymen openly opposed the activities of these societies in Spanish America. Despite this, these societies were welcome and even 'invited' by the new ruling elites to provide knowledge and expertise in the organisation of the new states. This was particularly evident in the case of the BFSS, whose agent James Thomson was hired by many of the new Spanish Americans governments, including that of Chile, to reorganise the educational systems on the basis of the Monitorial system.[2] On the other hand, the Catholic clergy in Chile did not react as one against the presence of these missionaries. The agents of the BFBS, James Thomson and Luke Matthews, who were circulating the Protestant version of the Bible throughout Spanish America, were welcomed by many low-ranking priests, while sometimes being openly criticised by members of the high clergy. They were not seen as imperial agents, but the fact that they were Britons was sometimes problematic, since they were immediately identified as Protestants and heretics.

The new political authorities fostered the presence and activities of these societies. As shown in the previous chapter, perceptions of Britain had changed by the beginning of the 1820s. 'Britain' acquired a new meaning, becoming a land from which ideas and expertise could be taken. This was reinforced by the fact that Chile was ruled by O'Higgins, who had been educated in London. In addition, both Bibles and schools were lacking and needed, and British Protestant societies promised to provide them. Spanish American leaders considered it more urgent to reform the educational systems inherited from the colonial period rather than to distribute Bibles among the population. The new authorities thus welcomed James Thomson

2 I am using the term 'Monitorial' as it represents the main characteristics of this system: the use of 'monitors', who were also students, to collaborate with the teacher in the classroom. Notwithstanding, the system is also known as the 'Lancaster' system, after 'Bell-Lancaster', to emphasise that in spite of their differences both Lancaster and Bell are the authors of one single system, or simply the 'British system', to signal its origins. However, it is also common to use the term 'Mutual system' to stress the fact that students are taught by other students.

because he had the expertise necessary to organise the educational system, and not because he was selling Bibles.[3] This was more evident in Chile, where the power of the Catholic clergy was relatively strong. Education was in fact a matter of major concern, due to its close connection to the consolidation of the new political project, which was the creation of the republic. By means of education, the new republic would count on new citizens who were individuals responsible for their own destiny but with a clear commitment to the future of the entire community. The Monitorial system of education, designed by Joseph Lancaster and Andrew Bell, in Southwark and Madras respectively, provided a reasonable means to rapidly expand primary schooling at low cost. This system only required one teacher per school with the aid of many 'monitors' who delivered the lessons to the rest of the pupils. Besides these practical considerations, Chilean leaders were eager to adopt this system because it was the most common in what they called the 'civilised world'. Thus, Britain acquired a new meaning for Chileans. It became a sort of 'cultural model', which Chileans followed in reforming their educational system, although they adopted it to their local circumstances.[4] This is what scholars like Marcelo Caruso and Eugenia Roldán Vera have called a 'cultural approach', which emphasised the local conditions and the active role of the receptors of the system in its adoption and adaptation.[5] They have also made it clear that by adopting this system, Spanish America entered into a process of 'internationalisation', since this was the first 'global' educational system.[6]

The role of missionaries remains overlooked in the historiography, apart from some apologetic acknowledgement of James Thomson's role as the first colporteur in Spanish America and Chile, and the valuable contributions of Roldán Vera on his mission and of Racine on the commercial interests of the

3 The most well-known and quoted work on the adoption of this system in Chile is Domingo Amunátegui Solar, *El sistema de Lancaster en Chile i en otros países sudamericanos* (Santiago: Imprenta Cervantes, 1895); Webster Browning, 'Joseph Lancaster, James Thomson, and the Lancasterian System of Mutual Instruction, with Special Reference to Hispanic America', *Hispanic American Historical Review*, 4 (1921), 49–98.

4 The term 'cultural model' is used by Racine, 'This England and This Now', p. 423.

5 Marcelo Caruso and Eugenia Roldán Vera, 'Pluralizing Meanings: The Monitorial System of Education in Latin America in the Early Nineteenth Century', *Paedagogica Historica: International Journal of the History of Education*, 41:6 (2005), 645–54 (p. 651).

6 Eugenia Roldán Vera, 'Internacionalización pedagógica y comunicación en perspectiva histórica: La introducción del método de enseñanza mutua en Hispanoamérica independiente', in *Internacionalización. Políticas educativas y reflexión pedagógica en un medio global*, ed. by Marcelo Caruso and Heinz Elmar-Tenorth (Buenos Aires: Editorial Gránica, 2011), pp. 297–344.

BFBS in Spanish America.[7] Both Thomson and Matthews travelled across South America following different strategies and 'encountered' a reality that was much more diverse than most historians recognise.[8] As in the previous case study in chapter two, different types of encounters are analysed here. In most cases these were short-lived 'contacts', due to the nature of the missions, which consisted in visiting as many places as possible. 'Collisions' were less usual, but they were experienced when these missionaries faced criticism from their Catholic counterparts. 'Relationships' were the usual outcome of these interactions since the initial contacts were prolonged in time by means of the Bibles or schools they left whenever they passed. All of these factors also shed light on the changing nature of British-Chilean relations, which at this stage tended to be more fluid, fostering exchanges, flows and movements of peoples, goods and ideas.

The consequences of these interactions did not concern issues of national identity as discussed in other chapters. These encounters provided some of the means by which the new ruling elites began to construct the new nation state. The adoption of the Monitorial system of education, closely linked in the minds of its Chilean adopters to British industrial and imperial realities, was a fundamental step in the organisation of a national educational system. It provided a homogeneous system and method for every school in the country and was adapted to the local conditions of poverty and the centralised Chilean state. In addition, this system was employed to educate a certain type of new citizen, according to certain features defined by the ruling elite, like order, discipline and usefulness. These concerns also shaped debates around national identity and the role of schools in forging the new nation. Lastly, the adoption of the Monitorial system also influenced the way Chileans perceived their place in the world. The image of Chile as a marginal, poor but well-connected country in comparison to the richer area of Peru was highlighted by the Chilean authorities as they sought to convince British agents to travel to Chile to assist them.

7 See Arnoldo Canclini, *Diego Thomson: Apóstol de la enseñanza y distribución de la Biblia en América Latina y España* (Buenos Aires: Sociedad Bíblica Argentina, 1987); David Muñoz Condell, *La influencia de Diego Thompson en Bernardo O'Higgins* (Valparaíso: Editorial Alba, 2010); Eugenia Roldán Vera, 'Export as Import: James Thomson's Civilising Mission in South America, 1818–1825', in *Imported Modernity*, ed. by Caruso and Roldán Vera (Frankfurt: Peter Lang, 2007), pp. 231–76; Karen Racine, 'Commercial Christianity: The British and Foreign Bible Society's Interest in Spanish America, 1805–1830', in *Informal Empire in Latin America: Culture, Commerce and Capital*, ed. by Matthew Brown (Oxford: Blackwell Publishing, 2008), pp. 78–98.

8 Browning, pp. 49–98. Browning stressed the idea that Chile was mostly a strong Catholic society, whereas Villalobos et al. stressed that Chilean society was mostly republican and that the Catholic Church and the clergy was mainly monarchical and after independence had to forcibly 'fall back'. See Sergio Villalobos et al., *Historia de Chile* (Santiago: Editorial Universitaria, 1974), pp. 420–37.

3.2 British Missionary Culture and its Global Scope

The Spanish American struggles for independence took place while a new missionary culture was emerging in Great Britain. This missionary culture, which embraced different Protestant denominations such as Baptist, Methodist, Quaker and Anglican, was characterised by its expansion outside the borders of Great Britain.[9] Historians have largely debated the reasons for the flourishing of a number of missionary groups and societies during the years 1780–1830 in Great Britain, and their role in the expansion of the British Empire.[10] In the context of rapid urban growth caused by industrialisation, and the subsequent emergence of a pauperised population, which could easily be attracted by the spread of French revolutionary ideas, these groups sought to transmit specific notions of morality that would prevent any attempt to disrupt the social order. This explains the flourishing of a wide range of missionary groups willing to evangelise to this population. The expansion of this missionary culture had strong links to the period of expansion of the British Empire. This also implies thinking about the extent to which Protestant missionaries might be regarded as agents of the British informal empire. As demonstrated by Andrew Porter, these missionaries were not necessarily supporting Empire. Moreover, they could even transmit an anti-colonial message since their particular theologies were contrary to colonialism.[11] As suggested above, these missionaries were acting as 'non-state' actors, pursuing the interests and projects of particular evangelical societies, rather than the interests of the British state.

In 1804, one particular group that encompassed people from different non-conformist and Anglican groups established the BFBS.[12] For this society, the principal means of evangelisation was to 'encourage a wider circulation of the Holy Scriptures' and more specifically the version 'without annotations and comments'.[13] This obeyed a particular understanding of the relationship between God and mankind, in which nothing was more important than knowing the word of God without mediation. It was necessary to make the reading of the Bible an easy task to reinforce an individual engagement with

---

9 Alison Twells, *The Civilising Mission and the English Middle Class, 1792–1850: The 'Heathen' at Home and Overseas* (London: Palgrave Macmillan, 2009).

10 See Hilary M. Carey, *God's Empire: Religion and Colonialism in the British World, c. 1801–1908* (Cambridge: Cambridge University Press, 2011); Catherine Hall, *Civilising Subjects: Metropole and Colony in the English Imagination 1830–1867* (Chicago, IL and London: University of Chicago Press, 2002); Andrew Porter, *Religion versus Empire? British Protestant Missionaries and Overseas Expansion, 1700–1914* (Manchester: Manchester University Press, 2004).

11 Porter, pp. 325–27.

12 See its Constitution in BFSS, *First Report of the British and Foreign School Society to General Meeting* (London: J.B.G. Voguel, 1805), pp. 3–5.

13 BFBS, 'Laws and Regulations', Art. IX, *First Annual Report* (1805), p. 26.

it. That is why this society aimed to make the word of God available to all of the people in the vernacular languages of 'all the nations' of the earth. This was against the doctrines established in the Council of Trent (1545–1563), which were still valid in the Catholic world in the 1820s. These doctrines included the definition of the *Vulgate*[14] as the official version of the Bible, the inclusion of the so-called 'Apocrypha'[15] in the official text of the Bible and the prohibition of the translation of the Bible into vernacular languages to avoid any misinterpretation and 'indiscriminate reading' of the text by the common people.[16]

When the Protestant missionary Luke Matthews travelled across South America in 1826, he reported that several Catholic priests had one or more copies of Felipe Scio's version of the Bible.[17] This was an authorised translation of the Bible into Spanish, which also preserved the text in Latin, that circulated widely in Spanish America.[18] It was a hardbound, multivolume and non-portable edition. It was thus unusual to find a copy of Scio outside of a library or a church; it was an item that was difficult for the common people to access. James Thomson described the disadvantages of Scio's Bible as follows:

> Two translations of the Bible have been made in Spain, and both by royal authority. They are published with ample annotations in many quarto volumes, and accompanied with the Latin text of the Vulgate, from which the translations are both made. These expensive works of course would come into few hands, and hence the general ignorance of the holy book of inspiration, in the mother country and in the colonies.[19]

Thomson's testimony also shed light on one problem that made access to these Bibles even more difficult: their high cost. The BFBS aimed to simplify the reading of the Bible, not only by translating it into vernacular languages but also by taking out all the comments and annotations from the 'founding fathers' of the Catholic Church. In addition, they printed it in a

---

14 This was the version translated into Latin by St Jerome in the year 382.

15 These books are: 1 Esdras, 2 Esdras, Additions to Esther, 1 Maccabees, 2 Maccabees, Tobias, Judith, Wisdom, Sirach, Baruch, Epistle of Jeremiah, Susanna, Prayer of Azaria, Prayer of Manasseh, Bel and the Dragon, Laodiceans.

16 James Waterworth, *The Canons and Decrees of the Sacred and Oecumenical Council of Trent Celebrated under the Sovereign Pontiffs, Paul III, Julius III, and Pius IV* (London: Burns and Oates, 1888).

17 Luke Matthews to the BFBS, Valparaíso, 20 February 1827, BFBS, *Annual Reports* (1828), p. 105.

18 Phelipe Scio de San Miguel (Bishop of Segovia), *La Biblia vulgata latina, traducida en español y anotada conforme al sentido de los santos padres y expositores catholicos por Rmo P. Scio de San Miguel, de las escuelas pías, electo obispo de Segovia* (Madrid: Imprenta de Benito Cano, 1797).

19 James Thomson, 'South America. N° V', *Evangelical Christendom*, 1 (1847), pp. 316–18.

single-volume edition to make it portable and cheaper than the multivolume editions. None of these strategies would have made sense if the receptor of the Bible was unable to read it or, as a 'respectable Minister in Holland' wrote to the BFBS, was capable only of 'reading with understanding'.[20] It was also necessary, therefore, to ensure that those who received a copy of the Bible acquired this skill. This explains the close links between the BFBS and her 'sister society', the British and Foreign School Society (BFSS), founded by the English Quaker educator Joseph Lancaster in 1808 under the name Society for Spreading the Lancasterian System of Education among the Poor. It was renamed in 1814, when Lancaster was accused of erratic and irresponsible financial behaviour and expelled from the society.[21] This was the beginning of a particular project which, despite being successful within Britain and gaining support from the monarchy, gradually began to lose ground.

The BFSS aimed to spread Monitorial schools and, more generally, the Monitorial system of education, throughout the world. This system had been designed by Lancaster in Southwark, an industrial district of London, in the context of the social changes arising from the Industrial Revolution. Lancaster was concerned about the number of impoverished and unoccupied children and youth in the streets who might potentially become delinquents. The use of the term 'system' was not insignificant. In effect, Joseph Lancaster designed a coherent set of ideas and practices to be implemented not only within a particular school, but also the entire educational system.[22] All of his ideas had been systematised in brief, clear and well-written manuals and pamphlets, which were often revised and re-edited by him. Yet Lancaster was not the only one involved in the design of the Monitorial system of education. Before he published his manual in 1803, another Briton, Rev. Andrew Bell, had published another crucial textbook in 1797, in which he explained a teaching method he had designed while in Madras.[23] This led to a controversy about who was the genuine creator of the Monitorial system, although Lancaster himself stated that he had been inspired by Bell's ideas. In addition, in 1811 Bell and his followers established another society in London, the National Society for the Education of the Poor (NSE), to spread Bell's variant of the Monitorial system.[24]

20 BFBS, *First Annual Report* (1805), pp. 42–43.
21 Carl F. Kaestle, *Joseph Lancaster and the Monitorial School Movement: A Documentary History* (New York: Teachers College Press, 1973), pp. 131–34.
22 Paul Sedra, 'Exposure to the Eyes of God: Monitorial Schools and Evangelicals in Early Nineteenth-century England', *Paedagogica Historica: International Journal of the History of Education*, 47:3 (2011), 263–81 (pp. 271–73).
23 See Andrew Bell, *An Experiment in Education Made at the Male Asylum in Madras. Suggesting a System by Which a School or Family May Teach Itself under the Superintendence of the Master or the Parent* (London: Cadell and Davies, 1797).
24 Kaestle, pp. 1–53.

In simple terms, the Monitorial school, in both its versions, aimed to teach reading, writing and arithmetic to a large group of up to one thousand children – in the Lancasterian variant, under the supervision of a single teacher aided by a group of monitors.[25] These monitors were chosen from amongst the most advanced pupils and were in charge of delivering lessons that the master had taught them in advance. In Lancaster's version, the school was organised as a sort of regiment in which the master acquired the role of the commander-in-chief, the monitors were the officers and the pupils were the troops. Every movement, every instruction was codified so that nobody talked or did more than was strictly necessary. The Monitorial school used the Bible – or a selection of passages – as the core textbook in the classroom. Lancaster, a Quaker himself, strongly believed that the correct approach to the Scriptures was an individual practice that required no mediation. He stated that 'it is an inviolable law to teach nothing but what is the standard of belief to all Christians, *the Scriptures themselves*'.[26] In his school, pupils had to read the Bible, but they had no religious lessons, and children from all denominations were equally accepted. Therefore, it was a non-confessional school and there was no room to incorporate practices from any particular denomination. In Lancaster's words, 'education ought not to be made subservient to the propagation of the peculiar tenets of any sect'.[27] In turn, Anglicanism occupied a central place in Andrew Bell's curriculum, and therefore specific lessons on religious doctrine were incorporated. This eventually led to the NSE receiving the official support of both the Church and the monarchy during the 1810s in England. Lancaster, who had initially rapidly and successfully expanded his system within Britain, began to lose ground to his rivals. This explains why the BFSS privileged a more overseas-oriented policy, extending its operations to all the continents up to 1820, including Spanish America.[28] This also reveals why in this particular case, the projects of the BFSS and the BFBS did not form part of an imperial project. Indeed, they had to look for opportunities outside the boundaries of the British Empire.

The BFSS and the BFBS formed part of the same evangelical project and together expanded their activities throughout the world. If the BFBS provided

---

25 Joseph Lancaster revised the editions of his works many times. In the third edition of his *Improvements* he claimed that a Lancasterian school could easily take in up to one thousand pupils. See Joseph Lancaster, *Improvements in Education; Abridged. Containing a Complete Epitome of the System of Education Invented and Practiced by the Author*, 3rd ed. (London: Free School, Borough Road, 1808), p. vii.

26 Joseph Lancaster, *Report of J. Lancaster's Progress from the Year 1798, with the Report of the Finance Committee for the Year 1810. To Which Is Prefixed an Address of the Committee for Promoting the Royal Lancasterian System for the Education of the Poor* (London: Royal Free School Press, 1811), p. v.

27 Lancaster, *Improvements in Education*, p. 1.

28 Kaestle, pp. 1–53.

the message for the evangelical mission, that is, the word of God printed in the Scriptures, the BFSS provided the 'means of instruction'.[29] Whenever a Monitorial school was established, an agent of the BFBS – if it was not the same person – would turn up to supply the Bibles and New Testaments to be used as textbooks. Insofar as pupils were learning to read by means of Bibles, they would receive the essentials of the word of God, rather than a set of doctrines defined beforehand by the Church and expressed in the annotations and comments on the Scriptures.[30] This approach was known as 'Scriptural education', that is, 'the promotion of general education [...] as a means to introduce the literacy that would make the reading of the Scriptures possible'.[31] This was the core element of the 'civilising' project of both societies, expressed in the conjunction of two intertwined aims: evangelisation and education. This also reveals that in spite of not being formally linked to British imperial projects, these societies also promoted a 'civilisational' discourse to legitimise their activities. Such a discourse was an essential part of the rationale of the expansion of the British Empire, which means that to some extent it was natural for Chileans to identify the British Protestant missionaries with the British imperial project. One particular missionary, the Scottish Baptist James Thomson, agent of both the BFSS and the BFBS, played a fundamental role in the diffusion of this mission in Spanish America.

3.3 A Land of Opportunities: Spanish America in the Independence Era

The context in which British Protestant missionaries found themselves in Spanish America and Chile was not uniformly 'Catholic'. There were liberals and freemasons, and also Catholics who were liberal, among the ruling elites who were much more open to religious tolerance than the clergy, as well as indigenous peoples seen as on the margins of institutionalised religion. The liberal elite, particularly in Chile, configured its own 'civilising' project, in which education was the keystone because of its potential to shape the new citizen that was the intended result. This is why they found the Monitorial system of education so useful and encouraged its implementation across the country. Moreover, this is why the new leaders like O'Higgins 'invited' missionaries like James Thomson to their countries despite him being Protestant. As shown in other chapters, regardless of their confession, Britons were praised as having knowledge and expertise that might be useful in the construction and consolidation of the new state.

This new educational model had been designed to produce disciplined and orderly children in the context of the Industrial Revolution, and aimed to educate the new labourers. The liberal ruling elite in Chile shared a common

---

29 BFSS, *Sixteenth Report of the British and Foreign School Society to the General Committee* (London: J.V.G. Vogel, 1821), p. 3.

30 Sedra, pp. 274–75.

31 Roldán Vera, 'Export as Import', p. 240.

conception with the designers of this system regarding 'order' and 'discipline', in a period of uncertainty after the struggles for independence which was common to all Spanish America.[32] Fears of social distress, the continuation of a form of guerrilla war in southern Chile and the danger represented by the many unoccupied soldiers after the war were crucial factors in explaining such fears. Spreading a universal educational system that offered to both 'moralise' (through the reading of the Bible) and 'discipline' the children (through a military organisation of the school) was seen as a means to accomplish the elite's own civilising project. This also implies that civilising discourses were not exclusively a manifestation of imperial expansion, but also the expression of a new political project in a former colony which bore many points in common with the Protestant global mission. Therefore, any attacks on the exporters of the Monitorial system of education and the Protestant version of the Bible were made on the grounds of them being representatives of another, rival confession, rather than on their belonging to the British Empire.

Upon James Thomson's arrival in South America in 1818, there were already some newly independent states, like the United Provinces of La Plata and Chile, whose leaders were willing to rebuild their old educational systems. There was a clear awareness of the importance of education for both economic progress and political stability, and it became evident that the old colonial system did not fit into the new political context.[33] Moreover, this old educational system was blamed for the state of ignorance of the population, which allegedly led to the economic backwardness of the old Spanish colonies, as shown in a statement by the Chilean Senate in 1819:

A farrago of absurd opinions, false ideas, vain words, preoccupations and mistakes was brought to us as science. Not only was the freedom of the press denied to us, but also the printing of books about America without authorisation from Spain; not only were the Economic Societies and lectures in mathematics, chemistry and public law forbidden, but we were even recently insulted by His Majesty, who added that popular instruction in America was inconvenient.[34]

This reveals that the Chilean state, by means of its representative bodies, was directly involved in the adoption of foreign ideas to be used in the

---

32 See Richard Graham, *Independence in Latin America: Contrasts and Comparisons* (Austin, TX: University of Texas Press, 2013), pp. 145–49; Marcelo Caruso, 'Latin American Independence: Education and the Invention of New Polities', *Paedagogica Historica: International Journal of the History of Education*, 46: 4 (2010), pp. 414–15.

33 See Caruso, 'Latin American Independence', pp. 412–13; Gregorio Weinberg, *Modelos educativos en la historia de América Latina* (Buenos Aires: Kapelusz and Unesco-Cepal-Pnud, 1984), pp. 90–111.

34 'Proclama del Senado Conservador a los padres de familia', 3 July 1819, *Gaceta Ministerial de Chile*, p. 99.

structuring of the new education system. However, the war for independence was not finished and most of the country's resources were spent on funding armies – and navies – rather than schools. In Chile, the organisation of the Liberating Expedition of Peru had been an expensive undertaking for the state and a loan from London was necessary to cover part of the costs of the war.[35] Something similar happened in Colombia, whose leader Simón Bolívar had also organised a Liberation Army. In this context of scarcity, the Monitorial system of education, which was low-cost since it needed only one teacher per school, seemed suitable for reforming and reorganising the old educational systems without representing a burden for the state. However, as I show in this chapter, there were also other reasons involved.

In Chile, for some intellectual leaders, educational reform was a powerful, if not the decisive tool for social transformation. The need to reform the educational system inherited from the colonial era was amply debated as early as 1810 by intellectuals like Camilo Henríquez, Juan Egaña and Manuel de Salas. The outcome was the merger of the old colonial elite's educational institutions into a new one, the *Instituto Nacional literario, económico, civil i eclesiástico del Estado* – simply known as the Instituto Nacional – inaugurated in August 1813. Such an institution was unprecedented in Spanish America. Firstly, because it was created during the independence process and not in the aftermath, and secondly, because in all the other countries the abolition of the colonial schools, colleges and universities and the funding of new ones took longer. When Thomson arrived in Chile the Instituto had just been reinaugurated after its closure during the Spanish restoration (1814–1817), and preserved the same regulations (*Ordenanzas*) with which it had been inaugurated in 1813. This meant that the Instituto was the leading and model educational institution in Chile, and its board was the main educational body of the country. Moreover, it was conceived as the cornerstone of the new republican educational project, and any decision made within the Instituto affected the whole system. Primary education policies, such as the adoption of the Monitorial system of education, would need to be decided within this institution first.[36] This confirms what João Paulo Pimenta has said regarding the role of the existent educational institutions in Spanish America in implementing new educational methods. For Pimenta, 'they were responsible for setting up a scenario of active educational practices which involved diverse agents and social strata, and which were articulated with other less formalised spaces of teaching and learning'.[37] As an institution of the Chilean state, the

---

35   The loan was granted by the London-based firm Hullet Brothers and Company. See Somarriva, Chapter 4, pp. 133–43.

36   See Raúl Silva Castro, *La fundación del Instituto Nacional, 1810–1813* (Santiago: Imprenta Universitaria, 1953), pp. 5–33.

37   João Paulo Pimenta, 'Education and the Historiography of Ibero-American Independence: Elusive Presences, Many Absences', *Paedagogica Historica: International Journal of the History of Education*, 46:4 (2010), 419–34 (p. 421).

Instituto Nacional was actively involved in the adoption and adaptation of foreign ideas and practices in the field of education.

From the perspective of both the BFBS and the BFSS, the situation of Spanish America, still struggling for independence, offered an attractive opportunity to expand their operations. Spanish America was an unexplored world, with more than a million people to be evangelised – who were also seen as potential Bible buyers. Quoting an agent of the American Bible Society (ABS) who travelled across South America in 1824, the BFBS stressed the importance of its mission in the continent: 'What do we behold! What do we behold, calculated to interest this noble Society? We behold, Sir, 15 millions of human beings – beings, too, professedly Christians, believing in Revelation, baptised in the name of the Trinity, and yet almost entirely without the Bible!'[38] The BFBS and the BFSS both saw Spanish America as a 'new market', following the assertions of scholars like Roldán Vera and Somarriva regarding the way Britons envisaged Spanish America during and after independence.[39] Since Spanish American homes lacked Bibles and given that the population was eminently Catholic, it was feasible to believe that they wanted to purchase a copy of the sacred text. In the eyes of the BFBS, the new political context would enable the spreading of the Bible more easily than during the colonial era.

The BFBS had hopes that the new liberal political elites would be more receptive to its mission. The same aforementioned ABS agent, quoted in the BFBS reports, said that 'the Bible was no longer excluded by Royal mandates and Papal bulls; the houses of the Inquisition had lost their territories, for they had been converted into public buildings and schools where the Bible itself might be read daily'.[40] Therefore, the belief that a mostly Catholic population would necessarily want personal copies of the Bible, plus the allegedly more permissive attitude to the circulation of texts than in previous years, were two key elements of the BFBS's expectations of success in the continent. Yet this assumption was too simple since, as Karen Racine has pointed out, some of the difficulties experienced by the BFBS in Spanish America arose because 'they were Christians evangelizing other Christians'.[41]

Knowledge about the Spanish American context was also the result of a series of communications between the agents of both London-based societies and their committees. Information sent by agents like James Thomson and Luke Matthews, who travelled across South America, John Armstrong, who

---

38 Quoted in William Canton, *A History of the British and Foreign Bible Society*, Vol. 2 (London: John Murray, 1904), pp. 86–87.

39 Eugenia Roldán Vera, *The British Book Trade and Spanish American Independence: Education and Knowledge Transmission in Transcontinental Perspective* (Aldershot: Ashgate, 2003), pp. 45–47; Somarriva, especially Chapter 1, 'A New World, a New Market: British Visions on the Southern Cone, 1808–1820', pp. 15–43.

40 Quoted in Canton, p. 87.

41 Racine, 'Commercial Christianity', pp. 78–98.

was settled in Buenos Aires, and by agents from other societies, was crucial in reinforcing the need for their missions. Their views on this last point diverged, a point that historians have overlooked and which had crucial repercussions for the way these societies worked. Thomson, for example, had a clear tendency to emphasise the wish of Spanish Americans to be educated and to get access to Scripture. As he wrote in a letter, 'there is in South America generally, I believe, a great desire for the increase of knowledge'.[42] For him, Spanish Americans were themselves keen to do whatever necessary to emerge from the darkness and to overcome their alleged state of ignorance. In an article, he expressed his satisfaction in this interest in being educated:

> I have had intercourse with all classes of society there, and through repeated conversations and otherwise, have come, I think, to understand what are the actual feelings and desires of the people upon this point. I have no hesitation in saying that the public voice is decidedly in favour of UNIVERSAL EDUCATION. I never heard even once, what is still to be heard elsewhere, 'that the poor should not be taught'. The very opposite feeling most undoubtedly exists, and prevails among the clergy and the laity, the governors and the governed.[43]

Luke Matthews was more critical of the condition of the Spanish American population, although his view was directed at what he called the 'lower classes' of society. In his reports he stressed their 'miserable condition' and their state of ignorance, which also explained the extended general indifference and lack of interest in his mission. This was particularly true in Chile, in places like Coquimbo and Quillota, where he identified 'very few respectable or educated people'.[44] This shows that despite representing the same society, these agents differed in their perceptions about the reality they were interacting with. Eventually, this led them to follow different strategies, as shown in the next section.

However, Thomson and Matthews shared a common perception about the origins of the condition of Spanish American society: the undisputed influence of the Catholic Church upon social life and its control over the education of the population. Matthews, for example, wrote that:

> such is the influence of the Catholic religion where it exists, as here, in the depth of its delusion and darkness, in extinguishing rational reflexion, in limiting all interest as it regards religion to its various ceremonies and observances, and producing perfect satisfaction and immovable self confidence in the performance of its outward rites and assent to its

---

42 James Thomson, *Letters on the Moral and Religious State of South America Written During a Residence of Nearly Seven Years in Buenos Aires, Chile, Perú and Colombia* (London: James Nisbet, 1827), p. 31.

43 Ibid., p. 291.

44 Luke Matthews, Coquimbo, 9 March 1827, BFBS, *Annual Report* (1827), p. 107.

unexamined and peculiar dogmas, that scarce any impression has been made.[45]

This was the main argument to justify the landing of both missionary societies in Spanish America, the necessity of helping its inhabitants to break free from such cultural dominion. In one of its reports, the BFSS stated that 'from that interesting region of the earth, the stain of civil despotism is at length happily cleansed away; and it may be confidently hoped that the diffusion of the sacred writings will, by the blessing of God, achieve that moral emancipation which ever accompanies true piety'.[46] It is not surprising, then, that the motives stated to explain why they must intervene in Spanish America were theological, as if they were accomplishing a divine mission, which consisted in liberating Spanish Americans from the 'oppression' of the Catholic Church. Beyond these shared motivations, however, missionaries mostly behaved as individuals guided by their own perceptions of the places they visited and the ways in which they understood this transcendental mission.

3.4 One Mission, Diverse Strategies: British Protestant Missionaries and Educators in Chile

The existence of a strong Catholic society, along with a powerful clergy, prevented Spanish Americans from being greatly influenced by these missionaries. Authors like David Muñoz Condell have claimed that there was a binary opposition between Catholics and Protestants.[47] However, testimonies suggest that these missionaries found a more tolerant society than they expected, even within the clergy. The very presence of these missionaries also fostered greater toleration of foreign people and ideas in a context in which Britons were identified as 'infidels'. In any case, and in spite of such tolerance, complaints about indifference towards their religious project were common in the missionaries' correspondence. However, according to the same sources, they found much more enthusiasm, especially Matthews, in the 'low clergy' based in isolated towns and villages. In many of these, as shown in this section, there were no Bibles at all and the presence of these missionaries was seen as a practical solution. When these missionaries presented themselves as educators, enthusiasm was more general. Spanish Americans, and particularly Chileans, seemed much more interested in the educational project these missionaries were spreading than in the diffusion of Bibles. This explains why they were ultimately more successful in spreading and establishing Monitorial schools than in selling Bibles.

---

45 Luke Matthews, Cordova, 5 December, 1826, BFBS Archive, Brunel University Archives, BSA/DI/2.
46 BFSS, *Annual Reports* (1826), p. 26.
47 Muñoz Condell, pp. 47–62.

The activities of the BFBS and the BFSS in Spanish America during the independence era were carried out by different agents. James Thomson and John Armstrong were agents of both societies and Luke Matthews was an agent only of the BFBS. Both Thomson and Matthews travelled across South America. Thomson travelled between 1818 and 1825 in the current territories of Uruguay, Argentina, Chile, Peru, Ecuador and Colombia. Matthews was commissioned to follow Thomson's route in 1826, although he had visited more places by his death in 1829. Besides the aforementioned territories, he also visited what is now Bolivia and made a brief stop in Brazil at the beginning of his journey, although this was not part of his plan. Armstrong, who had spent 12 years in Honduras, became an agent of the BFBS in 1824 (although he also corresponded with the BFSS), but remained settled in Buenos Aires. He was designated chaplain of the British community based in that city and the BFBS agreed to keep him as its agent.[48]

Prior to this, there is little knowledge of the activities of these societies in Spanish America and Chile. Early in 1807 the first agent, David Hill Creighton, was sent to Buenos Aires by the London Missionary Society with 600 copies of the Bible.[49] At that time, the BFBS circulated Bibles and New Testaments by means of several soldiers, seamen and merchants who travelled to Spanish America, rather than through its own agents. A clear example was John James Barnard, mentioned in chapters 1 and 4, who in the 1820s would become one of the most important British merchants in that area. Between 1813 and 1826 he corresponded with the BFBS about the distribution of Bibles in Chile. In his first letter, dated 2 August 1813, he wrote to Samuel Mills, member of the BFBS Committee, to request 'a small quantity not exceeding 150 or 200' Bibles to be distributed in this country after getting news that 'a few Spanish Testaments' had already been distributed and 'received with eagerness'.[50] This shows that there were already copies circulating in Chile before he started to act as an agent of the BFBS. Barnard's correspondence was limited to reporting his efforts to sell Bibles and he said little on any other subject. Despite this, these letters prove that even before the opening of trade between Great Britain and Chile, and the emergence of the more liberal environment of the 1820s, the BFBS had managed to put into circulation some of their Bibles and New Testaments. This has not been explored by historians, however, who often focus on the processes unfolding during the 1820s, that is, once independence was achieved.[51]

---

48 BFBS, *Annual Reports* (1825), p. liv.

49 Justice C. Anderson, *An Evangelical Saga: Baptists and their Precursors in Latin America* (Maitland, FL: Xulon Press, 2005), pp. 29–30.

50 J.J. Barnard to Samuel Mills, 2 August 1813, BFBS Archive, Foreign Correspondence Inwards, Rev. J.J. Barnard, Cambridge University Library. BSA/1/2.

51 An exception to this is Karen Racine, who reported the early circulation of Bibles throughout Spanish America, including Chile in the 1810s, although she does not

In contrast, there is no news about any activity of the BFSS in Spanish America before the arrival of Thomson, although it has been said that the school established by the military leader José Artigas in Montevideo (1815), the Escuela de la Patria, was the first one to use the Monitorial method in Spanish America.[52] In Chile, the first attempt to use this system was made in the primary school adjoined to the Instituto Nacional in 1818. Its rector, the Catholic priest Manuel José Verdugo, had received a copy of one of Lancaster's manuals from Antonio Alvarez Jonte and designated Pedro Nolasco to take responsibility for its implementation. However, the need to search for someone experienced in the system, so as to implement it in Chile in accordance with the original model, became evident.[53] This is where the figure of James Thomson emerged, and yet he was not the first to be considered for this responsibility. Antonio Irisarri, envoy of Chile in London, had made contact with the headquarters of the BFSS and visited Borough Road School in September 1820. The nature of this relationship is significant, as it reveals the importance that the Chilean government placed in the appointment of someone with expertise in the Monitorial system: an agent of the Chilean state was directly involved in Thomson's recruitment.

According to his report to the Chilean government, there were many teachers interested in going to Chile, but all of them demanded conditions 'that obliged me to make payments which my pecuniary condition did not allow me to do'. The BFSS then suggested the name of Antony Eaton, whose terms were 'pretty moderate'.[54] Irisarri and Eaton signed a contract according to which the latter would travel to Chile in November 1820 and be paid 500 pesos a year. In the same report, Irisarri said that he had been informed that 'in Buenos Aires a school under this method has already been established'. He did not know, however, whether the person in charge of this school was an experienced teacher, or if he was, he might find 'one thousand problems to go to Chile'. That is why he considered it much better to send someone from London 'straight [to Chile] to teach to others'.[55] Although apparently Irisarri did not know it, James Thomson was such a person. He had arrived in Buenos Aires in October 1818 as part of his own missionary project. Minister Echeverría did seem to have considered Eaton's conditions too expensive though, since in his reply to Irisarri he stressed the need to 'reconcile this appointment with the scarcity of our public funds'. This is why he suggested the appointment of Eaton, but under the following conditions:

mention the particular case of Barnard. See Racine, 'Commercial Christianity', pp. 84–85.

52 Caruso and Roldán Vera, 'Pluralizing Meanings', p. 651.
53 Amunátegui, *El Sistema de Lancaster*, pp. 15–16.
54 'Irisarri to Echeverría', London, 13 September 1820, *ABO*, vol. 3, pp. 189–90.
55 Ibid.

Should the capital of Peru be free soon, and being rich, populous and enlightened, the one who went there to teach the mentioned method might be provided with great benefits. With this capital [Santiago] being a pathway to that one [Lima], he could stay here [in Chile] one year or less while Peru is being pacified, going there at the government's recommendation and expense, teaching the method in the meantime.[56]

Peru was presented as wealthier, more populated and even more enlightened than Chile, which was relegated to a marginal position. Rather than promoting the attractiveness of their country, the Chilean authorities highlighted its geographical position as a 'pathway' to the richer territory of Peru. Chile was regarded as a pathway to other markets rather than as a market itself. Thus, the Chilean case at least did not entirely fit the definition of a 'new market' as stated by Somarriva and Roldán Vera when referring to the Southern Cone (which included Argentina) and Spanish America in general.[57] The appointment was a good opportunity for Eaton, therefore, to spend a brief period in Chile and then go to Peru. Yet this strategy was not unusual. As I showed in the previous chapters, a negative image had already been used defensively in the colonial period. Since Chile could not count on an army to defend its coasts from pirates and privateers, locals used to publicise the poverty of the country to make it an unattractive target. This approach was also used to prevent an attack by Great Britain after the invasion of Buenos Aires, which means that it was already usual to stress that in Chile there was nothing worth considering, beyond its strategic position on the map. Craufurd's plan to invade Chile did not praise it as an attractive destination in itself, but as a key point for establishing a trade route between Buenos Aires and Peru. In this case, that attractiveness consisted of the riches of Peru and the fact that it would be easy to get there from Chile once liberation had been completed.

Despite Eaton's hiring as the official agent of the BFSS in Chile, his trip suffered a delay and he could not depart on time. In the meantime, the Chilean envoy in Buenos Aires informed the government that a trained agent from the BFSS, James Thomson, had established some schools and was willing to go to Chile if the government requested his services.[58] Zañartu also stressed the 'promising benefits from the opening of Peru',[59] to convince Thomson and hoped that 'for less than one thousand pesos per annum, he will introduce the method in all of the towns of that state'.[60] It was agreed that

---

56 'Joaquín Echeverría to Antonio Irisarri', Santiago, 5 December 1820, *ABO*, vol. 3, p. 131.

57 Somarriva, pp. 15–16; Roldán Vera, *The British Book Trade*, pp. 45–47.

58 Miguel Zañartu to Joaquín Echeverría, Buenos Aires, 1 January 1821, *ABO*, ed. by Archivo Nacional de Chile, Vol. 5 (Santiago: Imprenta Universitaria, 1949), pp. 225–26.

59 Ibid.

60 Ibid.

Thomson would travel in February 1821, but it was not until July 1821 that he eventually arrived in Chile, taking office as Director of Public Education. Eaton arrived only a few weeks after Thomson and became his subordinate. He was commissioned to organise a Monitorial school in Concepción, but eventually had to remain in Santiago, replacing Thomson when he went to Mendoza. There is also information confirming that Eaton was appointed as the English teacher of the Instituto Nacional.[61]

Beyond their roles in establishing Monitorial schools, there are some differences between the two educators, which allow for a better understanding of their roles in Chile. Eaton was hired by Irisarri in London and was exclusively appointed to establish schools under the Monitorial system of education. His knowledge of the Spanish language was the main reason the Chilean government appointed him.[62] In fact, that was the only actual reason the BFBS recommended his appointment, since he was not an 'expert' in the system. The Chilean government had to pay the costs of his training in the Monitorial system at Borough Road School, which shows the extent to which the Chilean authorities were interested in adopting this system.[63] No other Spanish American government had searched for an agent of the BFSS in London, although some Spanish Americans, like Simón Bolívar himself, at least toured Borough Road School.[64] The case of Thomson is different, which confirms the interpretation advanced here that, in spite of being agents of the same society, their interactions with locals were determined by the way they perceived their own role as individuals. Thomson had embarked on his own personal project, which went beyond the establishment of Monitorial schools. Despite claiming that this was his main mission in South America, he perceived himself as a missionary who was evangelising and civilising Spanish Americans by means of schools and Bibles. Unlike Eaton, Thomson travelled to South America as a missionary, not only as an educator. He was carrying out a transcendental mission, as he wrote in a letter to the BFSS: 'I have resolved in the name and strength of the Almighty, in whom I trust through Christ Jesus, I have resolved to spend that life which he gave, so long as he shall please to continue it, in his great and good work in South America'.[65] In this mission, Chile was not a destination in itself, apart from being a 'step forward' on his plan to 'see all South America if practicable'.[66]

61 'Manuel José Verdugo to Echeverría', Santiago, 7 March 1822, Archivo Nacional Histórico de Chile, Fondo Ministerio del Interior (ANH-MI), vol. 52, fol. 39.

62 'Irisarri to Echeverría', London, 13 September 1820, *ABO*, vol. 3, pp. 189–90.

63 'Expediente de contratación de Antony Eaton', September 1820, Archivo Nacional Fondo Sergio Fernández Larraín (ANH-SFL), vol. 42, piece 42.

64 Racine, 'This England and This Now', p. 438.

65 'James Thomson to Millar', Santiago, 26 February 1822, BFSS, Foreign Correspondence, File: Chile, n.fol.

66 'Thomson to Millar', Santiago, 6 August 1821, BFSS, *Annual Reports*, 17 (1822), p. 123.

Thomson was quite careful about portraying himself as a missionary whose main purpose was the distribution of Bibles and New Testaments. In a letter to the BFBS agent he wrote, 'the little influence I have thus acquired and the confidence reposed in me [as a BFSS agent], enable me more effectually to promote the circulation of the Scriptures, than if I acted ostensibly and exclusively as your agent'.[67] Thus, in some parts of South America – specifically Chile – it was easier for him to say that he was arriving in the territory to establish primary schools than that he was selling Bibles. However, he later wrote that when he arrived in Buenos Aires, 'he was agreeably surprised to find a greater degree of liberality than he had anticipated'. Then he wrote something similar about Chile, where 'the Scriptures were admitted, and had a similar unobstructed circulation'.[68] In other countries, like Colombia, this seemed not to be a problem and he even founded a Bible Society in Bogotá in 1825, with the collaboration of Pedro Gual, who became its president, and some members of the local Church hierarchy.[69]

The relevance of Thomson's role as an educator, especially in Chile, led local authorities to grant him Chilean citizenship, putting him at the same level as Thomas Cochrane, who as the commander of the newly created navy had also been honoured with citizenship. This reveals not only the importance assigned to education, but the capacity of Thomson to construct networks amongst the political elites. Compared to other missionaries like Luke Matthews, he met several key political figures of the period, such as José de San Martín, Bernardo O'Higgins, Bernardino Rivadavia, Pedro Gual and Simón Bolívar, and managed to expand his networks amongst the elites in the main cities of the continent.[70] These connections even made possible for him to discuss some plans that went beyond his Protestant mission. In Chile he proposed to O'Higgins in 1822 to attract and settle skilled artisans, merchants and peasants from Britain and Switzerland to Chile. This led to the Franciscan Friar Joseph Xavier de Guzmán to write a report opposing such plan on the grounds that it would be a threat to the religious unity of Chile and demanding the government the due protection of the Catholic religion.[71]

Such a strategy was also an expression of Thomson's 'top-down' approach to his civilising mission, which was not entirely consistent with the ideas of the societies he was representing. These societies were much more concerned about the universal diffusion of Scriptural knowledge and education, especially amongst the poor, as shown by Roldán Vera.[72] In Thomson's view, however,

67 'Thomson to Owen, Santiago', 8 October 1821, *Letters*, pp. 14–21.
68 James Thomson, 'South America V', *Evangelical Christendom*, 1 (October 1847), 316–18.
69 'Thomson to the BFBS', Bogotá, 5 April 1825, *Letters*, pp. 252–61.
70 James Thomson, 'Report to the British and Foreign Bible Society', London, 25 May 1826, *Letters*, pp. 266–96.
71 See Muñoz Condell, pp. 89–97.
72 Roldán Vera, 'Export as Import', pp. 231–76.

it was more effective to prioritise the education of the elites so that they could disseminate their knowledge to the rest of the population. This emphasis on the elite's education (and evangelisation) has not been considered by Roldán Vera, who was more concerned about the way Thomson carried out the BFBS and BFSS missions than his own perceptions of it.[73] In a letter Thomson stated that 'the more the higher classes are instructed, and rightly instructed, the more will the lower classes seek after knowledge'.[74] The basis of this assumption was his belief that 'knowledge is power', which would lead those who were at the bottom of the social structure to seek knowledge if they wanted to ascend to the top. Therefore, for Thomson it was not necessary to visit every single town or village in each territory, but only the most important cities in order to obtain the support of the local elites. In Chile, he even said that his purpose was 'to promote as far as I am able, the education of the higher classes in this country'.[75] The foundation of both Bible and Lancasterian societies in places like Colombia and Chile, which were formed by politicians and clerks, was also an expression of this view. This conception, prioritising the education of the elites, would fit perfectly into the conception of the Chilean authorities regarding the role of the Instituto Nacional in leading the elite's education. The consequences of this are discussed in the following section.

Luke Matthews, the BFBS missionary who travelled across South America between 1826 and 1829, had a different approach. We know little about Matthews's life (apart from his journey to South America), but we know more about his death. His activities in Spanish America have only been mentioned by historians of Protestantism, but without any thorough analysis of his interactions with locals or his own perception of his mission.[76] He died in January 1829, presumably murdered, on his way from Bogotá to Mompox in Colombia.[77] He has thus been praised as the first Protestant 'martyr' in Latin America.[78] His journey started in Buenos Aires on 30 October 1826 and his instructions stated that he had to circulate Bibles and New Testaments in all the towns between Buenos Aires and Chile. Once in Peru, he had to follow the steps taken by Thomson between Lima and Bogotá a couple of years before.[79] The first contrast with Thomson is Matthews's level of engagement, visiting every single village or town he

73 Ibid.
74 'Thomson to Millar', Santiago, 26 February 1822, BFSS Archive, Foreign Correspondence, Chile, n.fol.
75 Ibid.
76 Arnaldo Canclini, *La Biblia en Argentina. Su distribución e influencia hasta 1853* (Buenos Aires: Asociación Sociedad Bíblica Argentina, 1987); Canclini, *Diego Thompson*; Justice C. Anderson, *An Evangelical Saga*.
77 BFBS, *Annual Reports* (1830), p. lxxxi; and (1831), pp. lii–liii.
78 Anderson, pp. 57–58.
79 BFBS, *Annual Reports* (1827), pp. lxv–lxvi.

found during his travels. Whereas Thomson focused his mission on cities like Buenos Aires, Lima and Bogotá, Matthews visited towns like Salta, Mendoza (Argentina), Quillota, Rancagua (Chile), Puno, Chucuito (Peru), Tupiza and Cotagaita (Bolivia), and many unnamed villages (see Map 2). One of the last people that Matthews met before his departure from Bogotá, the British consul James Henderson, said that 'he was very desirous that the Bible should be put into circulation by any quiet means, notwithstanding obstacles thrown in the way'.[80] As a result, he had closer relations with the 'lower clergy' than Thomson, who mostly established relations with the main urban authorities, including the 'higher clergy'. This contrast has also been overlooked by historians, who have dealt with Protestant missionary activities in Spanish America.[81]

Matthews faced many more obstacles than Thomson. He travelled to South America with the exclusive mission of circulating Bibles and New Testaments, which aroused little interest in the political leaders of independence, in contrast to the much more pressing need to reform education. Matthews's reports show little enthusiasm for his mission and he complained about indifference in some places like Coquimbo, where he perceived that 'the apathy of the people precluded every hope of doing anything among them'.[82] In addition, in contrast to Thomson, the date of Matthews's arrival also had a negative impact on his journey. In October 1824 Pope Leo XII published an encyclical titled *Urbi Primum* in which he condemned the translation of the Bible into vernacular tongues and, more specifically, blamed the BFBS for turning the Scriptures into a 'gospel of man' and, even worse, a 'gospel of the devil'.[83] Despite Matthews not reporting any mention by the clergy of this encyclical, it is plausible that it played a role in the animosity he found in Spanish America. Also, in 1825 the BFBS decided to withdraw the Apocrypha from the edition of the Bible to be circulated. From a Catholic perspective this was a serious problem, since it was against the stipulations of the Council of Trent regarding the Vulgate. The translation of the Bible into Spanish, and the lack of annotations and comments, were not as serious as the omission of the Apocrypha, which would be sharply criticised by the clergy. According to Bill Mitchell, Thomson had suggested that the Committee of the BFBS should avoid such a measure because 'it would be regarded as a Protestant Bible and would not be acceptable to the clergy in

80 BFBS, *Annual Reports*, (1832), pp. lxxx–lxxxi.
81 Canclini, *La Biblia en Argentina*; Canclini, *Diego Thompson*; Canton, *A History of the British and Foreign Bible Society*; Anderson, *An Evangelical Saga*; Eugenia Roldán Vera, 'Export as Import', pp. 231–76.
82 'Matthews to the BFBS', Coquimbo, 9 March 1827, BFBS, *Annual Reports* (1828), p. 107.
83 León XII, *Carta encíclica de nuestro santísimo padre el Papa León XII a todos los patriarcas, primados, arzobispos y obispos y bula de jubileo para el año 1825* (Barcelona: Imprenta de José Torner, 1824), pp. 26–27.

Map 3 Places visited by James Thomson in South America, 1818–1825

Places visited by Luke Matthews
in South America

◆ Rio de Janeiro

◆ Montevideo

◆ Buenos Aires

◆ Córdoba

◆ San Luis

◆ Mendoza

◆ San Juan

◆ Valparaiso

◆ Quillota

◆ Santiago

◆ Rancagua

◆ Coquimbo

◆ La Rioja

◆ Catarmarca

◆ San Miguel de Tucuman

◆ Salta

◆ San Salvador de Jujuy

◆ Tupiza

◆ Santiago de Cotagaita

◆ Caiza

◆ Potosi

◆ Arica

◆ Oruro

◆ Sucre

◆ Cochabamba

◆ Nuestra Señora de La Paz

◆ Puno

◆ Chucuito

◆ Arequipa

◆ Lima

◆ Guayaquil

◆ Panama

◆ Taboga

◆ Babahoyo

◆ Bogota

◆ Mompos

Map 4 Places visited by Luke Matthews in South America, 1826–1829

South America'.[84] Matthews's letters provide many examples of an evident opposition to the circulation of Bibles without the Apocrypha and, to a lesser extent, the lack of annotations and comments. On 18 January 1828 he wrote from Lima:

> I am sorry to confirm, from what I have since learned, the observations already made respecting the injurious effect produced upon the sale of Bibles by the omission of the Apocrypha. Had the Bibles contained the Apocrypha, the number sold would have been very great: I am told 1,000 might have been disposed of. The prejudices against the incomplete editions, as ours are called, is very strong and very general. I hope I shall find things different in the interior.[85]

This casts doubt on what Fernando Armas said about Matthews facing opposition because 'the people were reluctant to buy [the Bibles] since they were not the Catholic version of Father Scio of San Miguel, but replicas of the Protestant version of Reina Valera, which were printed from 1825 by the British Society for Latin America'.[86] The BFBS reports make clear that during the years of Matthews's travels, the Scio Bible remained the Spanish version distributed in Spanish America.[87] At best, both versions coexisted, but Valera's version did not replace Scio's at that time.

Even though Matthews faced more difficulties than Thomson, mainly because the latter circulated Scio's Bible with the Apocrypha, the opposition to his mission was not as strong as historians like Armas and Canton claim.[88] It is true that several clergymen openly and publicly opposed Matthews and did everything possible to hinder his mission. This was the case, for example, in Oruro, where 'the clergy made a strong opposition; some because the notes of the Church were wanting, and some because of the suppression of the Apocrypha'. In Arica, he claimed, 'the Bible was publicly burnt, by order of the ecclesiastical authorities'.[89] However, it is also true that other clergymen, mainly those who lived in small and isolated towns and villages were more willing to purchase a copy of the Bible, even without the Apocrypha. This

84 Bill Mitchell, 'Diego Thomson: A Study in Scotland and South America (1818–1825)', *Bulletin of the Scottish Institute of Missionary Studies*, 6–7 (1991), 66–75, available online: http://www.jamesdiegothomson.com/diego-thomson-a-study-in-scotland-and-south-america-1818-1825/ (accessed 21 July 2015).

85 'Matthews to the BFBS', Lima, 18 January 1828, in BFBS, *Annual Reports* (1828), p. 80.

86 Fernando Armas, *Liberales, protestantes y masones: Modernidad y tolerancia religiosa. Perú siglo XIX* (Lima: Fondo Editorial PUCP, 1998), p. 41. A similar approach is found in Anderson, *An Evangelical Saga*, pp. 57–58.

87 BFBS, *Annual Reports* (1827), p. xv.

88 Armas, p. 41; Canton, pp. 89–90.

89 'Matthews to the BFBS', Chuquisaca, 23 September 1827, BFBS, *Annual Reports* (1828), p. 116.

was also because, all things considered, missionaries were fulfilling a role that
the other actors were unable to carry out. One priest in Cotagaita 'purchased
half a dozen, all that I had of the large print, with the utmost joy and reiterated thanks, for distribution among his friends'.[90] In other villages, like Puno
and Chuquito, Matthews reported similar experiences.[91] One reason might
be that those local priests were also engaged in their own evangelical mission
and having copies of the Bible made their work easier. As Matthews said in
some reports, their usual reaction was to examine the book before purchasing
it. In most cases the omission of the Apocrypha was considered irrelevant.
Few complained about the lack of annotations and comments, and none about
it being a Spanish translation. In Córdoba, an important city in Argentina,
Matthews reported,

> In the conversations I had with the heads of the Church here they expressed
> no opposition to the circulation of the Bible [...] The Dean expressed his
> surprise that the apocryphal books were left out and a clergyman present,
> the most intolerant, I believe, in the place observed they might at least have
> been placed at the end. Neither of them however considered the omission
> as fatal to the propriety of disseminating the book, considering it as part
> of the Bible.[92]

Another priest in Panama said that 'each part of the Bible is valuable
itself'.[93] Whatever reason we accept, the fact is that Matthews's encounters
with these priests provide evidence that in the 1820s the reality was complex
and not simply a binary opposition between Catholics and Protestants, or
conservatives and liberals. Not all the clergymen had the same opinion about
the Apocrypha or the presence of Protestant missionaries in their localities.
Reactions, attitudes and ideas about the presence of these missionaries were
not monolithic. In some cases, priests received these missionaries favourably
because they were supplying Bibles that neither the state nor the Catholic
Church had been able to supply them with.

Unlike Thomson – and here I make the second contrast – Matthews
believed that his mission should be carried out amongst the lower classes,
and not on a 'top-down' basis. Matthews's opinion was much closer to the
aims of the BFBS than the views expressed by Thomson about the elites.
That is why in Matthews's letters – most of which have not previously been
consulted by historians – we find a number of references about the condition
of the indigenous population, 'half-indians' and 'people of colour', but only

90 Ibid., p. 113.
91 'Matthews to the BFBS', Lima, 18 January, 1828, BFBS, *Annual Reports* (1828),
   p. 112.
92 'Matthews, to the BFBS', Cordova, 5 December 1826, BFBS Archive, Foreign
   Correspondence inwards, Luke Matthews, BSA/D1/2.
93 'Matthews to the BFBS', Guayaquil, 30 June 1828, BFBS, *Annual Reports* (1829),
   p. 93.

few mentions of the elites. On several occasions, Matthews manifested his will to distribute Bibles amongst the poor, for whom he was more concerned than for the wealthiest people, who were 'more inclined to supply themselves'.[94] In Santiago, he made a deal with a 'very respectable man' to whom he stated 'that he should commence by taking to his account the case sent to the city, the half of which he should pay for, and the other distributed among the poor'.[95] At the same time, he was surprised to find much more interest in the Bible amongst the poor than in the other classes. Most of his buyers were in fact indigenous, 'half-Indians' or black. In Panama, for example, he said that Bibles 'are read attentively' amongst the 'people of colour'.[96] He expressed his surprise about the interest shown by the 'Indian postmaster' in Oruro:

> Having ascertained that the Indian postmaster could read, a circumstance at which I was much surprised, I sent him a Bible. In the morning I asked him how he liked the book, he said, exceedingly, and asked if I would sell it. I told him I would; and he has complained of the smallness of the print, that I had some of a larger size in my box, from which I took him out one, and he immediately purchased it.[97]

On the other hand, Matthews also sold several Bibles to the directors of both Monitorial schools and colleges. Those in charge of these institutions did not express any inconvenience in a copy of the Bible without the Apocrypha. Matthews reportedly sold 1,500 copies of the Bible in schools in Tucuman, Valparaíso, Coquimbo, Cochabamba and Guayaquil.[98] This means that in the mid-1820s, the process started by Thomson a few years before was still having repercussions, not only because of the spread of Monitorial schools, but because the Bibles that the BFBS was circulating were read in several schools across the continent, including in Chile. The role of Matthews in providing Bibles to schools was not considered by Amunátegui in his study on the Lancasterian system of education either.[99]

Thomson stayed almost a year in Chile, whereas Matthews stayed for four months. John Armstrong was always based in Buenos Aires, from where he coordinated the selling of Bibles and the activities of missionaries like Matthews. Others, like J.J. Barnard, were still acting as correspondents for the BFBS, but there are only ten letters from the 1820s sent to the BFBS. There is no news about other agents in Chile during the 1820s. The BFBS Archive only holds letters from three other agents who passed through Chile

---

94 'Matthews to the BFBS', Panama, 12 May 1827, BFBS, *Annual Report* (1828), p. 89.
95 'Matthews to the BFBS', Coquimbo, 9 March 1827, BFBS, *Annual Reports* (1828), p. 107.
96 'Matthews to the BFBS', Panama, 12 May 1827, BFBS, *Annual Report* (1828), p. 91.
97 'Matthews to the BFBS', Chuquisaca, 23 September 1827, BFBS, *Annual Reports* (1828), p. 116.
98 BFBS, *Annual Reports* (1829), p. liii.
99 See Amunátegui, *El sistema de Lancaster*.

in the 1830s. Although these missionaries' encounters with locals were often brief, they could have far-reaching consequences. This was particularly relevant for the construction of the educational system, for which the adoption of the Monitorial system was seen as a fundamental step.

3.5 Civilising Citizens: The Adoption of the Monitorial System of Education in Chile

There are many reasons why the new Chilean authorities decided to adopt the Monitorial system of education to reorganise primary schooling. Scholars have provided many explanations, which can be divided into practical and ideological reasons. Practical reasons refer to features of the Monitorial system, like its low cost and its efficiency. The fact that one teacher could educate up to a thousand children and that the system could expand rapidly across the territory were strong reasons to adopt it in a context of the economic constraints following the war.[100] Ideological reasons were less evident and were not openly defended by the promoters of the system. The most recurrent was the manner in which the Monitorial school fostered discipline and order as core values of education, in a period in which the Chilean authorities also aimed to preserve social order and stability. Another lesser-known ideological reason had to do with the system's 'Britishness' and the assumption that it was adopted because it embedded certain values of British society which were to be imitated.[101] Besides, some of the Spanish Americans who had lived and been educated in London were acquainted with this system because they attended schools that used it.[102]

Although the sources show that it was usual to refer to this system as the 'British System of Education', the correspondence between the agents involved in its adoption reveal that they chose it because it had been adopted in the 'civilised world'. This can be read in two ways. The first concerns identifying the notion of 'civilisation' with Britain, since the system had been created there. The second refers to the use of the idea of civilisation allegorically, which means that Chilean leaders believed that by adopting this system, Chile would be able to emulate the 'civilised' nations of the world. In either case, Britain was not seen as an empire expanding its sphere of influence by means of education, but as an example to follow by a part of the elite. This perception coexisted with another generalised view, particularly among the high clergy, that Britain was synonymous with heresy and evil. This was because most Britons who arrived in Chile were Protestants, but also because of the long-standing imperial rivalry between Spain and Britain.[103]

---

100 A good summary of this can be found in Weinberg, pp. 98–100.
101 This argument has been mainly pointed out by Racine, 'This England and This Now', pp. 439–40.
102 Racine, 'The Childhood Shows the Man', pp. 294–99.
103 On British-Spanish imperial rivalry see Elliott, pp. 400–01; Liss, pp. 1–26.

However, missionaries like Thomson managed to separate these two dimensions of their mission and presented themselves mainly as educators. In doing so, they were not seen as a threat to the religious cohesion of the country. These reasons were not contradictory and were accepted by those in charge of implementing this system because, ultimately, it was a good fit for their political project.

From this point of view, it has been suggested that due to the adoption of the republican regime, it was necessary to 'reshape' political identity, abandoning that of 'subject' of a monarchy for that of 'citizen' of a new republic.[104] Primary education seemed to be the most suitable means as it aimed to educate the 'people' in a broad sense and not in the manner of secondary and higher education, represented by the Instituto Nacional, which privileged the elite. In practical terms, reading and writing were two key skills for exercising the right to vote and both were at the centre of teaching in primary schools. A good example is the Constitution of Chile enacted in 1822 which, in Article 14, decreed that only married and literate men over twenty-five could vote. The same article fixed a period of time, 1822–1833, to allow schools to teach reading and writing to prospective citizens.[105] Primary schooling, therefore, became a source of political legitimacy for the new republican regime. Historians such as Eugenia Roldán Vera have also suggested that Monitorial schools actually taught children how to behave in a republic.[106] Camilo Henríquez, one of the intellectual leaders of Chilean independence, witnessed Thomson's activities during a stay in Buenos Aires and circulated a pamphlet in Chile titled 'Bosquejo compendioso de la enseñanza mutua'. He recommended the adoption of the 'Monitorian' school, as he called it, because it 'was a republic in miniature'.[107] Chilean independence leaders found in the ideas disseminated by Thomson a suitable means to carry out their own project. This project had already been designed, and if they adopted the Monitorial System of education it was because it fitted well into their own pre-existing set of ideas about how to educate the new generation of citizens.

The Monitorial system offered a good opportunity to teach reading and writing in a rapid, economical and efficient way due to its capacity to

104 Marcelo Caruso, 'Latin American Independence: Education and the Invention of New Polities', *Paedagogica Historica: International Journal of the History of Education*, 46:4 (2010), 409–17; Sol Serrano et al., *Historia de la Educación en Chile (1810–2010)*, 2 vols (Santiago: Editorial Taurus, 2012), I, pp. 61–84.

105 *Constitución Política del Estado de Chile*, 1822.

106 Roldán Vera, *The British Book Trade* and 'Order in the Classroom: The Spanish American Appropriation of the Monitorial System of Education', *Paedagogica Historica: International Journal of the History of Education*, 41:6 (2005), 655–75.

107 Camilo Henríquez, 'Bosquejo compendioso del sistema de enseñanza mutua', Colección Manuscritos de Camilo Henríquez, Biblioteca Nacional de Chile (Santiago, 1822), fols 6–11.

educate hundreds of children at once under the supervision of one teacher. In Chile, philanthropist, politician, intellectual and educator Manuel de Salas praised the adoption of the Monitorial system, stressing the 'readiness with which this mode of education has been generally adopted, its economy, and the quickness and order with which children learn by it reading, writing, arithmetic, and the principles of grammar'.[108] His support was highlighted by Thomson, who described him as a gentleman who 'takes a deep interest in this object and who makes the instruction of youth the amusement of his declining days [...] He is always to be found in one or other of our schools'.[109] In addition, while living in London before the outbreak of the struggle for independence, Bernardo O'Higgins, Supreme Director of Chile, had been acquainted with this system and it is plausible to think that he truly believed that it was an efficient way to improve the education of the Chilean population once in government.[110] According to Racine, O'Higgins, like other Spanish Americans settled in England at that time, regarded the Monitorial system as 'a hallmark of British-style aristocratic reformism, and it proved just as irresistible to them as it did to citizens in Russia, the United States, and France who were adopting it at the same time'.[111]

Nevertheless, the need to educate new citizens under new republican parameters is not enough to explain why this particular system was eventually adopted. If we take into account that the Monitorial system was born in a monarchical and imperial context and not in a republican one, it is hard to believe that a Monitorial school would necessarily fit into the republican project of the new ruling elites as stated by Roldán Vera.[112] Tuschnerev has even demonstrated that this system was 're-exported' from Britain to India and Africa as a means to consolidate its imperial project.[113] The republican purpose of the Chilean elites could be accomplished perfectly well by adapting the old colonial schools to the new political context, as most Spanish American republics did in the educational institutions of the elites like universities, seminaries and colleges. From such a perspective, the Monitorial system of education only solved the problem of the efficient establishment of primary schools. Colonial schools used the 'individual method', by which one teacher had to deal with many students in the same room, devoting a specific amount of time to each one. Compared to the Monitorial system,

---

108 Manuel de Salas, 'Educación Publica', in *Gazeta Ministerial de Chile*, 4 August 1821, p. 17.
109 'Thomson to Millar', Santiago, 26 February 1822, BFSS Archive, Foreign Correspondence, Chile, n.fol.
110 Racine, 'This England and This Now', p. 438.
111 Ibid.
112 Roldán Vera, 'Order in the Classroom', pp. 667–70.
113 Jana Tschurenev, 'Diffusing Useful Knowledge: The Monitorial System of Education in Madras, London and Bengal, 1789–1840', *Paedagogica Historica: International Journal of the History of Education*, 44:3 (2008), 245–64.

this was much less effective, since in the latter, large groups were taught by one teacher at the same time. In addition, Lancaster not only conceived a teaching method, but a complete educational system by which schools could spread easily and rapidly. The establishment of a 'central school' to train future teachers and to provide the guidance to implement the method elsewhere was a fundamental part of this. Beyond this, the Monitorial system was adopted mainly because it had a good reputation after being spread all over the world by means of a network of agents, coordinated by the BFSS, specifically devoted to promoting its adoption, who were able to identify the needs of the elite.[114] There was clearly a confluence of interests in these years between a new political elite eager to rebuild Chile's educational system and a society whose aim was to export its educational system throughout the world.

In the case of Chile, the correspondence of those in charge of seeking someone to implement this system – Antonio José de Irisarri in London and Miguel Zañartu in Buenos Aires – shows that the process also fit the political conceptions of the elite about the place of Europe and Great Britain in the world. In a letter to Joaquín Echeverría, the Minister of Foreign Affairs Antonio Irisarri highlighted the pedagogical features of the Monitorial system, saying that 'a child is able in six months to learn how to read, write and count [...] each school can take in as many pupils as you like under the direction of only one teacher, because this teaching system is conceived so that pupils can teach each other'.[115] Andrés Bello, at that time secretary of the Chilean delegation in London, had suggested not adopting it due to its pedagogical failings, such as the key role played by the inexperienced monitors in the delivery of lessons.[116] Irisarri, in turn, was enthusiastic about its implementation in Chile because it was 'the most widespread in the civilised world' and he believed that it was 'absolutely necessary to get that degree of culture, without which freedom has always been dangerous'.[117] This was how the members of the Chilean liberal elite conceived their own civilising project. It was not by education itself, but by the adoption of this specific British model that Chile would join the 'civilised world'.

The Monitorial system was designed to educate 'useful citizens' in the context of the Industrial Revolution in England.[118] Lancaster had described the school as a means to keep children busy, learning 'useful knowledge', and not

114 See Racine, 'This England and this Now', pp. 434–38.
115 'Irisarri to Echeverría', London, 13 September 1820, *ABO*, vol. 3, pp. 189–90.
116 'Andrés Bello to Antonio Irisarri', London, 11 September 1820, reproduced by Edgard Vaughan, *Joseph Lancaster in Caracas 1824–1827: And His Relations with the Liberator Simon Bolivar: With Some Accounts of Lancasterian Schools in Spanish America in the Nineteenth Century and Some Notes on the Efforts of the British and Foreign Bible Society to Distribute the Scriptures in Spanish in the Same Territory* (Caracas: Ministerio de Educacion, 1987), pp. 148–49.
117 'Irisarri to Echeverría', London, 13 September 1820, *ABO*, vol. 3, pp. 189–90.
118 Tschurenev, pp. 245–64.

only as a means of evangelisation. In Chile, Henríquez, besides assimilating the Monitorial school to a republic, described what was most characteristic of such a school in his view. After explaining how students must spend their time in reading and writing, he concluded that 'being, then, completely busy all the time they are at school, the children are less predisposed to be idle and to make mischief'. In Henríquez's view children must be kept busy at all times, learning and doing useful things rather than wasting their free time. The concept of 'usefulness' has been absent from debates about the role of education in Chile during this period, which has mainly been approached from the perspective of 'citizenship' by scholars like Sol Serrano and Carlos Ruiz.[119]

Preserving the social order seemed to be one of the most important aims of the new ruling elites.[120] The 'useful citizen' in this new political context was therefore an obedient and disciplined one who would help to preserve the social order of the republic. In this respect, Henríquez also highlighted the similarity of the Monitorial school to a military regiment: 'Anyone who has seen and admired the good order that is maintained in a regiment and the steadiness of its motions, is soon to believe the good effects of this system of education run by monitors under the rule of a master'. In his view, discipline and order were the two features that must prevail in a school, similar to a regiment. 'There must always be silence at the school', he added, '[...] everything must be done with the utmost order, whatever it is'.[121] If the school was both a republic in microcosm and a regiment, the republic could also be assimilated into a regiment. This reveals that notions of discipline and social control among the ruling elite were fundamental elements of the educational system in Chile since its very origins.

3.6 The Local Reception of a Global Missionary Project

Recent historiography, led by scholars like Marcelo Caruso and Eugenia Roldán Vera, has insisted that just as important as the diffusion of the Monitorial system of education itself was the role of the receptors, who were not merely passive imitators of a given foreign model, but active agents who adopted it and adapted it according to their local circumstances. This has been called a 'cultural approach', based on 'the production of differences in processes of reception, reinterpretation and re-articulation of ideas and institutions'.[122] Such an approach has been absent from analysis of the Monitorial system of education in Chile, mainly because scholars have tended to base any mention of the system on Domingo Amunátegui's classic work.[123]

119 See Serrano et al., 1, pp. 61–84; Carlos Ruiz Schneider, *De la República al mercado. Ideas educacionales y política en Chile* (Santiago: Lom Ediciones, 2010), pp. 15–40.
120 Roldán Vera, 'Order in the Classroom', pp. 667–75.
121 Camilo Henríquez, 'Bosquejo compendioso', pp. 6–11.
122 Caruso and Roldán Vera, 'Pluralizing Meanings', p. 648.
123 Amunátegui, *El sistema de Lancaster.*

In the particular case of Spanish America, the conditions in which this system began to be implemented during the 1820s were completely different to those in which the Monitorial system had been created in England. Neither an industrial revolution nor rapid urban population growth was taking place in those years. Husbandry and mining were still the most important economic activities and the population remained mostly rural. However, this system was the cornerstone on which further national educational systems were built, and the Monitorial system remained in place for different periods depending on the country. In Ecuador, Peru, Mexico and Argentina the Monitorial system was implemented until 1828, 1850, 1870 and 1873, respectively.[124] In Chile, although some scholars suggest that it was officially abolished in 1833, it lasted until 1860 in a mixed form. This, however, remains an unexplored area for further research.[125]

The particular local circumstances also conditioned the way the Monitorial system of education was implemented in Chile. The prevalence of a strong high clergy was seen by Thomson as a threat to his purposes. However, the opposition of the clergy was not as strong as has been suggested by some scholars, like Browning.[126] The prominence assigned to the education of the elite to the detriment of mass primary education was another factor, which allows for an explanation of why the implementation of this system in Chile was mediated by the Instituto Nacional. This institution had been created following the French model of institutes created in 1795 during the French Revolution. Thus, the idea that the Monitorial system was adopted mainly because of its Britishness must be considered carefully, since the evidence shows that the Chilean elite was open to receiving influences from different cultural models. In addition, the scarcity of resources, most of which had been exhausted during the war, represented a major challenge for the establishment of new schools even considering that the Monitorial system had been designed to be low-cost.

The Monitorial system was implemented in Chile under the auspices of the Instituto Nacional. James Thomson was appointed first to run a primary school attached to the Instituto, which would become the 'central school', where teachers were trained in the system. This meant transforming it into a model school, similar to the Borough Road School founded by Lancaster in London. This method of introducing the Monitorial system under the supervision of a secondary education institution did not occur in other Spanish American countries. The prominence of the Instituto reveals the importance of elite education for the Chilean authorities, to the detriment

124 Carlos Newland, 'La educación elemental en Hispanoamérica: desde la Independencia hasta la centralización de los sistemas educativos nacionales', *Hispanic American Historical Review*, 71:2 (1991), 335–64 (p. 345).
125 María Loreto Egaña, *La educación primaria popular en Chile en el siglo XIX: Una práctica de política estatal* (Santiago: Ediciones DIBAM, 2000), pp. 160–63.
126 Browning, p. 76.

of 'education for the poor' or 'universal education', which was the objective of the BFSS. However, as mentioned before, this was not a problem for Thomson, whose personal 'top-down' approach to education privileged the education of the elites as a first step to 'civilising' the rest of society. Thomson and the Chilean authorities had similar views regarding the priority of the elites, which in part explains why primary schooling progress more slowly in Chile than in other Spanish American countries in the 1820s. A clear choice was made to prioritise the establishment of secondary education institutions in the different provinces, following the model of the Instituto Nacional, which according to its regulations was the model elite institution for any other to be founded.[127]

This choice was made on the grounds that it was more pressing to educate the ruling elite of the future than the rest of the citizenry. This also explains one of the adaptations of the Monitorial system in Chile, which consisted of its being used for a new elite educational institution, the Liceo de Chile, founded by the Spanish liberal exile José Joaquín de Mora in 1829, as shown by Roldán Vera.[128] This institution was established under the liberal administration of President Francisco Antonio Pinto to 'compete' with the Instituto Nacional, as demonstrated by scholars like Gertrude Yeager, Ivan Jaksic and Sol Serrano.[129] At that time, the Instituto was regarded as a conservative bastion of the Catholic Church, since its major figures were all priests. Mora adapted the main features of the Monitorial system to organise the Liceo, which eventually worked as a military regiment. As Mora stressed in his inaugural speech, 'the organisation of the students will be purely military; subordination will be practised by the different grades of authority among the students themselves; the transition from one task to the other will be done in a slow and orderly way, in which each student should always know the place he is to occupy'.[130] In another article Mora explicitly stated that the Liceo would have a primary school attached based on the 'mutual teaching system'.[131]

127 Silva Castro, *La fundación del Instituto Nacional*, pp. 5–33.
128 Roldán Vera, 'Order in the Classroom', pp. 666–67. For an excellent account of the key role played by Mora in Chile during the 1820s see Graciela Iglesias-Rogers, 'José Joaquín de Mora in Chile: From Neo-Europe to the "*Beocia Americana*"', *Bulletin of Latin American Research*, 36:3 (2017), 326–39.
129 Gertrude Yeager, 'Elite Education in Nineteenth Century Chile', *Hispanic American Historical Review*, 71:1 (1991), 73–105 (p. 76); Iván Jaksic and Sol Serrano, 'In the Service of the Nation: The Establishment and Consolidation of the University of Chile, 1842–1872,' *Hispanic American Historical Review*, 70 (1990), 139–71 (p. 142).
130 'Plan de estudios del Liceo de Chile con algunos pormenores para su ejecución y sobre la disciplina del establecimiento', *El Mercurio Chileno*, 10, 1 January 1829.
131 Quoted by Alamiro de Ávila Martel, *Bello y Mora en Chile* (Santiago: Ediciones de la Universidad de Chile, 1982), p. 24.

Thus, in terms of organisation, the Liceo had a similar structure to the Instituto, being an institution which offered both primary and secondary education.

The hopes that the Monitorial system of education would be the definitive step for the construction of the first 'national' system of education led O'Higgins to decree on 22 November 1821 that it was mandatory for 'all the schools of the state'.[132] This decree obliged all teachers to attend the model school established in Santiago in order to be instructed in the new system. Any new school must be founded under this system too. This meant that the adoption of the Monitorial system, and its imposition as the only system permitted, was a first attempt at homogenising primary schooling. In addition, the role of the central school attached to the Instituto reinforced the centralism with which this institution had been conceived in 1813, as both the cornerstone of the new educational project and the model institution for the rest of the provinces of Chile. The Constitution of 1822, enacted shortly after the aforementioned decree, and which was the first to devote an entire chapter to education, would reinforce these centralising principles by declaring that 'public education will be uniform in all the schools, and will be given the greatest possible extension, as circumstances permit'.[133]

To reinforce this idea, a Lancasterian Society (Sociedad Lancasteriana) was founded by Bernardo O'Higgins on 17 January 1822. The decree stated that 'the government intends to protect [the Monitorial system] with fondness, and believes that it fulfils its wishes by partnering with people who have the same feelings along with the activity, zeal and prudence that it demands'.[134] In this case, the society was founded in order for the government to take direct control over education and not to sponsor a particular initiative as many monarchs, nobles and politicians did in Europe. In Chile, it was the government itself who was directly involved in the formation of the Lancasterian Society and not O'Higgins as an individual. This was contrary to one of the principles defended by the BFSS, by which schools were to work independently of the state's supervision and run by private societies. This principle was clearly set out in an annual report of the Committee of the BFSS: 'to confine the management of the public schools, for the education of the poor, to official superintendence, would weaken the interest of Public in these institutions, and thus check those feelings which ought to be cherished, strengthened, and universally diffused'.[135] This also followed the pattern by which that Spanish American elites nurtured their policies from different liberal models, mainly French and British, as stated

132 *Gazeta Ministerial de Chile*, 24 November 1822, p. 93.
133 Constitución Política del Estado de Chile, art. 230.
134 *Gazeta Ministerial de Chile*, 19 January 1822, p. 131.
135 BFSS, *Annual Reports* (1821), pp. 23–24.

by H.S. Jones. The former was much more 'statist' than the latter, which emphasised the role of private agency in providing education.[136]

In his reports, Thomson mentioned the establishment of five schools in Santiago, Valparaíso and Coquimbo. There was also a plan to establish a school in Concepción under the supervision of Antony Eaton, the BFSS agent who eventually travelled to Chile and became Thomson's assistant. However, Thomson said that, taking into account that 'it would be better to concentrate our labours in the capital, and from thence to send qualified masters to the various provinces, it was acceded that Mr. Eaton should remain in Santiago'.[137] In any case, compared to the 50 schools that the BFSS reported for the United Provinces of La Plata in 1827,[138] this was a rather small number. Also, if we consider that the regulation enacted by the Cabildo of Santiago back in 1813 stated that there were 'no more than four schools'[139] in that city, Thomson's mission was not an evident improvement. Anthony Eaton remained in the country for a few months after Thomson's departure. In his letters he provided some information about the schools that Thomson had already established in Santiago, but nothing else about his particular role in charge of them:

> There are three schools in this City on the British and Foreign plan. One is attended by about one hundred and twenty boys, part of whom pay a dollar a month and the others only pay for a slate on admission. Another school has about sixty boys, fifty of whom pay a dollar per month. The remaining school is gratuitous and the Master's salary is paid by the Magistracy. There have been difficulties and delays but the schools are now going on well and the boys improve pretty fast.[140]

These early years were far from fruitful in terms of the quantity of schools established. However, the implementation of the Monitorial system was a first attempt to set the principles for a single and homogenous system of education for the entire country. This was first attempted through the aforementioned decree, which declared it mandatory for all the schools, and a manual which defined the main criteria to be adopted in a Monitorial school. One of the few manuals published in Chile regarding this system was *Instrucciones para conducir escuelas bajo el sistema de enseñanza mutual*. It is plausible that it

136 H.S. Jones, 'Las variedades del liberalismo europeo en el siglo XIX: Perspectivas británicas y francesas', in *Liberalismo y poder. Latinoamérica en el siglo XIX*, ed. by Iván Jaksic and Eduardo Posada Carbó (Santiago: Editorial Fondo de Cultura Económica, 2011), pp. 43–62.

137 'Thomson to the Committee of the British and Foreign School Society', *BFSS Annual Reports* 21 (1826), pp. 118–19.

138 BFSS, *Annual Reports* 20 (1825), pp. 30–31.

139 'Reglamento para los maestros de primeras letras', p. 86.

140 'Antony Eaton to Millar', Santiago, 16 June 1822, BFSS Archive, Foreign Correspondence, file: Chile, n.fol.

was published by the Lancasterian Society that was founded by O'Higgins, but this remains unclear. This text does not provide many details about the functioning of the school itself, unlike the BFSS's *Manual to Teach Reading, Writing, Arithmetic and Needlework* which was published in 1816.[141] The main objective of the *Instrucciones* was to define the role and duties of the monitor, defined as 'an advanced boy [...] who must teach the children of the class and procure that all of them keep the good order',[142] and some guidance regarding the teaching of reading, writing and arithmetic. Nothing is said concerning the teaching of religion, perhaps one of the most controversial issues of the system. However, the Constitution of 1822, which was the only constitution of the period to define what students must learn in a (Monitorial) school, stated that 'principles of religion, reading, writing, counting [and] the duties of men in society' would be learned.[143]

In his report to the BFSS in London in 1825, Thomson recognised the difficulties that the introduction of the Monitorial system was facing in Chile. He wrote that 'the cause in Chili [*sic*], began to decline, and I believe at the present moment, the schools formerly established are in a very low state, if not given up altogether. It is much to be regretted, that things should be retarded there, whilst it is making progress in other quarters'.[144] Thomson never mentioned the opposition of the Catholic Church as a factor that undermined his mission. Elsewhere, in a letter, he had only reported his concerns about the Bishop of Santiago's censorship of all the books that were introduced in the territory, fearing that the Bibles would be banned in Chile.[145] However, in a classic work on the spread of this system in South America, Webster Browning stressed the opposition of the Catholic clergy as the main factor explaining its decline. Moreover, he said that such opposition sounded the 'death knell of the movement', an idea that has remained influential.[146] Thomson, however, claimed that in Peru, Buenos Aires and Chile he was 'treated with all liberality and confidence, and was never once asked whether he was a Roman Catholic or a Protestant'.[147]

Only one Catholic priest, the rector of the Instituto, Manuel Verdugo, openly opposed Thomson's dissemination of the Monitorial system of

141 BFSS, ed., *Manual of the British and Foreign School Society to Teach Reading, Writing, Arithmetic and Needlework in the Elementary Schools* (London: Longman and Co., 1816), p. 1.
142 *Instrucciones para conducir escuelas bajo el sistema de enseñanza mutua* (Santiago: [1823?]).
143 *Constitutcion Politica para el Estado de Chile*, 1822, art. 231.
144 'Thomson to the BFSS', BFSS, *Annual Reports* (1826), pp. 118–19.
145 'Thomson to Owen', Santiago, 8 October 1821, *Letters*, pp. 14–21.
146 Browning, p. 76. See also Ruth Aedo Richmond, *La educación privada en Chile. Un estudio histórico-analítico desde el periodo colonial hasta 1990* (Santiago: Ril editores, 2000), pp. 34–35.
147 James Thomson, 'South America IV', *Evangelical Christendom*, 1 (1847), 287–88.

education. His stance had less to do with a religious dispute, however, and much more with the way Verdugo perceived both Thomson's performance as the man in charge of the primary school at the Instituto, and the role of the state, embedded in the Instituto, in funding the working of the Monitorial system. Some of the official documents show that Verdugo criticised Thomson mainly for three reasons: his absence from Chile for four months to visit the schools he had already established in Mendoza; his attempt to establish a mixed school for boys and girls, and the excessive burden of the implementation of the plan on the Instituto's budget.[148] He never mentioned the alleged Protestant roots of the system to explain his opposition, although in another letter he expressed his concern about the excessive attention that, in his view, the Monitorial system was attracting, to the detriment of other domains of education. In Verdugo's view, 'the spread of Lancaster's method is very useful, but I think it should not be done with so remarkable a detriment to the mother establishment of sciences'.[149]

The situation within the Instituto after the end of Verdugo's time as rector saw some considerable changes to the benefit of the Monitorial system. A French engineer, Ambrosio Lozier, appointed rector of the Instituto in 1826, and the first civilian to take over, was a clear supporter of the system. A maths teacher, he founded the Society of the Students of the Modern Methods in order to encourage a modernisation of the pedagogical techniques used at the Instituto. This society also published regularly what was to be the first educational journal in the history of Chile: *El redactor de la educación* (The Editor of Education). In these activities, the Monitorial system occupied a central place along with other 'modern' methods such as that of Johan Heinrich Pestallozi. One of the articles of its constitution stated that 'by introducing the best teaching systems in its schools and classrooms, [society] will have comparative experiences to determine which ones must be preferentially adopted'.[150] This means that as early as 1825, the teachers of the Instituto were already studying the Monitorial system and comparing it to other methods, essentially performing a first exercise in 'comparative education'. Lozier also applied all of this as the Rector of the Instituto in 1826, including some variations that he had brought from France. For example, he incorporated the practice of singing the traditional Catholic Gregorian chant *Veni creator* every morning, at the beginning of each lesson.[151] This practice aimed to adapt the system to a Catholic environment, in which rites and exterior signs were as important as the cult itself.

The third rector of the Instituto, Francisco Meneses (1827–1829), was also favourably disposed to the Monitorial system. Considering his background,

---

148 All this correspondence is held at AHN-MI, vol. 52, February–June 1822.
149 'Verdugo to Echeverría', Santiago, 21 October 1822, ANH-SFL, vol. 9, piece 41.
150 *Diario de Documentos del Gobierno*, Santiago, 28 November 1825.
151 ANH-MI, 19 March 1826, vol. 52, fol. 308.

he was possibly one of the most 'conservative' clergymen appointed rector of the Instituto. During the wars of independence, Meneses had been a convinced royalist, and later on, a deputy to the National Congress for the conservatives. If we follow Browning's argument, he should have been an opponent of the Monitorial system because of its Protestant roots. However, he was a supporter and even suggested some measures to adapt it for use in secondary education. For instance, he approved the use of the Latin manual written by J.J. Ordinarie, which was based on the Monitorial system of education.[152] No criticisms of the Monitorial system are found in his correspondence or reports held at the National Archive of Chile.

All these examples show that the adoption of the Monitorial system of education within the Instituto Nacional, the cornerstone of the education system, was a complex process. No opposition to its Protestant roots was raised from within the Instituto, its rectors seemed proactive in supporting its use. Verdugo's opposition was not for doctrinal reasons, but his disagreement with Thomson's behaviour. This also shows that the implementation of the Monitorial system was strongly supported by the central state, which in this case was represented by the Instituto Nacional. Thus, in the field of education, interactions between Britons and Chileans occurred at different levels. On the one hand, Chilean state actors were represented by the agents, governors and educational authorities involved in its adoption and adaptation of the Monitorial system. On the other hand, British non-state actors were represented by Thomson, who disseminated the ideas and expertise required to carry out the new educational project.

3.7 The Reception of the Missionary Project in the Provinces of Chile

The implementation of the Monitorial system of education in the provinces of Chile did not differ considerably from the way it had been implemented in Santiago. Only minor variations are identified in the way it was adopted in other cities, which reveals the prominence of Santiago as the capital city, and of the Instituto Nacional as the cornerstone of the new educational project. Some testimonies from Manuel de Salas and travellers like Maria Graham have given clues as to how some Monitorial schools worked in this period. On 22 May 1822 Salas sent a report to the Minister of the Interior about the state of the Monitorial schools in Chile. He gave a general overview of Thomson's activities within the Instituto and the prospects of the Monitorial system in the country, saying that Valparaíso would have its own school 'thanks to the remarkable efforts of its philanthropist and active governor Mr José Ignacio Zenteno'. About Coquimbo he said that some 'other individual has gone

---

152 ANH-MI, 30 May 1828, vol. 52, fols 453–54. The textbook is titled *Gramática Latina dispuesta en forma de catecismo adaptada al método de enseñanza mutua y sacada de las mejores hasta ahora publicadas en Europa* (Santiago: Imprenta Republicana, 1831).

to deliver the first lessons', although he does not say who this was.[153] Salas also expressed his high expectations of the Monitorial system as a means to achieve general prosperity in 'all the classes, sexes and ages'.[154] However, another report dated 3 May 1828 reflected a conflicting reality. With regard to the possible appointment of the Spanish educator José León Cabezón to boost primary schooling in Chile by applying the 'Lancastrian method', Salas stressed the struggles and expenses undertaken by the government to implement it in the past, lamenting that it had been 'frustrated by accidents, whose knowledge will now serve to avoid them'.[155]

In Concepción, another Lancasterian Society was formed on 19 June 1824, to promote the diffusion of the Monitorial system in southern Chile. The Regulations stated that 'representative governments cannot exist until the people have received the first elements of human knowledge [reading, writing and calculus]'. At the same time, it stated that the Society was in charge of everything concerning 'physical and gymnastic, moral and intellectual, scientific and industrial education', introducing some new elements that were not originally included in the Monitorial curriculum.[156] Unlike the Lancasterian Society formed in Santiago in 1821, the state did not exert control over the Society in Concepción, but it was formed according to the principles of philanthropy defined by Lancaster, by which a group of people would contribute to establishing, maintaining and fostering Monitorial schools. This reveals that individual non-state agents were also engaged in the diffusion of the system, although to a lesser degree than in Santiago.

Some British travellers also wrote about the progress of the Monitorial system in Chile. Peter Schmidtmeyer, for example, reported on 'the introduction of the plan of mutual instruction, which if well understood, allowed a free course, and conducted with the abilities and incessant attention which it requires for success, would undoubtedly effect a considerable change here'.[157] Maria Graham, who witnessed the first year of its implementation in 1822, said that the school established by Thomson in Santiago was 'well attended' and that she had 'met many of the country people bringing in their children to go thither'.[158] Gilbert Farquhar Mathison also stated that Monitorial schools had been established in Santiago and other parts of the country, but added an appreciation worthy of mention. He was the only person to notice

---

153 *Escritos de don Manuel de Salas y documentos relativos a él y a su familia, Vol. 1*, ed. by University of Chile (Santiago: Imprenta de Cervantes, 1910), pp. 641–42.

154 Ibid.

155 Ibid., pp. 643–44.

156 'Regulations of the Society for the Mutual Teaching, Concepción', 19 June 1824, ANH-MI, vol. 5, fols 344–47.

157 Peter Schmidtmeyer, *Travels into Chile, over the Andes in the Years 1820 and 1821 Illustrated with 30 Plates* (London: Longman, Hurst, Rees, Orme, Brown, and Green, 1824), p. 322.

158 Graham, *Journal of a Residence in Chile*, p. 157.

that the implementation of the Monitorial system of education in Chile consisted of 'combining [...] with the Lancasterian method of instruction, the inculcation of the Roman Catholic religion'.[159] Other travellers were perhaps less aware of the non-confessional nature of Lancaster's plan, but Mathison did realised that the Chileans were adapting the Monitorial system to their context, confirming the plausibility of the idea of a 'cultural approach' suggested by Caruso and Roldán Vera.[160] In contrast, John Miers briefly mentioned a school founded in Valparaíso, saying that as soon as Thomson left the country 'the clergy immediately procur[ed] its abolition'.[161] With this statement Miers was reinforcing the idea that the Monitorial system failed due to opposition from the Catholic clergy.

However, in 1827 Luke Matthews visited Valparaíso, Quillota, Rancagua and Coquimbo, and his narrative differed from that of Miers. In his view, Catholic opposition was not as strong as it had been a few years previously, when the clergy openly opposed the circulation of missionary Bibles and even burnt them. In a letter to the BFBS he wrote:

> Twelve years back, the sale and possession of the Scriptures were prohibited by a public edict. Copies that had got into circulation were, as far as possible, recovered from their possessors, and then burnt. Such an edict would now excite the utmost contempt. There is, nevertheless, a party still violently opposed to the public use of the Scriptures. I am told that a number of bigots not long since met together and burnt the Bibles. This party is, however, entirely destitute of power to prevent the most public efforts of the friends of the Bible. They have the fullest liberty to distribute, and the people to receive.[162]

This testimony suggests that such recalcitrant Catholic opposition was not majoritarian, and that Protestant missionaries believed that the obstacles to spreading Scripture were not insurmountable. Matthews himself provided more information about the dissemination of the Scriptures in schools and how easy it was for him to sell Bibles and New Testaments to the 'large school' for the poor children of Valparaíso:

> I visited the schoolmaster and learned he was almost entirely destitute of books; he told me that the civil governor of the port, Ignacio Zenteno, took a great interest in the progress of the boys and was the principal supporter of the institution. I accordingly waited upon him, and proposed

---

159 Gilbert Farquhar Mathison, *Narrative of a Visit to Brazil, Chile, Peru, and the Sandwich Islands during the Years 1821 and 1822* (London: Charles Knight, 1825), p. 188.
160 Caruso and Roldán Vera, 'Pluralizing Meanings', p. 649.
161 Miers, I, p. 447.
162 'Matthews to the BFBS', Valparaíso, 20 January 1827, BFBS, *Annual Reports*, 23 (1827), p. 106.

the introduction of the New Testament into the school, offering a quantity gratuitously, if the governor would purchase an equal number. Upon his consulting the council of the town, who have the management, my proposition was immediately and thankfully acceded to; and we arranged that 100 New Testaments should be given and 100 purchased.[163]

In Coquimbo he had a similar experience. Despite expressing his frustration that 'purchasers were not to be found at any price', he managed to make a deal with the director of the local college:

I engaged to introduce the subject the next day to the cabildo, that is, the council of the town. I waited the following morning upon him, and he informed me that the cabildo had cheerfully closed with his proposal to take 100 copies of the Testaments on the principle I mentioned, and that they would also have taken 150 Bibles had they contained the Apocrypha. The senior Treasurer, a kind and intelligent ecclesiastic, waited on me this morning with the amount. I have just returned from visiting him at the college, where I found the books carefully arranged in the library. It is more than possible that the use of the Scriptures in this public institution may be the means of extending their circulation to a considerable extent.[164]

Matthews's testimony shows that by the mid-1820s the Bibles circulated by the BFBS were still used as textbooks in some Chilean schools. The use of this version of the Bible as a textbook posed a problem for the Catholic hierarchy because it contradicted the stipulations of both the Council of Trent, which was still the valid authority for the Catholic world, and the papal encyclical published in 1824.

James Thomson's version of the Bible contained the Apocrypha and was not resisted by the clergy. Most of the Bibles he carried with him were sold as textbooks and he even sold some 'Scriptural lessons' he had prepared with passages of the Bible for children's use. These lessons were central to his education plan, since it was 'the most adapted for the instruction of children in the truths and the virtues of the Christian religion'.[165] He also reported that the Scriptural lessons were printed by the governments in Buenos Aires, Chile and Peru, recognising that this 'exhibited a striking instance of liberality worthy of being mentioned in honour of the place and parties, and as exhibited by a Roman Catholic Government and community towards a Protestant and a foreigner'.[166] Hence if there was clerical opposition to the activities of Protestant missionaries, it was not entirely effective.

When assessing the way the Monitorial system of education was adopted and adapted to local circumstances, it becomes evident that the system in

163 Ibid.
164 Ibid., pp. 103–04.
165 James Thomson, 'South America, IV', *Evangelical Christendom*, 1 (1847), 287–88.
166 Ibid.

itself did not suffer a profound change from its original version. Some of the variations that were introduced – like the *veni creator* and its use in the Liceo de Chile – were not properly 'local'. They were introduced by foreigners appointed by the Chilean government as rectors of some of the leading educational institutions. Even the system's adoption in secondary education was not exclusive to Chile, since Thomson himself believed that the BFSS's efforts must first be directed to the education of the elites. The examples discussed here reveal a complex process of interaction and exchange of ideas that eventually led to the implementation of the Monitorial system of education according to the parameters that had been established by the new ruling elite of Santiago.

3.8 Conclusions

The interactions between the British missionaries and Spanish American populations reveal that during these years, Protestantism was not regarded as a threat to the extent that has been suggested by many scholars. Both Thomson's and Matthews's testimonies make clear that their encounters with locals resulted in a wide range of reactions. Strong opposition was also present, but this attitude coexisted with greater tolerance, not only within the liberal elites, but also within the Catholic clergy. Not all the priests they came across on their journeys, particularly in Matthews's case, were concerned about the presence of these missionaries, and nor were many of them worried about the circulation of Bibles without Apocrypha. This was because they were also engaged in their own evangelising mission, and the circulation of Bibles, which were really difficult to get, was seen as a good opportunity to supply their localities with texts that, although not 'orthodox', might also be useful.

A comparison between the strategies followed by Thomson and Matthews, as part of the same evangelical project, also reveals that they had different views on their role in this transcendental mission, and about their own role as individuals. Thomson privileged a more elite-oriented strategy, whereas Matthews preferred to make deals and agreements with shopkeepers and teachers in the different towns he visited, so that the Bibles could reach all of the inhabitants. This also influenced their respective perceptions of Spanish Americans. Thomson tended to stress their desire to foster universal education and the reading of the Bible, whereas Matthews was more sceptical about the genuine interest of Spanish Americans in reading the Bible.

These approaches also influenced the way they interacted with Chileans. Thomson's views on the priority of the education of the elites, so that ideas would trickle down to the rest of the population, fit well the educational project of the Chilean authorities. The role of the Instituto Nacional would be the masterpiece of their project and this also influenced the way they adopted and adapted the Monitorial system to local conditions. This excessively centralised approach, which would be the basis of the future educational system throughout the nineteenth century, was first debated during this period, along with ideas regarding the role of order, discipline and 'useful knowledge' in the shaping of the citizens of the new republic. This was the core of the educational project of the new ruling elite, which considered education as a means to prevent social upheaval and political distress.

The analysis of the interactions which made it possible to adopt and adapt the Monitorial system to local circumstances also reveals that the seeds of the 'national' system of education were sown in this period, a realisation that is made clearer when considering the fact that this was the first time that all of the existing and future schools were homogenised, under the same model and curriculum. Moreover, it can be argued that the configuration of a national system of education in Chile was inextricably linked to processes of the 'internationalisation' of educational models around the world. In other words, any reference to a national system of education in Chile has necessarily to be linked to the international dimension of the diffusion and circulation of knowledge.

Analysis of these multifaceted interactions reveals that in the eyes of Chilean authorities, the British roots of the Monitorial system were more important than its links to Protestantism. As shown in the first chapter, ever since the first diplomatic negotiations Chilean leaders had been keen on attracting skilled British and European workers, educators and 'wise men' to travel to Chile. They were convinced that by adopting the Monitorial system they were also entering into the 'civilised world', where this system was widely spread. A study of the realm of education policy shows how representations of Britain in Chile had changed radically since 1806, when it had been synonymous with evil.

CHAPTER 4

British Merchants, Private Interests and the Fostering of Free Trade in Chile, 1811–1831

4.1 Introduction

The final case study to be discussed is the role of the other British 'non-state' actors involved in Chile's independence era: merchants. The presence of merchants and traders of different nationalities had been very extensive along the Chilean coasts prior to the crisis of 1808, but their presence was illegal since Spain had adopted a trade monopoly policy after its conquest of America. The situation changed after 1811 thanks to the policies adopted by the new Chilean authorities, who gradually 'legalised' the status of these 'smugglers'. As a result, the activities of British merchants in Chile were no longer forbidden and their former status as illegal traders or smugglers shifted as they became legal merchants operating in Chile.

The role of merchants raises some interesting questions regarding the nature of the links between trade and British imperialism. It is difficult not to regard British merchants as agents of the British Empire, considering that trade was one of the main means of imperial expansion to the extent that Peggy K. Liss, a historian of the Atlantic empires, refers to imperial England as a 'trading nation'.[1] In a classic work on the relations between Latin America and Britain in the independence era, Charles Webster claimed that 'what the British government and people were really seeking was not territory, but trade and bullion'.[2] Webster's interpretation became the basis of one of the most widespread assumptions about British policy towards the Spanish American independence struggle, that Britain was simply trying to expand its commercial routes and markets to sell the goods it produced in the context of the Industrial Revolution. However, as discussed in the Introduction of this

---

1 Liss, pp. 1–25.
2 Charles Webster, *Britain and the Independence of Latin America, 1812–1830*, 2 vols (London, New York and Toronto: Oxford University Press, 1938), I, p. 9. See also Victor Bulmer-Thomas, 'Preface', in *Britain and Latin America: A Changing Relationship*, ed. by Victor Bulmer-Thomas (Cambridge and New York: Cambridge University Press), pp. x–xii.

book, there is an ongoing debate about the extent to which the interests of merchants and businessmen are coincident with the interests of government.[3]

As shown in Chapter 1, the plan to invade Chile in 1806 aimed to build up a trade route to connect the Atlantic and the Pacific with Chilean ports as key connection points. Even though the plan was outlined by the 'official mind', its actual aim was to open new trade routes for British merchants, who were not precisely agents of the state. In matters of commerce, the distinction between 'state' and 'non-state' actors is indistinct, since as they pursued their own personal interests, British merchants were also contributing to the imperial project. Furthermore, the aforementioned invasion plan was outlined in the context of imperial rivalry between Britain and Spain, and trade was consciously used as a means to weaken the Spanish empire. In R.A. Humphreys's words, 'Spain's enemies first exhausted her by plunder, then by trade'.[4]

This situation changed during the struggles for independence, however, in which the two powers became allies and Britain declared its neutrality. Thereafter, trade was no longer used as a means to undermine the power of the Spanish empire, and the 'official mind' did not exhibit a clear interest in persisting with its former policy. Of course, this did not prevent British merchants from taking part in the conflict; firstly, by exploiting the opening of trade in 1811 passed by the newly created National Congress of Chile, and secondly, by settling British communities in Chile in the 1820s, once independence was achieved and free trade was declared.

However, commercial relationships did not develop in a vacuum. For trade to take place, it was necessary that some people made transactions of goods, materials or money. In the independence era, this meant that there were people willing to travel, to transport the goods and to sell them in the local markets. This also implied interaction with the people who inhabited these new markets. In this period these 'encounters' had significant consequences. British merchants who travelled to Chile were fundamental in fostering and consolidating ideas of free trade that had not been well known there before their arrival. They used different mechanisms to influence the political life of Chile. One of the most important was the support of the Royal Navy stationed in the Pacific. Whenever the interests of the merchant community were under threat, the commander of one of the British ships of that station intervened to act as a mediator between them and the local government.

This was evident in the late 1820s, and particularly when political unrest led to the first civil war in 1829. In this conflict Royal Navy officers presented themselves as neutral actors, preserving their own personal interests without interfering in local conflicts. Diplomatic sources consulted for this book – which have not previously been consulted by historians of this subject – show

3 Rory Miller, *Britain and Latin America*, pp. 17–20.
4 R.A. Humphreys, *British Consular Reports on the Trade and Politics of Latin America, 1824–1826* (London: The Royal Historical Society, 1940), p. viii.

that merchants were not ideologically allied to any of the political factions, but simply supported the one which secured their personal safety and the integrity of their properties and business. These findings contradict the assumptions of historians such as Gabriel Salazar regarding connivance between British merchants and the conservative faction led by Diego Portales, with the aim of subjugating the Chilean economy to British commercial interests.[5] This assumption has been one of the main arguments to maintain that the role of British merchants during the independence era was the background that explains the subsequent neocolonial relationship of the mid-nineteenth century onwards. The presence of merchant companies like Anthony Gibbs & Sons in Chile and other parts of South America from 1820 might be regarded as an example of this. Gibbs & Sons became a powerful firm over the nineteenth century, especially after 1840, when they became involved in the guano trade. Their interest in guano and nitrates have led some scholars to claim that these were fundamental in explaining the start the War of the Pacific (1879–1883) between Chile and Peru and Bolivia.[6] Manuel Llorca-Jaña, however, has said that in the 1820s Gibbs & Sons were not as powerful as others like Huth & Co., which was the first merchant banking house to become global before 1840 and one of the first to start operations in Chile.[7] Rather, the key role played by merchants like John James Barnard demonstrates that the presence of British merchants in Chile had divergent and ambiguous meanings for contemporaries.

The main contribution of British merchants, as a group, to Chilean society was their fostering of the liberalisation of the Chilean economy although, as in the cases studied in chapters two and three, this was done in line with 'local conditions'. The formation of the Association of British Merchants in Valparaíso in 1819 was a way to influence the decisions of the government regarding eliminating customs barriers that impeded the free circulation of goods to other destinations like Peru. As Luz María Méndez has said, the establishment of free depots in Valparaíso in 1824 'boosted the expansion of international trade in Valparaíso because foreign ships could store their goods there while doing other trips'.[8] However, the fact that during the 1820s the Chilean economy was clearly oriented to free trade, to the extent

5 Salazar, *Mercaderes, empresarios y capitalistas*, pp. 79–160.

6 Manuel Ravest Mora, 'La casa Gibbs y el monopolio salitrero peruano, 1876–1878', *Historia*, 41:1 (2008), 63–77.

7 Manuel Llorca-Jaña, 'The Economic Activities of a Global Merchant-Banker in Chile: Huth & Co. of London, 1820s–1850s', *Historia*, 45:2 (2012), 399–432 (pp. 400–01). From the same author see also *The Globalization of Merchant Banking before 1850: The Case of Huth & Co.* (Oxford and New York: Routledge, 2016), especially Chapter 2, pp. 29–55.

8 Luz María Méndez, *La exportación minera en Chile. 1800–1840. Un estudio de historia económica y social en la transición de Colonia a Republica* (Santiago: Editorial Universitaria, 2004), p. 80.

that Llorca-Jaña suggests that it represented an 'early globalisation', also had internal consequences.[9] British merchants' opening trade to external actors had a negative impact on some, like urban artisans who could not compete with the low prices of imported goods. This led them to organise themselves for the first time in order to oppose such free-trade policies, which itself had long-term consequences for the rest of the nineteenth century.

4.2 British Merchants, Chile and the British Empire

In his work, Marcelo Somarriva wrote that during the independence era the relations between Great Britain and the 'Southern Cone' (including Chile) were 'eminently commercial'.[10] Indeed, most of the work that has dealt with the relations between Great Britain and Chile has focused mainly on the role of trade and commerce in the making of these relations. John Mayo, for example, has defined them as an 'informal dominion', whereby Chile became part of Britain's 'informal empire'.[11] Mayo argues that the seeds of such informal dominion, crucial to explaining the position of 'dependency' of the Chilean economy for the rest of the nineteenth century, were sown during these years. For Mayo, this was not the result of an intentional official policy towards Chile, a territory which was regarded by British authorities as commercially and strategically 'unimportant'. The configuration of this informal dominion was the result of the activities of a network of 'expatriate merchants' who went to Chile and 'sold foreign goods and services on the local market and organised the return trade that paid for them'.[12] Thus, according to Mayo, if informal imperialism was exerted upon Chile, this was mainly due to the critical role played by British merchants as agents of the Empire.

Mayo's approach is too constrained by the role that trade itself played in consolidating the peripheral condition of Chile in the global economy. His approach is clearly influenced by Gallagher and Robinson's ideas on British informal imperialism during the nineteenth century, eschewing other aspects and focusing on trade. He said little about the role of merchants themselves and their interactions with the locals in order to understand how this process was experienced by the people involved in this relationship. Unlike Mayo, Somarriva based his analysis on a cultural approach to determine the way commerce and trade became fundamental factors in the configuration of this relation, but did not analyse the role played by these merchants either. Just as important as trade and discourses about its significance is how merchants

---

9 Llorca-Jaña, 'The Economic Activities of a Global Merchant-Banker', p. 405.
10 Somarriva, p. 1.
11 Mayo, 'Britain and Chile, 1851–1886', pp. 95–120. An extended version of this analysis can be found in John Mayo, *British Merchants and Chilean Development, 1851–1886* (Boulder, CO: Westview Press, 1987).
12 Mayo, 'Britain and Chile, 1851–1886', p. 99.

behaved in their interactions with locals. This enables us to determine whether the preservation of their British identity on Chilean shores had any critical impact on the society they were interacting with. Ricardo Salvatore has taken a similar approach to the role of the US and its informal imperialism exerted upon Latin America by means of a network of missionaries, travellers, diplomats and merchants.[13]

For the Chilean case, historians who have tried to determine the role of merchants have focused on the way they influenced the economic development and the 'new mentality' of the Chilean bourgeoisie in order to explain the supposed economic success of Chile in the nineteenth century. Sergio Villalobos provided a first approach to the subject of the cultural influence of British (and foreign) merchants by highlighting their role in the making of a Chilean 'entrepreneurial class':

> They made a great contribution to audacity and imagination, because they had another economic mentality, based on entrepreneurship, that is, identification with the creative work and determination to carry it forward, overcoming difficulties and making a great effort and personal risk, to the intimate satisfaction of having reached the objectives proposed.[14]

Scholars like Eduardo Cavieres and John Rector share a similar approach, with their positive assessment of the role of British merchants in this period. For Cavieres, the presence and actions of British merchants in Chile as early as the 1820s were crucial for the 'modernisation of the Chilean economy'.[15] Rector argues that, 'had not outside influences entered the country in 1810, the republic's development would have suffered'.[16] On the other hand, Gabriel Salazar published a major work on the role of the 'entrepreneurial' class in the development of Chilean politics during the nineteenth century. His starting point is precisely the independence era and the role of British merchant houses in Chile, through their consignee agents. Salazar is very critical about such a role, arguing that the most important consequence of their activities in Chile, mainly in the 1820s, was the subjugation of Chilean trade to British economic interests. This also allegedly had long-term consequences in the making of the Chilean ruling class, who were allied with these merchant houses in order to consolidate the authoritarian political regime that commenced in 1830. One critical argument of Salazar is that many of the consignees were incorporated into Chilean society and became part of the ruling elite.[17] In contrast to other migrant communities, such

13 Salvatore, 'The Enterprise of Knowledge', pp. 71–104.

14 Sergio Villalobos, *Origen y Ascenso de la burguesía chilena* (Santiago: Editorial Universitaria, 2006), pp. 62–63.

15 Eduardo Cavieres, *Comercio chileno y comerciantes ingleses, 1820–1880 (Un ciclo de historia económica)* (Valparaíso: Universidad Católica de Valparaíso, 1988), p. 13.

16 Rector, p. xii.

17 Salazar, *Mercaderes, empresarios y capitalistas*, pp. 79–130.

as Germans or Italians, British merchants based in Chile did not maintain
a discrete community but tended to merge with their Chilean counterparts. This differs from what happened in other contexts, such as Buenos
Aires in Argentina and Bahia in Brazil, where it seems that at least in
the first decades of the nineteenth century, British settlers remained as a
community.[18] In Rector's words 'numerous foreign merchants established
permanent residence in Chile, married Chilean women, received citizenship,
and entered into business association with national merchants. To some
extent, therefore, the distinction between national and foreign merchants
diminished'.[19]

Beyond these works, it is hard to find research that has dealt with the role
of the British merchant communities settled in Chile and their interactions
with their local counterparts in the early nineteenth century. Most of the
work focuses on the settlement of such communities in a period of economic
transformation in the mid-nineteenth century, when Valparaíso became the
major port of Chile. Indeed, for the historian and politician – of British
descent himself – Benjamin Vicuña Mackenna, the prominent presence of
British settlers in Valparaíso determined the shaping of this city as a 'tiny
England'.[20] It is evident that such a presence formed part of Valparaíso's
identity as some research has shown from the point of view of heritage.
Architecture, religion, sports and education in Valparaíso seem to have
been influenced by British culture, a process whose results remain today.[21]
Something similar has been said with respect to some smaller communities
in Concepción. Leonardo Mazzei De Gracia has tracked the origins of the
British community in this city, and noted that in the 1820s, unlike Valparaíso,
'there was not in Concepción a homogenous nucleus of British traders
projected beyond the local ambit'.[22] This also differs from the situation in
Coquimbo, where British merchants arrived quite early due to mining activities. In this respect, John Mayo's work has been significant in identifying the
'influence' and 'interests' of this community, although here he avoids using
the concept of 'informal empire' as he had in previous works.[23]

Considering the close connection between the concept of informal empire
and trade, the very presence of British merchants and traders in Chile might
be regarded as a manifestation of British imperialism. This is what scholars,
like Mayo and Salazar, have done from different perspectives. They have
concluded that the Chilean economy was subjugated to British interests, even

---

18 See Guenther, pp. 111–35; Silveira, 'Ingleses y escoceses en Buenos Aires'.
19 Rector, p. 51.
20 Vicuña Mackenna, 'La Inglaterra chica i la Inglaterra grande'.
21 See *Legado Británico en Valparaíso = British Legacy in Valparaíso*, ed. by Prain.
22 Leonardo Mazzei De Grazia, 'Orígenes del establecimiento británico en la región
    de Concepción y su inserción en la molinería de trigo y en la minería de carbón',
    Historia, 28 (1994), 217–39 (p. 221).
23 Mayo, 'The Development of British Interests in Chile's Norte Chico', pp. 363–94.

during the independence era, as stated by Salazar, or as a background for late nineteenth-century imperialism.

However, in this period the presence of British merchants was not necessarily a manifestation of informal imperialism as it was in other places of the world. In this respect, I follow Louise H. Guenther's argument regarding Brazil:

> The informal empire model serves to explain many of the overall changes in world trade flows over two or three centuries. However, it does not really take into account what was happening between Brazilians and Britons throughout the nineteenth century, and most importantly, how this happened on a day-to-day basis, the uncertainties that were constantly struggled with, and the broad changes that took place in the relationship over time.[24]

The intensity of the historiographical debates about the nature of the commercial relationships between Britain and Chile in this period shows that issues of informal imperialism and trade have been constant. However, the extent to which the role played by individual British merchants shaped the relationship remains understudied. In this chapter, I focus on the 'uncertainties' that can be tracked in the sources about some of the merchants who were settled in Chile during this period, rather than the day-to-day basis as Guenther did. Analysis of individual merchants and their 'encounters' reinforces the interpretation developed in this book that the relationships between Britain and Chile during this period were characterised by their unpredictable and changing nature.

4.3 From Smugglers to Merchants

One crucial aspect of the role of British merchants in the independence of Chile is related to their own situation during the dynamic period that commenced in Spanish America in 1806. Given that the presence of such merchants was not legal, the status of British merchants in South America was that of smugglers. In the context of a war between Britain and Spain, British smugglers were officially regarded as Spain's enemies. For Villalobos, 'it was not really about plundering ports, assaulting shops or spreading terror. Enemy vessels intended to introduce contraband and only incidentally to commit crimes in case of being chased or as retaliation'.[25] The governor of Chile in 1806, Luis Muñoz de Guzmán, manifested his willingness to prosecute British smugglers, whom he considered an extension of the British forces in the context of the war. His official correspondence with the central Spanish authorities is filled with testimonies of his struggles against contraband.[26]

---

24 Guenther, p. 2.
25 Sergio Villalobos, *El comercio y la crisis colonial. Un mito de la independencia* (Santiago: Ediciones Universidad de Chile, 1968), p. 142.
26 AGI, File: Chile, vol. 206, n.fol.

This view was not shared by all Chileans. Most of the population benefited from this contraband, getting goods at low prices to the extent that, according to Villalobos, up to 1808 there was a sort of *de facto* free trade in Chile. This was because British (and French) goods were so abundant that the market was overstocked, and prices tended to fall, which clearly benefited consumers. The testimony of the British merchant George Cood, who was in Chile in 1812, in a letter to his employee Peter Schmidtmeyer confirms this idea. He claimed that he 'found it impossible to realise this hope [of selling his goods], for owing to the market of Chile being so overstocked I had sold but very few of my goods when the Cordilleiras shut'.[27] Despite this, British authorities still believed that free trade was extensively desired by Creoles, which would allow them to be persuaded about the benefits of accepting British rule. This was clearly shown in the plan to invade Chile (discussed in Chapter 1), whose aim was to secure new trade routes in South America for Britain and to define the role that Britain would play in securing free trade for Chileans.

The massive introduction of goods as contraband might not have been possible without two elements. The first of these was the connivance of the Spanish American authorities, who tolerated contraband because they benefited from it themselves. The second factor is the existence of merchant houses that made the exportation of goods possible, to the point of overstocking the market. It has been argued that British merchant houses, and not individual contrabandists, were in fact 'illegally' trading with Spanish America before independence. Manuel Llorca-Jaña has suggested this possibility, pointing out that 'it is apparent that the Southern Cone was importantly supplied by the British before the Independence, and the area was not alien to British merchants who opened houses after independence.[28] However, the clandestine nature of their operations, and the many troubles derived from it, led merchants to demand the legalisation of their activities. The unclear role of the authorities in Chile was one of the difficulties that traders had to face, which on some occasions was expressed in their own involvement in such trade. In addition, the context of warfare also made the way these smugglers were identified puzzling, and in some cases they were confused with privateers.

As discussed in Chapter 1, the new governor of Chile after the death of Muñoz de Guzmán, Francisco García Carrasco, held an erratic policy towards both free trade with Britain and contraband. In mid-1809 he supported free trade as a means to overcome the economic crisis caused by Napoleon's invasion of the Iberian Peninsula. One year before, in July 1808, he had been involved in a scandal in which the protagonists, including him, tried to cheat

27 'Cood, to Schimdtmeyer', Buenos Ayres, 15/03/1812, TBL, Manuscripts, Add MS 48212 M, n.fol.
28 Manuel Llorca-Jaña, *The British Textile Trade in South America in Nineteenth Century* (Cambridge: Cambridge University Press, 2012), p. 18.

a smuggler for their own benefit. This was known as the 'Scorpion affair', and reveals how the pretext of the threatening presence of foreign privateers and smugglers was used for García Carrasco's own personal ambitions. This episode also reveals the often contradictory behaviour of the actors involved, many of whom continued to pursue their own personal benefit despite acting as state-agents. The scandal is also a manifestation of the complex geopolitical context of the period, characterised by the changing roles of individuals and their shifting affiliations. This, as was shown in Chapter 1, was the result of the changing role of the actors involved in the Napoleonic wars in Europe, with Britain and Spain becoming allies against the growing power of France.[29]

The episode itself is well-known in Chilean historiography and versions do not differ considerably.[30] It was basically a bloody conspiracy by García Carrasco and some of his subordinates, with the aid of Henry Faulkner, a North American physician settled in Quillota, against Tristan Bunker, a British subject and commander of the *Scorpion* frigate. Bunker was a privateer and a smuggler, relatively well-known in the South Pacific, who had been in Chile for the first time in 1807.[31] In that year he met Henry Faulkner, with whom he agreed a deal to sell a load of textiles in Chile the following year. He would return in July 1808 and would meet Faulkner at the Topocalma estate, on the coast of Colchagua in central Chile. The estate owners were José de Fuenzalida and the local authority of Colchagua, Francisco de la Carrera. Faulkner, Fuenzalida and De la Carrera plotted against Bunker, cheating him and persuading him to finish the deal in October in Pichidangui Bay, on the northern coast of Chile. In the meantime, De la Carrera had informed García Carrasco about the situation. He decided to join the plot, and began to find legal excuses for the operation. Since the *Scorpion* was a privateer ship, the laws of war might be applied and if the ship were captured it would be regarded as a prize.[32] In García Carrasco's view, nobody would care since smugglers were considered criminals and privateers, enemies of Spain. However, Manuel Manso, the customs officer who also had to deal with the situation, claimed that all of this was untrue. In a testimony sent to the Junta Central de Sevilla on 4 February 1809, he wrote that the *Scorpion* was not a privateer ship, but a smuggling vessel, simply because it might not

29 Robson, pp. 214–26.

30 See Barros Arana, *Historia General de Chile*, VIII, pp. 55–70, Amunátegui, *La crónica de 1810*, I, pp. 225–55.

31 Historians tend to speak of both as being either English or North American. Miers believed that Faulkner was English. Bunker seemed to have born in North America as well, but he was the commander of a British ship and was serving as a British subject. It is likely that the fact that they spoke English led many Chileans to believe they were in fact English. See Miers, pp. 150–52.

32 'García Carrasco to the Junta Central de Sevilla', Santiago, 30 January 1809, AGI, Chile, vol. 206, n.fol. The Junta had officially been abolished one day before the date of this letter and was replaced by the Consejo de Regencia.

have a 'letter of marque and reprisal'.[33] The armistice between Spain and Great Britain had started on 6 June 1806 and in July the British king had declared that Spanish vessels must be treated as any others. Therefore, no letters of marque were given to pursue Spanish vessels, which would have been the case if the *Scorpion* had been a privateer ship.[34]

Bunker was warned about the conspiracy. One of his old friends and former surgeon on one of his travels was George (Jorge) Edwards, an Englishman settled in La Serena and married to a Chilean lady, Isabel de Ossandon.[35] Edwards had sent Bunker a letter in which he told him that rumours about the plot had spread throughout the country.[36] This made the plotters convince Bunker that José Toribio, the Marquis of Larraín, one of the most prominent and powerful figures of Santiago, was interested in buying a considerable part of the load. Pedro Arrue, one of García Carrasco's subordinates, had to pass himself off as Larraín. Bunker reached Pichidangui on 15 October 1808 as agreed. García Carrasco's role was to uncover the operation as a privateering affair, granting a letter of marque to two officers in charge of two boats in Valparaíso, from where they departed with 70 men to hunt and capture the *Scorpion* at Pichidangui. This was the way to make the operation appear licit. As a result, Bunker and eight of his men were killed and both the ship and the load were taken as a 'prize' to be divided between the plotters, including the governor. However, Manso claimed that in the context of the armistice, there were no reasons to give such a letter because the 'disposition of the supreme Junta of Seville towards the British nation proves more and more also what I have said in my writing: it was not the time to grant a letter of marque when Medina and Echeverría wanted to make themselves privateers'.[37] Despite Edward's warnings, Bunker trusted the fake Larraín and the plot was successful.

Details of the cruelty of the plot began to spread rapidly. According to Amunátegui, news about the capture of a smuggler ship was not as relevant for the people as the 'cruelty' with which the plot was carried out. The fact that the governor himself was involved was also unacceptable. Cheating,

---

33 A letter of marque is a permission granted by the state to attack vessels of another state in particular circumstances. See Matthew McCarthy, *Privateering, Piracy and British Policy in Spanish America, 1810–1830* (Woodbridge: Boydell Press, 2013), p. 29.

34 'Manso to the Junta Central de Sevilla', Santiago, 4 February 1809, AGI, Chile, vol. 206, n.fol.

35 A recent biography of Agustín Edwards Eastman, the owner of the most important newspaper in Chile, *El Mercurio*, provides details of how the 'legend' of the founder of the family has been assimilated by his descendants. See Víctor Herrero, *Agustín Edwards Eastman. Una biografía desclasificada del dueño de El Mercurio* (Santiago: Debate, 2014), pp. 9–15.

36 Reproduced in Amunátegui, *La crónica de 1810*, I, pp. 230–33.

37 'Manso to the Junta Central de Sevilla', Santiago, 4 February 1809, AGI, Chile, vol. 206, n.fol.

lying and killing were all behaviours that García Carrasco did not accept from a foreigner, as shown in the census of foreigners he had undertaken in July 1808 (see Chapter 1). Manso claimed that 'arbitrariness and despotism with which so serious a business was managed by the government has scandalised all the people'.[38] The second factor was the role of the real Marquis of Larraín. Once he learned that his name was involved in the plot, he complained to the Real Audiencia, the highest tribunal of the territory. Three English officers on the *Scorpion*, William Kennedy, Isaac Ellard and John Edward Wolleter, had survived the attack and were under arrest. All of them recognised Arrue and not José Toribio Larraín as the marquis who boarded the *Scorpion*.[39] Notwithstanding, Larraín raised the case and on 22 December 1808 reported it to Sidney Smith, the British commander of the Royal Navy station at Río de Janeiro.[40] At the same time, García Carrasco reported the capture of the *Scorpion* to the metropolitan authorities, the Consejo de Regencia, which was ruling the Spanish dominions on behalf of the king. On 23 March 1811 the Consejo stipulated that the case was actually a 'seizure' and not a prize, agreeing with Manso. The issue also had a diplomatic dimension, since the British government complained to the authorities of the metropolis. According to Matthew McMarthy, the British authorities were still demanding the return of the *Scorpion* from the Spanish government in 1823.[41] This confirms also that the plot was a manifestation of the geopolitics of the period and not simply an isolated action carried out by individuals.

The *Scorpion* affair reveals the confusing and contradictory nature of British-Chilean relations at that time. García Carrasco was aware that the situation in Europe had changed and that the war between Britain and Spain, which justified reactions during and after the invasions of Buenos Aires, had finished. As stated by Manso, before the plot was carried out, news about Spain's declaration of war on France, as well as the armistice with Britain, had already reached Chile. The *Scorpion* was thus not targeted because it was British, but because it was undertaking an illegal activity that might be exploited for personal benefit. García Carrasco even tried to link the incident to the international context of warfare by presenting it as a question of privateering. At the same time, he tried to benefit from the rhetoric he had used a couple of months before (July 1808) against foreigners, in which the British were depicted as enemies and criminals. But it was too late to present Britain as an enemy and the privateering argument did not convince the Spanish authorities on the Iberian Peninsula. The episode also makes it clear that by 1808 the presence of smugglers (many of whom were also privateers) was extensive, something that did not change over the short term

38 Ibid.
39 Amunátegui, *La cronica de 1810*, 1, pp. 242–44.
40 Ibid.
41 McCarthy, p. 123.

because free trade was not yet declared. In fact, when in 1825 Christopher Nugent reported to George Canning on his first months as Consul General in Valparaíso, he stressed that 'the total want of regularity in the public offices, the suspicions of the British merchants apprehensive of the imposition of new charges upon trade, the regular system of smuggling carried on throughout the country, are, amongst a variety of lesser ones, the obstacles that I have to contend with'.[42]

The 'want of regularity' was seen as a matter of priority by British merchants because hindering it would make their operations easier in Chile. Their identification as smugglers, or 'illegal' traders, caused several difficulties for their operations. The *Scorpion* affair was the most extreme example in the period, since it involved a governor who was willing to take advantage of this situation for his own benefit, drawing upon the 'anti-foreigner' rhetoric he had spread. The changes brought about by the situation in the Iberian Peninsula from May 1808 also affected trade. Once Britain stopped being Spain's enemy in the war, Chileans began to see commercial relationships with British merchants differently, and to debate about the necessity of open trade with other nations.

4.4 The Opening of Trade, 1811–1814

The role of British merchants in Chile was determined by changes in the regulations regarding trade passed by the Junta formed in September 1810. As shown above in the second section of this chapter, the Spanish American colonies were not permitted to trade freely with other nations. Up to 1778, there was a trade monopoly by which Spanish Americans were only allowed to trade with the port of Cádiz in Spain. The only changes to that regulation, via a decree of 'free trade' enacted in that year, were the authorisation to trade with other ports in Spain, and the opening up of some previously closed ports in Spanish America. In Chile, this new trade regulation led to the opening of Coquimbo in the north, along with Talcahuano in the south, to trade with Spanish ships only. Talcahuano had hitherto been the sole port authorised to trade with the metropolis. In practice, then, the trade monopoly between the Spanish crown and the Spanish American colonies did not change in itself, it was simply extended. This meant that trade with merchants from other nations, such as Britain, continued to be forbidden, and such merchants were considered to be smugglers, as shown above. This did not stop 'illegal' trade carried out by British smugglers, however. As demonstrated by scholars like Adrian Pearce and Sergio Villalobos, contraband was present in Spanish American and Chilean ports, and most smugglers were British merchants.[43]

---

42 'Nugent to Canning', Valparaíso, 17 April 1825, in *Britain and the Independence*, ed. by Webster.

43 Adrian Pearce, *British Trade with Spanish America, 1763–1808* (Liverpool: Liverpool University Press, 2007), pp. 161–90.

When the Junta was formed in Chile in 1810, the trade situation was a priority. This led the Junta to pass a new regulation on 21 February 1811 to open up trade to other 'friendly nations' on the grounds that at that moment they were still loyal to the Spanish crown and that Britain was its ally in the war against France. The decree stated that from that date onwards, 'the ports of Valdivia, Talcahuano, Valparaíso and Coquimbo are open to free trade with foreign powers, friend and allies of Spain, as well as neutral ones'.[44] The regulation was not an explicit declaration of free trade, but simply permission to trade with powers like Britain and the US, whose merchants were, along with the French, the most common along the Chilean coast. Thus, the new regulation changed the status of many smugglers, who now became legitimate merchants in the eyes of the Chilean authorities.

The enactment of this new regulation encouraged many more British merchants to travel to Chile. Among them was John James Barnard, who arrived in January 1812 as a supercargo on the *Emily*. His purpose was to sell guns and swords to the patriotic forces who were then already fighting the royalists (mostly sent from Peru). Yet this was not Barnard's only role, as seen in the previous chapter. He also brought Bibles and New Testaments to Chile as an agent of the BFBS. When the Spanish authorities retook the government after defeating the patriots in October 1814, Barnard was arrested. He was accused of illegally introducing 'one hundred and twenty pairs of guns and one hundred and twenty swords and fine sabres' to be sold to the patriots. Of these, 100 pairs of guns and 100 swords and sabres were purchased by Joaquín de Echeverría, who was later Minister of the Interior in the O'Higgins government (1817–1823).[45] In 1812–1813, when Barnard was operating, this meant that he was supporting one side in the conflict at a moment in which Britain had declared its neutrality. The Spanish authorities even accused him of violating the Treaty of Utrecht, signed by Spain and Britain in 1713. Barnard defended himself by claiming that he did not know that there was an ongoing war, and that he understood that the 'exportation of guns, sabres and swords to all friendly countries of England was allowed'.[46] Indeed, the Decree of 1811 declared that 'books, maps, plans, swords, guns, sabres, fusils, cannons, gunpowder, bullets' and other goods were exempt from tax.[47] He even suggested that they had been 'embarked in London with the intervention of a customs house'.[48] For the Spanish

---

44 'Decreto que establece la libertad de comercio', Santiago, 21 February 1811 in Villalobos, *El comercio y la crisis colonial*, pp. 373–76.

45 'Trial against Juan Diego Barnard', Santiago, November 1814, ANH-FV, vol. 440, fol. 34.

46 Ibid., fol. 35.

47 'Decreto que establece la libertad de comercio', in Villalobos, *El comercio y la crisis colonial*, p. 373.

48 'Trial against Juan Diego Barnard', Santiago, November 1814, ANH-FV, vol. 440, fol. 35.

authorities it was impossible that Barnard was unaware of the war, as he claimed, arguing that he could still have 'resisted its trade with the intruder government, whose evil one cannot ignore, upon arrival to the port, in a moment in which it was in a war against the royalist troops from Lima'.[49]

Spanish authorities accused Barnard of violating 'the pact of the nations', taking advantage of a situation allowed by 'an obscene regulation of free trade enacted by the insurgent government'.[50] However, although they did not explicitly blame the British government, the Spanish insinuated that the arrival of a 'multitude of foreigners who trade and go freely about the kingdom' was the result of governmental policy. As soon as British authorities learnt of the beginning of the independence process, it was claimed, they 'prepared mercantile expeditions to Chile', and it was argued that Barnard was one of those who arrived in this context. This also conformed, according to the Spanish, to the 'dominant ideas [in Britain] about Chile and other countries of South America, that they were rebel countries since the Inquisition had carried out its abominable atrocities'.[51]

The arrest and trial of Barnard shows that in 1814, amidst the independence struggles, Spanish authorities in Chile were still dubious about the intentions of the British Empire despite its declaration of neutrality. Barnard was accused of undertaking an illegal activity, which was even more serious considering that he was selling weapons to the 'insurgents'. The Spanish authorities also appealed to the treaties and pacts signed by both countries in the past to argue that the British must remain neutral in the conflict between Spain and its colonies. It was clear to them that this neutrality was not being respected, since Britain was trying to interfere in their internal matters by other means. The main activity was trade carried out by 'expeditions of merchants' sent to Chile after the opening of trade in 1811. In the Spanish authorities' view, trade became one of the means by which Britain would try to weaken the power of Spain, drawing benefits from the conflict in Spanish America. The Spanish authorities even claimed that British merchants travelling across the territory were 'getting knowledge about it [...], something that might be costly in the future'.[52]

Testimonies of merchants already settled in Chile between 1811 and 1814 reveal the uncertainty that they experienced amidst the conflict. Samuel Haigh, who had arrived in Chile early in 1817, witnessed the tension when royalist troops led by General Mariano Osorio were heading to Santiago to try to regain the power they had lost after the battle of Chacabuco. One of the merchants' main fears was losing their properties to confiscation, in the

---

49 Ibid.
50 Ibid., fol. 36.
51 Ibid., fol. 40. See also Ossa, *Armies, Politics and Revolutions*, pp. 62–64.
52 'Trial against Juan Diego Barnard', Santiago, November 1814, ANH-FV, vol. 440, fol. 37.

event that Osorio won the battle. This was a reason to support the patriots, even with money if necessary. According to Haigh:

A few months before, when the general patriotism was at its height, and everyone was vying with his neighbour to show his love of liberty and detestation of the troops of the tyrannical invader, the English merchants participated in the general enthusiasm. Upon one occasion, when the government was in the want of money to pay the army, they most generously came forward with a donation for that purpose, and each received a letter of thanks for his liberality.[53]

Haigh implies that British merchants even adhered to the patriots' cause beyond personal interests. When the threat of Osorio's triumph seemed most likely, these merchants were planning to take action even more radical than financial support: 'When the Spaniards commenced their march from Talcahuano, all the regular troops had taken the field, and we merchants had it in contemplation to form ourselves into a body of cavalry, for the protection of our property and the tranquillity of the town'.[54] They did not do so in the end; many of the British merchants in fact decided to leave for Mendoza in Argentina as a desperate measure. Only three remained in Chile, including Barnard. The main reason, as stated by Haigh, was to protect their property: '[...] I determined not to abandon it, whilst there was any hope of securing it'.[55] This also implied a more radical view on the outcome of the battle:

Having thus done everything in my power for the safety of the property, I began to think what to do for myself, and soon resolved that I would share the fate of the patriot army, and if, by its defeat, my mercantile prospects should vanish 'at one fell swoop,' then, in the event of escape, I would enter into the republican service.[56]

The image of Britain acquired different meanings for each side in the conflict as it developed. The Spanish authorities in Chile interpreted the extensive presence of merchants, some of whom were seen as nothing other than arms traffickers, as a manifestation of British attempts to weaken their power, whereas patriots saw Britain extend its 'helpful hands' to fight in the war.[57] Likewise, the view of British merchants themselves was not monolithic and they behaved in different ways as the war progressed. Their own personal interests and the need to defend their property – which in

---

53 Haigh, p. 202.
54 Ibid., p. 203.
55 Ibid., p. 204.
56 Ibid., p. 205.
57 'Trial against Juan Diego Barnard', Santiago, November 1814, ANH-FV, vol. 440, fol. 36.

most cases belonged to merchant houses based in Britain – seemed to be
their main reasons to support the patriotic faction during the war, rather
than shared principles.

4.5 The Association of British Merchants and the Role of John James Barnard, 1817–1820

After the Battle of Chacabuco, on 12 February 1817, the patriots retook
power, restoring the regulations and institutions they had established before
1814. The regulation of trade, which had been revised and amended in
1813, was re-enacted, which meant that British merchants were allowed to
trade in Chile again. The end of the Napoleonic wars in 1815 was also seen
by merchants as a new opportunity to expand their operations to Spanish
America. According to Humphreys, 'in the years after 1815, a war-weary
Europe saw in the fabled lands of the Spanish Empire a new El Dorado'.[58]
For their part, the Chileans were also interested in attracting foreigners to
the country, in order to contribute to the economy. As shown in Chapter
1, this project was revealed as early as 1813, when Francisco Antonio
Pinto was sent as an envoy to London with, among others, the mission to
encourage the migration of skilled European workers. In May 1817, Irisarri
wrote to O'Higgins from London that in order to win Britain's recognition
of Chilean independence, it might be advantageous to offer 'ten years of
exclusive trade with us'.[59] Although this idea was not pursued, it reveals
that the arrival of British merchants was seen by the Chilean authorities
as mutually beneficial.

There is no consensus about the number of Britons or, more specifically, British merchants who arrived and stayed in Chile during this period.
Most historians have repeated the estimate of one to three thousand Britons
arriving in Chile between 1817 and 1824. Yet the discrepancy of two thousand
people is too great to take these numbers seriously. Even Miers estimated
that there were no more than 400 Britons in Valparaíso upon his arrival in
1822, although the number of 'respectable' Britons was much smaller, since
most were 'sailors, or persons in the lower sphere of life'.[60] Gilbert Farquhar
Mathison, a traveller of the period, gave a clear (undated) opinion of his first
impression on arriving in Valparaíso:

> English and Americans, however, appeared to constitute the bulk of the
> population of the town; and so many naval officers, mates of merchantmen,
> sailors, and men of business, were everywhere seen, that, but for the mean

---

58 Humphreys, *British Consular Reports*, p. ix.
59 'Irisarri to O'Higgins', London, 27 May 1817, quoted by Jay Kinsbruner, 'The
   Political Influence of the British Merchants Resident in Chile during the O'Higgins
   Administration, 1817–1823', *The Americas*, 27:1 (1970), 26–39 (p. 28).
60 Miers, p. 446.

and dirty appearance of the place, a stranger might almost fancy himself arrived at a British settlement.[61]

Samuel Haigh, a merchant himself, paints a similar picture when narrating how foreign vessels began to arrive more frequently in Valparaíso after the establishment of O'Higgins in government: 'foreigners arrived in great numbers, and Valparaíso already began to look like an English port'.[62]

Although up to 1817 the presence of British merchants in Chile was still limited, Jay Kinsbruner has demonstrated it was under O'Higgins's government (1817–1823) that British merchants in Chile began to organise themselves in order to attain benefits.[63] On 5 July 1819, Admiral William Shirreff, commander of the *Andromeda* and of the Royal Navy station in the Pacific, wrote a letter to the 'British merchants resident in Chile'. He asked them to 'appoint a committee or some public agent who shall make known to me your wishes upon all subjects connected with the commerce and to whom I may also address my communications'.[64] He claimed that it was too difficult to hear their diverse interests at once, so it was much better to work as a group and appoint a secretary in charge of communications. The Association of British Merchants was established shortly thereafter (although we do not know the exact date) and John James Barnard, who was residing in Santiago, was appointed its secretary. If we follow Charles Webster's argument that the British influence in Spanish America was mainly exerted by means of trade and the presence of the Royal Navy, we can see that on this occasion both elements worked together.[65] It was the commander of the station in the Pacific who requested that the merchants form an association. This intervention also reveals the nature of the involvement of the British state during Chile's struggle for independence. The merchants organised themselves as an association of individuals pursuing their own benefits. However, they did so encouraged by a British state agent, a commander of the Royal Navy who not only acted to protect their interests, but also intervened to mediate with the Chilean government. Despite the argument being advanced that improvements in communications were required, it is clear that the association worked to put pressure on the new government to change trade regulations and to adapt these to British interests. According to Rector,

> the association of British merchants sought two goals, protection of property and modification of Chilean commercial institutions to English models. Protection of property ranged from preventing the seizure of ships

---

61 Mathison, p. 176.

62 Haigh, p. 253.

63 Kinsbruner, 'The Political Influence of British Merchants', pp. 30–38.

64 'Shirreff to the British Merchants Resident in Chile, Sir Majesty's ship *Andromeda*', Valparaíso, 5 July 1820, ANH-FV, vol. 440, fol. 56.

65 Charles Webster, *Britain and the Independence of Latin America, 1812–1830*, 2 vols (London, New York and Toronto: Oxford University Press, 1938), i, pp. 10–11.

to guarding the merchandise in the warehouse of Valparaíso. Modification of commercial institutions varied from tariff reductions to greater efficiency in customs handling.[66]

The role of the fleet stationed in the Pacific, that is, the naval representatives of the British state, was fundamental to both goals. In the first case, particularly during the campaigns of the Liberation Expedition of Peru, British navy officers appealed on many occasions to the Chilean authorities to protect the interests of British merchants in Callao. As shown in Chapter 2, the blockade of Callao had caused serious disputes between Cochrane and some Royal Navy officers, who considered it an illegal action. Something similar happened in Chile at the end of the 1820s, when the political turmoil generated by the opposition of different political groups to the liberal administration of Francisco Pinto led many British merchants to request help from the British fleet to protect their interests. In this matter, the role of John James Barnard was crucial.

As the secretary of the Association of British Merchants, Barnard was the mediator between the British merchants residing in Chile and the commanders of the Royal Navy stationed in the Pacific. The complaints and requirements of the former were transmitted to the latter so that they could ask the Chilean government act in favour of the merchants. Admiral Shirreff sent letters representing the merchants' interests in 1819 to O'Higgins, requesting his protection of their operations between Chile and Lima, in the context of the blockade of Callao.[67] On 10 February 1820, Captain Daniel O'Brien, another Royal Navy officer in the Pacific, suggested that

> there should not be any misunderstanding between the British merchants and the government of Chili [sic]. They at all times have given great proofs of their liberality in supporting it and more than would be either expected of them as consistent with their duty as the subjects of a nation which although possessing every wish to preserve harmony and good understanding with this country yet is most anxious to keep its state of neutrality inviolable.[68]

This testimony shows that for British officers, the role played by some merchants had gone beyond Britain's policy of neutrality, which was more evident in the case of the secretary of the association, John James Barnard. It also shows that in spite of protecting the interests of British merchants, Royal Navy officers stuck to the policy of neutrality declared by Britain, and sometimes intervened to defend that policy in the face of merchants' pleas.

As explained above, the very presence of Barnard in Chile was controversial, since he was accused of violating British neutrality when introducing

---

66 Rector, p. 121.
67 ANH-FV, vol. 440, fols 57–61.
68 'O'Brien to Barnard', Valparaíso, 10 February 1820, ANH-FV, vol. 440, fol. 62.

weapons for the patriotic forces. His behaviour as a merchant and as secretary of the association also reveals that he was building up his own career, and despite being the secretary of an association that represented the interests of a specific community, he acted on his own on many occasions. Although a foreigner, Barnard gained prestige and a reputation not only as a renowned merchant but also as a philanthropist. As such, his most important contribution was his donation of 500 pesos for the war, which was regarded as 'proof of his generosity for the prosperity and glory of this country'.[69] The government also requested that he intercede with the British merchants in order to obtain a loan of 10,000 pesos for the war as proof of their 'due fraternity with this republic'.[70] In addition, he contributed to other philanthropic causes, such as the establishment of a 'military hospital for the expeditionary army of Peru' in May 1820, and the Lancasterian Society in June 1822. In sum, Barnard's role as the secretary of the merchant association and his philanthropic contributions to different causes led the authorities to nominate him for different commissions, such as the 'commission of mercy',[71] the 'board of health',[72] the commission in charge of revising and reforming trade regulations[73] and even the commission to reform the Constitution.[74] In all these bodies he interacted with prominent figures in the political and social life of Chile. For example, the board of health was formed by people like José Toribio, the Marquis of Larraín mentioned above, who was the leader of one of the most powerful families of Santiago, Francisco Ruiz Tagle, chief of the urban police, Manuel Grajales and Agustin Nataniel Cox, the most important physicians in the country, and Camilo Henríquez, one of the intellectual leaders of the independence movement.[75]

Despite these considerations, Barnard's involvement in Chilean affairs was controversial. He emphasised his condition as a 'foreigner' in most of his correspondence with local authorities and never requested Chilean citizenship. Whenever he replied to an invitation to join the above commissions, he claimed that he was a foreigner without sufficient knowledge of the implementation of foreign ideas in a local context. In his reply to Agustin de Vial, who invited him to join the commission to reform trade regulation, he said he was

69 'José Miguel Infante, Domingo Eyzaguirre and Rafael Correa to Barnard', Santiago, 27 January 1818, ANH-FV, vol. 440, fol. 74.
70 'José Antonio Rodriguez to Barnard', Santiago, 12 July 1820, ANH-FV, vol. 440, fol. 76.
71 'Camilo Henríquez to Barnard', Santiago, 14 August 1822, ANH-FV, vol. 440, fol. 89.
72 'Joaquín Echeverría to Barnard', Santiago 23 August 1822, ANH-FV, vol. 440, fol. 90.
73 'Agustín de Vial to Barnard', Santiago 21 October 1821, ANH-FV, vol. 440, fol. 85.
74 'Mariano Egaña to Barnard', Santiago, 21 January 1823, ANH-FV, vol. 440, fol. 91.
75 'Joaquín Echeverría to Barnard', Santiago 23 August 1822, ANH-FV, vol. 440, fols 90–91.

reluctant to accept because of the 'envy and censorship of those individuals whose interests would be influenced by any disposition adopted'. In addition, he claimed that 'there must be naturals from Chile whose general knowledge is widely useful for this enterprise, while their local experience can be judiciously used to prevent a collision with radical ideas'.[76] In his reply to Juan Egaña, he also claimed that 'neither my education nor my local knowledge make me apt to accept such a position', arguing that 'Chile does not lack apt and prudent men to perform these duties with honour and judgment'.[77]

These testimonies suggest that Barnard behaved in different ways, which makes it difficult to label him simply a merchant acting in his own interests. His role as the secretary of the association of British merchants implied representing both the interests of many individuals like himself, who were simply trying to do business, and British interests at large. The involvement of Shirreff in the formation of the association and his regular communication with Barnard make it difficult not to consider Barnard an agent of the British Empire. According to Rector and Salazar, it was this association, plus the mediation of Royal Navy officers, that most influenced the liberalisation of the Chilean economy in the 1820s. This also explains the arrival of thousands of Britons, and the settling of about forty branches of merchant houses in Valparaíso during this decade. Barnard's role seemed critical, although the extent to which he was either acting on his own, or representing the rest of the merchants is not so clear. His insistence on conciliating the adoption of 'radical' liberal ideas did not necessarily fit into the conception that other merchants expressed regarding the need to eliminate any barriers to free trade. This was a much better fit for the Chilean government's own conception of how to adopt a liberal economic policy in the complex context of the independence struggles. At the same time, this was also another dimension of the 'cultural approach' mentioned in Chapter 3, which reveals that foreign economic ideas had to be adopted considering the local context.[78] When the O'Higgins government appointed the commission to revise the regulation of trade in 1813, the aim was 'to revise the regulation and subsequent decrees to form a sensible and clear law adaptable to our state'.[79] The local conditions that made it necessary to adapt the principles of economic liberalism in Chile were explained on the grounds that 'this government, always aware about the liberal ideas it had adopted, only tries to conciliate the advantages of trade and less obstacles for the trader, with the proportionate and more difficult to evade charge that these days the upholding of the republic demands'.[80]

Despite his expressed reluctance, Barnard eventually joined the commission to revise and reform trade regulations. As such, he wrote a piece about

76 'Barnard to de Vial', Santiago, 30 October 1821, ANH-FV, vol. 440, fol. 85.
77 'Barnard to Egaña', Santiago, January 1823, ANH-FV, vol. 440, fol. 93.
78 Caruso and Roldán Vera, 'Pluralizing Meanings', p. 649.
79 'O'Higgins communication', Santiago, 2 March 1821, ANH-FV, vol. 440, fol. 101.
80 Ibid.

'how to reach the prosperity of Chile' that he sent to O'Higgins on 7 August 1821. It is not clear whether this piece was written considering the point of view of other merchants or not, but it clearly outlines the place of Chile in the world trade system, reinforcing the image of Chile as a pathway to other places as suggested earlier in chapters 1 and 3 of this book. In his view, it was beneficial to Chile 'to attract to its ports foreign expeditions, which pass by the Cape Horn with Peru as the destination'.[81] This was fundamental because the attractiveness of Chile laid in the fact that it was an *entrepot* between the Atlantic and the Pacific, and a necessary stop for those whose final destination was Peru. As shown in other chapters, this idea of Chile being a pathway to Peru was not new and had been contested since the beginning of the independence era. When the Liberation Expedition departed Valparaíso for Callao in 1820, expectations regarding the fall of Lima increased. John Parish Robertson, a merchant who was in Chile as an agent of his grandfather's firm, John Parish, wrote in April 1821: 'the utmost anxiety prevails to hear from San Martín, who is besieging Lima. No doubt he is entertained of its ultimate fall, but the poverty of the Treasury and the large stock of goods in the hands of the merchants make the government impatient and the English uneasy about the delay'.[82] His brother William, based in Buenos Aires, also gave his opinion regarding the importance of the fall of Lima and the potential impact on the Chilean economy:

> You are fully aware of the immense advantages which must accrue to our commerce as well as to that of Chile, when the whole of Peru is incorporated in the general cause. It is by far the richest and most extensive part of the country, and while vessels going round to the Pacific supply all the coast and Lima itself, we shall have our trade extended to Potosi, Cochabumba [Cochabamba], and in short to all the interior of Peru.[83]

This reinforces the idea that the economic interests of Britain in Chile laid in its strategic position and its advantages as a pathway to Peru, rather than in being a market in itself as suggested by Somarriva.[84] This was the same image seen in the plan to invade Chile in 1806, although now it was becoming clearer that an invasion was no longer necessary in order to take advantage of the location.

In his writing, Barnard made a call for the restoration of the decree of 30 September 1820, which had declared Valparaíso a *puerto franco* (free port), implying that goods in transit could be deposited indefinitely in the depots

---

81 'Barnard to O'Higgins', Santiago, 7 August 1821, ANH-FV, vol. 440, fol. 83.
82 'John Parish Robertson to John Parish', Santiago, 17 April 1821, The Wellington Archive (hereafter, TWA), University of Southampton Library, Special Collections, WP1/685/20.
83 'William Parish Robertson to John Parish', Buenos Aires, 6 September 1821, TWA, WP1/685/20.
84 Somarriva, pp. 15–34.

for only a small fee. This decree had been abolished, restricting the duration of storage in the depots and raising the tariffs. In Barnard's view, the imposition of higher tariffs was 'opposite to the very idea of a market and as long as it persists, there will not be a market at all'. He claimed that the decree must be immediately restored as its abolition was 'the dagger that kills free trade'.[85] Barnard understood that said decree had been abolished in line with a protectionist policy, to foster local industry and agriculture. Although he did not completely oppose this idea, since it could bring some benefits to the treasury, he argued that 'it cannot be considered as a burden for trade'.[86]

Eventually, O'Higgins enacted the new *Reglamento de Comercio* (Trade Regulations) on 23 October 1822, which restored the depots in Valparaíso in order to foster free trade. Merchants were allowed to store their goods in transit without paying customs tariffs, only paying a small fee for depositing the goods.[87] Barnard's suggestion had been followed, which reveals the influential position he had reached in Chilean society. However, shortly afterwards, the government decided to abolish the measure due to the increasing presence of smugglers. It was eventually restored by Ramon Freire's government in 1824. This was a contested idea, difficult to reconcile with locals' views on the need to protect local production from the competition of foreign goods. Even so, this reveals that, as with the debates on the adoption of the Royal Navy's *Regulations*, and the Monitorial system of education, ideas about free trade were not simply imposed by the Chilean government, they had to be reconciled with local conditions.

4.6 Between Private Interests and Political Affairs

Merchants' day-to-day lives, and the local conditions they experienced daily, shaped their private interests. Some British travellers, like John Miers, who was also a merchant and a businessman in Chile, and Maria Graham, a British traveller who arrived in Chile in 1822, gave their views on the way Britons and foreigners behaved once settled in this new country. Graham, for example, said that 'as all Englishmen, from the highest to the lowest, love to have their *home* with them, the clerks, who fit naturally into these sort of employments, either bring or find suitable wives: therefore, society, as far as relates to the English, is of a very low tone'.[88] This impression confirms the idea that in the 1820s the British merchants who settled in Chile behaved as a community. However, in Kinsbruner's view, rather than behaving as a collective entity with common goals and interests, these merchants seemed to behave as individuals who sporadically requested intervention from the Chilean authorities to get benefit for their business or to preserve some

---

85 'Barnard to O'Higgins', Santiago, 7 August 1821, ANH-FV, vol. 440, fol. 83.
86 Ibid., fol. 80.
87 See Mendez, pp. 80–82.
88 Graham, *Journal of a Residence in Chile*, p. 179.

aspect of their life. Since the association of British merchants did not have a formal organisation, it is not clear if during this decade it still worked as such, but there are sources that show that in some cases they acted as a group in order to defend their common interests. In any case, either as individuals or as a group, merchants tended to behave as 'non-state' actors, distancing themselves from British imperial interests. However, when it was convenient, they still counted on the protection of the British state, represented by the ships of the Royal Navy stationed in the Pacific. This was one of the privileged means by which the firm Antony Gibbs & Sons started its operations in Chile in 1820. As argued by Salazar, they sent their consignee John Moens to Valparaíso, who began his business illegally, knowing he was under the protection of the Royal Navy. This enabled him to expand his operations to Lima, even during the blockade of Callao by the Chilean squadron commanded by Cochrane.[89]

The petition of 47 British merchants to O'Higgins in 1819, to preserve their religious liberties, is a good example of an occasion on which merchants chose to preserve and promote their collective identity as Britons. It is telling that the first signature on the petitions is that of Admiral Shirreff, the commander of the British fleet in the Pacific, which shows that these British state agents also put pressure on the government to obtain benefits for Britons. The British government was willing to protect its subjects, and also to intercede in their favour in order to get equal treatment with locals in terms of civil rights.[90] As stated in another chapter, religious toleration was also one of the critical spheres of autonomy that Thomas Cochrane's fellows managed to maintain while part of the Chilean navy. Despite these examples, Kinsbruner has argued that 'the British Protestants [...] were not crusading for religious toleration', but asking for 'something specific'.[91] However, he overlooks the fact that the granting of a certain degree of religious toleration was also a policy fostered by the Chilean government on its own initiative. From 1811, it became clear that attracting Europeans – not only Britons – was a fundamental step to improve the economic system. The opening of free trade was also a measure to attract foreigners to Chile, which means that the tolerance allowed by O'Higgins formed part of a set of measures to make Chile an attractive destination for British merchants. Also, as shown in Chapter 3, the extent to which Catholics opposed the presence of Protestants – considering that to Chileans eyes in the period, Briton and Protestant were synonymous – must not be exaggerated, since at least before 1825 the cases of open opposition to the presence of Protestant missionaries were isolated. Likewise, the role of these missionaries in fostering religious toleration by means of the spread of Monitorial schools and Bibles, as well as the granting of similar privileges from the government to the British seamen of the navy,

---

89 Salazar, *Mercaderes, empresarios y capitalistas*, pp. 98–100.
90 Kinsbruner, p. 34.
91 Ibid., p. 35.

seems to show that religious liberty was not simply a particular petition from an interested group but much more crucial. Maria Graham's impressions reveal that a certain degree of toleration was in fact experienced by Britons who were living in Chile in 1822:

> In Chile the Protestant worship in private houses was connived at, and the Protestants had been permitted to purchase ground for a burial place, both in the city and at the port; and something had been attempted as to facilitating marriages between Protestants and Roman Catholics, but it was too early as yet to hope for perfect and public toleration: yet the officers entering into the service, naval or military, were never incommoded on account of their form of worship, or even requested to change it.[92]

The fact that this group of Protestant merchants defended their liberties would have a significant impact in Chilean society. At least, during the tumultuous 1820s, the possibility existed to debate with the authorities, and even the potential to be granted some privileges. This also triggered major concern from some leading statesmen like Juan Egaña, who in 1823 published *Memoria* to oppose O'Higgins policies on religious tolerance on the grounds that it would undermine the state's unity and stability.[93] He also opposed such measures because, as argued by Racine, 'he viewed with apprehension the republican government's willingness to accommodate foreigners by guaranteeing freedom of religion as part of their overall modernising agenda'.[94] This became much more difficult during the authoritarian regime inaugurated in the 1830s by Diego Portales, who took a more restrictive and intolerant stance towards Protestants after the enactment of the Constitution of 1833, which consolidated the principle of religious uniformity.

On another occasion, a group of nine merchants made a representation on 4 September 1824 to the recently appointed British consul, Christopher Nugent, to complain about their situation. The letter was signed by Dickson Price, John James Barnard, Tyler Miller, Tayleur Newton, James Kirk, James Ingram, John Parish Robertson, Winter Brittain Waddington and Thomas Edward Brown. The representation aimed to state that their interests and 'their duties as subjects of His Britannic Majesty (merchants in the present relations of this country) [was] exposed to serious compromise'.[95] More

92 Graham, *Journal of a Residence in Chile*, p. 52.

93 Juan Egaña, *Memoria política sobre el conviene en Chile la libertad de cultos. Reimpreso en Lima y Bogotá con una breve apología del art. 8 y 9 de la constitución política del Perú de 1823* (Caracas: Imprenta G.V. Devisme, 1829).

94 Racine, 'Proxy Pasts', p. 872.

95 'Extracts from a Representation Addressed by the British Merchants in Chile to His Britannic Majesty's Consul-General', Santiago, 4 September 1824, Archivo Nacional Histórico de Chile, Fondo Ministerio de Hacienda (hereafter, ANH-MH), vol. 59, n. fol.

important than the reason for the complaint, which was their fear of a new change in trade regulations, the letter reveals some critical elements of their self-perception as merchants. Firstly, they considered themselves 'foreigners invited to Chile' by the Chilean government 'in the publication of the decree by which commerce was first opened to other nations in 1813'.[96] Although trade was actually opened in 1811, they considered 1813, when a new regulation was enacted, as the defining moment in which they were considered proper merchants residing in Chile. Before that, they could not consider themselves as such, because their activities were forbidden. This reinforces the idea that one of the aims of British merchants was to legalise what they had previously done illegally, and they considered the declaration of free trade the first step. A second element was the way they stressed that they 'came to this country as consignees, receiving and selling the property of persons residing outside of this country'.[97] This was one of the main arguments used to resist any attempt to subject them to 'personal contributions', or taxes, which the merchant houses based in Britain, whom they represented, had to pay in their place. They made this distinction because they were not the owners of the goods they were transporting, which led them to demand that they be permitted to 'reside in Chile, free as foreign merchants from all commercial impositions and contributions, except such as declared upon the goods, which may be imported and exported by them'.[98] They claimed that 'they only wished to be treated with justice, according to the customs of other nations, and that good faith be observed toward them'.[99] This testimony reveals that in the middle of the 1820s the British merchants defined themselves as a group of foreigners which was not still incorporated into Chilean society. They also used this differentiation to demonstrate that, as consignees, they were simply trading goods that belonged to other persons who lived in Britain, a reason to preserve their exemptions. They were much more concerned with the defence of their private interests than defending the interests of Britain in general. In fact, some of them, like John Parish Robertson were not actually based in Chile.[100]

Despite the increasing numbers of Britons arriving in Chile in the 1820s, the extent to which they played a critical role in Chilean political developments in the period has been debated. For Jay Kinsbruner, the political influence of British merchants during the O'Higgins government 'was limited in nature',

96 Ibid.
97 Ibid.
98 Ibid.
99 Ibid.
100 As noted before, Robertson was a renowned merchant in Buenos Aires and he and his brother William had extended their operations to different parts of South America, like Paraguay, Chile and Uruguay. See John Parish Robertson, *Letters on South America: Comprising Travels on the Banks of the Paraná and Río de la Plata*, 3 vols (London: John Murray, 1843).

the main reason being 'the resolute independence of mind demonstrated by the Chilean government'.[101] However, as shown in the previous section, the case of John James Barnard cannot be overlooked. He played a critical role in the definition of Chile's economic policy, which in the 1820s at least was clearly open to free trade. Rector maintains that, in this respect, Barnard was not acting on his own, but as the representative of the rest of the merchants based in Chile. For Salazar, the role of British merchants was critical to both the definition of the Chilean economy as a 'mercantilist' system and for the construction of the authoritarian regime inaugurated by Diego Portales in 1830. He identifies two different groups among these merchants: those who remained loyal to their merchant houses in Britain and those who broke free from them and were 'creolised' and incorporated into the Chilean elite. Both groups formed part of the same network, even those who gained their 'independence' and became part of the *patriciado* colonised the Chilean elite. This paved the way for the settlement of the 'subsidiary houses', which were fundamental agents in Chile's economic development during the late nineteenth-century nitrate era. In other words, the ties between these British merchants and the Chilean political elite were unbreakable, subjugating the Chilean economy to the imperial ambitions of Great Britain.

The extent to which British merchants were involved in Chilean political matters must not be exaggerated. Salazar implies that they were seeking to establish a form of alliance with one of the Chilean political factions with whom they had common interests.[102] This was the faction led by Diego Portales, formed by conservatives and *estanqueros* (former monopoly holders in tobacco and liqueurs), who were supported by these merchants in order to build a political regime in line with their interests, and which would enable them to conduct their business without trouble. However, this 'alliance' was not configured from the outset. During the 1820s, the British merchants in Chile did not behave as a single entity, but tried to defend their own interests and supported different factions alike, depending on how threatened they felt. On many occasions they even complained about Diego Portales's faction and requested protection from the Royal Navy station in the Pacific. They were therefore defending their own interests in a period of political turmoil and not establishing an alliance with a particular faction more sympathetic to their ideas, as shown in the following section.

4.7 British Merchants and Chilean Politics in the 1820s

One way to assess Salazar's interpretation of the undeniable link between Chile's ruling elite and British merchants is to analyse their behaviour at a particular moment after independence. The late 1820s saw increasing

---

101 Kinsbruner, p. 26.
102 Salazar, *Mercaderes, empresarios y capitalistas*, pp. 161–67.

political unrest due to the conflictive relations between different political factions. A revolution led by General Joaquín Prieto, commander of the military forces in Concepción and leader of the 'liberating army of the south', broke out in 1829 against the liberal government of Francisco Antonio Pinto. Prieto's forces represented the interests of different factions of the incipient Chilean political system: the conservatives and the *estanqueros* led by Diego Portales.[103] The British Consul General in Valparaíso, John White, appointed in 1828, wrote to Captain Coghlan, commander of the British ship *Forte*:

> Having this day received official news that a revolution had broken out in the South of Chile, and that General Prieto in command there was about to march upon the capital to depose the President, it is not unreasonable to suppose that this government will oppose his intentions, and withdraw the force here for that purpose to the Capital, should such be the case, to guard against the possibility of British subjects and their property being subjected to the attack of a licentious mob whom it may not be in the power of the civil authorities to overawe. I submit to your consideration the policy of one of His Majesty's ship being stationary in this port for the protection of British interests under the present state of affairs.[104]

This extract reflects one of the main concerns of the British consul: the threats to the safety of British merchants and their properties based in Coquimbo. It is not surprising that most of the consular reports about the safety of these merchants amidst the conflict refer to this port. Coquimbo was not only the main port in the north, but an important depot for the copper mined in northern Chile. As John Mayo has shown, it was a crucial place for British economic interests, which was sufficient reason to consider the possibility of stationing a warship off its coast.[105] This measure did not mean attacking the port if necessity, but having a ship ready in case British merchants needed to run away from the city. Such fears came not only from the consul, but from the merchants themselves, who wrote to the consul demanding protection of their interests.

There are several letters from British merchants based in Coquimbo, La Serena, Santiago and Valparaíso begging for protection, which have been overlooked by historians. On 14 December 1829, Alex Caldelaugh, John Falcon, Henry Cood, Geo Hormold, James Whitehead, Ralph Kirk, James Clark, J.C. Blakely, Charles S. Grey, George Bingley, Thomas Smith, Henry Doncaster, Thomas Bonnus, James Oliver, William Chenas, Francis M. Drexel, Geo Smith, Andrew Tomlin, Benjamin Smith, B. Miller, John Atkinson, James G. Hull and William Dartwell wrote from Santiago claiming that 'we

---

103 Collier, pp. 323–60.
104 'White to Coghlan', Valparaíso, 8 October 1829, TNA, Foreign Office (hereafter, FO), vol. 16, FO 16/10, fols 5–6.
105 Mayo, 'The Development of British Interests in Chile's Norte Chico', pp. 368–73.

find our lives and property exposed to the grasp of a lawless rabble, which government acknowledges at the present moment they cannot restrain'.[106] The main argument was the belief that foreigners were being targeted for the mere fact of being foreign and rich: 'foreigners have been especially selected as the objects of their vengeance, as the events of this day sufficiently show, dreadful attacks having been made on them by the mob headed by some soldiers'.[107] From La Serena, Thomas Kendall, Edward Abbot, David Ross, J. Walker and Willie Miller wrote to White 'that in consequence of the extremely disordered state of this city and province, we consider our lives to be in imminent peril, and the property of others intrusted to our care, every moment in danger of confiscation', reminding him of 'the atrocious acts committed on persons and property last Sunday night'.[108]

In all these cases, the aim of the British merchants in sending these letters to the consul was to request the protection that the Chilean government was unable to guarantee. The means of securing such protection was the intervention of one of the ships stationed in the Pacific, particularly that commanded by Captain Arthur Bingham, the *Thetis*. Letters requesting British protection were also sent by the Chilean authorities themselves. Ramón Picarte, commander of the military garrison at Valparaíso, wrote to White on 7 December 1829 to inform him that:

> Some common people who think only of causing harm to their neighbour's property, particularly if those neighbours are British subjects, are preparing to attack houses in the Almendral [Valparaíso]. Because the government troops under my command cannot hope to defend all these houses, I request that your nation's warships provide the necessary protection.[109]

More than requesting protection of the British merchants in Valparaíso, Picarte intended for White to reinforce the defence of the port with one of the British warships stationed in the Pacific. In a previous letter, White had already reminded the Minister of Foreign Affairs that to activate such a plan in Valparaíso 'could be contrary to the neutrality that His Britannic Majesty's government has ever professed to maintain in the friendly states wherever its authorities or subjects may be situated'.[110] This testimony reveals that the principle of neutrality was invoked even when the conflict did not involve different states, but in a civil war which confronted nationals of the same state. In consequence, White replied to Picarte: 'the Captain of His Britannic Majesty's ship Thetis will not land the force of his nation

106 'Caldelaugh et al. to White', Santiago, 14 December 1829, TNA, FO 16/10, fols 142–43.
107 Ibid.
108 'Kendall et al. to White', La Serena, 25 April 1830, TNA, FO 16/12A, fols 233–34.
109 'Picarte to White', 7 December 1829, TNA, FO 16/10, fol. 134.
110 'White to the Minister of Foreign Affairs', 2 December 1829, TNA, FO 16/10, fols 131–32.

for the protection of the little property and few houses belonging to British subjects situated in the Almendral, from whence the property they contain may be removed by those to whom it belongs'.[111] Almost simultaneously, the Intendant of Coquimbo, Joaquín Vicuña, wrote to the consul to that port, Matthew Carter, to ask for protection from a possible invasion by Facundo Quiroga's 'barbarian' and 'depraved' forces, who were fleeing the army of the United Provinces in northern Argentina. In this case, Vicuña did not hesitate to use the economic importance of British merchants as an excuse to request help:

> the greatest part of this commerce depends on British houses which in such a lamentable case would experience incalculable injuries, and in order to avoid them, it would be very proper for you to communicate with the Admiral of the British Force which is in our seas, to the end that he should station in this port one of the vessels of war under his command to watch any event and be able to protect the interest of your nation.[112]

On this occasion, neither White nor Bingham mentioned the principle of neutrality, but rather agreed that intervention was a 'justifiable measure'.[113]

In all these examples, we can see that White seemed reluctant to interfere in the course of the civil war. The principle of neutrality was the perfect reason to ignore the petitions of the authorities, with the exception of those cases in which it was more evident that 'British interests', rather than 'British subjects', were under threat. The most evident case was Coquimbo, where mining was a crucial economic activity. However, White did sometimes interfere, at least diplomatically, when there were imminent threats to the safety of British subjects. The most documented case occurred in Santiago, where the House of Sewell and Patrickson office was in danger of being attacked by the forces of General Prieto. White protested strongly and wrote a letter to Prieto warning him that:

> it is not necessary to remind the General that the subjects of His Britannic Majesty have never mixed themselves up with the political affairs of Chili [sic], nor have been wanting in respect to the laws and the authorities of the State, he therefore has every reason to hope that the General will afford them the protection that the undersigned has the right to claim for them.[114]

White reinforced the idea that the British subjects were neutrals who did not interfere in the political affairs of any country. This was also accompanied by a declaration of the values that a Chilean should expect from a British subject. He wrote of John Sewell and Thomas Patrickson that they:

---

111 'White to Picarte', 8 December 1829, TNA, FO 16/10, fols 138–39.
112 'Vicuña to Carter', 5 December 1829, TNA, FO 16/10, fols 220–21.
113 'Bingham to White', 21 December 1829, TNA, FO 16/10, fol. 223.
114 'White to Prieto', 12 December 1829, FO 16/10, fols 140–41.

have been very many years in South America, and several years resident as merchants in Chile. They are gentlemen of well known integrity, and have been variously connected with persons directing mining operations in many of the different districts in Chile, particularly those of Copiapo and Coquimbo. They are personally acquainted with the members of Government, and the official legal, and commercial gentlemen of the country.[115]

Shortly after voicing this opinion, he was disappointed by the role played by Mr Sewell, who was not happy with the letter that White had sent to Prieto. Sewell requested that White withdraw the letter, arguing that Prieto was threatening his properties, and claiming 'that I know of no English house that has been attacked nor of any Englishman'.[116] White interpreted this sudden change of view as a sort of betrayal of British values like integrity, honesty and honour. In so doing, he implied that with his request, Sewell represented those 'few who would not fail in my opinion to sacrifice our national honour and dignity to serve their own narrow, selfish, purposes'.[117] White believed that by breaking the principle of neutrality Sewell wanted 'to receive some privilege, perhaps a remission of custom house duties for a certain time, or a preference in supplying the government for such advantages' should Prieto rule the country.[118] This was not, in his view, the expected behaviour of a British subject amidst an internal conflict in a foreign country.

These testimonies show that British merchants were not aligned with one specific group during the conflict that took place at the end of the 1820s, which casts doubt on Salazar's assertions on this.[119] They were concerned about their personal safety and the future of their business. In 1829–1830 the British merchants did what they had done before in such cases, that is, to ask for protection from the British fleet stationed off the Chilean coast in the Pacific. This is what the British merchants in Callao did in 1819, when they felt that Cochrane was a threat to their commercial interests. Ten years later, they did the same in Chile when they felt that the civil war posed a similar threat. In some cases, British merchants identified General Prieto as the most important threat to their safety, denouncing his troops' willingness to attack their properties. They did not necessarily see Prieto and Portales, both in the same group during the war, as their natural allies. In the British merchants' view, Prieto and Portales were as responsible as Pinto for the political unrest in Chile. This calls into question the assumption that in this period at least British merchants formed part of the same alliance with Portales and Prieto, imposing their own political and economic interests, as

---

115 'White to the Earl of Aberdeen', TNA, FO 16/9, fols 92–93.
116 'Sewell to White', 21 December 1829, TNA, FO 16/10, fols 242–45.
117 'White to the Earl of Aberdeen, 23/12/1823, FO 16/10, fols 226–30.
118 Ibid.
119 Salazar, *Mercaderes, empresarios y capitalistas*, pp. 130–60.

Salazar claimed. If this happened, it was because one side triumphed in the war and this meant that British merchants that could keep running their business. The behaviour of the British merchants in this context must be explained on the grounds of the circumstances they experienced, rather than a set of ideas fixed beforehand.

The reorientation of the Chilean economy meant that those who worked to supply the internal demand for manufactured goods found themselves in a difficult situation. Since the colonial period, artisans like shoemakers, smiths and carpenters had made goods to be sold in the Chilean internal market. According to Sergio Grez, the natural reaction of these groups of artisans was to organise themselves politically in order to defend their interests against the government. They gradually configured a political discourse to demand protectionist measures, to prevent the influx of products manufactured abroad. As Rory Miller argues, these artisans voiced 'early critiques' of the role played by British merchants in Latin America.[120] Their demands for protectionist measures would be a constant among Chilean artisans throughout the nineteenth century, when free trade-oriented policy expanded and British influence in business became more significant.[121]

4.8 Conclusions

The role played by British merchants was crucial in terms of influencing the economic policy of the new government of Chile. At the beginning of the independence era, the Chilean Junta decided to open some ports to trade with foreign powers. Although Villalobos demonstrated that this was far from being a major factor in the independence movements, it is clear that the decision to declare the opening of trade had significant consequences. As a group of British merchants said in 1824, this decision was seen as an 'invitation' to travel to Chile and carry out their activities as individual actors. Before then, they had not been invited because their activities were considered illegal, at a moment in which trade was restricted to commerce between certain specific Spanish American ports and Spain. This 'invitation' attracted many merchant houses to Chile to start their operations. The fact that Valparaíso was one of the ports opened up was also seen as good opportunity, since it was a natural *entrepot* for ships travelling from the Atlantic to the Pacific via Cape Horn. One of the first merchants to 'accept' the invitation was John James Barnard, who was aware that guns and swords were needed in the war that had already started in Chile. His role was fundamental, because

---

120 Miller, p. 14.

121 Sergio Grez, *De la regeneración del pueblo a la huelga general. Génesis y evolución histórica del movimiento popular en Chile (1810–1890)* (Santiago: Ril Editores, 2007); James A. Wood, *The Society of Equality: Popular Republicanism and Democracy in Santiago de Chile, 1818–1851* (Albuquerque, NM: University of New Mexico Press, 2011), p. 54.

it signals the different meanings that the presence of a British merchant could have in Chile. As the secretary of the British association of merchants, formed under the auspices of Admiral W.H. Shirreff, Barnard represented the interests of merchants and, by extension, those of the British Empire, represented by Shirreff. Barnard was the intermediary between Shirreff and the merchants, but this did not prevent him from acting as an individual when he got involved in other affairs. This explains the reputation he gained, to the point that he was invited to join several political groupings, including the commission to reform trade regulations. In that position, he tried to convince the government to adopt a free trade-oriented policy, although he was conscious that this had to be done in consideration of the local reality. During the 1820s, this policy was decisive in defining British merchants as a single group. They would try, and were often able, to preserve their own identity as foreigners and to avoid intervening in internal Chilean conflicts. They often depicted themselves as preserving their own interests, which were restricted to commerce. However, even if we limit their sphere of influence to the field of economic policy, this had stark consequences for the political life of Chileans. Some of the latter, like the artisans, were affected by this free trade policy, and would become an increasingly politicised group demanding a more protectionist economic policy.

Finally, the assessment of British merchants' activities during the tumultuous 1820s reveals that they were focused on the short- and medium-term protection of their own interests and were therefore not necessarily aligned with any faction involved in the conflict. As a result, it is difficult to state that the role of British merchants in this period was the foundation for subsequent relations established by Britain and Chile in the late nineteenth century, as scholars like Mayo and Salazar argued.[122]

---

122 Mayo, 'Britain and Chile, 1851–1876', pp. 95–120, and *British Merchants and Chilean Development*, pp. 11–51; Salazar, *Mercaderes, empresarios y capitalistas*, pp. 593–95.

CHAPTER 5

Beyond Diplomacy

The Cultural Significance of British Recognition of Chile's Independence, 1817–1831

5.1 Introduction

Great Britain formally recognised the independence of Chile in 1831. This was the outcome of a long process of formal negotiations that began as early as 1813, when the first Chilean diplomatic envoys were sent to London to get support from Britain and to open up commercial relations.[1] Such negotiations took place in a context of warfare both in Europe and Spanish America. The Chileans did not initially succeed in the negotiations because Britain declared its neutrality in the conflict between Spain and its colonies and refused to negotiate with Chilean envoys as representatives of a state that did not exist. There is a general assumption about the expansion of foreign policy of Great Britain during these years by formal and informal means since the nineteenth century was coincident with the most expansionist period of the British Empire (1780–1830).[2] Also, it is generally assumed that diplomatic relations with Spanish America during this period were carried out on the grounds of the expansion of British 'commercial interests' around the globe and the need for merchant houses to expand their markets, which led to the configuration of a 'public policy; based on 'private interests'.[3] Gabriel Paquette has added that the intellectual context of British recognition was also a crucial factor to take into account, and it can be summarised in three major points:

> First, colonial monopoly was deemed unprofitable and unrestricted commerce's benefits were embraced; second, Spain's legitimacy as a colonial power was repudiated due to its unstable government, pernicious

---

1 Cristián Guerrero Lira, 'Chile en el mundo', in *América Latina en la Historia contemporánea. Chile, Vol. 1: 1808–1830. Crisis imperial e independencia* (Madrid: Fundación Mapfre, 2010), pp. 89–138 (p. 128).

2 Bayly, *Imperial Meridian.*

3 See Kaufmann, pp. 18–33.

degradation, and hostility to unregulated commerce; and third, the fledgling states' separation from Spain was justified because they accommodated British political and financial institutions.[4]

The policy of neutrality followed by Great Britain between Spain and the insurgent colonies is also understandable. It was a context in which the British wanted to take advantage of the possibilities that the opening of free trade from the new governments, like that of Chile, could bring to Great Britain.[5]

This is why, as has been explored and explained in the previous chapters, the relations between Britain and Chile between the declaration of neutrality in 1808 and the resumption of diplomatic negotiations from 1817 were upheld mainly by non-state actors. During that period, and beyond it into the 1820s, a number of soldiers, sailors, educators, missionaries and merchants travelled from Britain to Chile, interacted with locals in the different ways which have been defined in this book as contacts, collisions or relationships. These, at the same time, were different types of 'cultural encounters' that took place in different 'contact zones'.[6] These encounters had significant consequences in a wide range of domains, such as debates on national identity, the definition of the place of Chile in the world, the shaping of a new citizen, the educational system, debates on religious and commercial liberties, the use of the English or Spanish language to define belonging to a specific community and the strategic importance of Chile for British interests. All these topics were still under debate when formal diplomatic negotiations were reinstated in 1817. The main difference between these post-1817 'interstate' relations and those of 1806 is that Chile had declared its independence on 12 February 1818 and was now acting as a sovereign state demanding to be treated as such by Britain and to be accepted in the international arena.

These negotiations aimed to obtain formal British recognition of independence, far beyond the support that was sought in the initial negotiations that began in 1813. The very act of 'recognition' has many implications. Firstly, because this was one of the realms in which the 'official mind' revealed the interests of Britain itself regarding a new state that was coming into existence. In addition, it has been argued that in order to exist formally, a new political entity needs to be recognised by the already existent community of states.[7] This does not mean that a new state needs to be recognised by all states, but by at least a few of them who will recognise that such a political entity is a new member of the international community. The question in this case is, though, why the Chileans were so persistent in their efforts to get British

---

4   Gabriel Paquette, 'The Intellectual Context of British Diplomatic Recognition of the South American Republics, c. 1800–1830', *Journal of Transatlantic Studies*, 2:1 (2004), 75–95 (p. 95).

5   Roldán Vera, *The British Book Trade*, pp. 45–47.

6   See Bitterli, pp. 20–51; Pratt, p. 5.

7   See the discussion on 'constitutivists' in Section 5.2.

recognition in particular, if other states, like the US, had already recognised them early in 1818. This pattern was also followed by the other new nation states emerging from the independence struggles. The main difference is that, unlike the United Provinces of La Plata, Mexico or Gran Colombia, which were recognised by Britain in 1825, Chile was not recognised until 1831. Even so, negotiations continued until recognition was eventually granted. The persistence in pursuing British recognition reveals that for Chileans this was not simply a means to begin to 'exist' as a political entity, but was understood as a realm of negotiations where they could also obtain something.

It was at this stage that the Chileans began to make clear their interest in dominating trade in the Pacific – an idea already defined by O'Higgins and Cochrane, as shown in Chapter 2 – which, in turn, was the main area of influence of the United States. This was one of the main differences of the geopolitical context between the 1820s and the 1810s: the rising power of the US began to be seen as a threat to both British and Chilean commercial interests in the Pacific. Some Chileans became much more concerned about imperialism emanating from the US than from Britain and began to see recognition by the latter as a potential defence against the threat represented by the US. Britain for its part had its own interests in the Pacific, and was equally concerned about the rise of the United States. The experience of Buenos Aires showed Britons that in order to protect their interests in the Pacific, organising a new invasion of South America was not feasible; it was much better to establish new partnerships with governments on both formal and informal levels.

Nevertheless, the diplomatic negotiations of the 1820s tended to end in failure. In 1825 recognition was granted to the states that emerged from the former viceroyalties of La Plata, Nueva Granada, and Mexico, with the exception of Peru, whose independence had been achieved in December 1824. Chile was not considered for recognition despite a British consul being appointed in Valparaíso the same year. Reports from the consul, Christopher Nugent, reveal that he was not favourable to Chile's pretensions and that the image that both Britons and Chileans had configured about Chile in previous years remained that of a poor, isolated and marginal country. It is difficult to establish causation here, but it is possible to suggest, based on the evidence unearthed and discussed in this chapter, that these images led the British authorities to believe that Chile was less relevant to its interests in the Pacific than the former viceroyalties who were assumed to be richer territories. Thus, Chile was still not attractive enough for the definitive step, which involved signing free trade agreements. Also, by means of the very appointment of consuls and the massive settlement of British merchants in Chile, many British goals had been already achieved without recognition.

All this suggests that in order to be recognised by Britain, the Chileans had to reconfigure the image of Chile to convince the British authorities that it was a reliable country, characterised by political stability and economic progress and significant for its privileged location for trade. This meant leaving behind the traditional narrative of a poor and marginal country and constructing a new narrative of Chile's national identity that would have long-term consequences.

Beyond the diplomatic ambit, as with the realm of trade, these negotiations might be regarded as proper 'relationships' if we follow Bitterli's model of cultural encounters. In this case the nature of the interaction was to sign treaties and appoint specific representatives in each state, in order to consolidate the relationship for the future. It was not a mere 'contact', since there were moments that were more conflictive than others. From a cultural perspective, it was during these negotiations that – out of diplomatic necessity – a new image of Chile began to be clearly promoted, as a stable, prosperous and ordered country, which contrasted with that shaped by the British authorities.

5.2 Why the Need to Be 'Recognised'?

The political act of recognition has many implications, since it means that an already existing state accepts that a new one is coming into existence. This inherently implies an asymmetrical relationship between the two entities, since the new one is requesting something of the older one. In this particular case, all the new Spanish American states resulting after the dissolution of the Spanish empire were proactive in seeking the recognition of one specific power of the world: Great Britain. In other cases, recognition was almost automatically granted by other powers, like the US, without any negotiation. This means that when the US recognised the Spanish American new states, they had already 'come into existence', but even so, they persisted in seeking the recognition of the predominant empire. This also reveals that the act of recognition has many other implications that need to be clarified. Rapid recognition by the US was seen by many leaders as a manifestation of the latter's ambitions in Spanish America.[8]

It might now seem obvious to state that the outcome of the Chilean independence process was the creation of a new political entity called 'Chile', a new nation state that nominally did not exist until 12 February 1818. On that day, Bernardo O'Higgins, who had been designated as the Supreme Director of Chile the year before, read the *Acta de Proclamación de la Independencia de Chile*.[9] This document was the first to declare the 'existence' of Chile as

---

8 See below, Section 5.5.

9 The document has been widely published and diffused, but I take the online version of the Library of the Congress of Chile. See 'Acta de Proclamación de la Independencia de Chile' http://www.bcn.cl/bibliodigital/dhisto/acta (accessed 12 March 2017). There is a big controversy about the date and place of the Proclamation, because despite being publicly signed and read on 12 February 1818 in Talca, the text itself is dated 1 January 1818 in Concepción. During the war in the area around Concepción, O'Higgins allegedly 'declared' independence on 1 January 1818, although no

a distinct political entity and the first that explicitly declared 'the resolution of separating from the Spanish monarchy forever and of proclaiming its independence to the whole world'.[10] This proclamation was thus addressed to the 'entire world' and not only to Spain. It was a message directed to other powers which stated that Chile was coming into existence. This contradicts what David Armitage has argued about the global significance of the US Declaration of Independence, which was the first of its type. In his view, 'the authors of the [US] Declaration had claimed independence only for themselves and not for others'.[11] Chile, in turn, proclaimed its independence to be known by the rest of the world. In another passage this was even clearer, where along with the declaration of Chile as a new independent entity, the text included a definition of the territory that would constitute the new state:

> we have well considered, exercising the extraordinary power that for this particular case was authorised by the people, to declare solemnly on their behalf and in the presence of the Almighty, to let the great confederation of mankind know that mainland Chile and its adjacent islands are in fact and law, a free, independent and sovereign state, and remain forever separated from the monarchy of Spain, with full right to take the form of government that best suits their interests.[12]

It must be noted that the precise name of this state, 'the Republic of Chile', was not defined until 1823, when a new Constitution was enacted. Simon Collier notes that the proclamation of 1818 made a significant omission: it never mentioned the word 'Republic', but left undefined the political regime to be adopted. Collier argued that this was an intentional omission, since in 1818 there was no clear consensus about the regime to be adopted and therefore 'a final choice had still to be made'.[13] Thus, the proclamation was seemingly written in a way that left open the possibility of adopting a monarchical regime. This is not surprising, considering not only the

document survives. According to Cristián Guerrero Lira, this was not a formal declaration, but a desperate and symbolic act during a war the patriots were losing. He has also convincingly argued that the real date and location of the Proclamation were 12 February 1818 and Talca, as stated in the act of the Proclamation attached to the document. The reference to 1 January 1818 and Concepción was made retroactively because this city was in royalists hands and O'Higgins wanted to make clear that Concepción was also a part of the new independent state of Chile. See Cristián Guerrero Lira, 'Certezas y dudas en torno a la Proclamación de la Independencia: Una visión personal', in *La independencia de Chile y su celebración ¿Una polémica (aún) abierta?*, ed by Christian Hausser and Eduardo Bravo (Talca: Editorial Universidad de Talca, 2016), pp. 81–114.

10 Ibid.

11 David Armitage, *The Declaration of Independence: A Global History* (Cambridge, MA: Havard University Press, 2007), p. 4.

12 'Acta de Proclamación de la Independencia de Chile'.

13 Collier, p. 251.

monarchical tendencies of some leaders like José de San Martín, but also the pressure exerted by Great Britain to encourage these new states not to become republics. O'Higgins had been told by his envoy to London that recognition was a difficult issue, 'for nobody knows what it is that has to be recognised, whether it is a democratic republic, an aristocracy, a monarchy, or a government without principle'.[14] In addition, from the British point of view, there were still hopes that Britain would be able to 'strengthen monarchic and aristocratic principles in Peru, Mexico, and Chile'.[15] Thus, the possibility of establishing a monarchy was always latent, especially considering that early in 1812, José Miguel Carrera had already outlined a draft Chilean constitution establishing a constitutional monarchy,[16] and that the British monarchical model was seen as 'the best guarantor of social stability and gradual reform' by many Spanish American leaders.[17]

Despite these omissions and the quibbles about adopting a monarchy, as Montaner Bello maintains, this proclamation was an event of genuine international importance because 'Chile was ever since a subject and a person of the society of nations and a state amongst the states'.[18] This political act, from the point view of those who were proclaiming their independence, was a statement directed to the other nations, which had only to recognise something that already existed. This is what in international law is known as a 'declaratory' model of recognition, which could be understood as 'an acknowledgement of statehood already achieved'.[19] This implies that any pre-existing state must recognise the state that has declared its existence. However, this approach, although identifiable in the declarations of independence, coexisted with a second approach to recognition, which is known as the 'constitutive' model. For this model, 'whether or not an entity has become a state, [statehood] depends on the actions of existing states'.[20] Recognition, therefore, is the outcome of a relationship between a 'donor' state, which is pre-existent, and a 'recipient' state, which wants to be accepted by the international order. 'Constitutivists' believe that for the pre-existing state, recognition is not an obligation, but a voluntary act. In other words, for constitutivists 'statehood' is defined by the recognition of others, and by the new state itself for declaratorists.

14 Ibid.
15 Charles Centner, 'The Chilean Failure to Obtain British Recognition, 1823–1828', *Revista de Historia de América*, 15 (1942), 285–97 (p. 287).
16 See Juan Luis Ossa, 'Monarquismo(s) y militarismo republicano en Chile', in *Cádiz a debate. Actualidad, contexto y legado*, ed. by Roberto Breña (Mexico DF: Centro de Estudios Internacionales – El Colegio de México, 2014), pp. 409–29 (pp. 411–15).
17 Racine, 'This England and This Now', p. 429.
18 Montaner Bello, *Historia diplomática de la independencia*, p. 47.
19 Thomas D. Grant, *The Recognition of States: Law and Practice in Debate and Evolution* (Westport, CT: Praeger Publishers, 1999), p. 4.
20 Ibid., p. 3.

Both models coexisted in Chile during the struggles for independence. The proclamation only stated that Chileans wished to 'let the great confederation of mankind know' that Chile was a state, without explicitly mentioning the need for recognition, assuming that the declaration of independence itself was enough, or 'self-evident' in Armitage's words.[21] However, O'Higgins added a handwritten footnote to the first draft of the proclamation (which does not appear in the final text) to clarify that Chile would make 'opportunely demonstrable, in all its extension, the solid foundations of this just determination'.[22] Hence, O'Higgins was aware that the decision to declare Chilean independence must be justified to persuade the rest of the world of its legitimacy. Also, his government started a series of diplomatic procedures in order to gain recognition not only from some pre-existing states, but from the most powerful. Among them, Britain was by far the most privileged, as shown in the next section.

O'Higgins took a first measure to gain diplomatic recognition on the same day of the proclamation. On 12 February 1818 the Chilean government issued the *Manifiesto que hace a las naciones el supremo director de Chile de los motivos que justifican la revolución y la declaración de su independencia* (Manifest from the Supreme Director of Chile to the Nations on the Reasons that Justify the Revolution and the Declaration of Independence). This document contains the rationale for the declaration of independence, giving an account of all the events that in Chile following the 1808 crisis. Some of the statements reveal how radical the political language had become by the end of the independence struggles compared to the early years in which declarations of loyalty were usual. Thus, the preamble stated that 'we do not want to belong to a null nation. We do not need it at all'.[23] The addressee was again 'the rest of the nations' and not simply Spain, justifying Chilean independence to the entire world. In the first paragraph it is recognised that 'it seemed useless to express the reasons that Chile has had to declare its independence, if a constant practice and due to the dignity of the powers, whose rank we will enter too, does not force us to this step, which is also part of our own honour and respect'.[24] This reveals that O'Higgins did not consider it necessary to ask for recognition, he assumed that there was a sort of practice amongst the states that eventually obliged any new state to do so.

This manifesto, which was sent to both Europe and the US, never received a response. Neither did the series of letters that O'Higgins had already sent to the authorities of the same powers in 1817, before independence

---

21 Armitage, p. 6.
22 'Acta de proclamación de la independencia de Chile'.
23 Bernardo O'Higgins, 'Manifiesto que hace a las naciones el supremo director de Chile de los motivos que justifican la revolución y la declaración de su independencia', Santiago, 12 December 1818, in *Anales de la República* ed. by Luis Valencia Avaria (Santiago: Editorial Andrés Bello, 1951), vol. I, pp. 17–36.
24 O'Higgins, 'Manifiesto', p. 17.

was declared.[25] Thus, it was clear that in order to obtain recognition, extra effort was needed and the idea of sending diplomats to Europe was gaining importance. This also implied rethinking strategies and the need to promote an image of Chile that convinced other states to grant political recognition became evident. This meant shifting the traditional image of Chile as a poor and isolated country to one of a prosperous country with much to offer potential European and British migrants.

5.3 Pursuing Recognition and Shaping an Identity: Chilean Diplomatic Envoys in Britain

Chile and Britain behaved in divergent ways during the negotiations for British recognition of Chile's independence in the 1820s. Chile sent diplomatic envoys to negotiate recognition and other subjects such as the loan to fund the Liberation Expedition of Peru, the enlistment of mercenaries for this expedition and the appointment of a general director of education to reorganise the educational system.[26] These envoys were also charged with negotiating formal diplomatic recognition with the British authorities. This meant that the relations between Britain and Chile would now be carried out by state agents for the Chilean government, even though British seamen, educators, missionaries and merchants were already in Chile.

As shown in the first chapter, diplomatic contacts with foreign powers began as early as 1813, when even the aim of independence was not clearly defined. Francisco Antonio Pinto travelled as an envoy to London in order to win support for the war, but he was never taken seriously due to the policy of neutrality adopted by Lord Castlereagh. These early contacts made clear that, more than seeking external support in general, the main aim was to win British support. Several reasons explain why British recognition, and not French, Russian or even North American recognition, was so significant. The main reason was that Britain had the most powerful maritime empire and its support for independence would somehow guarantee it. In addition, as Racine has demonstrated, Britain itself represented a cultural model for many Spanish Americans who had lived in London in the late eighteenth and early nineteenth century.[27] For them, including O'Higgins, Britain was an admired power and winning its recognition could be a means to increase the circulation of ideas, peoples and practices to help in the construction of the new states. Scholars like Mario Barros have stressed O'Higgins 'Anglophilia' to explain the preference for British recognition, which he referred to as his 'golden dream'.[28] However, this explanation is quite simplistic since other

25 Montaner Bello, pp. 40–41.
26 All these cases have been studied in previous chapters of this book, especially chapters 2 and 3.
27 Racine, 'This England and This Now', p. 434 and 'Proxy Pasts', pp. 871–72.
28 Barros, p. 64.

critical geopolitical factors, like the growing power of the US, explain why the new Chilean government was eager to gain British recognition (see Section 5.5 of this chapter).[29] The ambitions of the US in the Pacific were also a powerful reason to request British recognition and to become allies by the signature of a treaty. Chileans did not only fear an expansion of US activities in the Pacific, they also had their own interest in becoming the rulers of trade in the South Pacific. As shown in Chapter 2, the idea that Chile could rule the Pacific was first stated by Cochrane as a result of Chile being the state who 'gave' independence to the rest of the continent by expelling the remaining Spanish fleet from its coast.

During the 1820s two diplomats had the 'mission' to obtain the recognition of Chile's independence from different European powers. Antonio José de Irisarri was appointed by O'Higgins in 1817 and remained in Europe until 1825. Mariano Egaña was appointed after O'Higgins's resignation, during the tumultuous years that followed his government, and stayed in Europe between 1824 and 1827. Although they made a big impact, both failed to gain recognition from Great Britain and it would be a third diplomat, José Miguel de la Barra, who eventually succeeded in this mission. However, unlike the previous two, he was not appointed to negotiate recognition. He was the secretary of the Chilean delegation in London, and had to remain after Pinto recalled Egaña to Chile, once he realised that recognition might take longer than expected. Compared to their British counterparts, whose rank was that of consul, the Chilean envoys used different denominations: 'Deputy', in the case of Irisarri and 'Plenipotentiary Minister' for Egaña. In one of his first letters to Castlereagh, Irisarri made it clear that he was 'completely authorised to represent before the ministers of HBM and the rest of the kingdoms of Europe whatever is convenient to the interests of this state [Chile]'.[30] However, they were never officially received as representatives of Chile, but as mere individuals or 'well-informed travellers', because this would mean formal or *de iure* recognition of the existence of Chile as an independent state.[31] At this point, the policy of neutrality still affected relations between Britain and the already independent Spanish American states.

Antonio José de Irisarri's life is perhaps one of the most vivid examples of how weak the sense of nationhood was in these years.[32] Born in Guatemala, he worked as a Chilean diplomat in Great Britain and France until 1824 and in the 1830s worked as an advisor to Andrés de Santa Cruz during the war of the Peru-Bolivian Confederation against Chile (1837–1839). He was not only a diplomat, but a renowned intellectual and one of the most

29 Blaufaurb, pp. 742–63.
30 'Irisarri to Castlereagh', London, 4 June 1819, in Montaner Bello, p. 446.
31 Montaner Bello, pp. 87–90.
32 Raúl Silva Castro, 'Antonio José de Irisarri: Fragmentos para una historia literaria de Chile en construcción', *Anales de la Universidad de Chile*, 83–84 (1951), 5–25.

well-known defenders of the independence cause in the newspapers.[33] In 1817 he became one of Bernardo O'Higgins's key advisors and even his Minister of the Interior in January 1818. His nomination to represent Chile in Europe was triggered by the news of the Congress of Aix-la-Chapelle in October 1818, in which representatives of the European powers were to debate the revolution in Spanish America. However, Irisarri arrived in London when the Congress had already finished, on 15 November. The only Spanish American representative to attend the Congress was Bernardo Rivadavia, who a few years later would be the Governor of Buenos Aires.[34]

Regardless of his late arrival, the 'Instructions' given to Irisarri provide great insight into the rationale behind the desire to gain recognition from the European powers, in particular Great Britain.[35] One of the means was to offer prerogatives and privileges to those states willing to recognise Chile as an independent state. These included 'the rights to export the fruits of the country, and less importation provided that such a privilege became necessary to get the protection of Great Britain'. In addition, the government was even willing to grant a 'concession of some of the islands, like Juan Fernández or Santa Maria', although not 'by any means a portion of territory from the continent'. The document also stated that 'Valdivia or Chiloe, which were considered integral parts of the territory', were not subject to negotiation.[36] A favourable image of Chile also had to be publicised by Irisarri. In particular, he had to stress 'all the favourable events from this part of the globe, the fertility of its lands, the hospitality of its naturals, the [mining] wealth of its territory, the good health of its temperament, the liberality of its laws and civil and religious tolerance'.[37] With respect to the political regime, he was authorised to demonstrate if necessary that Chile was not 'not far from adopting a moderate or consti-tutional monarchy',[38] which confirms what Collier said about the intentional omission of the declaration of independence. Finally, as with Pinto's 1813 instructions, Irisarri needed to attract skilled workers and 'wise men' to travel to Chile. In this case, the specific group targeted for skilled workers was the Germans, while the document did not specify any nationality for 'scientists in mineralogy, machinery, chemistry, political economy, maths,

33 See Castillo, *La creación de la República*; Susana Gazmuri, 'La lectura de los autores romanos y la construcción del discurso republicano: Citas, traducciones y adapta-ciones. Chile, 1810–1833', *Historia*, 49:2 (2016), 329–453.

34 Barros, *Historia diplomática de Chile*, pp. 51–2, Montaner Bello, pp. 55–57.

35 'Presupuesto de las instrucciones acordadas por el gobierno supremo de Chile para la conducta de su diputado en la Corte de Londres', reproduced in Diego Barros Arana, *Historia General de Chile*, 16 vols, 2nd ed. (Santiago: Editorial Universitaria-DIBAM, 1999), IX, pp. 37–39.

36 Ibid., p. 37.

37 Ibid., p. 37.

38 Ibid., p. 38.

history, geography and other useful sciences'.[39] These instructions show that the strategy followed by the government was, in the first place, to offer a good trade deal which included the concession of a strategic island in the Pacific, like Juan Fernández, and the promotion of a favourable image of Chile. The latter also included offering something in exchange, in terms of being a land of opportunities for people who sought to begin a new life. This also reveals that when diplomatic negotiations were reinstated in 1817, the necessity of configuring a new image of Chile became evident. This explains why Irisarri was commissioned to offer a wide range of benefits to those who wanted to travel to Chile. By doing so, Chile was being promoted as a much more attractive destination than simply an in-between state among other richer areas. The negotiations for recognition by the US did not include such offers. Neither an island nor immigration opportunities were offered to US agents,[40] the latter because the US itself was promoted as a land of opportunities for Europeans, and the former considering the economic interests of the US in the Pacific. These offers were made only to Britain, which makes clear the geopolitical uncertainty of the period for the Chileans and how they envisioned the US presence in the Pacific. They preferred to compromise their territorial integrity and part with an island in favour of Britain in order to defend their interests from US expansion.

There is a clear consensus that the main achievements of Irisarri's mission in London were the obtainment of a loan and the first informal conversations with Lord Castlereagh regarding the recognition of Chile by Great Britain.[41] The first achievement, however, was not attained free of trouble, since Irisarri was fiercely criticised for getting a loan with unfavourable conditions for Chile.[42] The second is arguably one of his most notable labours because, despite not achieving the desired recognition, he tried to persuade Castlereagh of the need to appoint consuls in Chile. In a letter he sent on 6 August 1819 Irisarri complained about the abusive behaviour of some British navy commanders in the past, who 'on the pretext of protecting trade some of HBM's warships have gone to such seas, whose commanders, without any diplomatic investiture, have tried several times to compromise that government, making statements against the policy of this office and asking

39 Ibid.
40 See the most recent contribution on the relations between Chile and the US during the independence era, Juan Luis Ossa Santa Cruz, 'El gobierno de Bernardo O'Higgins visto a través de cinco agentes estadounidenses, 1817–1823', *Co-Herencia*, 13:25 (2016), 139–66.
41 Barros, pp. 60–66; Montaner Bello, pp. 151–54.
42 The loan has been widely studied and I think it deserves further research, especially because of the number of sources available (at least four volumes of correspondence in the National Archive of Chile on this theme alone). The most recent work that deals with this is Marcelo Somarriva's dissertation. See Chapter IV 'Loans and Mines', pp. 125–58.

extravagant things of that supreme authority'.[43] Those commanders were Fleming, Hillyar and Shirreff, who acted as ruling powers in the Pacific, as shown in previous chapters. Irisarri argued that 'this evil has born from the lack of British consuls who looked after the interests of their nation, which has not happened with respect to US trade, there having existed from the beginning a Consul general of this state in the capital of Chile and others particular to each port'.[44] He knew that the appointment of consuls would be a first step towards recognition and Castlereagh was cautious precisely for this reason. Irisarri reported to the Minister of the Interior, Joaquín Echeverría, in Santiago that Castlereagh 'replied to me that the appointment of such consuls in Chile would lead us to appoint our own consuls in England, accomplishing by indirect means our ultimate goal, which is the recognition of our independence'.[45]

Irisarri's good understanding of diplomatic relations made him careful not to push for any measure that could put his mission in danger. For him, it was more important to pave the way by trying to gain a *de facto* recognition of Chile's independence than to exert pressure on the British government to get *de iure* recognition. Hence, the appointment of consuls in Chile alone would have been a sort of achievement for Irisarri, insofar as it implied recognition that Chile was a distinctive political entity. In addition, Irisarri used another strategy: to stress the importance of Britain maintaining the principle of neutrality. He would thus ensure that Great Britain would not support any attempt by Spain to regain the Spanish American territories. In a letter to Castlereagh, Irisarri argued that:

> Chile does not demand that either HBM or his ministers assist in the cause of the independence of South America at this moment, breaking the neutrality that is not convenient to break, although it is perhaps fair. However, it does hope that this neutrality [...] does not degenerate in protection for the enemies of such country.[46]

This was the only thing Irisarri knew for sure after the meeting. Maintaining the principle of neutrality, Great Britain was not obliged to recognise Chile as an independent state, but could accept the fact that a new government had been formed and that Chile's 'mercantile transactions, like the military and naval, would be regarded as a precedent from a competent authority'.[47] In addition, Britain would not support any attempt by Spain to reclaim these territories.

Mariano Egaña was appointed to replace Irisarri in April 1824, but according to his biographers he lacked diplomatic experience and understanding of

43 'Irisarri to Castlereagh', 6 August 1819, in Montaner Bello, p. 447.
44 Ibid.
45 'Irisarri to Echeverría', 23 August 1819, in Montaner Bello, p. 448.
46 'Irisarri to Castlereagh', 12 June 1819, in Montaner Bello, p. 447.
47 Ibid., p. 448.

international relations.[48] He travelled with a set of instructions, which included the specification of his duties as 'Plenipotentiary Minister', a 'memoir' to justify the Chilean cause, and instructions regarding Irisarri's mission. This document made clear that the new government wanted to remove Irisarri, but left the final decision to Egaña: 'Should Mr Egaña determine it to be more convenient to suspend Mr Antonio José Irisarri from his functions as plenipotentiary minister, it would equally suspend his assigned salary'.[49] Unlike the instructions for Irisarri, the *Instrucciones políticas* (Political Instructions) issued by the government for Egaña's mission were more explicit about the goal of recognition: 'the object of the mission of the envoy is to negotiate the end of the independence wars and [Chile's] subsequent recognition by the European Nations'.[50] Concerned about the reaction of the US government, the instructions issued by Chile's government also stated that 'as it is necessary to establish negotiations of alliance and confederation with the US, the envoy should prevent the distinctions and privileges conceded to Great Britain arousing the resentment of the US'.[51] A third aspect of the mission was to deal with the loan already obtained by Irisarri, meaning to 'liquidate all the accounts of such loan, collect all what remains in favour of Chile, and generate all the convenient charges of all what does not come from legal and positive agreements by the legislative body of Chile'.[52] Lastly, as with all the other missions to Europe, Egaña was commissioned to

> Attract to the country every class of useful men, offering protection, every kind of consideration and public employment according to their aptitudes, so as to especially look for men instructed in public affairs and other economic matters. Above all, teachers for the industrial and scientific institutes and the museum.[53]

48 Barros, *Historia diplomática*, p. 84.
49 'Instrucción reservada que el gobierno de Chile comunica al enviado don Mariano de Egaña', Santiago, 27 April 1824, in *Documentos de la misión de don Mariano Egaña en Londres (1824–1829)*, ed. by Javier González Echeñique (Santiago: Ministerio de Relaciones Exteriores, 1984), p. 40.
50 'Instrucciones políticas que el gobierno de Chile comunica a don Mariano Egaña, oficial de la Legión de Merito, su Ministro de Estado del Departamento de Relaciones Exteriores y nombrado enviado y Ministro Plenipotenciario acerca del Reino Unido de la Gran Bretaña y otras provincias de Europa, conforme a las cuales deberá obrar en el desempeño de su misión', Santiago, 27 April 1824, in *Documentos de la misión Mariano Egaña*, ed. by González Echeñique, p. 33.
51 Ibid., p. 36.
52 'Instrucciones que dan los directores de la Caja Nacional de Descuentos a su apoderado y representante del Supremo Gobierno y Senado de Chile en las cortes de Europa doctor do Mariano Egaña', Santiago, 27 April 1824, in *Documentos de la misión Mariano Egaña*, ed. by González Echeñique, p. 40.
53 'Instrucciones que el gobierno de Chile comunica a don Mariano Egaña, oficial de la Legión de Merito, su Ministro de Estado del Departamento de Relaciones

Egaña's mission was also a failure, since he did not achieve the target stated in his instructions.[54] In fact, it was during his mission in 1825 that George Canning, the new British Minister of Foreign Affairs, decided to grant recognition to other states (United Provinces of La Plata, Mexico and Colombia), but not to Chile. In his letters Egaña suggested that the main reason was the negative image that Canning had of Chile, blaming the British Consul to Chile, Christopher Nugent, for this: 'I guess Mr Nugent has realised that the success of the war of Peru cannot be assured, and therefore, he considers that the independence of Chile is threatened and that amongst the Chilean people there are divergent opinions'.[55] In his view, 'the opinion that there is no order, no calm, no consolidated and tranquil government order in Chile gets stronger'.[56] The failure to obtain recognition arose, in Egaña's view, from bad publicity about the internal situation of Chile, fostered by the press, the British Consul (see the next section below) and by some travellers like John Miers, referred to as a 'furious detractor of Chile'.[57] Indeed, Miers made some harsh judgements on the state of Chile in 1824 compared to that of Buenos Aires, emphasising its lack of political organisation and stability:

> Chile is still in a state of revolution, while Buenos Ayres, from the experience gained by her legislators, has attained a sufficient importance, a better administration of justice, sound commercial views, and has displayed such punctuality and good faith in all her engagements, as fully to entitle the government of that country to rank with the regular government of other nations. Chile, on the contrary, has been for some time past retrograding, and can scarcely be said to possess any government at all; all its affairs are mismanaged, its revenues are misapplied, its commerce has decayed; and a great change, probably a violent one, must take place before it can again be restored to the state in which it was even under the administration of Bernardo O'Higgins.[58]

Eventually, Egaña abandoned the negotiations for recognition and focused on both the plan to attract British 'colonisers' and the renegotiation of the loan that Irisarri had obtained. The latter was a new difficulty for Egaña, because

Exteriores y nombrado enviado y Ministro Plenipotenciario acerca del Reino Unido de la Gran Bretaña y otras provincias de Europa, conforme a las cuales deberá obrar en el desempeño de su misión', Santiago, 27 April 1824, in *Documentos de la misión Mariano Egaña*, ed. by González Echeñique, p. 34.

54 See Barros, *Historia diplomática de Chile*, pp. 76–77 and Montaner Bello, pp. 266–67.

55 'Mariano Egaña to Joaquín Campino', London, 20 July 1825, in *Documentos de la misión Mariano Egaña*, ed. by González Echeñique, p. 123.

56 'Mariano Egaña to Joaquín Campino', London, 20 October 1825, in *Documentos de la misión Mariano Egaña*, ed. by González Echeñique, p. 199.

57 Ibid., p. 209.

58 Miers, p. 120.

it became evident that Chile was facing serious trouble in paying. 'There is no other country with more financial discredit than Chile', he wrote in a letter in which he also repeated the idea that the news that circulated about Chile's 'interior disorder' and 'miserable' treasury were the main cause of this lack of credit.[59]

News of his unsuccessful negotiations reached Chile. The negative views of this country that circulated in Britain, and the failure to obtain recognition, convinced the Chilean authorities that it was futile to persist. Besides, if we take into account that recognition itself was a juridical mechanism to bring a political entity into existence, other states had already recognised Chile's independence: the US (1822) and Portugal (1821). Thus, on these terms, Chile did not need British recognition. In fact, Francisco Antonio Pinto, one of the first agents in London and President of Chile in 1827, did not persist in the pursuit of recognition from Great Britain or any other state. In a letter from his Minister of Foreign Affairs Juan Francisco de Zegers to Egaña, the reasons were clearly stated:

> The Chilean government is convinced that it is not possible to sustain in England a plenipotentiary minister of this republic any longer without compromising the honour of the nation, and extremely taxing the treasury. The British cabinet, having recognised the independence of other states of America, has not only ceased studying it with respect to Chile, but, which is most notable, has not even recognised the public character of this envoy thus far, so it has been decided in accordance with the national commission that he must stop in his duties and come back to this republic.[60]

The same letter also stated that the former secretary of the legation, José Miguel de la Barra, would remain in London as a 'general consul' and not as a 'Plenipotentiary Minister' like Egaña. This means that De la Barra was only going to represent Chile for commercial affairs and, unlike Irisarri and Egaña, was not commissioned with special instructions for pursuing recognition. Furthermore, he left London shortly afterwards and settled in Paris to negotiate French recognition in 1830. He only returned to London after being informed that the British government was willing to negotiate recognition again.

Negotiations for recognition, carried out by state agents, were troubled and by the mid-1820s the Chilean authorities were convinced that gaining recognition from Britain was going to be a complex matter. The persistence of traditional images of Chile as well as its reputation as a weak and instable state undermined any pretension to be recognised. The attempts to promote

---

59 'Egaña to Campino', 19 December 1825, in *Documentos de la misión Mariano Egaña*, ed. by González Echenique, p. 278.
60 'Zegers to Egaña', Santiago, 12 November 1827, in *Documentos de la misión Mariano Egaña*, ed. by González Echeñique, p. 443.

a favourable image of Chile did not succeed either. Therefore, the British authorities saw no need to recognise Chile at this time. Chile was not seen as an important or rich area like the former viceroyalties of Mexico, Buenos Aires and Nueva Granada, and the commercial interests of British merchants could be secured by other means, without taking this definitive step. In the meantime, the appointment of a consul concerned with British commercial affairs seemed to be enough.

5.4 Consolidating Commercial Interests: British Consuls and the Construction of a Negative Image of Chile

One of the first diplomatic steps taken by the British government during the wars of independence was the appointment of consuls in Spanish America. I have said that Irisarri tried to persuade Castlereagh to do this early in 1819, but without success. George Canning would finally make this decision in 1824. In British diplomatic history the figure of the consul has a specific meaning. Until 13 February 1649, when the Act of Parliament for 'Constituting a Counsel of State for the Commonwealth of England' was passed, the figure of consul was primarily devoted to commercial affairs, not a representative of the state.[61] Indeed, as John Dickie points out in his work on the history of the British consul, 'the early consuls were traders selected by the merchant community, not by the royal government, to represent the particular interests of the merchants and not those of the nation in general'.[62] The Act, passed under Cromwell, meant a significant change in terms of who the consul represented, but not in the nature of his duties. From then on, the consul would be a representative of the state and no longer of a particular community, but his most important duties would still relate to commercial affairs: 'You are to use all the Good ways and means for the securing advancement, and the encouragement of the trade of England and Ireland, and the dominions to them belonging, and to promote the Good of all foreign plantations and factories belonging to this Commonwealth or any of the natives thereof'.[63] Therefore, during the independence era the nomination of a British consul had a clear purpose: the fostering of commercial relations to the direct benefit of British merchants, although it officially represented the interests of the British state.

On 10 October 1823 Christopher Nugent was appointed as a 'Consul General in Chili [sic]',[64] while Matthew Charter and Henry W. Rouse were

---

61 John Dickie, *The British Consul: Heir to a Great Tradition* (New York: Columbia University Press, 2008), p. 9.

62 Ibid., p. 8.

63 'Act of Parliament for Constituting a Counsell of State for the Commonwealth of England', 12 February 1659, quoted by Dickie, *The British Consul*, p. 9.

64 'George Canning to Christopher Nugent', London, 10 October 1823, in Webster, *Britain and the Independence of Latin America*, I, p. 351.

designated Vice consuls for Concepción and Coquimbo respectively.[65] Similar appointments were made for Buenos Aires, Colombia, Peru and Mexico, all of them nominated on the same date as Nugent. This followed the reaction of George Canning, who in 1823 had replaced Castlereagh as the Minister of Foreign Affairs, to the recognition of Spanish American independence by the US on 22 March 1822. Thus, Montaner Bello's claims that Irisarri had persuaded Castlereagh of the need to appoint consuls must be called into question, as it was the outcome of a plan that the British government had already devised.[66] Canning was simply appointing functionaries as representatives of the British state in the key ports of Spanish America, in a context of commercial rivalry with the increasingly powerful US. British merchants were already settled in all these ports, including Valparaíso, Talcahuano (near Concepción) and Coquimbo, but the presence of North American merchants was also extensive.[67] Gilbert F. Mathison also pointed out that the designation of a consul was an urgent matter for the British merchants since the only British agent that had previously mediated between them and the Chilean government was the Pacific naval station. This alone was not enough to protect their interests because commanders could only try prevent acts of violence against merchants. For Mathison, therefore, it was evident that 'a regular Consular establishment ought to be appointed by the British Government, and that, again, backed by a naval force of sufficient consideration to ensure prompt attention and respect to every reasonable demand that may be made on behalf of the British subjects'.[68]

The appointment of consuls was a measure taken to protect British interests in the Pacific, an ocean the British did not dominate as they did the Atlantic. That is why Nugent's instructions made clear that his duties should be performed 'for the benefit of His Majesty's commercial subjects',[69] which also explains why he had been appointed to Valparaíso, Chile's main port, and not to Santiago. The instructions also stated that one of his duties was 'to collect and transmit to' the Minister of Foreign Affairs 'information on all matters of interest and importance in the State of Chili [sic] and its dependencies'.[70]

This also responded to the interest of the British government in expanding its commercial networks in a period of increasing competition with the US. When Canning decided on 5 July of 1825 to grant recognition only to the

65 Humphreys, *British Consular Reports*, p. xviii.
66 Montaner Bello, pp. 87–90.
67 Kinsbruner, 'The Political Influence of the British Merchants Resident in Chile', pp. 26–39.
68 Mathison, p. 264.
69 'Canning to Nugent', London, 10 October 1823, in *Britain and the Independence of Latin America*, vol. 1, ed. by Webster, p. 351.
70 'Canning to Nugent', London, 15 December 1823, *Britain and the Independence of Latin America*, ed. by Webster, p. 352.

United Provinces of Río de la Plata, Colombia and Mexico, despite the negotiations already undertaken with Irisarri, it was clear that the strategic geographical location of Chile and its ports was not a sufficient reason. The decision to grant recognition to these states was unilateral and even unexpected, but provoked delusions among the Chilean authorities, who were convinced that recognition was imminent.[71] George Canning's foreign policy regarding the situation of the former Spanish colonies was clear in this respect: these states had gained recognition because they had attained a certain degree of political stability, cohesion and territorial integrity.[72] Scholars like Charles Centner and Theodor E. Nichols have stressed the lack of political stability as the main factor explaining Chile's failure to secure recognition, along with Chile's hesitations about adopting a political regime, either federalist or centralist.[73] In the 1820s, such stability was still difficult to achieve, due to the formation of different political factions with divergent interests, like the *pipiolos* (liberals), *pelucones* (conservatives), federalists and *estanqueros*. Likewise, the extension of the territory and the rivalries between cities like Concepción in the south and La Serena in the north against Santiago, also seemed to be factors that made British authorities doubt the stability of Chile. This was precisely the context described by Miers that was so publicised in London.

Nugent's appointment came nine months after O'Higgins's resignation, which occurred on 23 January 1823 to prevent a civil war. He resigned because the march to Santiago started by General Ramón Freire, the Intendant of Concepción, and his troops some days before would have led to his overthrow. Eventually, Freire took over, inaugurating a new political phase under a new Constitution enacted the same year. Upon Nugent's arrival, the situation had calmed down and he believed that Freire might be capable of being the Supreme Director of Chile. In the first months Nugent devoted himself to collecting information about the state of the country and sent a questionnaire to the Minister of Foreign Affairs, Diego José Benavente, with some questions about the situation of Chile. This was the same questionnaire that other consuls sent to the governors of the other new Spanish American states:

> 1st. Is the Government of Chile established as a single State, and that State Independent, or is it connected by subordinate or any federal union or incorporation with any other State or system of States?

71 Montaner Bello, p. 355.

72 Leslie Bethell, *George Canning and the Independence of Latin America: A Lecture Delivered at Canning House* (London: The Hispanic and Luzo Brazilian Councils, 1970), p. 11.

73 Centner, pp. 287–88; Theodore E. Nichols, 'The Establishment of Political Relations between Chile and Great Britain', *The Hispanic American Historical Review*, 28:1 (1948), 137–43 (pp. 138–39).

2nd. Has the Government, if constituted as an independent State, notified, by a public Act, its determination to remain independent of Spain and to admit no terms of accommodation with the Mother Country?

3rd. Is it in military possession of the country, and also in a condition of military defence against any probable attack from Europe?

4th Has it abjured and abolished the Slave Trade, and by what public Act?[74]

The questions did not aim to find out to what extent Chile was a stable country, but to determine its definition as a single state and its capacity to maintain such a condition. This was particularly relevant considering the circumstances in which O'Higgins had to resign, which almost led to a civil war between Santiago and Concepción. The response was issued shortly afterwards and reproduced by Nugent in his report:

It is replied that Chile has established itself as an independent State under the Constitution herewith, Marked N°1 (Constitución Política del Estado de Chile, promulgada en 29 de Diciembre de 1823).

That the Government of Chile constituted itself independent on the 1st January 1818, as appears by the Act a copy of which is annexed under the N°2 (Copy of 'Proclamación de la Independencia de Chile' of, 1st January, 1818).

That the State of Chile is at present entirely free from hostile troops, and in a condition to repel every attack which Spain may wish to attempt in order to return Chile to her ancient domination, or to that of any other Foreign Power. The little Island of Chiloé that still finds itself for the moment under the enemy's yoke, as much on account of its climate as of its little political importance can inspire the Government of Chile with no anxiety, nor alter the tranquillity which it enjoys.

That Chile has abjured and abolished the commerce in Slaves since the year 1811, as appears by the documents accompanying under Nos. 1 and 3 ('Boletin de Ordenes y Decretos del Gobierno, Santiago', of 31st July 1823).[75]

On this occasion, it was the British government who encouraged the Chilean authorities to promote a favourable image of their newborn state. They had not only to stress the fact that Chile was already an independent country that had declared its independence to the rest of the world, but also that such independence would not be threatened in the future. The situation of Chiloé, where Spanish royalist troops were still stationed, made it difficult to believe that Chile was 'in a condition to repel every attack'. It is clear that on the British side, there was a need to be sure that this was a

---

74 'Nugent to Canning', Valparaíso, 4 June 1824, in *Britain and the Independence of Latin America*, ed. by Webster, p. 354.

75 Ibid., p. 355.

truly independent country with whom they could establish formal relations to negotiate, among other things, the opening of free trade.

In spite of the favourable image presented in the reply, the image that Nugent configured of Chile stressed other less favourable aspects. Nugent was sceptical about the real capacity of Chile to maintain its independence as a discrete entity, especially because the war in Peru had not yet finished (it only ended on 9 December 1824, after the Battle of Ayacucho). Also, most of the negative characteristics which Nugent stressed about Chile were related to the third point in the response. He was not convinced about Chile's military defence capacity, 'either to invade with any prospect of success the possessions of the royalists, or even its ability, in the event of attack from Europe, to resist. Indeed the military appearance of the country is not imposing'.[76] Other reports stressed the situation of political unrest in Chile, its poverty and its struggle to consolidate itself as a single political entity: 'The trade of Chile has, upon the whole, been steady and profitable, and in proportion as the country becomes organised, and the form of government more precisely defined and settled, will indisputably increase'.[77] Perhaps informed by some merchants or travellers who had returned to Britain, Canning also expressed concern about the liberties of Britons who were settled in Chile. In his view, Nugent's role was to secure that British subjects could enjoy 'the unmolested exercise of religious worship along with other civil rights'. Then he added that 'the toleration of religious opinions, the unmolested exercise of religious worship, and the decent celebration of the rites of sepulture according to their own persuasion are no less indispensable to the comfort and well-being of the members of a Christian community'.[78] However, Canning's view differed starkly with the reality, since O'Higgins's government had already passed some decrees that allowed Britons who joined the navy and settlers to exercise their religion in the private sphere and to bury their dead in a cemetery. In contrast, other British travellers like Luke Matthews had given clear testimony about the religious tolerance across Spanish America, particularly in small towns.[79]

In a letter to Canning on 23 September 1825, Nugent gave an account of his meeting with Ramón Freire:

I availed myself of the occasion to impress on His Excellency's mind the absolute necessity of a perfect union in the Government of Chile, whether as a consolidated republic or one to be formed, as the late secession of Concepción and Coquimbo would imply, upon a Federal system of States, and gave it as my opinion that the delay in the Recognition of Chile, on

76 Ibid., p. 354.
77 'Nugent to Canning', Valparaíso, 17 April 1825, in *British Consular Reports*, ed. by Humphreys, p. 93.
78 'Canning to Nugent', London, 24 April 1824, in *Britain and the Independence of Latin America*, ed. by Webster, pp. 352–53.
79 See Chapter 3 and Baeza, 'Circulación de biblias protestantes', pp. 24–26.

the part of Great Britain, could solely arise from a desire to treat with a de facto Government, in either of the two before-recited forms.[80]

Nugent was still sceptical about the union and stability of Chile, and gave his personal opinion about this as a reason to delay recognition by Great Britain. The letter was written several months after the recognition of other Spanish American states and reveals that Freire expressed his disappointment at Chile not being recognised. Nugent responded that Great Britain was still waiting for 'that stability and political union in Chile evinced in the States already recognised'.[81] However, we know that it is at least an exaggeration to suggest that the United Provinces, Mexico and Colombia had an image as stable and unified states. In the United Provinces, for example, the 1820s was a decade of constant tension between Buenos Aires and the provinces, including civil wars, and there were still serious doubts about the capacity to consolidate a 'national government'. The General Congress of Buenos Aires, celebrated in December 1824, was the first serious attempt to solve that problem. However, following Klaus Gallo's argument, it was Canning himself who lobbied for such recognition 'on the grounds that the Holy Alliance powers had persuaded France to remain in Spain, and that this represented a continuing menace to British interests in South America'.[82] This lobby was more intense from mid-December 1824, that is, when the Congress of Buenos Aires had just been inaugurated and the problem of unity had not yet been resolved.[83] In Mexico, the dissolution of the Mexican empire ruled by Agustín de Iturbide took place between February and March 1823 after a rebellion led by Antonio López de Santa Anna. This meant that Mexico was facing a phase of political unrest at the same time O'Higgins was forced to resign in Chile. In both cases, a new leader took over – Guadalupe Victoria and Ramón Freire respectively – and a new Constitution was enacted – the Federal Constitution in Mexico (1824) and the Constitution of 1823 in Chile.

Therefore, the lack of internal stability in Chile could not be sufficient reason to postpone recognition. Moreover, in the announcement of the recognition of Buenos Aires, Mexico and Colombia, Canning did not give a clear explanation of the Chilean case. He only claimed that 'we have not sufficient information to enable us to form any opinion as to the fitness or expediency of any further measure of approximation to that Province, at the present moment'.[84] Indeed, most of Canning and Nugent's

---

80 'Nugent to Canning, Valparaíso, 23 September 1825, in *Britain and the Independence of Latin America*, ed. by Webster, p. 362.

81 Ibid. See also Guerrero Lira, 'Chile en el mundo', p. 132.

82 Gallo, pp. 155–56.

83 Ibid., p. 156.

84 Quoted by Harold Temperley, *The Foreign Policy of Canning, 1822–1827: England, the Neo-Holy Alliance and the New World*, 2nd ed. (Oxford: Frank Cass & Co., 1966), p. 150.

correspondence on the internal situation of Chile was held in 1825, that is, the year after the recognition of these three states. If Canning knew anything about the internal situation of Chile it was from other sources, like testimonies of British travellers.

Notwithstanding, there is only one relevant feature shared by the three states recognised in 1825: all had been viceroyalties during the Spanish dominion and were commercial and administrative centres, which meant that to the eyes of Britons they were much more important than Chile. Peru was also a viceroyalty, but it only gained its independence in December 1824, which was too close to the date when Canning granted the recognition to these three states. Chile was a General Captaincy, and did not have the economic importance of the aforementioned former viceroyalties. It seems therefore that recognition started gradually with those states that presented a specific political and economic trajectory while others like Chile were seen as marginal territories with less to offer. However, a minimal level of stability was also required.

The reports that Nugent sent to Canning tended to stress the internal instability rather than the poverty of Chile. For Nugent, tensions between the provinces of Coquimbo and Concepción and Santiago were even more serious than those in the United Provinces of La Plata. In the same letter mentioned above, he gave details about the central government's attempts to reach a certain degree of unity at a moment in which federalist ideas had gained ground. According to his account of his meeting with Freire, the outcome was a *Discourse Addressed to the Assemblies of Concepción and Coquimbo*, in which the central government claimed that 'the Republic being de facto one and indivisible, the Deputies from all Chile ought to meet in one Congress'.[85] Among many other petitions regarding the representativeness of the Congress, the government pointed out that 'the present state of anarchy presents to the world a spectacle humiliating to Chile, and one which must diminish the good opinion and confidence of foreign powers'.[86] The account of the responses from provincial assemblies of Concepción and Coquimbo did not help to promote a good image of Chile. Of Concepción, Nugent said that its assembly 'acknowledges that a General Congress can alone consolidate the free institutions of Chile, but urges the necessity of first putting down that *violent party spirit* which influenced former elections, and brought on the dissolution of the last Congress'.[87] The italicised phrase refers to an element that made it difficult to attain stability in Chile: the existence of antagonistic groups of interests which characterised the politics of the 1820s. In Nugent's view, this party

85 'Nugent to Canning', Valparaíso, 23 September 1825, in *Britain and the Independence of Latin America*, ed. by Webster, p. 363.

86 Ibid.

87 'Nugent to Canning', Valparaíso, 30 October 1825, in *Britain and the Independence of Latin America*, ed. by Webster, p. 365.

spirit was violent and was also embedded in the 'extreme jealously of the two other Provinces to the superior talent, influence, and supposed aim at domination of that of Santiago'.[88] The US diplomatic agents offered similar descriptions of the disputes between the factions led by O'Higgins and Carrera during the wars of independence. One of these agents, William D.G. Worthington, divided the political spectrum into two factions: the *buenosayrean* (the Party of Buenos Aires) and the Chilean. The former made reference to the role played by San Martín and the *Logia Lautaro* in Chilean politics through the government of O'Higgins, whereas the latter was the Carreras faction, the most popular within Chile. For Worthington this explained O'Higgins's evident preference for European politics to the detriment of the republican model of the US.[89]

The outbreak of the civil war on 7 November 1829 between the different factions represented by the *pipiolos* and *pelucones*, allied with other minor groups like the *estanqueros* did not allow the promotion of a better image of Chile. On 4 January 1830 John White, the vice consul who had arrived in Chile on February 1825, wrote to the Earl of Aberdeen that 'the State is so generally convulsed that it may be said there is no Government in the country'.[90] Ten days later, he went further, suggesting that the British government take some measures to protect the interests of the British community settled in Valparaíso: 'the present distracted state of Chile will require for a long time the presence of a frigate in the port of Valparaíso, from its being the depot of immense British property, so that the British interest laying on the coastline between Chile and Mexico will have to be protected by two ships only ...'.[91] The reply to these letters was sent by John Bidwell, on behalf of Aberdeen, and suggests that he considered the picture painted by White to be exaggerated. Despite 'the melancholy account of the disturbed state of affairs in Chili [*sic*]', Bidwell made clear that such accounts 'have impressed on the minds of the British residents there an extreme degree of apprehension [...], which the fact that no actual attack had been made upon the persons or property of His Majesty's subjects does not appear to justify'.[92] The civil war ended on 17 April 1830 with the triumph of the conservative forces led by General Joaquín Prieto and the civilian Diego Portales. White sent a brief note to Aberdeen on 30 June 1830 in which he stressed that Chile 'has remained undisturbed, and that the Government has been zealously employed in organizing and disciplining the militia of the

88 Ibid.
89 Ossa, 'El gobierno de Bernardo O'Higgins visto a través de cinco agentes diplomáticos', 145–46.
90 'White to Aberdeen', Valparaíso, 14 January 1830, in *Britain and the Independence of Latin America*, ed. by Webster, p. 368.
91 Ibid., pp. 369–70.
92 'Bidwell to White', London, 21 June 1830, in *Britain and the Independence of Latin America*, ed. by Webster, p. 370.

country'.[93] In the same letter he added other ideas regarding the political regime that he suggested should be adopted by Chileans:

> Many of the most intelligent, most wealthy and influential people of the Capital are quite unreserved in declaring that the country cannot long remain undisturbed under a republican government, and that the only means of securing respect to it both at home and abroad would be by its assuming a monarchical Government. Señor Portales, the present Minister of Foreign Affairs, has so expressed himself to Mr. Caldcleugh, and even authorised him to make these sentiments known to His Majesty's Ministers ...[94]

This must be one of very few testimonies regarding the allegedly monarchical adherence of Portales, since none of his letters contains an explicit preference for such a regime. However, it might be understandable that, as Minister of Foreign Affairs, he wanted to send signals to the British government in order to obtain recognition.

Another point that deserves special attention is the mention of Chiloé in the Chilean government's reply to Nugent's inquiries. The possibility of annexing Chiloé to British formal dominion might also be regarded as a reason explaining why Britain delayed the recognition of Chile. The knowledge that Chiloé Island was still controlled by the Spanish royalist General Antonio Quintanilla in 1825 was a powerful argument against the territorial integrity of Chile. Moreover, it could be used to argue that Chile was not completely free of Spanish dominion, and thus to reinforce the policy of neutrality in the conflict. However, as the same letter from Nugent shows, the reference to Chiloé reflected other interests: 'It is covered with timber, fit for all naval purposes, and has a fine harbour. In the hands of Great Britain it would be the key to the whole western side of South America'.[95] In addition, there were serious concerns about the expansionist plans of Bolívar, who after taking power in Peru began to look to the south. Since Chiloé belonged to the Viceroyalty of Peru, despite being geographically attached to Chile, Bolívar urged the Chileans to invade the island and defeat the remaining royalist forces that were still there. Nugent reported in a letter to Canning on 25 July 1825 that 'General Bolivar [...] signified to the Government of Chile his intention of employing an expedition for the reduction of the Island of Chiloé to the Government of Peru, if the State of Chile take not measures, on their own part, to regain so desirable an occupation within three months from the date of such notification'.[96] The threat of Bolívar is another factor to take into account regarding the representations of

---

93 'White to Aberdeen', Valparaíso, 30 June 1830, in *Britain and the Independence of Latin America*, ed. by Webster, p. 370.

94 Ibid., pp. 370–71.

95 Ibid., p. 353.

96 'Nugent to Canning', Valparaíso 25 July 1825, in *Britain and the Independence of Latin America*, ed. by Webster, pp. 359–60.

Chile in this period. According to Daniel Gutiérrez Ardila, Bolívar's triumph in Peru and Upper Peru conferred upon him an extraordinary military power that would even represent an 'existential threat' for the Republic of Chile. This led Chileans to express 'repulsion' at Bolívar, which explains better why some preferred to be under the protection of the British Empire.[97]

Nugent was convinced of the necessity of transferring Chiloé to the British. 'The more I take the subject into consideration', he wrote to Canning, 'proportionately am I confirmed and strengthened in such opinion'.[98] To reinforce his view he argued that 'General Quintanilla has expressed a wish to put Chiloé into the hands of the English', and that its inhabitants preferred 'the protection of Great Britain to that of Chile or Peru'.[99] The official response was eloquent and consistent with the policy of neutrality which the government had previously defended: 'the policy which has guided His Majesty's Government in its intercourse with the late Spanish Provinces of America, is founded upon principles which would not permit Great Britain to assume to herself the Government or exclusive protection of any of the States which may arise in those Colonies'.[100]

However, these words were written in 1826. The geopolitical context was quite different to that of 1808, when the conflict between Spain and its colonies began. Most of them had already declared their independence, and some had even been recognised by Britain. Why then remain stuck to the policy of neutrality in order not to invade Chiloé, as suggested by Nugent? Chiloé was an entrance to the Pacific and offered good possibilities for controlling trade in that ocean. Nugent knew well that the isolation of the territory and the Chilean government's delay in formally annexing it could be beneficial to British interests, and he considered it plausible to think of incorporating Chiloé into the formal British dominions. Even so, the British government held back to do so, evidencing a clear ambiguity about any alleged 'imperial' policy towards Chile in the period.

Despite this response, John White persisted. He was concerned about the constant presence of French vessels willing to negotiate with the islanders to exploit timber. In a letter to Lord Aberdeen written on 14 January 1830 he repeated the reference to 'the desire of the inhabitants for a change of Government', adding that there was also a 'seeming anxiety of the Government of France in persevering to keep up an intercourse with it'.[101] White was trying

---

97 Daniel Gutiérrez Ardila, 'The Chilean Republic in the Face of Bolívar's Expansionism (1823–1828)', *Bulletin of Latin American Research*, 36:3 (2017), 313–25.

98 Ibid., p. 360.

99 'Nugent to Canning', Valparaíso, 15 November 1825, in *Britain and the Independence of Latin America*, ed. by Webster, p. 366.

100 'John Bidwell to Nugent', London, 26 May 1826, in *Britain and the Independence of Latin America*, ed. by Webster, pp. 366–67.

101 'White to Lord Aberdeen', Valparaíso, 14 January 1830, in *Britain and the Independence of Latin America*, ed. by Webster, p. 369.

to persuade his government to reinforce the British presence along the coast and stressing the relevance of Chiloé and its location in the Pacific. Despite this, and unlike in 1806, the British government did not make any plan to invade Chiloé, which reveals that its imperial policy towards the region had changed. By 1826, however, Chilean forces had already occupied the island, and the remaining Spanish authorities had been expelled from the territory. Since then, under these circumstances there was no reason to change the 'official mind' about neutrality. In addition, both the Spanish and French presences on the island, along with Chile's interests on it made any everything much more complex. A British invasion of Chiloé would certainly have led to a large-scale conflict, a major break in any 'imperialist' policy. This reveals the uncertainties experienced during the period, which also explains the different possibilities that British and Chilean relations could experience, even in the diplomatic realm.

Order, stability and the definition of the political regime were not sufficient reasons to explain the denial of recognition to Chile, as has been claimed in the most important contributions to the historiography of British recognition of Chile's independence.[102] These problems were shared by other states, like the United Provinces, and no objection was made to their recognition. Furthermore, Chile was less politically stable in 1831, when recognition was eventually granted, than it had been in 1825. Nugent's correspondence also shows that he had many other concerns about Chile, regarding its territorial integrity and the possibility of an invasion from Peru. It might be argued, therefore, that the non-recognition of Chile had to be justified with different arguments simply because there was no serious reason to deny such recognition. Had these arguments been true, the United Provinces should not have been recognised so early. Colombia was certainly not an example of political stability either. Thus, Nugent had to construct a narrative to convince public opinion why Chile did not deserve recognition, at a moment in which Canning was only considering recognition of the former viceroyalties because of their economic and political significance.

5.5 Chile Between Empires: The United States, Britain and the Future of a New Nation

Some historians, like Theodore E. Nichols, have stressed the idea that the Chileans' persistence in pushing for British recognition reflected a desire to protect their own interests from the threats represented by other powers. The constant possibility of a Spanish invasion in the early 1820s was perhaps the most valid reason.[103] However, the geographical position of Chile, more distant than other destinations like Buenos Aires, made this

---

102 Centner, pp. 287–91; Nichols, pp. 138–42.
103 Nichols, pp. 137–43.

unlikely. United States interests in Spanish American and Chilean affairs came up as early as 1812, when the 'special agent' Joel Robert Poinsett arrived in Chile.[104] At that point, Chile was under the leadership of the military dictator José Miguel Carrera, who unlike his 'rival' Bernardo O'Higgins, was always keen to get any help possible from the United States. In fact, as claimed by Collier, while representing the US in Chile, Poinsett 'became an intimate friend of the Carreras, presented a draft constitution, and accompanied the patriot troops in their first campaign against the royalists'.[105] Poinsett remained in Chile until 1814, when he left for Buenos Aires, after the triumph of the royalist forces restored Spanish rule. For his part, Carrera eventually travelled to the US after this defeat and spent a short time in Mendoza. In Washington he met Poinsett and was introduced to some top military figures and even to James Monroe, all of whom helped him to return to South America to join the war of independence.[106] These years were seemingly the 'high point of early US-Chilean relations'[107] and show that the need for military aid, and the admiration that some patriots expressed for the US republican system, led them to consider it as a possible ally.

In 1817, though, the context was different. The patriots' victory in Chacabuco on 12 February and the establishment of the new O'Higgins government diminished the importance of the US for the consolidation of Chilean independence. For the new Supreme Director, it was much more important to establish good relations with Great Britain than any other state and he was reluctant to meet with US diplomatic agents.[108] As shown in this book, Bernardo O'Higgins was a declared admirer of British culture and politics; his father Ambrose (Ambrosio) – a former governor of Chile and viceroy of Peru in the eighteenth century – was Irish and he had himself been educated in London. In terms of diplomatic relations, his government also represented a continuation of what Pinto had tried to do in his failed mission to London in 1813, that is, the establishment of formal and long-standing

104 Ossa, 'El gobierno de Bernardo O'Higgins visto a través de cinco agentes estadounidenses, 1817–1823', 139–66; Liss, pp. 213–15.

105 Collier, pp. 97–98.

106 Tomás de Iriarte, *Biografía Del Brigadier General D. José Miguel Carrera, dos veces magistrado de la República de Chile* (Buenos Aires: Imprenta de Mayo, 1863), pp. 31–34. The most recent biographical work on Carrera is Beatriz Bragoni, *José Miguel Carrera. Un revolucionario chileno en el Río de la Plata* (Buenos Aires: Edhasa, 2012).

107 T. Ray Shurbutt, 'Personnel Diplomacy: The United States and Chile: 1812–1850', in *United States-Latin American Relations: The Formative Generations*, ed. by T. Ray Shurbutt (Tuscaloosa and London: University of Alabama Press, 1991), pp. 228–60 (p. 231).

108 Ossa, 'El gobierno de Bernardo O'Higgins visto a través de cinco agentes estadounidenses, 1817–1823', 149.

relations with Great Britain. This approach was also an expression of the place that Chile played in the shifting geopolitical dynamics that characterised the 1820s, in which the growing power of the US would be a significant factor in understanding the approach of Great Britain to the former colonies of the Spanish empire.

On 22 March 1822, President James Monroe granted recognition to all the already independent Spanish American states. This move was quite controversial and seen with suspicion in Spanish America, due to increasing fears about the expansion of US ambitions. However, as demonstrated by Ossa, there were brief, but crucial negotiations on the Chilean case that demonstrate the mutual interests of both parties: while O'Higgins asked for a loan in order to fund the Liberation Army of Peru, the agent Jeremy Robinson recommended the adoption of the republican system.[109]

On December 1823 Monroe read an address to the US Congress in which he stated his famous 'doctrine' regarding US and Latin American relations, as summarised in the phrase 'America is for the Americans'. The controversy of both decisions must be understood in the wider context of the complex international relations between the US and Great Britain. Liss has argued that British and US commercial rivalry was a crucial factor to consider.[110] In a recent work, Jay Sexton has addressed the long-term significance of the Monroe Doctrine in terms of the US's internal process of unification, nation-building and its imperialistic ambitions. The threat represented by the British Empire was fundamental in understanding the configuration of such a doctrine, with which the US authorities sought to 'consolidate their independence from an increasingly powerful British Empire, as well as to advance their interests in regions of the crumbling Spanish Empire'.[111] From the British point of view, fears of US expansionism were also significant. As argued by Harold Temperley, 'Canning's great fear was that the United States would head a "General Transatlantic League" to prevent Europe from cooperating with America, or America from cooperating in Europe. Hence, his future policy was to break down the barrier of partition that the Monroe Doctrine might erect between the two Hemispheres'.[112] For Spanish Americans this doctrine was not precisely a proof of the US's will to defend their sovereignty from the European threat. Piero Gleijeses argues that 'territorial expansion had been part of the mission of the United States from the very outset – expansion

---

109 Ossa, 'El gobierno de Bernardo O'Higgins visto a través de cinco agentes estadounidenses, 1817–1823', pp. 150–53.

110 Liss, pp. 212–14.

111 Jay Sexton, *The Monroe Doctrine: Empire and Nation in Nineteenth Century America* (New York: Hill and Wang, 2009), p. 16.

112 Harold Temperley, 'The Foreign Policy of George Canning', in *The Cambridge History of British Foreign Policy*, ed. by Adolphus William Ward and George Peabody Gooch, 2 vols (New York: Cambridge University Press, 1923), I, pp. 51–118 (p. 73).

against the decaying Spanish empire, and expansion into the lands of the Spanish Americans'.[113]

There are many examples to support the idea that the US was considered a threat to Spanish Americans' sovereignty, rather than an ally. From Peru, Diego Portales wrote to his friend José Miguel Cea in 1822:

> The President of the North American Federation, Mr Monroe, has said 'It is recognised that America is for these people'. Be careful not to exchange one form of domination for another. We should distrust these gentlemen who say they admire our liberators, when they did not assist us at all – that makes me anxious. Why should the United States accredit Ministers and representatives, and recognise America's independence, while they do nothing? What an odd system this is, my friend! I believe that there is a strategy here, which is to conquer America not by arms, but by influence. This will happen: perhaps not today, but certainly tomorrow.[114]

The growing US power was more threatening in closer areas, like the Caribbean or even Central America, than in the isolated territory of Chile in the extreme south of the continent.[115] If some Chileans were circumspect about the recognition granted by the US in 1822, it was because Chile's commercial interests, but not necessarily its sovereignty in the area, were under threat. O'Higgins had outlined a plan with Cochrane to rule the Pacific and even to conquer the Philippines. Thus, the Chilean authorities were not simply behaving as 'victims' of foreign imperial powers, but were trying to protect Chile's own ambitions in the Pacific.

In addition, the creation of the Chilean navy, as early as 1817, made Chileans enthusiastic about their capacity not only to defend the seas, but to become the second sea power in the world after Great Britain. O'Higgins analysed these possibilities in a manuscript titled 'Comparative State of the Natural and Other Advantages Possessed by the United States and Chili Respectively for Constituting a Maritime Power of the First Class in the New World' written during his exile in Peru on 20 August 1831.[116] His aim was to demonstrate why Chile's geographic situation gave it a better chance than the US of becoming the most respected sea power after Great Britain, whose

113 Piero Gleijeses, 'The Limits of Sympathy: The United States and the Independence of Spanish America', *Journal of Latin American Studies*, 24:3 (1992), 481–505 (p. 489).

114 'Diego Portales to José Miguel Cea', Lima, March 1822, in Raúl Silva Castro, *Diego Portales: Ideas y confesiones* (Santiago: Editorial del Pacífico, 1954), p. 61.

115 Gleijeses, p. 490.

116 Bernardo O'Higgins, 'Comparative State of the Natural and Other Advantages Possessed by the United States and Chili Respectively for Constituting a Maritime Power of the First Class in the New World', TNA, FO 96/150/6, fols 35–66. This document was translated into Spanish by Carlos Silva Vildósola, 'Papeles de O'Higgins. Un proyecto de alianza chileno-británica', *Boletín de la Academia Chilena de la Historia*, 17 (1923), 209–29.

global supremacy was not doubted. The document also stated the difficulty of becoming such a power due to the lack of a population dedicated to certain activities, like agriculture and fishing. The solution was to bring 20,000 Irish nationals to settle southern Chile, which at the same time allowed them to escape destitution.

All of this led O'Higgins to believe that Chile was in a good position to compete with the US and to become a paramount maritime power. He did not want to compete with Great Britain, but to establish an alliance to rule the seas together. The document states that 'the only thing which [Chile] requires [is] to unite her to Great Britain in the closest bonds of interest and of friendship and to render her in fact the second naval power in the world, second only to Great Britain, whose lofty and commanding position would thus be secured forever'.[117] Thus, on an initial level, the relationship was beneficial to Chile, as it would secure its place as the second naval power in the world. On a second level, the relationship was also beneficial to Great Britain, as it was through its union with Chile – perhaps its only potential competitor – that its supremacy would also be secured. There was also a third level on which an alliance between Great Britain and Chile was beneficial:

> These facts and prospects are most consoling to humanity as calculated to fortify the hope that future wars between the human race will be few and of short duration. England and Chili [sic], thus prosperous, powerful and united would have nothing to wish for but peace and to profess that, they would have the power whereas without such a union of which the Irish colonists would be the bond, such hope it is to be feared would prove unfounded.[118]

Therefore, it was thought that an alliance between both 'powers' would benefit the whole of humanity. For the author, Chile could not only become a naval power in the world, but a ruling power capable of bringing peace to the world along with its British partner. This also shows the extent to which representations of Britain had changed over the years of the struggles for the independence: from being depicted as an enemy to an ally with whom Chile might dominate the Pacific while Britain dominated the Atlantic. The linkage, as stated in O'Higgins's document, was the Irish settler population that would colonise the territory and boost the Chilean economy. In sum, this document shows that, in the context of imperial rivalries, for some, like O'Higgins, the future of Chile depended on its relations with Great Britain. This shows how the self-image of Chile had gradually changed. In the past Chile had been represented as a poor and isolated colony and was now being represented as potential maritime power.

This project was known and discussed in Britain. The Duke of Wellington received a letter from an anonymous writer, who signed as 'Amicus', with

117 O'Higgins, 'Comparative State', fol. 60.
118 Ibid., fol. 63.

clear details of the project and favourable opinions about it. 'Amicus' wrote that 'at present my object is to profit by the laudable anxiety of General O'Higgins to colonise the south of Chili [*sic*] with Irish emigrants, a measure which if carried into execution must prove of incalculable advantage to the British empire, as well as to the Chilean Republic'.[119] In another section of the letter, the writer expressed his confidence that it 'will be [the Mayor of Dublin's] most ardent wish, to do everything in his power to relieve the distress of the Irish poor and consequently to promote emigration on a large scale as the most effectual means for accomplishing that object'.[120] This confirms that one of the images that Britons had of Chile during the independence era stressed its character as a land of opportunities. This had been prompted earlier by Pinto in the first diplomatic mission to London and was again being discussed in 1830.

I explained earlier how O'Higgins, perhaps influenced by Cochrane, dreamed of creating a new naval empire in the Pacific that would even reach the Philippines. These projections were discussed in his correspondence of the 1820s. Notwithstanding, O'Higgins' letter analysed in this chapter reveals that such ambitions became even grander. Chile was not only destined to dominate the Pacific, but the Atlantic too. It must be remembered that in the 1830s the Chilean territory was not defined in its current shape. The region of 'Patagonia' in the south appeared as part of its territory on Chilean maps, embracing a vast area that reached the Atlantic. However, it is unlikely that O'Higgins genuinely thought Chile might be capable of challenging British supremacy in the Atlantic. As the same document shows, the power of Great Britain in the Atlantic was undisputed and at best he wanted Chile to be the second naval power after Britain. Hence, more than fearing the expansionism of the US, O'Higgins was imagining his country as a competitor in his projected dominion of the Pacific. That is why, beyond his 'Anglophilia', his approach to Great Britain might be understood as a means to establish an alliance with Great Britain, whose fleet would dominate the Atlantic, allowing Chile to rule the Pacific.

5.6 The Delayed British Recognition of Chile's Independence

As said above, José Miguel de la Barra had been commissioned by the Chilean President Francisco Antonio Pinto to remain in London as a 'general consul' in 1827. This was a decision made on the pragmatic grounds that Chile was not going to persist in seeking recognition from Great Britain but hoped that there would be a certain degree of reciprocity between the two states: Chile had accepted the appointment of British consuls, the British government should do the same. However, the British government was not willing to

---

119 'Anonymous letter, from Amicus, to Arthur Wellesley, first Duke of Wellington', Lima, 24 August 1830, TWA, WP1/11529, n.fol.
120 Ibid.

accept this nomination, since it implied recognition of Chile as an independent state and at the time there was no interest in granting such recognition. A controversy arose between De la Barra and the British authorities when the *Exequatur*, that is, the official permission by which a representative of another state was entitled to act as such, was considered 'offensive' by De la Barra. That document did not mention Chile as a state, but as a 'Province' and De la Barra was not granted all the 'privileges, immunities and advantages' of the Consul of Buenos Aires, but only 'assistance when required'.[121] De la Barra was then commissioned by Pinto to remain in Paris as a Plenipotentiary Minister and only returned to London in 1831.[122]

It was not until 24 February 1831 that Great Britain, with Lord Palmerston as the Minister of Foreign Affairs, decided to recognise three states that had not been recognised by Canning in 1824: Chile, Peru and Guatemala. De la Barra was informed by General Robert Wilson, a Member of Parliament, that the British government was about to recognise Chile as an independent state. He sent a letter to Portales, who was the Minister of Foreign Affairs at the time. According to Montaner Bello, had this news reached Chile a few years earlier, the reception would arguably have been joyful, but this was not the case in 1831. One year earlier France had already granted its recognition to Chile, mainly because of the pressure exerted by French merchants and bankers on their government. At that point, in addition, many other European countries, like the Netherlands and Prussia, had sent envoys and consuls to establish formal relations with the new Spanish American states.[123] This can explain why 'the legislative bodies replied with rather cold dispatches with respect to recognition'.[124] In addition, by 1830 the political context had changed and the initial enthusiasm and admiration for Britain had gradually faded. Neither Francisco Antonio Pinto nor his successor Joaquín Prieto was willing to persist in the negotiations for recognition. At most they would accept it, but would not persist in pursuing it.

The recognition was granted a few months after the end of the civil war of 1829–1830, which led Prieto as President and Diego Portales as Minister of the Interior to power. Chile's continuing political instability seemed less relevant than it had been in 1824, when Canning refused to grant recognition on the grounds of the alleged political divisions and violent factionalism reported by Nugent. That was shortly after O'Higgins resigned from power and in the eyes of Nugent and other travellers, Chile was facing a phase of political stability. Recognition was granted in the aftermath of a civil war, in contrast, when the situation of Chile was far from enjoying the stability of 1823. British recognition came because of the pressure exerted by the French recognition one year before, and the persistent lobbying by some merchant

121 All this is explained by Montaner Bello, pp. 359–61.
122 Barros, p. 87.
123 Guerrero Lira, 'Chile en el mundo', p. 138.
124 Montaner Bello, p. 379.

houses that wanted to open up this trade route.[125] In addition, none of the other factors explained above regarding the delay of recognition remained in 1831. Chilean forces had occupied Chiloé in 1826, Peru had achieved its independence and the end of the civil war by 1830 guaranteed freedom from political unrest in Chile, at least in the short term.

Historians do not agree on the meaning of this recognition. One of the elements stated in the official document of recognition was the need to sign a Treaty of Friendship and Trade, a further step that would not be easy to solve. This was a condition that the British government imposed on every new country seeking to be recognised, to secure its commercial interests. The treaty was only signed in 1839 and for some historians, like Charles Centner, it was not until this act that recognition was a fact: 'On 19 January, 1839, diplomatic representatives of the Chilean and British Governments signed a treaty for the cessation of any participation by Chilean nationals in the international slave trade. By this act, the British Government officially recognised Chile'.[126] For others, like Nichols, recognition was definitive only when Britain appointed a proper ambassador to Chile, which only occurred in 1930.[127] However, for the purposes of this study, I assume the recognition granted in 1831 to be at least symbolic, because this had been the aim of Chilean authorities from the beginning of diplomatic negotiations. The signing of treaties and appointment of ambassadors were merely consequences of this decision. This, however, must not obscure the importance of such treaties, which reinforced the aim of the British state to expand its commercial networks by means of free trade agreements.

The very act of recognition also had a symbolic meaning: it was the first manifestation of 'interstate' relations in which both states were at least nominally 'equals'. In 1806, the situation had been quite different, since one of the states openly aimed to conquer the other, which was still a colony subject to Spanish power. In 1831, two political entities entered into a long-standing 'relationship' through the actions of their diplomatic representatives. As historians such as Salazar and Mayo have shown, this relationship was configured upon unequal and asymmetrical foundations.

5.7 Conclusion

These negotiations show that there was an evident acceptance by Chileans of the geopolitical role played by Great Britain, as the paramount empire in the world. The persistent attempts to gain British recognition of Chile's independence between 1817 and 1827 is a clear proof of that. In all the diplomatic instructions we find explicit references to the need to bring Europeans and Britons to Chile in order to develop different economic activities. This

---

125 Kaufmann, pp. 180–85.
126 Centner, p. 296.
127 Nichols, p. 143.

was even considered by O'Higgins, for whom the Irish colonisers were the bond that would consolidate an alliance between Great Britain and Chile. Considering that these ideas were stated in documents dating from 1813, it is not surprising that from 1817, the Chilean authorities decided to adopt the British models of education and organisation of the navy.

The insistence of the British authorities that Chile must demonstrate that it was a stable and ordered country had significant consequences. The 'exceptionality' of Chile, that is, the image of Chile that is typically linked to the regime inaugurated in 1830 for its alleged uninterrupted political stability (just four elected presidents subsequently ruled the country between 1831 and 1871), was configured during the independence era. It was in these negotiations and debates that the image of Chile as a stable country was promoted and contested. Chileans tried to persuade the British authorities that the political situation was not as serious as they thought; for their part, British consuls did not promote a friendly image of Chile, which made it much more difficult to gain the desired recognition. Despite the role played by the British missionaries, merchants and seamen who were in Chile between 1806 and 1831, the image of Chile was not sufficiently positively promoted to persuade the British authorities that Chile deserved to be recognised as an independent state. This explains, in part, the need to send different diplomatic missions with clear instructions to offer whatever necessary. The role played by the US, and its increasingly expansionist ambitions, also explains the desire for British recognition. Chileans preferred to have closer connections with the most powerful contemporary empire, which had made it clear that it only wanted to trade, than with the US, whose intentions were less clear. All of these factors reveal that the image of Britain as the ruling empire of the world also had diverse meanings in this sphere. The Chilean authorities did not fear compromising their sovereignty; indeed, they were willing to concede part of their territory in order to gain Britain as an ally in the changing international geopolitical context, and considering the threat represented by the US. This eventually reinforced the image of Britain as the ruling power, who would see in Chile an ally in the expansion of its operations in the Pacific. However, in these interactions the Chilean authorities were also demonstrating that they were not merely concerned about being 'colonised' by a new empire, but were struggling to preserve and expand their own commercial ambitions in the Pacific so as to become rulers of its trade. This also demonstrates that in this period, even when relationships were established at an 'interstate' level, it would be far from accurate to speak of a British informal empire to define these relationships. As shown in this chapter, there were clear opportunities for Britain to expand its imperial interests in Chile, by occupying Chiloé or Juan Fernández (offered by the Chilean government itself). However, considerations of the fragile relationships amongst the European powers seemed to be more important.

Conclusion

This book has demonstrated the insights that can be found in the analysis of British-Chilean relations in the independence period, which in the case of Chile have been mostly studied relating to the second half of the nineteenth century. The fact that British investments and flows of peoples and goods became increasingly important after 1850, has led scholars like John Mayo to maintain that 'informal imperialism' is the appropriate term to describe the 'anatomy' of such a relationship. However, such a view is restrictive, allowing an examination of the traditional ambits by which informal empire has been regarded as an analytical tool when approaching the relations between Britain and Latin America. This is to say, the economic and diplomatic means that helped to preserve the subordinate condition of the former Spanish colonies to the interests of the British Empire. In recent years, approaches to the problematic nature of informal imperialism have made it clear that these elements are not enough, that they cannot be the only aspects imbricated in this problem. The cultural dimension must also form part of the analysis of a relationship that, at first glance, seemed to be determined by informal imperialism. This is particularly relevant in a period like the independence era, in which the economic and diplomatic means used by Great Britain to exert its dominion were not as evident as in subsequent years. Indeed, as I showed in the last chapter, Britain was not willing to recognise Chile's independence, even though this would have facilitated its alleged aim of trading at any cost. Therefore, the cultural dimension helps to demonstrate that in the realm of interpersonal relations, in the everyday lives of those who were supposedly affected by British expansionist ambitions, the idea of imperialism or, better, the idea of Britain as an empire that was threating Chile's sovereignty, had different and divergent meanings.

That is why it is so relevant to return to one of the ideas stated in the Introduction to this book, about the persistence of 'dependency theory' as an explanatory model of the relations between Britain and Chile. I am not denying that in the long-term study of this history, this could serve as an explanatory model to grasp the way Chile was subordinated to a marginal place in the world economic system. I argue that even though we are certain that this was 'the outcome' of the independence process, we cannot say that this was the 'obvious' outcome, predetermined due to the mere existence of Britain as an empire. In fact, when assessing the extent to which imperialism was exerted upon Chile during this period, it becomes clear that this was a short-lived policy and varied according to the circumstances. Thus, Windham's plan to invade Chile in 1806 was the clearest example that before the crisis of 1808, British policymakers were willing to use force and power to invade Chile and incorporate it into the British dominions. This was also the only moment, until negotiations for recognition in the 1820s, when British-Chilean relations were carried out on an interstate level. When Britain declared its neutrality in 1808, things changed radically and interactions between Chileans and Britons were on a non-state level, occurring via cultural encounters between Britons and Chileans in different contact zones. These spaces of interaction were configured by different actors, such as individuals and associations, with a wide range of interests and projects.

This book has demonstrated that at this level, Chileans had different and changing perceptions of the role played by Britain in the international order and how this could affect their lives. If, at the beginning of the process, Britain was seen as an enemy due to its undeniable role as an enemy of Spain, this image changed as the war in Europe developed. When Britain and Spain became allies, Chileans perceptions about their condition as subjects of Ferdinand VII also began to change. If their initial reaction after the invasion of Buenos Aires had been to organise the defence of their territory from a possible invasion by Britain, they would later move on to a more ambiguous representation of what to expect from Britain. It was one thing to be subjects of the Spanish king and defend their territory on his behalf, but another to defend their own territory when they assumed that the political ties with Spain had to be broken. That is why representations of Britain and Britons changed so rapidly, to the extent that, during the war, the latter began to be accepted as soldiers and seamen. This led to the building up of a navy, not only under the 'British model', but also under the direction of British officers who tried to reproduce their naval system in the newly created Chilean navy. This inevitably led to a cultural 'collision' with the Chilean seamen who formed the crews. Such collisions were the result of a relation that was necessarily conflictive, since there were two groups in contact with different cultural parameters such as language and religion. This had nothing to do with imperialism, or Chilean resistance to the cultural imposition of English language and customs on board ship. Chileans in the navy were led to configure an image of Britons composed of divergent elements, and which in many cases was determined by their position in the ranks as much as their origins. Anyway, this instance of encounter also revealed that any contact between individuals from different cultures required mediation, especially when language seemed to be an insurmountable barrier. The role of interpreters and translators, who were also cultural translators, was one of the elements that eventually allowed this navy to be successful, despite all of the difficulties they faced, such as a lack of basic resources for survival.

The case of British missionaries, who travelled to Chile in order to spread the Monitorial system of education and the Protestant Bible, was similar. Contact was physical in the travels of Thomson and Matthews, but also took place in a non-physical sphere. Chileans had to investigate the new educational system that they were to adopt and determine whether it suited their local conditions. This was also an exercise in cultural translation. A system that was originally created to educate children in the context of the Industrial Revolution, and had been conceived in religiously neutral terms, had now to be adapted to a different reality. Although this reality was different in some aspects, such as economic structure and the prominent place of the Catholic religion, it was not excessively different. Matthews's testimonies reveal that opposition to the introduction of foreign and allegedly Protestant ideas was not as strong as historians have claimed. Different attitudes among the clergy, and Chilean society in general, allowed the rapid spread of the Monitorial system and Protestant vernacular Bibles, at least before the doctrinal changes that took place within the BFBS. Although the implementation of the Monitorial system was short-lived, the interaction between these missionaries and educators and their Chilean counterparts had significant consequences. Many ideas that were debated during this process, such as the role of the central state in the provision of education, the preference for educating the elites and the role of philanthropy in contributing to the establishment of schools, were first debated in this context. In addition, the conception of a disciplined citizen, educated under a system characterised by an emphasis on order, was also configured as a result of this process.

With regard to the role of merchants, usually characterised as agents of the British informal empire *par excellence*, this book has demonstrated that their experiences affected the lives of those people with whom they interacted during these years in different ways. It is clear that, as merchants, they were expanding the commercial routes and economic markets of Britain, which led to them being understood as eminent examples of imperialists. However, once in Chile some, like John James Barnard, not only represented the interests of Britain and referred to themselves as a different community, but also began to be incorporated into Chilean society. Barnard, as a representative of the British merchants, did show a clear willingness to open up free trade to the benefit of Britain, but he also participated in the discussion to reform trade regulations on the invitation of the Chilean government. In this role, he also insisted that it was necessary to consider local conditions in order to adapt foreign ideas to a new context. That was, for him, the only way in which liberal economic ideas could prevail, and required even greater caution than the other British merchants, who were more willing to eliminate any kind of customs barrier. The consolidation of an economic policy oriented towards foreign trade also had repercussions for Chilean society, whose artisans would be affected by the introduction of manufacturers. In this case, in addition, the role of Barnard was essential to understanding that, even in the field of trade, the cultural mediation of an agent was a crucial element in applying foreign ideas. Barnard spoke Spanish, as did Thomson and Matthews, and his understanding of the language allowed him to take a key position as intermediary between Chileans and merchants. More important than language though was perhaps his consciousness of the importance of reconciling a foreign set of ideas with a local reality.

None of the above would have occurred without the political dimension. Although there is a debate about the extent to which all of these interventions in Chile conformed with official policy directed by the British government, it is undeniable that the political dimension was a permanent element in this relationship. In the first instance, this is because this was a relationship mediated by power, which is an essential element of the political sphere. The independence struggles were mainly a battle to change the conditions in which power was exerted in Chilean society. The active role of Britain in this conflict was also a struggle for power, in terms of who would become the hegemonic empire. All of this was also imbricated in the relationship between Chileans and Britons, and from the outset this would be manifested in the negotiations to obtain support and, later, political recognition from Britain. To ask for recognition immediately implies that the actor who is granting recognition has more power than the new entity, but in this case this was even more evident, since Chile was determined to get British recognition as a priority. This consideration was inserted into a complex geopolitical scenario, in which there was fear of invasion from Europe and the rising power of the US represented a threat to Chilean sovereignty. The evidence suggests that Chileans had ceased to consider Britain as a threat to its sovereignty and that they were even willing to compromise their economic liberty to gain British recognition.

All in all, these considerations permit one to answer the initial questions that this book intended to answer. The role of the British Empire in the making of Chile cannot be reduced to an alleged 'influence' from outside. Yet it is undeniable that a wide range of ideas and notions concerning education, seamanship and economics were disseminated by Britons; it is also true that these ideas were contested, debated and adapted to the local context. If such influence existed, it was neither linear nor unidirectional, but expressed in divergent ways. It can be said that the 'encounters' between Chileans and Britons in the different domains considered in this book catalysed a wide range of reactions, perceptions, representations and discourses that changed as the geopolitical role of Britain changed. In such encounters, images of Chile and Chileans were contested and debated and some, like the image of Chile as an example of order and stability, would later be used in the making of a 'national identity'. The nature of the encounters between Britons and Chileans was also divergent. As shown throughout this book, such encounters were experienced as a contact, a collision or a relationship. Thus, it is hard to sustain the contention that Chileans perceived Britain and Britons solely as 'imperialists'. As shown, this was only one of the many ways in which Chileans represented their experiences when interacting with Britons during this period. Indeed, Britons were seldom perceived as imperial agents and Britain was not always seen as an empire. Perceptions were also mediated by other factors like class – as shown in Chapter 2 – and not simply by origins. At the same time, Britons configured their own images of Chile as a result of these encounters. Britain thus regarded Chile as a territory with evident advantages due to its location in the South Pacific and the key role that this could play in transoceanic trade. All this had consequences in the subsequent nation-building process. Chileans debated their identity when they had to defend themselves from a possible invasion, and discussed whether they should only defend their own territory or whether they had fight in Buenos Aires when it was occupied by Britons. Images of Chile's place in the world were also debated and contested. These representations changed according to the political and military strategies that were adopted at different times. If the early strategy was to prevent an invasion and later on to attract immigrants, in the 1820s it shifted to a more active campaign regarding the stability and prosperity of the country. All this had consequences for the ways in which Chileans began to think about themselves as a distinct community.

Bibliography

Archives

Archivo General de Indias, Fondo Chile, vol. 206
Archivo Nacional Histórico de Chile,
    Fondo Capitanía General, vol. 819
    Fondo Ministerio de Hacienda, vol. 59
    Fondo Ministerio del Interior, vols 5 and 52
    Fondo Ministerio de Marina, vols 8, 30 and 35
    Fondo Sergio Fernández Larraín, vol. 144
    Fondo Varios, vols 237, 239 and 440
British and Foreign Bible Society Archive, Cambridge University Library, Foreign Correspondence Inwards: Luke Matthews and J.J. Barnard
British and Foreign School Society Archive, Brunel University Archives, Foreign Correspondence, Chile
National Archives of Scotland, Dundonald Papers, GD233/31–36
The British Library, Additional Manuscripts, 3268 and 48212
The National Archives at Kew
    Foreign Office, 16/9; 16/10; 16/12A and 96/150
    War Office, 1/161
The Wellington Archive, University of Southampton Library, WP1/685/20, WP1/115/29

Newspapers

El Mercurio chileno (1829)
Gazeta Ministerial de Chile (1819–1821)

Published Sources

Academia Chilena de la Historia (ed.), *Archivo de don Bernardo O'Higgins (ABO)*, vols 3, 5, 12 and 35 (Santiago: Academia Chilena de la Historia, 1946–2001).
'Acta de Proclamación de la Independencia de Chile', available at: http://www.bcn.cl/bibliodigital/dhisto/acta (accessed 20 March 2014).

An Authentic Narrative of the Proceedings of the Expedition Under the Command of Brigadier–Gen. Craufurd, Untils its Arrival to Montevideo, With an Account of the Operations Against Buenos Aires Under the Command of Liut. Gen. WhiteLocke. By an Officer of the Expedition (London: G.E. Miles, 1808).

'Actas del Cabildo de Santiago', 30 July 1807, available at: http://www.historia.uchile.cl/CDA/fh_indice/0,1387,JNID%253D27,00.html (accessed 20 March 2014).

'Acuerdo del Congreso Nacional de Chile', Santiago, 11 October 1811, available at: http://www.historia.uchile.cl/CDA/fh_article/0,1389,SCID%253D13577%2526ISID%253D405%2526PRT%253D13004%2526JNID%253D12,00.html (accessed 20 March 2014).

Bell, Andrew, *An Experiment in Education Made at the Male Asylum in Madras. Suggesting a System by Which a School or Family May Teach Itself under the Superintendence of the Master or the Parent* (London: Cadell and Davies, 1797).

Blanco Encalada, Manuel, *Contestación del Vice-Almirante Blanco Encalda a la vindicación apolojética del Capitán Wooster inserta en el número 37 de* El Barómetro de Chile (Santiago: Imprenta de la opinión, 1836).

Bowell Longeville, Richard, *Memorias de un official ingles al servicio de Chile, 1821–1829*, edited and trans. by José Toribio Medina (Santiago: Septiembre Ediciones, 2011).

British and Foreign Bible Society, *Annual Reports* (1821–1827).

——, *Annual Reports* (1821–1831).

——, *Manual of the British and Foreign School Society to Teach Reading, Writing, Arithmetic and Needlework in the Elementary Schools* (London: Longman and Co., 1816).

Cochrane, Thomas, *Observations on Naval Affairs and on Some Collateral Subjects; including Instances of Injustice Experienced by the Author: With a Summary of his Naval Service: and a Copious Appendix* (London: James Ridgway, 1857).

Cochrane, Thomas and H.R. Fox Bourne, *The Life of Thomas Cochrane, Tenth Earl of Dundonald G.C.B., Vol. 1* (London: Richard Bentley, 1869).

Constitución Política del Estado de Chile, 1822.

De la Cruz, Luis, *Viage a su costa, del Alcalde Provincial del muy Ilustre Cabildo de la Concepción de Chile, D. Luis de la Cruz* (Buenos Aires: Imprenta del Estado, 1835).

De Mora, José Joaquín, 'Plan de estudios del Liceo de Chile con algunos pormenores para su ejecución y sobre la disciplina del establecimiento', *El Mercurio Chileno*, 10, 1 January 1829.

Egaña, Juan, 'Elogio del Lord Alejandro Cochrane, Vicealmirante de Chile y General en jefe de la Marina pronunciado en el *Instituto Nacional*', Santiago, 1819, Memoria Chilena, Biblioteca Nacional de Chile, available at: http://www.memoriachilena.cl/602/w3-article-71971.html (accessed 2 June 2015).

——, *Memoria política sobre el conviene en Chile la libertad de cultos. Reimpreso en Lima y Bogotá con una breve apología del art. 8 y 9 de la constitución política del Perú de 1823* (Caracas: Imprenta G.V. Devisme, 1829).

Feliú Cruz, Guillermo (ed.), *Colección de Historiadores y Documentos relativos a la Independencia de Chile, Vol. 30* (Santiago: Imprenta Universitaria, 1939).

García Reyes, Antonio, *Memoria sobre la primera Escuadra nacional* (Santiago: Imprenta del Progreso, 1846).

Graham, Maria, *Journal of a Residence in Chile in the year 1822 and a Voyage from Chile to Brazil in 1823* (London: Longman, 1824).

Gramática Latina dispuesta en forma de catecismo adaptada al método de enseñanza mutua y sacada de las mejores hasta ahora publicadas en Europa (Santiago: Imprenta Republicana, 1831).

González Echeñique, Javier, *Documentos de la misión de don Mariano Egaña en Londres (1824–1829)* (Santiago: Ministerio de Relaciones Exteriores, 1984).

Henríquez, Camilo, 'Bosquejo compendioso del sistema de enseñanza mutua', Colección Manuscritos de Camilo Henríquez, Biblioteca Nacional de Chile, Santiago, Chile, 1822, fols 6–11.

Instrucciones para conducir escuelas bajo el sistema de enseñanza mutua (Santiago: [1823?]).

Lancaster, Joseph, *Improvements in Education; Abridged. Containing a Complete Epitome of the System of Education Invented and Practiced by the Author*, 3rd ed. (London: Free School, Borough Road, 1808).

——, *Report of J. Lancaster's Progress from the Year 1798, with the Report of the Finance Committee for the Year 1810. To Which Is Prefixed an Address of the Committee for Promoting the Royal Lancasterian System for the Education of the Poor* (London: Royal Free School Press, 1811).

Letelier, Valentín (ed.), *Sesiones de los cuerpos lejislativos de la República de Chile (SCL), Vol. 3 (1819–1820)* (Santiago: Imprenta Cervantes, 1867).

Martínez, Melchor, *Memoria histórica sobre la revolución de Chile: desde el cautiverio de Fernando VII hasta 1814* (Valparaíso: Imprenta europea, 1848).

Mathison, Gilbert Farquhar, *Narrative of a visit to Brazil, Chile, Peru, and the Sandwich Islands during the Years 1821 and 1822* (London: Charles Knight, 1825).

Matta Vial, Enrique (ed.), *Colección de historiadores i de documentos relativos a la independencia de Chile, Vol. 9* (Santiago, Imprenta Cervantes, 1909).

Miers, John, *Travels in Chile and La Plata. Including Accounts Respecting the Geology, Statistics, Government, Finances, Agriculture, Manners and Costumes and the Mining Operations in Chile. Collected During a Residence of Several Years in These Countries, Vol. 2* (London: Baldwin Cradock and Joy, 1826).

Miller, John, *Memoirs of General William Miller in the Service of the Republic of Peru* (London: Longman, 1828).

The Proceedings of a General Court Martial Held at Chelsea Hospital … for the Trial of Lieut. Gen. Whitelocke (London: J.C. Mottley, 1808).

'Proceso seguido por el Gobierno de Chile en 25 de Mayo de 1810, contra don Juan Antonio Ovalle, don José Antonio Rojas y el doctor don Bernardo Vera y Pintado por el delito de conspiración', in *Colección de Historiadores y Documentos relativos a la Independencia de Chile, Vol. 30*, ed. by Guillermo Feliú Cruz (Santiago: Imprenta Universitaria, 1939).

Real ordenanza naval para el servicio de los baxeles de S.M (Madrid: Imprenta Real, 1802).

Regulations and Instructions relating to his Majesty's Service at Sea (London, 1808).

Robertson, John Parish, *Letters on South America. Comprising Travels on the Banks of the Paraná and Río de la Plata, 3 Vols* (London: John Murray, 1843).

Salas, Manuel de, *Escritos de don Manuel de Salas y documentos relativos a él y a su familia, Vol. 1* (Santiago: Imprenta de Cervantes, 1910).

Scio de San, Phelipe Miguel (Bishop of Segovia), *La Biblia vulgata latina, traducida en español y anotada conforme al sentido de los santos padres y expositores catholicos por Rmo P. Scio de San Miguel, de las escuelas pías, electo obispo de Segovia* (Madrid: Imprenta de Benito Cano, 1797).

Schmidtmeyer, Peter, *Travel into Chile over the Andes in the Years 1820 and 1821, with Some Sketches of the Production of Agriculture; Mines and Metallurgy; Inhabitants, History, and Other Features of America, Particularly of Chile, and Arauco* (London: Longman, Hurst, Rees, Orme, Brown & Green, 1824).

Thomson, James, *Letters on the Moral and Religious State of South America Written During a Residence of Nearly Seven Years in Buenos Aires, Chile, Perú and Colombia* (London: James Nisbet, 1827).

——, 'South America IV', *Evangelical Christendom*, 1 (1847): 287–88.

Valencia Avaria, Luis, *Anales de la República*, vol. 1 (Santiago: Editorial Andrés Bello, 1951).

Secondary Sources

Aedo Richmond, Ruth, *La educación privada en Chile. Un estudio histórico–analítico desde el periodo colonial hasta 1990* (Santiago: Ril Editores, 2000).

Amunátegui, Domingo, *El sistema de Lancaster en Chile y otros países sudamericanos* (Santiago: Imprenta Cervantes, 1895).

Amunátegui, Miguel Luis, 'D. Bernardo Vera i Pintado', *La Semana. Revista noticiosa, literaria i científica*, 10 (23 July 1859), 147–50.

——, *La crónica de 1810*, 3 vols (Santiago: Imprenta de la República de Jacinto Núñez, 1876).

Anderson, Justice C., *An Evangelical Saga: Baptists and their Precursors in Latin America* (Maitland, FL: Xulon Press, 2005).

Arcangeli, Alessandro, *Cultural History: A Concise Introduction* (Abingdon: Routledge, 2012).

Armas, Fernando, *Liberales, protestantes y masones: Modernidad y tolerancia religiosa. Perú siglo XIX* (Lima: Fondo Editorial PUCP, 1998).

Armitage, David, *The Declaration of Independence: A Global History* (Cambridge, MA: Harvard University Press, 2007).

Ávila Martel, Alamiro, *Bello y Mora en Chile* (Santiago: Ediciones de la Universidad de Chile, 1982).

——, *Cochrane y la independencia del Pacífico* (Santiago: Editorial Universitaria, 1976).

Baeza, Andrés, 'Educational Reform, Political Change, and Penury: Primary Schooling and the Monitorial System of Education in Chile, approx. 1810–1833', in *Classroom Struggle: Organizing Elementary School Teaching in the 19th Century*, ed. by Marcelo Caruso, Studia Educationis Historica, Vol. 2 (Frankfurt am Main: Peter Lang, 2015), pp. 67–90.

——, 'Circulación de biblias protestantes y tolerancia religiosa en la América post-independiente: La mirada de Luke Matthews, un misionero protestante británico, 1826–1829', *Economía y Política*, 3:2 (2016), 5–35.

——, 'One Local Dimension of a Global Project: The Introduction of the Monitorial System of Education in Post-Independent Chile, 1821–1833', *Bulletin of Latin American Research*, 36:3 (2017) special issue: 'New Perspectives on Political Ideas and Practices in Post-Independence Chile (1818–1830)', ed. by Joanna Crow, 340–53.

Baeza, Andrés and Paula Caffarena, 'La independencia de Chile en su Bicentenario', *Tiempos de America: Revista de Historia, Cultura y Territorio*, 20 (2013) special issue: 'Las Revoluciones de Independencia: un bicentenario a debate', ed. by Manuel Chust, pp. 91–98.

Balmelli, J. Horacio, 'Juan José Tortel: Nuestro primer capitán de puerto', *Revista de Marina*, 2 (1999), available at: http://revistamarina.cl/revistas/1999/2/balmelli.pdf (accessed 14 July 2015).

Barros, Mario, *Historia diplomática de Chile, 1541–1938* (Santiago: Andrés Bello, 1970).

Barros Arana, Diego, *Historia general de Chile*, 16 vols, 2nd ed. (Santiago: Santiago: Editorial Universitaria–DIBAM, 1999), vols VIII–IX.

——, *Historia jeneral de la Independencia de Chile*, 2 vols (Santiago: Imprenta Chilena, 1854).

Barry, Douglas and Patricio Vergara, 'De revolucionarios a libertadores. Los oficiales europeos y norteamericanos en el Ejército de Chile 1817–1830', *Anuario de historia militar*, 27 (2013), 87–131.

Bayly, C.A., *Imperial Meridian: The British Empire and the World, 1780–1830* (London: Longman, 1989).

——, *The Birth of the Modern World, 1780-1914: Global Connections and Comparisons* (Malden, MA, Oxford and Carlton, Blackwell Publishing, 2004).

Bayly, C.A., Sven Beckert, Matthew Connelly, Isabel Hofmeyr, Wendy Kozol and Patricia Seed, 'AHR Conversation: On Transnational History', *The American Historical Review*, 111:5 (2006), 1441–64.

Benton, Lauren, 'No Longer Odd Region Out: Repositioning Latin America in World history', *Hispanic American Historical Review*, 84:3 (2004), 423–30.

Besseghini, Deborah, 'Commercio britannico e imperialismo informale in America latina. Robert P. Staples tra Río de la Plata, Perù e Messico (1808–1824)' (unpublished doctoral dissertation, University of Trieste, 2015).

Bethell, Leslie, 'Britain and Latin America in Historical Perspective', in *Britain and Latin America: A Changing Relationship*, ed. by Victor Bulmer-Thomas (Cambridge and New York: Cambridge University Press, 1989), pp. x–xii.

——, *George Canning and the Independence of Latin America: A Lecture Delivered at Canning House* (London: The Hispanic and Luzo Brazilian Councils, 1970).

Bickers, Robert (ed.), *Settlers and Expatriates: Britons over the Seas*, The Oxford History of the British Empire, Companion Series (Oxford and New York: Oxford University Press, 2010).

Bitterli, Urs, *Cultures in Conflict: Encounters between European and Non-European Cultures, 1492–1800*, trans. by Ritchie Robertson (Stanford, CA: Stanford University Press, 1989).

Blaufarb, Rafe, 'The Western Question: The Geopolitics of Latin American Independence', *The American Historical Review*, 112:3 (2007), 742–63.

Bragoni, Beatriz, *José Miguel Carrera. Un revolucionario chileno en el Río de la Plata* (Buenos Aires: Edhasa, 2012).

Brown, Matthew, 'Adventurers, Foreign Woman and Masculinity in the Colombian Wars of Independence', *Feminist Review*, 79 (2005), 36–51.

——, *Adventuring through Spanish Colonies: Simón Bolívar, Foreign Mercenaries and the Birth of New Nations* (Liverpool: Liverpool University Press, 2006).

——, 'Introduction', in *Informal Empire in Latin America: Culture, Commerce and Capital*, ed. by Matthew Brown (Oxford: Blackwell Publishing, 2008), pp. 1–22.

——, 'Not Forging Nations but Foraging for them: Uncertain Collective Identities in Gran Colombia', *Nations and Nationalism*, 12:2 (2006), 223–40.

Brown, Matthew and Gabriel Paquette (eds), *Connections after Colonialism: Europe and Latin America in the 1820s* (Tuscaloosa, AL: The University of Alabama Press, 2013), 1–28.

——, 'The Persistence of Mutual Influence: Europe and Latin America in the 1820s', *European History Quarterly*, 41:3 (2011) special issue: 'Europe and Latin America in the 1820s', ed. by Matthew Brown and Gabriel Paquette, 387–96.

Browning, Webster, 'Joseph Lancaster, James Thomson, and the Lancasterian System of Mutual Instruction, with Special Reference to Hispanic America', *Hispanic American Historical Review*, 4 (1921), 49–98.

Bulmer-Thomas, Victor, 'Preface', in *Britain and Latin America: A Changing Relationship*, ed. by Victor Bulmer-Thomas (Cambridge and New York: Cambridge University Press, 1989), pp. x–xii.

Burke, Peter, 'Strengths and Weaknesses of Cultural History', in *Cultural History. Journal of the International Society of Cultural History*, 1:1 (2012), 1–13.

Caffarena, Paula, 'Las Cortes de Cádiz y Chile. Encuentros y desencuentros a partir de sus diputados Joaquín Fernández de Leiva y Miguel Riesco', *Historia 396*, 2:2 (2012), 223–44.

——, 'Viruela y vacuna. Difusión y circulación de una práctica médica. Chile en el contexto hispanoamericano, 1780–1830' (unpublished doctoral dissertation. Pontificia Universidad Católica de Chile, 2015).

Canclini, Arnaldo, *La Biblia en Argentina. Su distribución e influencia hasta 1853* (Buenos Aires: Asociación Sociedad Bíblica Argentina, 1987).

——, *Diego Thomson, apóstol de la enseñanza y distribución de la Biblia en América Latina y España* (Buenos Aires: Asociación Sociedad Bíblica Argentina, 1987).

Canton, William, *A History of the British and Foreign Bible Society* (London: John Murray, 1904).

Carey, Hilary M., *God's Empire: Religion and Colonialism in the British World, c. 1801–1908* (Cambridge: Cambridge University Press, 2011).

Caruso, Marcelo, 'Latin American Independence: Education and the Invention of New Polities', *Paedagogica Historica: International Journal of the History of Education*, 46:4 (2010), 409–17.

Caruso, Marcelo and Eugenia Roldán Vera, *Imported Modernity in Post-colonial State Formation: The Appropriation of Political, Educational and Cultural Models in Nineteenth Century Latin America* (Frankfurt: Peter Lang, 2007), pp. 7–30.

——, 'Pluralizing Meanings: The Monitorial System of Education in Latin America in the Early Nineteenth Century', *Paedagogica Historica: International Journal of the History of Education*, 41:6 (2005), 645–54.

Castillo, Vasco, *La creación de la Republica. La filosofia publica en Chile, 1810–1830* (Santiago: Lom ediciones, 2009).

Cavieres, Eduardo, *Comercio chileno y comerciantes ingleses, 1820–1880 (Un ciclo de historia económica)* (Valparaíso: Universidad Católica de Valparaíso, 1988).

——, *Sobre la independencia en Chile. El fin del antiguo régimen y los orígenes de la representación moderna* (Valparaíso: Ediciones Universitarias de Valparaíso, 2012).

Centner, Charles, 'The Chilean Failure to Obtain British Recognition, 1823–1828', *Revista de Historia de América*, 15 (1942), 285–97.

Chambers, Sarah, *Families in War and Peace: Chile from Colony to Nation* (Durham, NC: Duke University Press, 2015).

Chust, Manuel and José Antonio Serrano, 'Un debate actual, una revisión necesaria', in *Debates sobre las independencias iberoamericanas*, ed. by Manuel Chust and José Antonio Serrano (Madrid: Iberoamericana – AHILA, 2007), pp. 9–26.

Colley, Linda, *Britons: Forging the Nation, 1707–1837*, 3rd ed. (London: Vintage Books, 1996).

Collier, Simon, *Ideas and Politics of Chilean Independence (1808–1833)* (New York: Cambridge University Press, 1967).

Contreras, Hugo, 'Artesanos mulatos y soldados beneméritos. El batallón de infantes de la patria en la guerra de independencia de Chile', *Historia*, 44: 1 (2011), 51–89.

Cordingly, David, *Cochrane The Dauntless: The Life and Adventures of Thomas Cochrane, 1775–1860*, 2nd ed. (London, Berlin and New York: Bloomsbury, 2008).

Cubitt, David, 'Lord Cochrane and the Chilean Navy, 1818–1823, with an Inventory of the Dundonald Papers Relating to his Service with the Chilean Navy', 2 vols (PhD dissertation: University of Edinburgh, 1974).

Dale, Richard, *Napoleon Is Dead: Lord Cochrane and the Great Stock Exchange Scandal* (Stroud: The History Press, 2006).

Darwin, John, *After Tamerlane: The Global History of Empire since 1405* (New York: Bloomsbury Press, 2008).

——, 'Imperialism and the Victorians: The Dynamics of Territorial Expansion', *English Historical Review*, 112:447 (1997), 614–42.

Davey, James, 'Atlantic Empire, European War and the Naval Expeditions to South America, 1806–1807', in *The Royal Navy and the British Atlantic World, c. 1750–1820*, ed. by John McAleer and Christer Petley (London: Palgrave Macmillan, 2016), pp. 147–73.

——, *In Nelson's Wake: The Navy and the Napoleonic Wars* (London: Yale University Press, 2015).

Davies, Catherine, Claire Brewster and Hilary Owen (eds), *South American Independence: Gender, Politics, Text* (Liverpool: Liverpool University Press, 2006).

De Iriarte, Tomás, *Biografía Del Brigadier General D. José Miguel Carrera, dos veces magistrado de la República de Chile* (Buenos Aires: Imprenta de Mayo, 1863).

De Vries, John, 'Reflections on Doing Global History', in *Writing the History of the Global: Challenges for the 21ˢᵗ Century*, ed. by Maxine Berg (Oxford: Oxford University Press, 2013), pp. 32–47.

Dickie, John, *The British Consul: Heir to a Great Tradition* (New York: Columbia University Press, 2008).

Edmundson, William, *A History of the British Presence in Chile: From Bloody Mary to Charles Darwin and the Decline of the British Influence* (New York: Palgrave Macmillan, 2009).

Egaña, María Loreto, *La educación primaria popular en Chile en el siglo XIX: Una práctica de política estatal* (Santiago: Ediciones DIBAM, 2000).

Elliott, John, *Empires of the Atlantic World: Britain and Spain in America, 1492–1830* (New Haven, CT: Yale University Press, 2006).

Felstiner, Mary Lowenthal, 'Kinship Politics in Chilean Independence Movement', *Hispanic American Historical Review*, 56:1 (1976), 58–80.

Fernández, Luis E. Iñigo, *Breve historia de la Batalla de Trafalgar. La batalla naval que cambió el destino del mundo* (Madrid: Ediciones Nowtilus, 2014).

Gallagher, John and Ronald Robinson, 'The Imperialism of Free Trade', *The Economic History Review*, 6:1 (1953), 1–15.

Gallo, Klaus, *Great Britain and Argentina: From Invasion to Recognition (1806–1826)* (Basingstoke and New York: Palgrave-St Antony's College, Oxford, 2001).

Gazmuri, Susana, 'La lectura de los autores romanos y la construcción del discurso republicano: Citas, traducciones y adaptaciones. Chile, 1810–1833', *Historia*, 49:2 (2016), 329–453.

Gentzler, Edwin, 'Introduction: New Definitions', in *Translation and Identity in the Americas: New Directions in Translation Theory* (London and New York: Routledge, 2008).

Gleijeses, Piero, 'The Limits of Sympathy: The United States and the Independence of Spanish America', *Journal of Latin American Studies*, 24:3 (1992), 481–505.

Góngora, Mario, *Ensayo histórico sobre la noción de Estado en Chile en los siglos XIX y XX* (Santiago: Editorial Universitaria, 1981).

Gould, Eliga, H., 'Entangled Histories, Entangled Worlds: The English Speaking Atlantic as a Spanish Periphery', *The American Historical Review*, 112:3 (2007), 764–86.

Graham, Gerald and R.A. Humphreys (eds), *The Navy in South America, 1807–1823. Correspondence of the Commanders-in-Chief on the South American Station* (London and Colchester: Navy Records Society, 1952).

Graham, Richard, *Independence in Latin America: Contrasts and Comparisons* (Austin, TX: University of Texas Press, 2013).

Grant, Thomas D., *The Recognition of States: Law and Practice in Debate and Evolution* (Westport, CT: Praeger Publishers, 1999).

Grez, Sergio, *De la regeneración del pueblo a la huelga general. Génesis y evolución histórica del movimiento popular en Chile (1810–1890)* (Santiago: Ril Editores, 2007).

Grimble, Ian, *The Seawolf: The Life of Admiral Cochrane* (London: Blond & Briggs, 1978).

Guenther, Louise H., *British Merchants in Nineteenth-Century Brazil. Business, Culture, and Identity in Bahia, 1808–50* (Oxford: Centre for Brazilian Studies, University of Oxford, 2004).

Guerrero Lira, Cristián, 'Certezas y dudas en torno a la Proclamación de la Independencia: una visión personal', in *La independencia de Chile y su celebración. ¿Una polémica (aún) abierta?*, ed. by Christian Hausser and Eduardo Bravo (Talca: Editorial Universidad de Talca, 2016), pp. 81–114.

——, 'Chile en el mundo', in *América Latina en la Historia contemporánea. Chile, Vol. 1: 1808–1830. Crisis imperial e independencia* (Madrid: Fundación Mapfre, 2010), pp. 89–138.

Gutiérrez Ardila, Daniel, *El reconocimiento de Colombia: diplomacia y propaganda en la coyuntura de las restauraciones (1819–1831)* (Bogotá: Universidad Externado de Colombia, 2012).

——, 'The Chilean Republic in the Face of Bolivar's Expansionism (1823–1828)', *Bulletin of Latin American Research*, 36:3 (2017), 313–25.

Hall, Catherine, *Civilising Subjects: Metropole and Colony in the English Imagination 1830–1867* (Chicago and London: University of Chicago Press, 2002).

Harmer, Tanya and Alfredo Riquelme (eds), *Chile y la Guerra fría global* (Santiago: Ril Editores-Instituto de Historia Universidad Católica, 2015).

Hernández Ponce, Roberto, 'Carlota Joaquina de Borbón. Apuntes en torno al epistolario carlotino y a un epistolario chileno inédito, 1808–1816', *Historia*, 20 (1985), 137–65.

Herrero, Víctor, *Agustín Edwards Eastman. Una biografía desclasificada del dueño de El Mercurio* (Santiago: Debate, 2014).

Howe, Stephen, 'Minding the Gaps: New Directions in the Study of Ireland and Empire', *The Journal of Imperial and Commonwealth History*, 37:1 (2009), 135–49.

Hughes, Ben, *The British Invasions of the River Plate, 1806–1807: How the Redcoats Were Humbled and a Nation Was Born* (Barnsley: Pen and Sword, 2013).

Humphreys, R.A., *British Consular Reports on the Trade and Politics of Latin America, 1824–1826* (London: Offices of the Royal Historical Society, 1940).

——, *Liberation in South America, 1806–1827: The Career of James Paroissien* (London: The Athlone Press, 1952).

——, 'Presidential Address: Anglo-American Rivalries and Spanish American Emancipation', *Transactions of the Royal Historical Society*, Fifth Series, 16 (1966), 131–56.

Iglesias-Rogers, Graciela, 'José Joaquín de Mora in Chile: From Neo-Europe to the "Beocia Americana"', *Bulletin of Latin American Research*, 36:3 (2017), 326–39.

Jaksic, Iván and Sol Serrano, 'In the Service of the Nation: The Establishment and Consolidation of the University of Chile, 1842–1872', *Hispanic American Historical Review*, 70 (1990), 139–71.

Jocelyn–Holt, Alfredo, *La independencia de Chile. Tradición, modernización y mito*, 3rd ed. (Santiago: Debolsillo, 2010).

Jones, H.S., 'Las variedades del liberalismo europeo en el siglo XIX: Perspectivas británicas y francesas', in *Liberalismo y poder. Latinoamérica en el siglo XIX*, ed. by Iván Jaksic and Eduardo Posada Carbó (Santiago: Editorial Fondo de Cultura Económica, 2011), pp. 43–62.

Kaestle, Carl F., *Joseph Lancaster and the Monitorial School Movement: A Documentary History* (New York: Teachers College Press, 1973).

Kaufman, William W., *British Policy and Latin American Independence, 1808–1824* (New Haven, CT: Yale University Press, 1951).

Kemp, Peter, *The British Sailor: A Social History of the Lower Deck* (London: J.M. Dent & Sons Ltd, 1970).

Kinsbruner, Jay, *Diego Portales: Interpretative Essays on the Man and Times* (The Hague: Springer Science, 1967).

——, 'The Political Influence of the British Merchants Resident in Chile during the O'Higgins' Administration, 1817–1823', *The Americas*, 27:1 (1970), 26–39.

Knight, Alan, 'Rethinking Informal Empire in Latin America (Especially Argentina)', in *Informal Empire in Latin America: Culture, Commerce and Capital*, ed. by Matthew Brown (Oxford: Blackwell Publishing, 2008), pp. 23–48.

Lempérière, Annick, 'Presentación: Hacia una nueva historia transnacional de las independencias hispanoamericanas', in *Las revoluciones americanas y la formación de los estados nacionales*, ed. by Jaime Rosenblitt (Santiago: DIBAM, 2013), pp. 13–27.

León, Leonardo, *Ni patriotas ni realistas. El bajo pueblo durante la independencia de Chile: 1810–1822* (Santiago: Centro Diego Barros Arana, 2012).

León XII, *Carta encíclica de nuestro santísimo padre el Papa León XII a todos los patriarcas, primados, arzobispos y obispos y bula de jubileo para el año 1825* (Barcelona: Imprenta de José Torner, 1824).

Lincoln, Margarette, *Representing the Royal Navy: British Sea Power, 1750–1815* (Aldershot and Burlington, VT: Naval Maritime Museum-Ashgate, 2002).

Liss, Peggy K., *Atlantic Empires: The Network of Trade and Revolution, 1713–1826* (Baltimore, MD: Johns Hopkins University Press, 1983).

Llorca-Jaña, Manuel, *The British Textile Trade in South America in the Nineteenth Century* (Cambridge: Cambridge University Press, 2012).

——, 'The Economic Activities of a Global Merchant-Banker in Chile: Huth & Co. of London, 1820s–1850s', *Historia*, 45:2 (2012), 399–432.

——, *The Globalization of Merchant Banking before 1850: The Case of Huth & Co.* (Oxford and New York, 2016).

Lloyd, Christopher, *Lord Cochrane: Seaman, Radical and Liberator. A Life of Thomas, Lord Cochrane, 10th Earl of Dundonald* (London, New York and Toronto: Longmans, 1947).

López Urrutia, Carlos, 'El Bergantín Intrépido', *Revista de Marina*, 1 (2007), 66–75.

——, *Historia de la marina de Chile* (Santiago: El Ciprés Editores, 2007).

Lucio Torres, Juan, *El español como soldado argentino. Participación en las campanas militares por la libertad e independencia* (Madrid: Ediciones de la Torre, 2014).

McCarthy, Matthew, *Privateering, Piracy and British Policy in Spanish America, 1810–1830* (Woodbridge: Boydell Press, 2013).

McFarlane, Antony, *The British in the Americas, 1480–1815*, Studies in Modern History (London and New York: Longman, 1994).

——, *War and Independence in Spanish America* (New York: Routledge, 2014).

Mariátegui, Francisco Javier, *Anotaciones a la Historia del Perú independiente de don Mariano F. Paz-Soldan* (Lima: Imprenta de El Nacional, 1869).

Marshall, Peter, *The Making and Unmaking of Empires: Britain, India and America, c. 1750–1783* (New York: Oxford University Press, 2005).

Mayo, John, 'Britain and Chile, 1851–1886: Anatomy of a Relationship', *Journal of Inter-American Studies and World Affairs*, 23:1 (1981), 95–120.

——, *British Merchants and Chilean Development, 1851–1886* (Boulder, CO: Westview Press, 1987).

——, 'The Development of British Interests in Chile's Norte Chico in the Early Nineteenth Century', *The Americas*, 57 (2001), 363–94.

Mazzei De Grazia, Leonardo, 'Orígenes del establecimiento británico en la región de Concepción y su inserción en la molinería de trigo y en la minería de carbón', *Historia*, 28 (1994), 217–39.

Medina, José Toribio, *Historia de la Real Universidad de San Felipe de Santiago de Chile*, 2 vols (Santiago: Sociedad Imprenta y Litografia Universo, 1928).

Méndez, Luz María, *La exportación minera en Chile. 1800–1840. Un estudio de historia económica y social en la transición de Colonia a Republica* (Santiago: Editorial Universitaria, 2004).

Miller, Nicola, 'The Historiography of Nationalism and National Identity in Latin America', *Nations and Nationalism*, 12:2 (2006), 201–21.

Miller, Rory, *Britain and Latin America in the 19th and 20th Centuries* (Oxford and New York: Routledge, 2013).

Mitchell, Bill, 'Diego Thomson: A Study in Scotland and South America (1818–1825)', *Bulletin of the Scottish Institute of Missionary Studies*, 6–7 (1991), 66–75, available at: http://www.jamesdiegothomson.com/diego-thomson-a-study-in-scotland-and-south-america-1818-1825/ (accessed 21 July 2015).

Montaner Bello, Ricardo, *Historia diplomática de la independencia de Chile* (Santiago: Editorial Andrés Bello, 1961).

Moraña, Mabel, Enrique Dussel and Carlos Jáuregui, *Coloniality at Large: Latin America and the Postcolonial Debate* (Durham, NC and London: Duke University Press, 2008).

Mulhall, Michael G., *The English in South America* (Buenos Aires: Standard Office; London: Ed. Stanford, 1878).

Muñoz Condell, David, *La influencia de Diego Thompson en Bernardo O'Higgins* (Valparaíso: Editorial Alba, 2010).

Newland, Carlos, 'La educación elemental en Hispanoamérica: desde la Independencia hasta la centralización de los sistemas educativos nacionales', *Hispanic American Historical Review*, 71:2 (1991), 335–64.

Nichols, Theodore E., 'The Establishment of Political Relations between Chile and Great Britain', *The Hispanic American Historical Review*, 28:1 (1948), 137–43.

Ortega, Francisco, *Logia* (Buenos Aires, 2014).

Ossa, Juan Luis, *Armies, Politics and Revolution: Chile, 1808–1826* (Liverpool: Liverpool University Press, 2014).

——, 'La Criollización de un Ejército Periférico, Chile, 1768–1810', *Historia (Santiago)*, 43 (2010), 413–48.

——, 'Francisco Antonio Pinto en los albores de la República, 1785–1828' (Unpublished dissertation, Santiago, Universidad Católica de Chile, 2006).

——, El gobierno de Bernardo O'Higgins visto a través de cinco agentes estadounidenses, 1817–1823', *Co-Herencia*, 13:25 (2016), 139–66.

——, 'Miguel Eyzaguirre: las redes de un chileno reformista en la Lima del virrey Abascal, 1803–1816', *Revista de Indias*, 57:269 (2017), 137–67.

——, 'Monarquismo(s) y militarismo republicano en Chile', in *Cádiz a debate. Actualidad, contexto y legado*, ed. by Roberto Breña (Mexico DF: Centro de Estudios Internacionales – El Colegio de México, 2014), pp. 409–29.

Páez Víctor, María, *Liberty or Death. The Life and Campaigns of Richard L. Vowell: British Legionnaire and Commander-Hero and Patriot of the Americas* (Ticehurst: Tattered Flag Press, 2013).

Paquette, Gabriel, 'The Dissolution of the Spanish Atlantic Monarchy', *The Historical Journal*, 52:1 (2009), 175–212.

Parra, Waldo, *Masones y libertadores* (Buenos Aires: Planeta, 2016).

Pearce, Adrian, *British Trade with Spanish America, 1763–1808* (Liverpool: Liverpool University Press, 2007).

Peña, Patricia, 'Y las mujeres, ¿dónde estuvieron? Mujeres en el proceso independentista chileno', *Anuario de Posgrado Universidad de Chile*, 2 (1997), 235–52.

Pimenta, João Paulo, 'Education and the Historiography of Ibero-American Independence: Elusive Presences, Many Absences', *Paedagogica Historica: International Journal of the History of Education*, 46:4 (2010), 419–34.

Pinto, Julio and Verónica Valdivia Ortiz de Zarate, *¿Chilenos todos? La construcción social de la nación (1810–1840)* (Santiago: Ediciones Lom, 2009).

Porter, Andrew, *Religion Versus Empire? British Protestant Missionaries and Overseas Expansion, 1700–1914* (Manchester: Manchester University Press, 2004).

Potter, Simon, *British Imperial History* (London: Palgrave, 2015).

Prain Brice, Michelle (ed.), *El legado británico en Valparaíso* (Santiago: Ril–Instituto Chileno Británico de Cultura, 2011).

Quijano, Aníbal, 'Coloniality of Power, Eurocentrism and Social Classification', in *Coloniality at Large: Latin America and the Postcolonial Debate*, ed. by Mabel Moraña, Enrique Dussel and Carlos Jáuregui (Durham, NC and London: Duke University Press, 2008), pp. 181–224.

Racine, Karen, 'The Childhood Shows the Man: Latin American Children in Great Britain, 1790–1830', *The Americas*, 72:2 (2015), 279–308.

——, 'Commercial Christianity: The British and Foreign Bible Society's Interest in Spanish America, 1805–1830', *Informal Empire in Latin America*, ed. by Brown, pp. 78–98.

——, 'Proxy Pasts: The Use of British Historical References in Spanish American Independence Rhetoric, 1808–1828', *The English Historical Review*, 132:557 (2017), 863–84.

——, 'This England and This Now: British Cultural and Intellectual Influence in the Spanish American Independence Era', *Hispanic American Historical Review*, 90:3 (2010), 423–54.

Ramírez Necochea, Hernán, *Historia del imperialismo en* Chile, 2nd ed. (Havana: Edición revolucionaria, 1966).

Ravest Mora, Manuel, 'La casa Gibbs y el monopolio salitrero peruano, 1876–1878', *Historia*, 41:1 (2008), 63–77.

Recio Morales, Oscar, *Ireland and the Spanish Empire, 1600–1815* (Dublin: Four Court Press, 2009).

Rector, John L., 'Merchants, Trade, and Commercial Policy in Chile: 1810–1840' (unpublished doctoral dissertation, Indiana University, August 1976).

Robson, Martin, *Britain, Portugal and South America in the Napoleonic War* (London: I.B. Tauris, 2012).

Rodríguez, Moises Enrique, *Freedom's Mercenaries: British Volunteers in the Wars of Independence of Latin America*, 2 vols (Lanham, MD: Hamilton Books, 2006).

Roldán Vera, Eugenia, *The British Book Trade and Spanish American Independence: Education and Knowledge Transmission in Transcontinental Perspective* (Aldershot: Ashgate, 2003).

——, 'Export as Import: James Thomson's Civilizing Mission in South America, 1818–1825', *Imported Modernity Imported Modernity in Post-colonial State Formation: The Appropriation of Political, Educational and Cultural Models in Nineteenth Century Latin America*, ed. by Caruso and Roldán Vera (Frankfurt: Peter Lang, 2007), pp. 231–76.

——, 'Internacionalización pedagógica y comunicación en perspectiva histórica: la introducción del método de enseñanza mutua en Hispanoamérica independiente', in *Internacionalización. Políticas educativas y reflexión pedagógica en un medio global*, ed. by Marcelo Caruso y Heinz Elmar–Tenorth (Buenos Aires: Editorial Gránica, 2011), pp. 297–344.

——, 'Order in the Classroom: The Spanish American Appropriation of the Monitorial System of Education', *Paedagogica Historica: International Journal of the History of Education*, 41:6 (2005), 655–75.

Rojas, Ximena, *Lord Cochrane y la liberación de Valdivia* (Santiago: Instituto de Historia de la Pontificia Universidad Católica de Chile–Instituto Chileno–Británico de Cultura, 1970).

Salazar, Gabriel, *Construcción de estado en Chile (1760–1860): democracia de 'los pueblos', militarismo ciudadano, golpismo oligárquico* (Santiago: Editorial Sudamericana, 2005).

——, *Mercaderes, empresarios y capitalistas: Chile, siglo XIX*, 2nd ed. (Santiago: Editorial Sudamericana, 2011).

Salvatore, Ricardo, 'The Enterprise of Knowledge. Representational Machines of Informal Empire', in *Close Encounters of Empire: Writing the Cultural History of U.S.-Latin American Relations*, ed. by Gilbert Michael Joseph, Catherine LeGrand and Ricardo Donato Salvatore (Durham, NC: Duke University Press, 1998), pp. 71–104.

Sanhueza, María Carolina, 'La primera división politico-admnistrativa de Chile', *Historia*, 41:2 (2008), 447–93.

Schell, Patience, 'Idols, Altars, Slippers, and Stockings: Heritage Debates and Displays in Nineteenth-Century Chile', *Past and Present*, 226:10 (2015), 326–48.

——. *The Sociable Sciences: Darwin and his Contemporaries in Chile* (New York: Palgrave Macmillan, 2013).

Schneuer, María José, 'Los ingleses del Pacífico. Identidad, guerra y superioridad en el discurso político chileno durante el siglo XIX' (unpublished doctoral dissertation, Pontificia Universidad Católica de Chile, 2014).

Sedra, Paul, 'Exposure to the Eyes of God: Monitorial Schools and Evangelicals in Early Nineteenth-century England', *Paedagogica Historica: International Journal of the History of Education*, 47:3 (2011), 263–81.

Serrano, Sol, *¿Qué hacer con Dios en la república? Política y secularización en Chile (1845–1885)* (Santiago: Fondo de Cultura Económica, 2008).

Serrano, Sol, Macarena Ponce de Léon and Francisca Rengifo, *Historia de la Educación en Chile (1810–2010)*, 2 vols (Santiago: Editorial Taurus, 2012).

Sexton, Jay, *The Monroe Doctrine: Empire and Nation in Nineteenth Century America* (New York: Hill and Wang, 2009).

Shurbutt, T. Ray, 'Personnel Diplomacy: The United States and Chile: 1812–1850', in *United States-Latin American Relations: The Formative Generations*, ed. by T. Ray Shurbutt (Tuscaloosa, AL and London: University of Alabama Press, 1991), pp. 228–60.

Silva Castro, Raúl, 'Antonio José de Irisarri: Fragmentos para una historia literaria de Chile en construcción', in *Anales de la Universidad de Chile*, 83–84 (1951), 5–25.

——, *Diego Portales: Ideas y confesiones* (Santiago: Editorial del Pacífico, 1954).

——, *La fundación del Instituto Nacional, 1810–1813* (Santiago: Imprenta Universitaria, 1953).

Silva Vildósola, Carlos, 'Papeles de O'Higgins. Un proyecto de alianza chileno–británica', *Boletín de la Academia Chilena de la Historia*, 17 (1923), 209–29.

Silveira, Alina, 'Ingleses y escoceses en Buenos Aires. Movimientos poblacionales, integración y prácticas asociativas (1800–1880)' (unpublished doctoral dissertation, University of San Andrés, Buenos Aires, 2014).

Sobrevilla, Natalia, *The Caudillo of the Andes: Andrés de Santa Cruz* (Cambridge: Cambridge University Press, 2011).

Somarriva, Marcelo, '"An Open Field and Fair Play": The Relationship between Britain and the Southern Cone of America between 1808 and 1830' (unpublished doctoral dissertation, University College London, 2012).

Stein, Stanley J. and Barbara H. Stein, *The Colonial Heritage of Latin America: Essays on Economic Dependence in Historical Perspective* (New York: Oxford University Press, 1970).

Temperley, H.W.A, 'The Foreign Policy of George Canning', in *The Cambridge History of British Foreign Policy*, ed. by Adolphus William Ward and George Peabody Gooch (New York: Cambridge University Press, 1923), I, pp. 51–118.

——, *The Foreign Policy of Canning, 1822–1827: England, the Neo-Holy Alliance and the New World*, 2nd ed. (Oxford: Frank Cass & Co., 1966).

Ternavasio, Marcela, *Candidata a la Corona. La infanta Carlota Joaquina en el laberinto de las revoluciones hispanoamericanas* (Buenos Aires: Siglo veintiuno editores, 2015).

Terragno, Rodolfo H, *Maitland y San Martín*, 3rd ed. (Bernal: Universidad Nacional de Quilmes Ediciones, 2001).

Thibaud, Clément, *Repúblicas en armas. Los ejércitos bolivarianos en la Guerra de independencia en Colombia y Venezuela* (Bogotá: Instituto Francés de Estudios Andinos, 2003).

Thompson, Carl E., *Travel Writing* (London: Routledge, 2011).

Tirifilo, S. Samuel, 'Early Nineteenth-Century British Travelers in Chile: Impressions of Santiago and Valparaíso', *Journal of Inter-American Studies*, 11:3 (1969), 391–424.

Trainafyllidou, Anna, 'National Identity and the Other', *Ethnic and Racial Studies*, 21:4 (1998), 593–612.

Tschurenev, Jana 'Diffusing Useful Knowledge: The Monitorial System of Education in Madras, London and Bengal, 1789–1840', *Paedagogica Historica: International Journal of the History of Education*, 44:3 (2008), 245–64.

Vale, Brian, *The Audacious Admiral Cochrane: The True Life of a Naval Legend* (London: Conway Maritime Press, 2004).

——, *Cochrane in the Pacific: Fortune and Freedom in Spanish America* (London: I.B. Tauris, 2008).

Valencia Avaria, Luis, 'Las Filipinas habrían podido ser para Chile', *En Viaje*, 99 (January 1942).

Valenzuela, Samuel, 'Caudillismo, democracia y la excepcionalidad chilena en América Hispana', *Revista de Occidente*, 305 (2006), 11–28.

Valenzuela Ugarte, Renato, *Bernardo O'Higgins. El Estado de Chile y el poder naval* (Santiago: Editorial Andrés Bello, 1999).

Vaughan, Edgard, *Joseph Lancaster in Caracas 1824–1827: And His Relations with the Liberator Simon Bolivar: With Some Accounts of Lancasterian Schools in Spanish America in the Nineteenth Century and Some Notes on the Efforts of the British and Foreign Bible Society to Distribute the Scriptures in Spanish in the Same Territory* (Caracas: Ministerio de Educación, 1987).

Vicuña Mackenna, Benjamín, 'La Inglaterra chica i la Inglaterra grande. Como un sarjento de artillería contribuyo al reconocimiento de la independencia de Chile por la Gran Bretaña', in Benjamín Vicuña Mackenna, *Chile. Relaciones históricas. Colección de artículos I tradiciones sobre asuntos nacionales*, 2nd series (Santiago, Lima and Valparaíso: Rafael Jover editor, 1818), 615–47.

Villalobos River, Sergio, *El comercio y la crisis colonial. Un mito de la independencia* (Santiago: Ediciones Universidad de Chile, 1968).

——, *Origen y Ascenso de la burguesía chilena* (Editorial Universitaria, 2006).

——, *Tradición y reforma en 1810*, 2nd ed. (Santiago: Ril Editores, 2006).

Villalobos Rivera, Sergio, Osvaldo Silva G., Fernando Silva Vargas and Patricio Estellé Méndez, *Historia de Chile* (Santiago: Editorial Universitaria, 1974).

Waddell, D.A.G., 'British Neutrality and Spanish-American Independence: The Problem of Foreign Enlistment', *Journal of Latin American Studies*, 19:1 (1987), 1–18.

Waterworth, James, *The Canons and Decrees of the Sacred and Oecumenical Council of Trent Celebrated under the Sovereign Pontiffs, Paul III, Julius III, and Pius IV* (London: Burns and Oates, 1888).

Webster, Charles K., *Britain and the Independence of Latin America, 1812–1830*, vol. 1 (London, New York and Toronto: Oxford University Press, 1938).

Weinberg, Gregorio, *Modelos educativos en la historia de América Latina* (Buenos Aires: Kapelusz and Unesco-Cepal-Pnud, 1984).

Welch, Chris, *Introduction to Chile (A Cartoon History)*, 2nd ed. (London: Chile40YearsOn, 2013).

Williams, Raymond, 'The Analysis of Culture', in *Cultural Theory and Popular Culture. A Reader*, ed. by John Storey, 2nd ed. (Athens, GA: The University of Georgia Press, 1998), 48–56.

——, 'Culture is Ordinary', in *The Everyday Life Reader*, ed. by Ben Highmore (London and New York: Routledge, 2002).

Wood, James A., *The Society of Equality: Popular Republicanism and Democracy in Santiago de Chile, 1818–1851* (Albuquerque, NM: University of New Mexico Press, 2011).

Worcester, Donald, *El poder naval y la independencia de Chile* (Santiago: Editorial Francisco de Aguirre, 1971).

Yeager, Gertrude, 'Elite Education in Nineteenth Century Chile', *Hispanic American Historical Review*, 71:1 (1991), 73–105.

Index